Hiking
New Mexico

Laurence Parent

FALCON®

GUILFORD, CONNECTICUT
HELENA, MONTANA

AN IMPRINT OF THE GLOBE PEQUOT PRESS

A FALCON GUIDE®

All photos by Laurence Parent unless otherwise noted.
Cover photo by Laurence Parent.

Library of Congress Cataloging-in-Publication Data

Parent, Laurence.
   Hiking New Mexico / by Laurence Parent.
       p. cm. — (A Falcon guide)
   Includes bibliographical references.
   ISBN 1-56044-676-5 (pbk.)
   1. Hiking—New Mexico—Guidebooks. 2. Trails—New Mexico—
Guidebooks. 3. New Mexico—Guidebooks. I. Title. II. Series.
GV199.42N6P377 1998
917.8904'53—dc21   98-11817
                                                                             CIP

♻ Text pages printed on recycled paper.
Manufactured in the United States of America
First edition/Fourth printing

CAUTION
Outdoor recreational activities are by their very nature potentially hazardous. All participants in such activities must assume the responsibility for their own actions and safety. The information contained in this guidebook cannot replace sound judgment and good decision-making skills, which help reduce risk exposure, nor does the scope of this book allow for disclosure of all the potential hazards and risks involved in such activities.

Learn as much as possible about the outdoor recreational activities in which you participate, prepare for the unexpected, and be cautious. The reward will be a safer and more enjoyable experience.

Contents

Acknowledgments

Many people contributed to this book, more than can be listed here. Special thanks go to my wife Patricia, John Sanders, Tonya Sanders Hays, and Pat Fischer for accompanying me on many hikes.

The following friends and family offered me their hospitality and logistical assistance with my hiking: my parents Hiram and Annette Parent, my sister Anne Fischer, and her husband Pat Fischer, David and Debbie Dozier, John and Adamina Morlock, Jack Shlachter, Cathy Bowman, Teresa Sanders, and Nancy Wizner.

Steve and Peg Fleming helped with photos. The REI store in Albuquerque graciously allowed me to use their extensive map collection. Many Forest Service, Park Service, and Bureau of Land Management (BLM) personnel endured numerous questions. Particularly helpful were Ron Henderson, formerly of the Gila National Forest, and Phil Dano of the Cibola National Forest. I would also like to thank Bill Blackard of the BLM and Cindy Ott-Jones, formerly of El Malpais National Monument.

Hike Locator Map

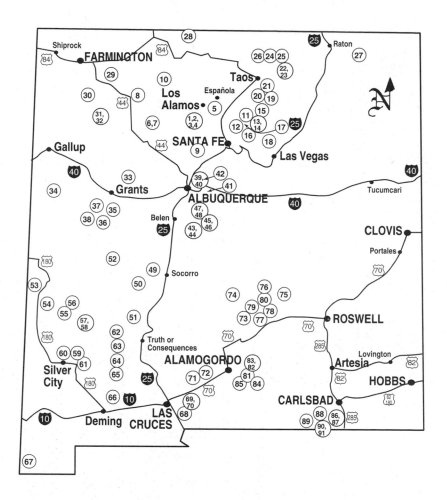

A Douglas fir clings to life on Sandia Crest.

Introduction

New Mexico is a diverse state, with almost every kind of terrain and climate imaginable. One day you can be sweltering in the desert backcountry of Carlsbad Caverns National Park, the next you can be shivering at an alpine lake as snow flurries shroud the peaks above. The ancient ruins of Bandelier National Monument lie in stark contrast to the government labs in adjacent Los Alamos. The skyscrapers of Albuquerque rise into the sky only sixty miles south of Santa Fe's almost 400-year-old Palace of the Governors. The lush spruce forests of the Sangre de Cristo Mountains seem worlds away from the sere desert along the Jornada del Muerto, the Journey of Death.

New Mexico's great range of elevations, from about 3,000 feet to over 13,000 feet, creates a wide variety of climates, vegetation, and terrain. People unfamiliar with the state often believe that most of New Mexico is little more than desert. Many are surprised to find that more than a quarter of the state is forested. In northern New Mexico, southern extensions of the Rocky Mountains boast peaks higher than 13,000 feet. Many other mountain ranges pepper the rest of the state, most with elevations of 10,000 feet or higher.

Elevation largely controls climate in New Mexico. The state's broad range gives rise to six life zones, from the Lower Sonoran, with its creosote, cacti, and other desert plants, to the Alpine Zone, with its tundra. The mountains attract most of the rainfall, with some receiving 40 inches of precipitation per year. In contrast, some desert areas receive as little as 8 inches annually. Likewise, temperatures vary widely, with record extremes of –50 degrees to 116 degrees. The wide variation in elevation and climate provide year-round hiking opportunities.

Most of the hikes in this guide lie in mountain areas because of their scenic beauty and the high concentrations of public land there. Also, most developed trails lie in the mountains.

A guidebook of manageable size can include only a fraction of the possible hikes in a state the size of New Mexico. One thousand miles of trail stretch across the Santa Fe National Forest alone. However, I have tried to include a cross section of hikes from all parts of the state. I have included popular hikes, such as the La Luz Trail, but also many obscure hikes, such as Cooks Peak. All of the hikes lie on public land, especially the national forests and national parks. The vast majority of trailheads are accessible by any type of vehicle; only a few require high clearance or 4-wheel-drive.

If you are a beginning hiker, do not let the length of some of these hikes intimidate you. Do not restrict yourself to only the short ones. Most of the long hikes are very beautiful and rewarding even if you go only a half mile down the trail.

Although the hikes in this guide may keep you busy for years, many of the hikes suggest additional nearby routes or extensions of the described hike. Do not be afraid to try them. This book serves best as an introduction to many of the most beautiful backcountry areas of New Mexico.

USING THIS GUIDE

Hiking New Mexico describes 91 hikes scattered widely across the state. The map at the start of this book indicates their locations. Several categories of information describe each hike. The **general description** gives a brief one-sentence description of the hike, along with its degree of difficulty. The **general location** gives the hike's location in regard to the closest significant town or park. The **length** gives the approximate length of the hike as a round trip; that is, the distance from the trailhead to the destination and back to the trailhead. The **elevation** lists the highest and lowest points reached on the hike. The **maps** category suggests maps to use for the hike. The **best season** gives the best time of year, weatherwise, for the hike. **Water availability** lists sites on the hike where water can be found. **Special attractions** describe some of the high points of the hike. **Permit** information is listed if permits are required to enter or camp in an area.

Finding the trailhead provides detailed directions for locating the start of each hike. **The hike** provides a detailed description of the hike itself, usually with some introductory information about the area.

Detailed maps accompany each hike. The map information was taken from USGS topo maps, national forest maps, BLM maps, and national park maps. Use the guidebook's maps in conjunction with the government maps.

Elevation charts are included with each hike if there is a gain or loss of more than about 300 feet in altitude on the trail. The **elevation** section mentioned above tells the highest and lowest points along the trail. The charts give a more detailed view of the ups and downs along the hike.

GENERAL DESCRIPTION

This section provides three categories of information. Besides giving a brief summary of the hike, it assigns the hike its degree of difficulty and suggests the amount of time required for the hike.

Assessing a hike's difficulty is very subjective. Not only do the elevation, elevation change, and length play a role, but trail condition, weather, and physical condition of the hiker are important. I probably rated some of the first hikes that I did for this book as more difficult than they are and some of the last hikes, when I was in much better physical condition, as easier than they really are. However, even my subjective ratings will give some idea of difficulty. To me, elevation gain was the most significant variable in establishing levels of difficulty.

In general, if a hike gains less than 1,000 feet and is less than 8 miles round trip, I usually rated it as easy. Within each category there are many degrees of difficulty, of course. Obviously a 2-mile hike gaining 200 feet is

Shiprock, an extinct volcano, lies west of Farmington.

going to be much easier than an 8-mile hike gaining 900 feet.

Moderate hikes, probably the most common in this book, usually gain somewhere between 1,000 and 2,000 feet and run longer than 8 miles. The strenuous hikes usually gain over 2,000 feet and are fairly long. Poor trails, excessive heat, high elevations with thin air, cross-country travel, and other factors may result in a more difficult designation than would otherwise seem to be the case.

Carrying a heavy backpack can make even an "easy" day hike fairly strenuous. All the designations assume snow-free trails. Early- and late-season hikes in the high mountains will be considerably more difficult if you are having to trudge through snow drifts.

The hiking speed of different people varies considerably. A hike is loosely classified as a day hike if most reasonably fit people can easily complete it in one day or less. Likewise, two- or three-day hikes can be easily done by most reasonably fit people in two or three days. Many of the day hikes, although easily done in one day, have attractions that make them worthy of longer, more relaxed stays. A few of the day hikes, particularly in some of the National Park Service areas, must be done in a day because overnight camping is not allowed.

LENGTH

The length specified in each description is listed as a round-trip distance from the trailhead to the end of the route and back. As mentioned in the individual hike descriptions, some of the hikes work well with car shuttles. Setting up such shuttles with two cars can halve the round-trip mileage of some of the hikes. Alternatively, someone can pick up your group at a set time at the end of the route. Another method involves splitting the group, dropping off the first half at one end, and parking the car and starting the other half from the other end of the hike. When the two groups meet in the middle, they exchange car keys, allowing the first group to later pick up the second. All hike mileages assume, however, that you are unable to arrange a shuttle.

Hike lengths have been estimated as closely as possible using topographic maps and government measurements. However, the different sources do not always agree, so the final figure is sometimes the author's best estimate.

ELEVATION

This is generally the most important factor in determining a hike's difficulty. The two numbers listed are the highest and lowest points reached on the hike. Often, but not always, the trailhead lies at the low point and the end lies at the highest point. With canyon hikes, the numbers are sometimes reversed. Many of the hikes have a fairly steady climb going out and a fairly steady downhill coming back. Some of the hikes have several ups and downs along the way, requiring more elevation gain and physical effort than the highest and lowest elevation numbers would seem to indicate. The Bandelier Wilderness hike is a notable example. The elevation charts associated with each hike will help identify such trails. The detailed hike descriptions will also mention multiple ups and downs. Hikes with no elevation chart have a net change in altitude of less than 300 feet.

Absolute elevation affects difficulty also. New Mexico is very high state, with its lowest point lying at almost 3,000 feet. At high elevations, lower atmospheric pressure creates thin air. The thin air requires higher breathing rates and more effort to pull enough oxygen into lungs. Since most of these hikes lie in the mountains, many lie at elevations of 8,000 feet or more. A good number of the hikes in the northern part of the state climb as high as 11,000, 12,000, or 13,000 feet. Most people will at least partially acclimate to the thin air after a few days. Hikers coming from low elevation areas, such as neighboring Texas, may want to do easy hikes at moderate altitudes for the first couple of days.

MAPS

The maps in this guide are as accurate and current as possible. When used in conjunction with the description and the maps listed in each hike's heading, you should have little trouble following the route.

Generally, up to three types of maps are listed. The national forest maps usually show the trails, but, because of their small scale, rarely give enough detail to be especially helpful. However, they are very useful for locating forest roads, trailheads, and campgrounds. They are generally more current than the USGS topographic maps and usually show the level of improvement of the forest roads. The National Park Service often has maps or brochures showing the trails. They vary in their usefulness.

USGS topographic quadrangles are generally the most detailed and accurate maps available of natural features. With practice, you can visualize peaks, canyons, cliffs, and many other features. With a little experience, a topographic map, and a compass, you should never become lost. Topographic

Map Legend

Interstate	(00)	Peak & Elevation	9,782 ft. ✕
US Highway	(00)	Cliff	
State or Other Principal Road	(00) (000)	Pass or Saddle	
Forest Road	[000]	River/Creek	
Interstate Highway	⟹	Spring	σ
Paved Road	⟹		
Improved Dirt Road	⟹	Lake	
Unimproved Road	====⟹	Marsh or Meadow	
Trailhead	◯	Mine or Tunnel	
Campground/Trailhead	◬	Bridge	
Campground	▲	Locked gate	==╪==:
Main Trail/Route		Wilderness Boundary	
Alternate/Secondary Trail/Route		State Boundary	
Cross-Crountry Route		Map Orientation	N
Cabins/Buildings	■		
		Scale	0 .5 1

maps are particularly useful for little-used trails and off-trail travel. Unfortunately, many of the quadrangles, particularly in the New Mexico hinterlands, are way out-of-date and do not show current man-made features such as roads and trails. However, they are still useful for their topographic information.

In recent years, government agencies have drawn up maps of many of the state's wilderness areas. All are set on topographic maps, although sometimes at a smaller scale than the USGS maps. So you not only get topographic data, but also fairly current road and trail information. When available for a given hike, the wilderness maps are probably adequate for all but off-trail hikes. The maps are a good compromise and cheaper to buy and easier to carry than a forest map and several USGS quads.

The wilderness and forest maps are usually available at ranger stations and at many outdoor shops in the larger cities. Currently most cost $3 to $4 each, but some, on plastic stock, are a little more expensive. National Park Service and BLM maps and brochures are usually available at no or small cost at the park visitor centers.

USGS quads can usually be found at outdoor shops or ordered directly from USGS. To order, list the state, the number desired of each map, the exact map name as listed in the hike heading, and the scale. Send your order to Map Distribution, U.S. Geological Survey Map Sales, Box 25286, Federal Center, Building 810, Denver, CO 80225. The phone number is 1-800-HELP-MAP. Call before sending your order to determine current prices.

BEST SEASON

This is the optimum or ideal season to take a particular hike. For instance, most of the mountain hikes are covered with snow much of the year. The months specified are those in which little or no snowpack covers the trail in normal years. The areas are not closed during winter months; however, experience with skis or snowshoes and winter travel is required. Several of the hikes, as noted in the descriptions, are marked for use as cross-country ski trails in winter.

The months specified are average; heavy spring snows can sometimes cover trails at the highest elevations well into summer and early winters can close trails ahead of time. Conversely, dry winters can greatly extend the optimum hiking season. At the highest elevations, especially in northern New Mexico, snow flurries can come even in the middle of summer, so be prepared. Local Forest Service ranger stations can tell you trail conditions for early- or late-season hikes.

The low elevation and desert hikes can usually be hiked year round. However, summers can be very hot, especially at places like Carlsbad Caverns and White Sands. Snow falls occasionally at the low elevations, but usually melts off within a day or two. Spring can be dry and windy, making desert hikes unpleasant at times. Fall is probably the premier time for low elevation hikes. Always check weather forecasts before starting your hike.

WATER AVAILABILITY

Sources of water are listed if they are known to usually be reliable. Any water obtained on a hike should be purified before use. Be sure to check with a ranger station about the status of water sources before depending on them. Droughts, livestock and wildlife use, and other factors can change their status.

PERMITS

Permits are not usually required for wilderness or backcountry entry in New Mexico. Several of the National Park Service areas allow only day use on certain trails. Generally all National Park Service areas require you to obtain a free permit for overnight trips.

FINDING THE TRAILHEAD

This section provides detailed descriptions for finding the trailheads. With a current state highway map, you can easily locate the starting point from the directions. In general, the nearest significant town was used as the starting point.

One warning: be sure to get a reasonably current highway map. For unfathomable bureaucratic reasons, the state highway department changed the numbers on most of New Mexico's state highways during the late 1980s. Thus, state highways shown on older U.S. Forest Service, National Park Service, USGS, and highway maps will be numbered incorrectly. This guide uses the new numbers throughout.

Driving distances were measured with a car odometer. Realize that different cars will vary slightly in their measurements. Even the same car will read slightly differently driving up a dirt road versus down a dirt road. So be sure to keep an eye open for the specific signs, junctions, and landmarks mentioned in the directions.

Most of this guide's hikes were selected to have trailheads that could be reached by a sedan. A few, as noted, require high clearance and, except in wet or snowy weather, none require a four-wheel-drive vehicle. Rain or snow can temporarily make some roads impassable. Before venturing onto unimproved forest roads, you should check with the local ranger station. On less traveled back roads, you should carry basic emergency equipment, such as a shovel, chains, water, a spare tire, a jack, blankets, and some extra food and clothing. Make sure that your vehicle is in good operating condition with a full tank of gas.

Theft and vandalism occasionally occur at trailheads. The local ranger station or sheriff's office can tell you of any recent problems. Try not to leave valuables in the car at all; if you must, lock them out of sight in the trunk. If I have enough room in the trunk, I usually put everything in to give the car an overall empty appearance. In my many years of parking and hiking at remote trailheads, I have never had my vehicle disturbed.

THE HIKE

All of the hikes selected for this guide can be done easily by people in good physical condition. A little scrambling may be necessary in a few, but none requires any rock climbing skills. A few of the hikes, as noted in their descriptions, travel across country or on very faint trails. You should have an experienced hiker, along with a compass and USGS quad, with your group before doing those hikes.

The trails are often marked with rock cairns or blazes. Most of the time, the paths are very obvious and easy to follow, but the marks help when the trails are little-used and faint. Cairns are piles of rock built along the route. Tree blazes are i-shaped carvings on trees, usually at shoulder or head height. Blazes can be especially useful when a forest trail is obscured by snow. Be sure not to add your own blazes or cairns; it can confuse the route. Leave such markings to the official trail workers.

Possible campsites are often suggested in the descriptions. Many others are usually available. Except for a few of the National Park Service areas, few restrictions usually exist in selecting a campsite, provided that it is well away from the trail or any water source.

After reading the descriptions, pick the hike that appeals most. Go only as far as ability and desire allow. There is no obligation to complete any hike. Remember, you are out hiking to enjoy yourself, not to prove anything.

HIKING WITH CHILDREN

Do not automatically hunt for the baby-sitter the next time that you want to go hiking. Kids of almost any age will enjoy a hiking trip if they aren't pushed beyond their ability.

The following hikes should entice children. A few may be difficult if hiked in their entirety, but most are easy and all are interesting even if only hiked a short distance.

You can't lose taking children of any age on either of the White Sands hikes. Of course you may spend the next two days getting the sand out of everything. In summer, the swarms of ladybugs that descend on the crest of Capulin Volcano along the trail will delight children.

The ladders, caves, and stream on the easy hike to Ceremonial Cave are great for older children. The cliffs and long ladders that create much of its appeal necessitate close supervision. The Gila Cliff Dwellings hike is another easy trail through caves and Indian ruins.

Some good hikes along streams include three in the Pecos Wilderness (Holy Ghost Creek, Cave Creek, and Trampas Lakes), Whitewater Creek, the Mimbres River, Argentina Canyon, and Bonito Creek. Children will love the hike along the east fork of the Jemez River—you *have* to wade.

Sitting Bull Falls is a sure winner. The water is much warmer than most of the high mountain streams and invites wading and swimming. However, unless your kids are older and very responsible, do not take them to the top of the falls; stay at the stream below the falls.

8

Vandals damage many trail signs; this one is in the Pecos Wilderness.

The rock formations and slot canyons on the Tent Rocks and Chavez Canyon hikes will appeal to many children. The historic wooden railroad trestles along the Cloud Climbing Rail Trail should also prove interesting. With close supervision, older children will enjoy exploring the lava tubes on the Big Skylight Cave hike.

Wilderness Ethics

A few simple rules and courtesies will help in both preserving the wilderness environment and allowing others to enjoy their outdoor experience. Every hiker has at least a slight impact on the land and other visitors. Your goal should be to minimize that impact. Some of the rules and suggestions may seem overly restrictive and confining, but with increasing use of shrinking wild areas, such rules have become more necessary. All can be followed with little inconvenience and will contribute to a better outdoors experience for you and others.

CAMPING

Camp at least 100 yards away from water sources. The vegetation at creeks, lakes, and springs is often the most fragile. Camping well away prevents trampling and destruction of the plant life. Destruction of vegetation usually leads to erosion and muddying of water sources. Additionally, camping 100 yards away limits runoff of wash water, food scraps, and human waste. An advantage to dry camps is that they are usually warmer and have fewer insects. Additionally, in desert areas, a spring may be the only water source for miles. If you camp too close, you may keep wildlife from reaching vital water.

Pick a level site that won't require modification to be usable. Do not destroy vegetation in setting up camp. The ideal camp is probably on a bare forest floor carpeted with pine needles. Do not trench around the tent site. Pick a spot with good natural drainage. If possible pick a site that has already been used so that you won't trample another. If you remove rock, sticks, or other debris, replace them when you depart. You want to leave no trace of your passage.

Do not pitch your tent right next to someone else's camp. Remember, they are probably out here to get away from people, too. Likewise, set up camp out of sight of trails and avoid creating excessive noise.

If backcountry toilets are available, use them. Otherwise, dig a six- to eight-inch-deep hole as far away from water, campsites, and trails as possible and bury human wastes. At that depth, it will quickly decompose. If weather and forest conditions allow, carefully burn toilet paper; otherwise, carry it out with you in plastic bags. Remember, New Mexico is a dry state and forest fires start easily. Burning should only be done when forests are very damp, the air is still, and there is absolutely no risk of starting a wildfire. Most often you should carry paper out with you. Fish entrails should be buried. Do not dispose of them in the water.

Carry out all of your trash. Other than paper, most trash, including foil freeze-dried food packages, will not burn completely. Plus, you run the risk of starting a wildfire. Animals will dig up any garbage that you bury. Im-

Backpackers should camp at least 100 yards from any water source. Lake Katherine, at the foot of Santa Fe Baldy.

prove the area for future visitors and take out trash that others have left behind.

Campfires leave permanent scars. If you must build one, do it on bare soil without a fire ring. Use only dead and fallen wood. Put it out thoroughly with water and never leave it unattended. Buried fires can sometimes escape from under the soil. Do not start a fire on dry or windy days. The forests of New Mexico are notoriously dry in late spring and early summer before the rainy season. The national forests often limit the use of fires during this time. Be sure to honor the restrictions.

Except in an emergency, do not use campfires in areas near timberline. Trees grow very slowly in the harsh conditions at high elevations, making firewood very limited. Likewise, do not use fires in any other areas, such as deserts, where wood is obviously scarce. For cooking purposes, backpacking stoves are much easier, quicker, and more efficient.

Carry an extra empty gallon jug or wash basin to use for washing yourself or cooking utensils. Use the jug to carry water and wash well away from the water source to keep soap and other pollutants from flowing into the water.

THE TRAIL

Do not shortcut switchbacks on the trail. Switchbacks were built to ease the grade on climbs and to limit erosion. Shortcutting, although it may be shorter, usually takes more effort and unquestionably creates additional erosion.

Always give horses and other pack animals the right-of-way. Stand well away from the trail and make no sudden movements or noises that could spook the animals.

If you smoke, stop in a safe spot and make sure that cigarettes and matches are dead out before proceeding. Be sure to take your butts with you. Do not smoke in windy and dry conditions.

Motorized and mechanized vehicles, including mountain bikes, are prohibited from all wilderness and most national park trails. Other areas may also have restrictions.

Do not do anything to disturb the natural environment. Do not cut live trees or plants. Resist the temptation to pick wildflowers. Do not blaze trees, carve initials on aspens, build bridges, or add improvements to campsites. Do not remove any Indian relics or other historic items. All historic items are protected by law on government lands.

If you take your dog, please be courteous. Dogs will often annoy other hikers seeking a wilderness experience. Leash him if other hikers are around. Keep him away from water sources to avoid possible contamination. Keep him from disturbing wildlife. Keep him quiet, especially at night. In general, it is probably best to leave your pet at home.

NATIONAL PARKS

Rules in National Park Service areas are generally more restrictive than in other government lands. Some park areas do not permit backcountry camping. Others require campsites to be located in specific areas. All require that free overnight permits be obtained. Dogs are not allowed on trails, nor may any plants, rocks, or other items be removed. Use of campfires is usually more restricted. Because of dry conditions and lack of wood, Carlsbad Caverns National Park prohibits the use of campfires altogether. Hunting is prohibited in park areas, but fishing is usually permitted with appropriate state licenses.

Other restrictions may apply at certain areas. Local ranger stations and signs at trailheads can inform you of any requirements.

Safety

With common sense and good judgment, few mishaps should occur. Do not push yourself or companions beyond physical ability. Be aware of changing weather. Know basic first aid techniques.

The following list elaborates on some of the potential hazards that you may encounter on your hikes. Do not let the list scare you. I have been hiking for more than 25 years without any serious mishap. The few incidents that have occurred usually were due to carelessness on my part: carrying too little water; not using sunscreen; pushing beyond my limits; and so on.

WEATHER

More problems and emergencies in the outdoors are probably related to weather than any other factor. Even in hot desert areas, sudden thunderstorms in late summer can drench you, and at the least, make you uncomfortably cool. In the high mountains, temperatures can plummet in storms. When combined with wet clothes or lack of shelter, a life threatening situation can develop.

It is easy to prepare for most weather problems. Always take extra warm clothes, especially on extended hikes. Wool and many synthetics still retain some insulating capability when wet; cotton is worthless. Rain gear is essential, especially on hikes in the higher mountains in late summer. Carry a reliable tent on the longer hikes. Hole up and wait for the bad weather to pass, rather than attempting a long hike out. Most storms in New Mexico, especially in summer, are of short duration.

Hypothermia develops when the body's temperature falls. New Mexico is usually thought of as a desert state, but many of these hikes are in high mountain areas where hypothermia is a risk. If conditions turn wet and cold and a member of your party begins to slur speech, shiver constantly, or becomes clumsy, sleepy, or unreasonable, it is wise to assume hypothermia is the cause and to immediately get the hiker into shelter and out of wet clothes. Give the victim warm liquids to drink and get him into a sleeping bag with one or more people. Skin-to-skin contact conducts body heat to the victim most effectively. This isn't a time for modesty; you may save the victim's life.

At the other extreme, heat can cause problems, particularly in summer in the low elevation areas of southern New Mexico. On hot-weather hikes, carry and drink adequate water. For long hikes in hot weather, plan to carry at least a gallon of water per person per day. Hikes in New Mexico can be quite hot even as high as 7,000 feet or more in May and June, before the summer rains begin. If you do desert hikes in summer, try to get a very early start to avoid the worst of the heat. Do not push as hard; take frequent breaks.

Thunderstorms are a constant danger in the New Mexico mountains. A storm builds up over the Black Range.

With heat exhaustion, the skin is still moist and sweaty, but the victim may feel weak, dizzy, nauseated, or have muscle cramps. Find a cool, shady place to rest and feed him plenty of liquids and a few crackers or other source of salt. After the victim feels better, keep him drinking plenty of liquids and limit physical activity. Hike out during a cooler time of day. The condition usually isn't serious, but take the hiker to a doctor as soon as possible.

Heatstroke is less common, but can develop with prolonged exposure to very hot conditions. The body's temperature regulation system stops functioning, resulting in a rapid rise in body temperature. The skin is hot, flushed, and bone-dry. Confusion and unconsciousness can quickly follow. The situation is life-threatening. Immediately get the victim into the coolest available place. Remove excess clothes and dampen skin and remaining clothes with water. Fan the victim for additional cooling. If a cool stream or pond is nearby, consider immersing the victim. You must get the body temperature down quickly. Seek medical help immediately.

Lightning poses another threat. New Mexico has the notorious distinction of having the highest number of lightning deaths per capita in the country. When thunderstorms develop, seek lower ground. Stay off ridges and peaks and away from lone trees, lakes, and open areas. Lightning makes high areas above timberline especially hazardous. Plan to start your hikes early to reach high peaks and ridges by lunchtime and head down promptly. The most common thunderstorms in New Mexico develop in the afternoons of late summer. If you get caught in a lightning storm, seek shelter in a low-lying grove of small equal-sized trees if possible. Put down your metal-framed packs, tripods, and metal tent poles well away from you.

Heavy rains can also cause flooding. Stay out of narrow canyons boxed in by cliffs during heavy rains. Even though you may be in sunshine, watch the weather upstream from you. Camp well above and away from streams and rivers. Never camp in that tempting sandy site in the bottom of a dry desert wash. Storms upstream from you can send water sweeping down desert washes with unbelievable fury.

PHYSICAL PREPARATION

Good physical condition will not only make your trip safer, but much more pleasant. Do not push yourself too hard, especially at high altitudes. If you have been sedentary for a long time, consider getting a physical exam before starting hiking. Ease into it; start with easy hikes and graduate to more difficult ones. Do not push your party any harder or faster than the weakest member feels comfortable with. Know your limits. When you get tired, rest or turn back. Remember, you are out there to have fun.

Be mentally prepared. Read this guidebook and the specific hike description. Study maps and other books on the area. Every effort has been made to create a guidebook that is as accurate and current as possible, but a few errors may still creep in. Additionally, roads and trails can be rerouted. Signs can disappear and other changes occur with time. Talk to rangers about current road and trail conditions and water sources. Check the weather forecast. Find out the abilities and desires of your hiking companions before hitting the trail.

ALTITUDE

Many of New Mexico's mountains are relatively high. People coming from low elevations, especially out of state, may have some trouble at altitudes above 8,000 feet. Until you acclimate, you may suffer from shortness of breath and tire more easily. A few hikers may develop headaches, nausea, fatigue, or other mild symptoms such as swelling of the face, hands, ankles, or other body areas at the highest altitudes. Mild symptoms should not change your plans. Rest for a day or two to acclimate. Retreating 1,000 feet or so will often clear up any symptoms. New Mexico residents should have less trouble than most since more than half of the people in the state already live at 5,000 feet or higher. Spending several days at moderate altitude before climbing high will often prevent any problems.

New Mexico's mountains are not high enough to cause the serious symptoms of altitude sickness, such as pulmonary edema (fluid collecting in the lungs) or cerebral edema (fluid accumulating in the brain), except in very rare cases. Should these symptoms develop, immediately get the victim to lower elevations and medical attention.

COMPANIONS

Pick your companions wisely. Consider their experience and physical and mental fitness. Try to form groups of relatively similar physical ability. Pick a leader, especially on long trips or with large groups. Ideally, have at least one experienced hiker with the group.

Too large a group is unwieldy and diminishes the wilderness experience for yourself and others. An ideal size is probably four. In case of injury, one can stay with the victim, while the other two can hike out for help. No one is left alone. Leave your travel plans with friends so that they can send help if you do not return. Allow plenty of time for your hike; trips often run later than expected.

Never hike alone, especially cross-country or on little-traveled routes. That said, I must confess that I did most of the hikes in this guide alone. However, I religiously informed family or friends of my travel plans on a daily basis and did not deviate from them. Upon returning from a hike I immediately called to let them know that I was back. Never forget to check in at the end of your hike. Nothing will aggravate rescuers more than to find that you were at the local bar relaxing with a beer while they were stumbling around in the rain and dark looking for you.

The only time that I did not worry about informing friends of my travel plans was when I did popular hikes on summer weekends. Plenty of other people were on the trail if a mishap occurred.

WATER

Unfortunately, with the heavy use that many backcountry areas are receiving, all water sources should be purified before use. Most hikers will not get sick if the water is obtained directly from springs or from streams near their source in little-used areas. However, it is best to play it safe and always treat your water. Boiling vigorously for ten minutes (more at higher altitudes) is a reliable method, but slow and consumes a lot fuel.

Mechanical filtration units are available at most outdoors shops. Filters with a very small pore size strain out bacteria, cysts, and other microorganisms. Their ability to filter out the smallest organisms, such as viruses, varies from model to model. For very contaminated water, filtration should probably be used in conjunction with chemical treatment.

Chemical treatment is probably the easiest method, but may not be quite as effective as boiling or filtration. Chlorination is the method used by most municipal water systems, but the use of hyperiodide tablets is probably safer and more reliable for backpackers. They can be purchased at any outdoors store. Follow the directions carefully. Cold or cloudy water requires more chemical use or longer treatment times.

The cleaner your water is from the start, the better. Get your water from springs or upstream from trails and camps if possible. For day hikes, it is usually easiest just to carry sufficient water for the day.

STREAM CROSSINGS

Crossing all but the smallest of streams poses several hazards. Except in flood stage, few of the streams along the trails in this guide are big enough to pose much of a risk to hikers. However, do not underestimate the power of fast-flowing rivers, such as the Rio Grande, Pecos, Gila, or smaller streams in flood. Avoid crossing high-volume waterways when possible. If you must cross them, try to find rocks or logs to use, although they may be slippery. Or try to find a broad, slow moving shallow stretch for your ford. Undo the waist strap on your backpack for quick removal if necessary. Use a stout walking stick or even ropes for stability and safety.

Since the vast majority of the streams in New Mexico are too small to sweep you away, the biggest risk probably lies in jumping from rock to rock or crossing on logs to avoid wet feet. Often the rocks or logs are unstable or slippery, making falls possible. A heavy pack makes such crossings even more tricky. While such a fall might not be life threatening, a twisted ankle or broken leg would present problems. It is often best just to wade. Use extra care and assist each other across streams.

INSECTS

Insects present more of a nuisance than threat in New Mexico. Summer is the most likely time for problems. Mosquitoes will hatch after heavy summer rains, even in desert regions. In general, mosquitoes are more of a problem in the high, lush mountains than in the desert. A repellent containing DEET in high percentages will discourage mosquitoes and gnats from bothering you. Camp well away from streams, marshes, and other wet areas. Good mosquito netting on your tent will allow a pleasant night's sleep. I have camped many a time in dry areas without a tent or netting with no problems at all.

Scorpions and centipedes have a painful sting, but generally do not cause any lasting harm in New Mexico. Unless you turn over rocks and logs, you are unlikely to see any. Bees and wasps will sometimes be seen, especially near water sources and wildflowers, but will rarely do any harm unless disturbed. If you are one of the few people that has an allergic reaction to their stings, be sure to carry medicines with you that control such reactions.

Ticks create only a minor problem in New Mexico. However, they do carry serious diseases, such as Rocky Mountain spotted fever and Lyme disease, so be aware of them. Use insect repellent, wear clothing that fits snugly around the waist, ankles, and wrists, and check yourself and pets every night. If a tick attaches, remove it promptly. Use tweezers and avoid squeezing the tick as you pull it out. Do not leave the head embedded and do not handle the tick. Apply antiseptic to the bite and wash thoroughly. Ticks are probably most common in livestock areas. If you develop any sickness within two or three weeks of the bite, see a doctor.

One of the pleasures of growing up in New Mexico was its paucity of nuisance insects. In all of my years of hiking and camping in the state, I have had only two ticks on my body. I got one after sitting for a half hour in a cave entrance near some packrat nests. I'm not sure how I got the other, but it did make me sick.

BEARS

Grizzlies have not roamed the mountains of New Mexico for decades, so bear attacks are extremely unlikely. Black bears are fairly common in many of the mountain ranges, although you are unlikely to encounter them. A little prevention will prevent any problems. Give bears a wide berth, especially those with cubs.

Put food and other smelly items, such as soap, toothpaste, and garbage, into a stuffsack and hang it from a tree well away from your tent. Hang it at least 10 feet above the ground and out from the trunk. Let it dangle a few feet below the limb to prevent access from above. Hanging your food will also discourage rodents and raccoons. Leave your packs unzipped to prevent damage to them by a nosy animal. Never cook in your tent or keep food in your tent or sleeping bag. If a bear does take your food, do not even think about trying to get it back.

SNAKES

The vast majority of snakes that you will encounter (usually you will see none) are nonpoisonous. On rare occasions you may encounter a rattlesnake, generally at elevations below about 8,000 or 9,000 feet. Most are not aggressive and will not strike unless stepped on or otherwise provoked. In daytime or cold weather they are usually holed up under rocks and in cracks. The most likely time to see them is in summer evenings in the desert. If you watch your step, do not hike at night, and do not put your hands or feet under rocks, ledges, and other places that you can't see, you should never have any problem. Do not hurt or kill any that you find. Remember, they are important predators.

If bitten, get medical help as soon as possible. Treatment methods are very controversial and beyond the scope of this book. Fortunately, the majority of bites do not inject a significant amount of venom. For basic treatment, tie a shoelace or other cord around the affected extremity between the bite and the rest of the body. Tie it only tight enough to dent the skin; do not cut off circulation. Apply ice if available. Get to a doctor. Do not use a snakebite kit unless you are very far from medical help.

EQUIPMENT

The most important outdoor equipment is probably your footwear. Hiking boots should be sturdy and comfortable. The lightweight boots are probably adequate for all but rugged trails and routes and for carrying heavy packs. Proper clothing, plenty of food and water, and a pack are other necessities. Other vital items for every trip include waterproof matches, rain gear or some sort of emergency shelter, a pocketknife, a signal mirror and whistle, a first-aid kit, a detailed map, and a compass.

In general, all of your outdoor equipment should be as light and small as possible. Many excellent books and outdoor shops will help you select the proper boots, tents, sleeping bags, cooking utensils, and other equipment necessary for your hike.

GETTING LOST

Careful use of the maps and hike descriptions should prevent you from ever getting lost. However, if you should become lost or disoriented, immediately stop. Charging around blindly will only worsen the problem. Careful study of the map, compass, and surrounding landmarks will often reorient you. If you can retrace your route, follow it until you are oriented again. Do not proceed unless you are sure of your location. If you left travel plans with friends or family, rescuers should find you soon. In an emergency, follow a drainage downstream. In most areas, it will eventually lead you to a trail, road, or town. Remember, however, that it will probably take you farther away from rescuers. In a few of the largest wilderness areas, in particular the Gila Wilderness, it may take you deeper into the backcountry. Some of the drainages in the Gila go 30 miles or more before hitting civilization.

Use of signals may help rescuers find you. A series of three flashes or noises is the universal distress signal. Use the whistle or signal mirror. Provided that it can be done safely, a small, smoky fire may help rescuers find you.

HUNTING

National forest and BLM lands all generally allow hunting during the various seasons set up by state agencies. Fall in particular can bring out large numbers of deer and elk hunters. The seasons vary from year to year and in different parts of the state. Check with local ranger stations before your hike to determine what, if any, seasons might be in effect. If you hike during a hunting season, inquire locally to find areas that are less popular with hunters and wear bright-colored clothing.

SUMMARY

Use of good judgment, adequate preparation, and common sense should keep all of your trips problem free. Get out there and enjoy New Mexico's great outdoors.

1 Upper and Lower Falls

General description:	An easy day hike down Frijoles Canyon to two large waterfalls and the Rio Grande.
General location:	Bandelier National Monument.
Length:	About 5 miles round trip.
Elevation:	6,066–5,360 feet.
Maps:	Falls Trail Guidebook; Bandelier National Monument "Trails Illustrated" topo map; Bandelier National Monument brochure; Frijoles 7.5-minute USGS quad.
Best season:	All year.
Water availability:	Frijoles Creek.
Special attractions:	Two large waterfalls.

Finding the trailhead: Bandelier National Monument lies about 11 miles southwest of White Rock (near Los Alamos) on NM 4. Park at park headquarters in the bottom of Frijoles Canyon.

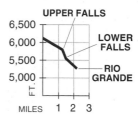

The hike: Bandelier is famous for its extensive Indian ruins. Few visitors are aware that 90 percent of the park is virtually undisturbed wild land. Over 70 miles of maintained trails cross Bandelier. This hike is the park's most popular hike, other than the archaeological trails, and makes an easy introduction to Bandelier's wilderness area.

Bandelier consists chiefly of a large sloping plateau, cut by deep, narrow canyons flowing to the Rio Grande. Massive volcanic eruptions from a huge crater in the Jemez Mountains built up a thick layer of consolidated volcanic ash, or tuff. To deposit such massive volumes of rock, the explosions had to have been about 600 times larger than those of Mount St. Helens. The collapsed summit of the volcano, the present day Valle Grande, forms one of the largest calderas in the world. Elevations in the park range from 5,300 feet at the river to over 10,000 feet in the Jemez Mountains.

The permanent stream of Frijoles Creek has easily cut a deep canyon through the soft tuff. At the Upper and Lower Falls, the stream encountered much harder layers of basalt. Since the creek was unable to erode the basalt as quickly as the surrounding tuff, waterfalls formed.

From the visitor center, cross the creek and walk downstream through the backcountry parking area to the well marked trail. The trail descends at an easy grade along Frijoles Creek through lush riparian vegetation, such as boxelder and ponderosa pine. About 1.5 miles down the trail you reach Upper Falls. The trail overlooks the large waterfall from above, before making a short, steep descent to the creek below the falls. The Lower Falls are only another 0.25 mile further, with a view from above. The Park Service does not allow hikers to approach the base of either waterfall because of the danger of rocks falling from the trail above.

Upper Frijoles Falls is one of the two large waterfalls along the Lower Falls hike at Bandelier National Monument.

After another short, steep descent at Lower Falls, the trail continues about 0.75 mile down the canyon to the Rio Grande. The last part of the hike is less shaded and hotter. At trail's end, the muddy Rio Grande flows by. Many of the trees are dead along the river, killed during the rare times that Cochiti Reservoir fills up. The lake, built in a fit of government pork barrel excess, usually consists of more mud flats than water.

The hike can be quite hot in summer, especially on the uphill return leg. Be sure to carry plenty of water and start early, if possible. If necessary, water can be obtained from Frijoles Creek and purified, but, since the hike is short and the area very heavily used, carrying water is recommended.

Upper and Lower Falls

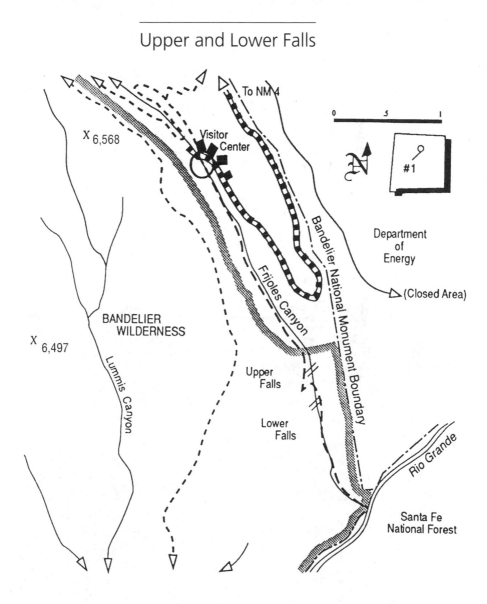

② Ceremonial Cave

General description:	An easy day hike to an Indian ruin high above the floor of Frijoles Canyon.
General location:	About 15 miles south of Los Alamos.
Length:	About 2 miles round trip.
Elevation:	6,066–6,400 feet.
Maps:	Bandelier National Monument "Trails Illustrated" topo map; Bandelier National Monument brochure; Frijoles 7.5-minute USGS quad.
Best season:	Spring through fall.
Water availability:	Visitor Center; Frijoles Creek.
Special attractions:	Restored Indian kiva in a shelter cave high above the canyon.

Finding the trailhead: The trail begins at the visitor center of Bandelier National Monument. Drive about 11 miles southwest of White Rock (near Los Alamos) on NM 4 to get to the monument.

The rebuilt kiva in Ceremonial Cave is one of many prehistoric ruins in Bandelier National Monument.

Ceremonial Cave

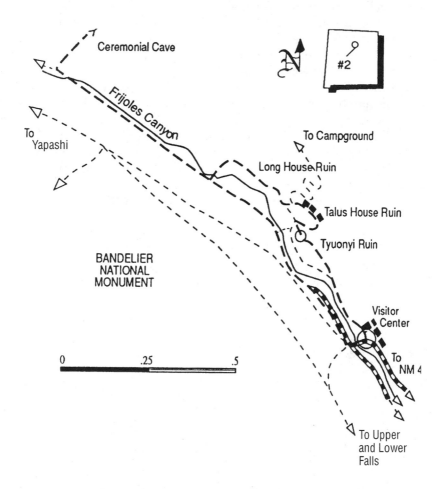

Ceremonial Cave

Frijoles Canyon

To Yapashi

To Campground

Long House Ruin

Talus House Ruin

Tyuonyi Ruin

BANDELIER
NATIONAL
MONUMENT

Visitor
Center

To
NM 4

To Upper
and Lower
Falls

N
#2

0   .25   .5

The hike: Frijoles Canyon, a narrow steep-walled canyon cut into the Pajarito Plateau, was home to a large community of Indians from about A.D. 1100 to 1550. The Indians raised corn, beans, and squash in the canyons and on the mesa tops of Bandelier and built impressive villages. The soft tuff (consolidated volcanic ash) was easy to carve, and the Indians honeycombed the cliffs of Frijoles Canyon and other canyons for cave homes. Ancient Indian trails sometimes wore several feet deep into the tuff. Archaeologists believe that soil exhaustion and depletion of natural resources, such as game, firewood, and useful plants, caused the residents to abandon their Bandelier home and create new villages at Cochiti and Santo Domingo.

To start, walk through the visitor center up the canyon on the main paved ruins trail. Stay on the north side of the creek. Within a few hundred yards, the trail forks. Keep right and walk through the large pueblo ruin of Tyuonyi.

On the far side of Tyuonyi, the right fork will take you on the short loop through Talus House. Stay left at the Frey Trail junction. It climbs up to the campground on the mesa. Immediately after, at the next junction, take the right fork up canyon to Long House. After passing Long House, you will cross the permanent stream flowing down Frijoles Canyon. Continue on the trail up the canyon after crossing the creek.

The trail up the canyon is an easy walk along the stream through shady stands of ponderosa pine, box elder, and many other trees. About 0.5 mile up canyon from the first creek crossing, signs indicate the climb up to Ceremonial Cave, high above the creek bottom in the north wall of the canyon. A series of four Indian-style ladders and connecting trail segments leads to the large natural shelter 140 feet above the canyon floor. The highlight of the cave is the restored kiva in the cave floor. If you are acrophobic, you may want to pass on the ladders.

Return to the visitor center via the same route. At the junction to Long House and Tyuonyi, do not cross the creek. Rather, stay right and continue to follow the creek trail back to the visitor center, passing through the picnic area. The trail can be followed many miles farther upstream from Ceremonial Cave into the Bandelier Wilderness, an area of lush forests and beaver dams. Although water can be obtained from the creek, the canyon trail is heavily utilized up as far as Ceremonial Cave and carrying of water is recommended.

3 Bandelier Wilderness

General description:	A strenuous two- or three-day loop hike deep into the scenic Bandelier Wilderness.
General location:	Bandelier National Monument.
Length:	About 18 miles round trip.
Elevation:	5,920–7,480 feet.
Maps:	Bandelier National Monument "Trails Illustrated" topo map; Frijoles 7.5-minute USGS quad.
Best season:	March through November.
Water availability:	Upper Alamo Creek; Frijoles Creek.
Special attractions:	Ancient Indian pueblo; deep gorges; solitude.
Permits:	Required for overnight camping; obtain at monument visitor center.

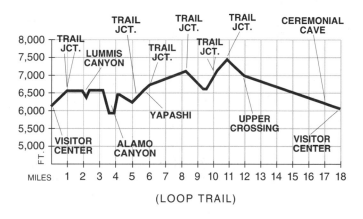

(LOOP TRAIL)

Finding the trailhead: Bandelier National Monument lies about 11 miles southwest of White Rock (near Los Alamos) along NM 4. Park in the designated backcountry parking area near the visitor center.

The hike: The ruins in Frijoles Canyon are usually mobbed with people in summer, especially on weekends. Within minutes of starting this hike, however, you will leave the vast majority behind. This hike makes a large loop into the heart of the Bandelier Wilderness. Along the way it visits a large unexcavated pueblo, scenic viewpoints, running streams, and dense forest.

In summer, plan on using at least one gallon of water per day per person, especially on overnight hikes. The first half of the hike travels mostly through pinyon-juniper woodland and is very hot and exposed. The scrubby trees do not cast much shade on the trail itself. Try to get an early start to avoid the worst of the heat. The first water is not reached until Upper Alamo Canyon about 9 miles into the hike, so prepare accordingly. The creek there is usually reliable, but inquire at the visitor center before starting. The hike is more difficult than the elevation and distance indicate because of several crossings of deep canyons. The first half of the loop is the hardest; it gets easier and more scenic the farther you go.

I foolishly did not follow my own advice when I made the hike. I started alone at noon on a hot summer day with only 3 quarts of water and no means of purifying more. I did the entire 18 miles in about 7 hours, having run out of water far from the end. I arrived intact, but exhausted and dehydrated, just before dark. The one smart thing that I did do was to let friends know when I expected to be back, in case I did not make it.

Although the hike can be done in one day as I did, it is much more enjoyable as a two- or three-day trip. Several side trails allow an even longer trek within the wilderness. The trail can generally be hiked all year, but in winter it can be very cold, especially at night. Snows, although not usually very deep, can obscure the trail on the flat mesa tops. If there is snow on the ground, it is best to go only if you are familiar with the trail and adept with a map and compass.

From the picnic area just across the creek from the visitor center, take the trail marked with signs for Yapashi, an abandoned pueblo ruin. The first mile is a long, fairly steep climb up out of Frijoles Canyon. A side trail or two right after the start stay in the canyon bottom. Follow the Yapashi signs. At a fork on the canyon rim, turn right toward Yapashi and enter the wilderness. Another 100 yards further, the trail forks again. Go left toward Yapashi. The trail traverses the relatively flat mesa top, crossing Lummis Canyon on the way.

Alamo Canyon is somewhat of a halfway point on the way to Yapashi. The narrow, sheer-walled, 600-foot deep canyon is spectacular but a major obstacle. The trail down is basically a set of rugged stairs, with the ascent only slightly better. Be sure to rest in the shade of the ponderosas lining the bottom. The canyon is usually dry here.

After you struggle out of Alamo Canyon, there is only one more small canyon to cross before reaching Yapashi. The ruined walls and rubble of the ancient pueblo cover a large area on the left side of the trail. Do not disturb or remove any artifacts from the unexcavated site. Little remains standing and vegetation covers much of it. Like many ruins at Bandelier National Monument, it has not been excavated and reconstructed. The Indians who reside today at Cochiti Pueblo say that their ancestors lived in this village. The Park Service does not permit camping within 0.25 mile of Yapashi Pueblo or other archaeological sites.

The trail forks 0.5 mile or so beyond Yapashi. Stay right, following the sign to Upper Crossing. A few hundred yards farther, another trail forks off to the left, to Painted Cave. Stay right again, toward Upper Crossing. The next 0.5 mile climbs steeply up onto a higher mesa level, through an attractive shady canyon wooded largely with ponderosa pine. The canyon tops out in open ponderosa woodland that is much cooler than the first part of the hike. Here and there are open patches left by the large La Mesa forest fire of 1977. At the top of a divide at about 8 miles, good views open up of

Bandelier Wilderness

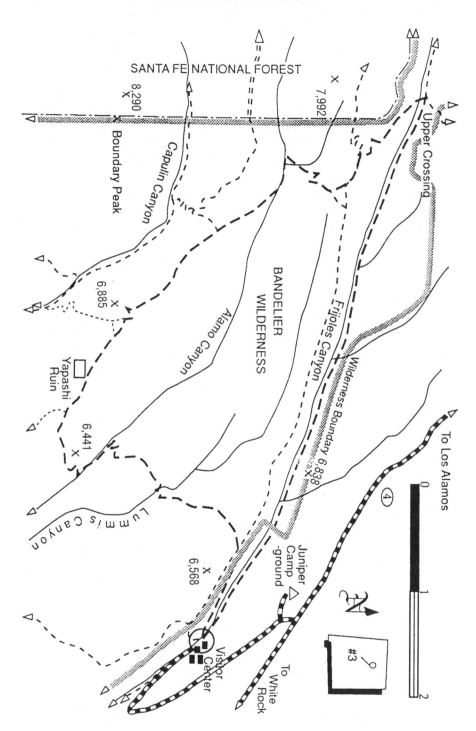

SANTA FE NATIONAL FOREST

Boundary Peak

8,290
X

X 7,992

Capulin Canyon

Upper Crossing

X 6,885

BANDELIER
WILDERNESS

Alamo Canyon

Frijoles Canyon

Yapashi
Ruin

Wilderness Boundary 6,838
X

6,441
X

Lummis Canyon

Juniper
Camp
-ground

To Los Alamos

④

X 6,568

#3

To
White
Rock

Visitor
Center

N

0   1   2

the high Jemez Mountains to the west. Also at the divide, another trail cuts left to Painted Cave. Bear right to Upper Crossing.

The crossing of Upper Alamo Canyon is much more pleasant than the lower crossing. The trail has a much gentler grade and is forested with ponderosa pine and Douglas-fir. The stream at the bottom is usually reliable. If you camp here, move well away from the stream and practice good sanitation. Watch for poison ivy.

The climb out of Alamo Canyon is not too bad. Go left toward Upper Crossing at the next junction reached in a large old burned area. The right fork follows the rim of Frijoles Canyon all the way back to the visitor center. It cuts off about 3 miles, if you are tired or short on time, but is much less scenic. Within another 0.25 mile, another fork cuts off to the right, following the same route as the previous fork. Bear left again toward Upper Crossing. After a short climb up through an old burned area, a third junction is reached. The left fork goes to the Alamo Springs trailhead. Turn right toward Upper Crossing. About 0.5 mile from the junction, the trail descends 600 feet into heavily wooded Frijoles Canyon.

From Upper Crossing, at 12 miles, only a long, gentle descent of 6 miles down Frijoles Canyon remains. At the junction in the canyon bottom, turn right toward park headquarters. Beware the poison ivy lining the trail for the first 3 miles or so. The canyon provides a lush, cool, peaceful walk beside a permanent stream. Do not camp at Upper Crossing; wait until you are at least 0.5 mile down the canyon and in a designated camping zone. At Ceremonial Cave (See Ceremonial Cave hike), only 1 mile from the visitor center, the crowds will reappear, making the long peaceful hike worthwhile.

4   Apache Spring

General description:	An easy day hike into the little-known, lush, high country of the Bandelier Wilderness.
General location:	Bandelier National Monument.
Length:	About 5 miles round trip.
Elevation:	7,720–8,600 feet.
Maps:	Bandelier National Monument "Trails Illustrated" topo map; Bland 7.5-minute USGS quad.
Best season:	April through November.
Water availability:	Apache Spring; Frijoles Creek.
Special attractions:	Lush forests; permanent stream.
Permits:	Required for camping; obtain at monument headquarters.

Finding the trailhead: From either Los Alamos or Bandelier National Monument headquarters, go to the junction of NM 4 and NM 501 along the north side of the monument. Go west 1.5 miles up into the mountains on NM 4 to the trailhead on the left (an unmarked parking area in front of a gate marked "Gate 10"). A Forest Service road goes off to the right across the highway from it.

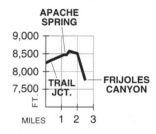

The hike: Bandelier is well known for its extensive Indian ruins, but few people leave the lower area of Frijoles Canyon surrounding the visitor center. Most people see only the scrubby pinyon-juniper woodland of the main archaeological area, not realizing that most of the park lies in the Bandelier Wilderness. The park's backcountry rises as high as 10,199 feet and some is lushly wooded with aspen, fir, and spruce. This hike provides an introduction to the little-known high country of the monument.

The hike starts at about 8,180 feet. The first part of the hike follows an old dirt road, closed to vehicle traffic, through ponderosa pine and Douglas-fir. Very quickly the road drops down to a meadow. It then climbs gradually up to a ridge top and hits a four-way junction. Turn right onto the most-used route, marked by a sign to Apache Spring. A few recovering burned patches mark the upper extent of the large 1977 La Mesa fire. At about 1.25 miles, the old road ends at the Bandelier Wilderness boundary. Signs indicate the boundary and trail distances.

The trail drops down a short distance into a small canyon. At the canyon bottom, a sign marks the very short side trail downstream to Apache Spring. If you obtain water, purify it. Take the trail up the canyon bottom, following the sign to Upper Crossing. About 0.25 mile up, a faint trail crosses the main trail. Ignore it and continue up the canyon bottom. The trail reaches

Apache Spring

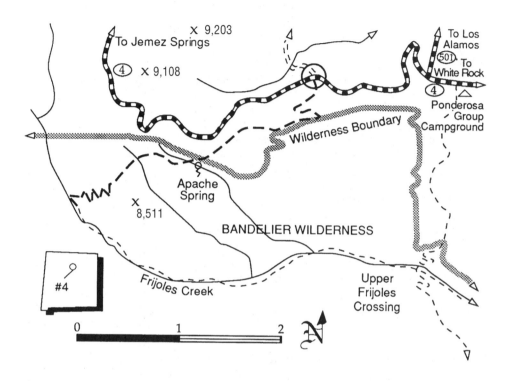

its high point shortly after climbing up out of the canyon. The trail follows a relatively level path through woods until it abruptly reaches the rim of Frijoles Canyon at about 2 miles. The next 0.5 mile is the only difficult part of the hike, as the trail steeply descends 750 feet to the bottom of the canyon.

The canyon bottom is lushly wooded and has a permanent bubbling stream. Return the same way you came, unless you want a longer hike. The easy trail in the canyon bottom can be followed downstream as far as desired. Some inactive beaver dams will be encountered as you go. Beware the thriving poison ivy lining much of the trail in the creek bottom. A loop can be made by following the canyon trail down the 3-plus miles to Upper Crossing, climbing out of the canyon 1.5 miles to Ponderosa Campground on NM 4, and walking 1.7 miles back up NM 4 past the NM 501 junction to your car. With a car shuttle, you can hike the long, but easy, 6 miles from Upper Crossing all the way down Frijoles Creek to the monument visitor center (see Bandelier Wilderness hike).

5 Tsankawi Ruin

General description:	An easy day hike along ancient Indian trails to a large unexcavated pueblo ruin in Bandelier National Monument.
General location:	Bandelier National Monument.
Length:	About 1.5 miles round trip.
Elevation:	6,490–6,680 feet (no elevation graph).
Maps:	Bandelier National Monument "Trails Illustrated" topo map; Tsankawi trail guide; White Rock 7.5-minute USGS quad.
Best season:	All year.
Water availability:	None.
Special attractions:	Indian pueblo ruin and caves; ancient trails; petroglyphs; views.

Finding the trailhead: Drive about 1 mile southwest on NM 4 from its intersection with NM 502 about 2.5 miles north of White Rock (near Los Alamos). Stop at the marked parking area on the left side of the road. Tsankawi ruin is a detached unit of the main park, which lies 12 miles away.

Tsankawi Ruin

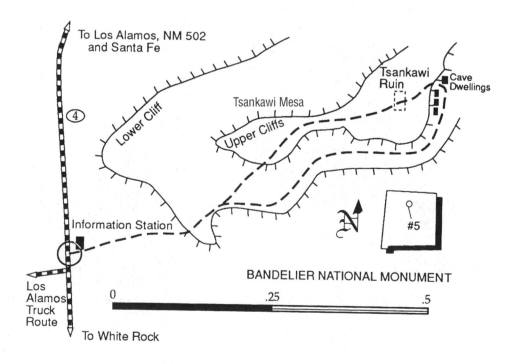

The feet of numerous prehistoric residents wore deep trails into the soft volcanic tuff of Tsankawi Mesa.

The hike: The separate Bandelier unit of Tsankawi contains a large mesa with surrounding valley land. Pinyon pine and juniper, along with a scattering of ponderosa pine, forest the area. This hike is one of the shortest in the book, but has many unique features.

Much of the trail follows prehistoric routes up onto the mesa top. Thousands of people's feet, using the trails for centuries, have worn deeply into the soft volcanic tuff. In places the old trails cut several feet into the rock. The large pueblo on the mesa top was probably built during the 1400s and occupied until the late 1500s.

The trail climbs up to the mesa top in two steps. After the first level, the trail forks, forming a loop. Stay left and climb up onto the mesa. A ladder must be climbed up the final ledge to the top. The mesa top itself has a very flat surface. The 350-room pueblo lies in the middle of the long narrow mesa. Only tumbled-down walls and a tremendous view of the Rio Grande Valley remain. Please do not disturb any of the ruins or artifacts.

After passing the pueblo, the trail drops down another ladder onto a ledge on the side of the mesa. Caves carved into the soft tuff line the cliffs by the ladder. The pueblo people built masonry buildings in front of the caves and lived in them. The trail curves back around the mesa, following ancient trails to the end of the loop. At sunset, watch the towering Sangre de Cristo Mountains across the Rio Grande Valley turn red and orange just before the sun drops below the horizon. Be sure to leave right afterwards, since Tsankawi closes at dusk.

6 McCauley Hot Springs

General description:	An easy day hike to a large hot spring in the Jemez Mountains.
General location:	About 35 miles west of Los Alamos.
Length:	About 3.5 miles round trip.
Elevation:	6,760–7,340 feet.
Maps:	Santa Fe National Forest; Jemez Springs and Redondo Peak 7.5 USGS quads.
Best season:	All year.
Water availability:	McCauley Hot Spring.
Special attractions:	Hot spring.

Finding the trailhead: From the junction of NM 501 and NM 4 about 5 miles southwest of Los Alamos, drive west 27.8 miles on NM 4 up into the mountains. Park at the Battleship Rock Picnic Ground. There is a small parking fee.

McCauley Hot Springs

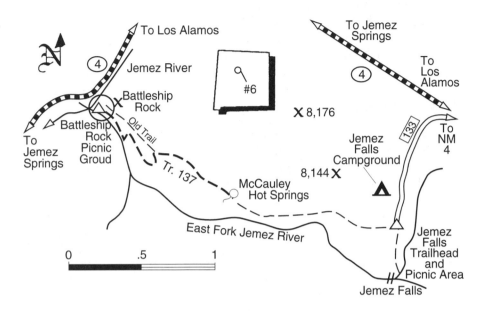

The hike: A huge caldera, or crater, created when an enormous volcano collapsed, forms the heart of the Jemez Mountains. Ash erupting from the mountain covered 400 square miles to depths of 1,000 feet. The crater rim is about 15 miles in diameter, one of the largest in the world. Although the volcano is no longer active, magma still lies fairly close to the surface under the mountains. The hot rock heats groundwater that surfaces as numerous hot springs throughout the mountains. In a search for potential geothermal energy sources, a number of test wells have been drilled in the Jemez.

This popular hike goes to a large hot spring, ideal for relaxing regardless of the time of year. Snows in winter may temporarily make the trail hard to find, but nothing feels better than a hot soak on a cold day.

Walk to the back of the picnic ground under the "prow" of the huge formation known as Battleship Rock. Trail 137 starts up the East Fork of the Jemez River from behind a round, gazebo-like picnic shelter. A "Trail 137" sign marks the spot. The trail follows along the left bank of the river for the first 0.25 mile or so. Watch for Trail 137 signs to help you find your way through the maze of social trails along the heavily used creek. An old trail climbs up to the spring just after you pass the base of Battleship Rock, but the new trail is easier. The new trail continues a little farther up the canyon bottom before beginning the climb up away from the river. A few large switchbacks help moderate the fairly steep grade. After you get partway up the side of the south facing slope of the canyon, the confusing side trails disappear.

At about the halfway point, the trail's grade lessens, making the rest of the walk very easy. Shortly before the spring, observant hikers will notice the ruined walls and rubble of an old Indian pueblo near the trail. Please do not disturb the site.

The spring, at about 1.75 miles, lies on a ponderosa pine-covered slope. The clear sandy-bottomed pool, created by a large rock wall, is about 30 feet across and 3 feet deep. Relax and enjoy the flowing warm water with the guppies, tetras, and other tropical fish that people have introduced.

Be sure not to get the pool water up inside your nose. On very rare occasions at other hot springs in the west, an amoeba has been known to pass through the mucous membranes, causing a very serious illness. If you are not too relaxed by the warm water, consider following Trail 137 another 1.75 miles to spectacular Jemez Falls.

7 Jemez River

General description: An easy day hike along the East Fork of the Jemez River.

General location: About 25 miles west of Los Alamos.

Length: About 3 miles round trip.

Elevation: 8,230–7,920 feet.

Maps: Santa Fe National Forest; Redondo Peak 7.5-minute USGS quad.

Best season: April through November.

Water availability: Jemez River.

Special attractions: Mountain stream in a narrow canyon; cross-country ski route.

Finding the trailhead: From the junction of NM 4 and NM 501, about 5 miles southwest of Los Alamos, drive west 18.1 miles on NM 4 up into the mountains. Stop at the well-marked East Fork trailhead parking area.

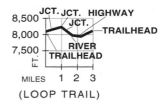

The hike: The East Fork of the Jemez River drains a large part of Valle Grande. The large circular valley, ringed with peaks as high as 11,500 feet, formed after an enormous eruption several million years ago. The explosion blew the heart of the mountain out, causing it to collapse into a large caldera, or crater. Eventually, several streams and rivers, such as the East Fork, cut through the crater wall. This hike follows an easy loop along part of the river. The trail is fairly new and does not show on older maps. Prepare to wade for a short part of the hike.

From the trailhead, follow the Trail 137 signs through second-growth ponderosa pine across a fairly level hilltop. Blue plastic diamonds nailed to

Jemez River

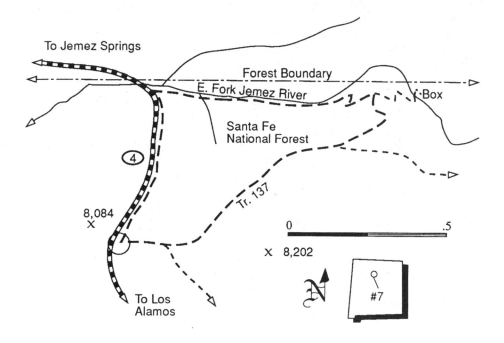

trees mark the route along an abandoned logging road. The diamonds mark the route for cross-country ski use in winter.

About 0.25 mile along the trail, a less-used blue diamond route forks to the right. Stay left on the main route. At just over 1 mile, Trail 137 forks. Go left, downhill, following the sign to East Fork Box. The trail descends steeply through dense Douglas-fir about another 0.25 mile to a second junction. The left fork, Trail 137A, is the proper route, going to the marked "East Fork River." The sign at the junction says 2 miles back to the East Fork Trailhead, but it is really less than 1.5 miles. If you have time, be sure to make the short side hike to the right to the East Fork Box. At the Box, the river squeezes into a narrow rocky gorge, impassable because of deep pools and waterfalls.

The left fork reaches the river after another short steep descent. A small footbridge crosses the small river, at least until the next flood washes it away. Follow the river downstream along its narrow, but lush grassy bottom. Soon the river narrows into a short section of small gorge. Plan to get your feet wet; the trail crosses from bank to bank in the rocky defile. In cold weather bring an extra pair of shoes. The canyon then widens for the last stretch before crossing NM 4 at about 2.25 miles. On summer weekends, you will encounter quite a few people on the last part of the trail. At the highway, hike left up the road about 0.5 mile to the trailhead or retrace the same route for your return.

8 San Pedro Parks

General description:	An easy two- or three-day hike into the lush meadows and forests of the San Pedro Parks Wilderness.
General location:	About 90 miles northwest of Albuquerque.
Length:	About 15 miles round trip.
Elevation:	9,200–10,300 feet.
Maps:	San Pedro Parks Wilderness; Santa Fe National Forest; Nacimiento Peak 7.5-minute USGS quad.
Best season:	May through October.
Water availability:	Rio de las Vacas; Clear Creek.
Special attractions:	Large meadows; solitude; winter cross-country ski potential.

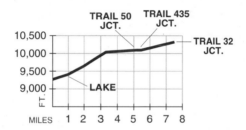

Finding the trailhead: From Cuba, drive east on NM 126 up into the mountains about 6 miles to the end of the pavement. About 0.25 mile from the end of the pavement, turn left onto gravel FR 70 and drive 2.8 miles to the parking lot, marked with signs for Trail 51 and the San Pedro Parks Wilderness.

From Los Alamos, start at the junction of NM 4 and NM 501 a few miles southwest of town. Drive west on NM 4 into the mountains for 24.5 miles to the junction of NM 126. Turn right onto NM 126 and follow it 29.8 very scenic miles to the turnoff of FR 70 above. The first 9 miles of NM 126 is paved, the remainder dirt. The gravel surface is generally good in dry conditions, but 1 or 2 miles in the middle are treacherous in wet weather. The dirt section of NM 126 is closed in winter.

The hike: This is one of my favorite hikes in New Mexico, in part because it is so different from most of the state's mountain areas. The 41,132-acre San Pedro Parks Wilderness is basically a big, relatively level area of forest and meadows. Crystal-clear, slow-moving mountain streams meander down through broad, marshy valley bottoms. Multiple large meadows give the area a manicured, park-like atmosphere. Instead of having a few high peaks, much of the entire wilderness lies at about 10,000 feet. No sheer cliffs or jagged peaks break up the terrain. Most New Mexico mountains are very steep, with level areas few and far between.

Boulders dot one of many meadows in the San Pedro Parks Wilderness.

Because the area is not very steep and mountainous, hiking is very easy, even over long distances. Additionally, plentiful water is available in the many creeks (as usual, treat it before using). This 15-mile hike gains only about 1,100 feet and can be done in a day fairly easily by someone in reasonable shape. However, you will regret not spending 2 or 3 days once you see it. Potential campsites are almost innumerable.

From the parking lot, follow Trail 51, the Vacas Trail, through spruce and fir about 0.75 mile to San Gregorio Reservoir. On summer weekends, the lake and trail to it can be busy. Once you leave the reservoir behind, you probably will not see many hikers. Weekdays are even better. When I did the hike on a summer weekday, I saw only one couple and one family in the entire 13 miles of hiking past the lake.

Follow the trail around the right (east) side of the small reservoir and away to the north. A little past the lake, a trail forks back to the lake on the left. Keep going north. At almost 2 miles you will hit Clear Creek, marked by a sign. The trail follows the creek for more than a mile, before climbing out a tributary into a long, flat, wooded stretch. Here and there a few faint old trails fork off, but the main trail is obvious.

Occasionally the trail crosses marshy meadows and creek bottoms. It is sometimes difficult to keep your feet dry during the crossings, especially right after the snow melts in the spring and after late summer rains. For overnight trips, you might want to carry an extra pair of tennis shoes. The trail sometimes gets faint in the marshy areas. Look carefully for the trail on the opposite side of the meadow and you should not have any problem.

San Pedro Parks

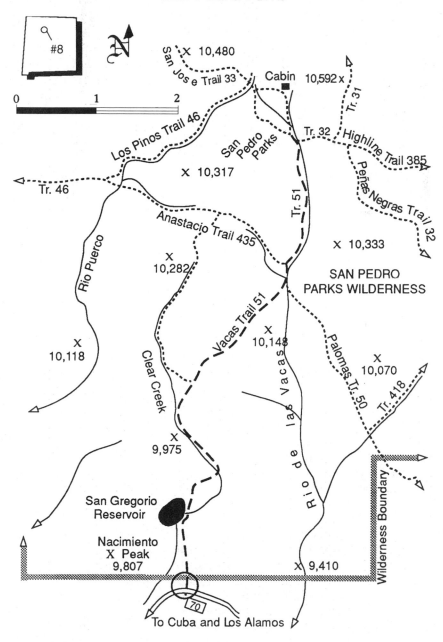

#8

N

0   1   2

X 10,480

San Jose Trail 33

Cabin   10,592 x

Tr. 31

Los Pinos Trail 46

San Pedro Parks

Tr. 32   Highline Trail 385

X 10,317

Peñas Negras Trail 32

Tr. 46

Anastacio Trail 435

Tr. 51

X 10,333

SAN PEDRO
PARKS WILDERNESS

Rio Puerco

X
10,282

X
10,118

Vacas Trail 51

X
10,148

Palomas Tr. 50

X
10,070

Tr. 418

Clear Creek

Rio de las Vacas

X
9,975

San Gregorio
Reservoir

Nacimiento
X Peak
9,807

Wilderness Boundary

X 9,410

70

To Cuba and Los Alamos

Also, wooden posts often mark the way in confusing sections. The junctions are generally fairly well marked, but having a copy of the San Pedro Parks Wilderness map will help immensely in avoiding any confusion in the large, open meadow areas.

At about 5.25 miles, the trail reaches the Rio de las Vacas. After this point, you will mostly be hiking across meadows. Be careful of lightning in the open areas, especially in late summer. Right after crossing the stream, Palomas Trail 50 forks off to the right. Turn left up the creek, staying on Trail 51 toward San Pedro Parks. About 0.25 mile up the creek, the Anastacio Trail 435, forks off to the left. Stay right on Trail 51 toward San Pedro Park. The rest of the hike follows the broad, grassy creek bottom of the Rio de las Vacas.

At about 7.5 miles, the trail reaches the junction with the Penas Negras Trail 32 on the right. From here, either return the same way, or continue as far as time and energy allow. By adding an easy 3 or 4 miles, a loop can be done by following Trail 51 a mile further up to Trail 46. Turn left on Trail 46, follow it for about 2.5 miles, and turn left again on the Anastacio Trail 435 to make a loop back to the 5.5-mile point on Trail 51.

9 Tent Rocks

General description:	An easy day hike through eroded rock pinnacles and a slot canyon.
General location:	About 35 miles west of Santa Fe.
Length:	About 3 miles round trip.
Elevation:	5,750–6,381 feet.
Maps:	Canada 7.5-minute USGS quad.
Best season:	All year.
Water availability:	None.
Special attractions:	Eroded volcanic spires and pinnacles; slot canyon; views.

Finding the trailhead: Take I-25 about 18 miles south of Santa Fe to Exit 264 (Cochiti Pueblo) and follow NM 16 about 8.2 miles to its junction with NM 22. Turn right onto NM 22. (If you are coming from Albuquerque, take Exit 259 for NM 22 and follow NM 22 to this junction.) Follow NM 22 for 2.7 miles to another junction. You will start seeing signs for Tent Rocks. Turn left, staying on NM 22. Go 1.7 miles and turn right onto gravel FR 266. The road has a washboard surface but is okay for sedans. Follow FR 266 for 4.8 miles to a small side road on the right that immediately opens up into a parking area. The eroded shapes of Tent Rocks are

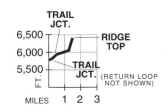

Tent Rocks

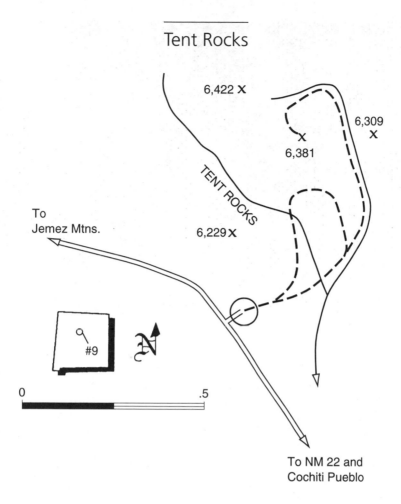

6,422 X

6,309 X

6,381 X

TENT ROCKS

To
Jemez Mtns.

6,229 X

#9

0 .5

To NM 22 and
Cochiti Pueblo

visible in the cliffs above. The trail starts by a large signboard at the back of the parking lot.

The hike: The interesting rock formations along this trail were named for their tepee- or tent-like shape. The formations were carved by water and wind out of a soft layer of pumice and ash deposited by massive volcanoes about 6.8 million years ago. The volcanoes are located a few miles northwest, part of the Jemez Mountains. The interesting terrain has attracted several movie makers; *Lonesome Dove, Young Guns II,* and *Silverado* are among the films with scenes shot here.

Do not try to climb on any of the formations. The rock is soft and crumbly, making it treacherous and easily damaged. The hike can be quite hot in summer, especially at midday. In winter, occasional snowstorms can make hiking difficult, but the white stuff usually melts off quickly.

Hikers admire the strange formations at Tent Rocks.

The hike consists of an easy loop with a somewhat more difficult spur trail. The trail begins behind the signboard and starts climbing at a moderate grade almost immediately. It quickly splits at the start of the loop. I arbitrarily took the right fork, which leads toward a narrow canyon mouth in a wall of cliffs. The spur forks to the right off of the loop near the canyon mouth.

The spur leads to some of the most interesting parts of the hike, but gets steeper and more treacherous than the loop. It follows the dry, sandy wash into the canyon. The walls quickly narrow into a dramatic slot canyon, similar to those commonly found in Arizona and Utah. The rock is so soft that if the wind is blowing, some sand and gravel may rain down on you. It almost goes without saying, but do not enter the canyon if rain threatens.

The trail winds up the narrow canyon bottom and then climbs steeply out, eventually reaching the ridge crest above. It offers great views of the Tent Rocks formations from above, plus far out over the Rio Grande Valley to the south. From the ridge, retrace your path to the loop and follow the rest of it back to the parking area.

10 Chavez Canyon

General description:	An easy off-trail day hike into a Utah-style red rock slot canyon.
General location:	About 50 miles northwest of Espanola.
Length:	About 2 miles round trip.
Elevation:	6,450–6,900 feet.
Maps:	Santa Fe National Forest; Laguna Peak and Navajo Peak 7.5-minute USGS quads.
Best season:	All year.
Water availability:	None.
Special attractions:	Sandstone slot canyon; solitude.

Finding the trailhead: Drive northwest of Abiquiu and Espanola on US 84 past Abiquiu Reservoir. Turn left (west) on FR 151 toward the Rio Chama. The turnoff lies about 1 mile north of the Ghost Ranch Museum and about 1.5 miles south of Echo Amphitheater. FR 151 is dusty, but usually in good enough condition for most vehicles. It may be muddy and slick when wet. Follow FR 151 12.8 miles to the Christ in the Desert Monastery entrance gate. Turn around and backtrack down the road 0.3 mile to where a faint old road turns off to the east (away from the river) and park. The old road is FR 151M, now closed to vehicles.

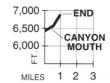

The hike: Although part of this hike is off-trail, most of it is quite easy. It takes you up a small tributary of the Chama River into a narrow sandstone slot canyon. The area, part of the Chama River Canyon Wilderness, is only lightly visited overall. Because this is not an improved trail, it sees minimal use.

Part of the drive to the trailhead follows the Chama River where it has cut a broad, scenic canyon into thick layers of red and buff-colored sandstone. The river is lined with cottonwoods, and pinyon pine and juniper cloak the mountain slopes and mesa tops. Chavez Canyon is a small, usually dry tributary that carries water down from the mesa above. Because part of the canyon is very narrow with sheer walls, flash floods can be a hazard if it rains. Check the weather carefully before doing the hike, especially on late summer afternoons.

Follow the old closed road (FR 151M) east toward the walls of the Chama River Canyon. It ends in about 0.5 mile or less; continue to follow the trail up into red rock Chavez Canyon. The trail, such as it is, soon disappears where it drops into the canyon bottom. Depending on the time of year and recent precipitation, there is sometimes a small trickle of water. The narrow canyon is more moist and shady than the surrounding area, so scattered

Chavez Canyon

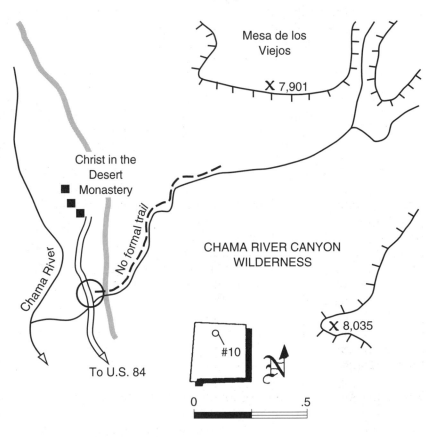

cottonwoods, ponderosa pines, and Douglas-firs grow here. The canyon narrows into a slickrock slot for a short distance and then widens some again. It then narrows once again and begins to climb more steeply. The walls tower overhead while the canyon shrinks to 10 feet in width. At this point, pools may require wading or even swimming to cross to continue traveling upstream.

I did the hike at the end of the rainy season (early fall) and was stopped by deep, muddy pools. If it is dry or you feel adventurous, give it a try. It is also possible that the canyon will become impassable at some point upstream because of unclimbable pouroffs (dry waterfalls). Do not try difficult climbing unless you have experience and the proper climbing equipment. Even if water or climbing soon ends your progress, the hike makes a scenic trip to a little-known area.

Chavez Canyon forms a narrow slot in places.

11 Santa Fe Baldy

General description:	A strenuous day hike or moderate overnight hike to a high summit in the Pecos Wilderness.
General location:	About 15 miles northeast of Santa Fe.
Length:	About 14 miles round trip.
Elevation:	10,300–12,622 feet.
Maps:	Pecos Wilderness; Santa Fe National Forest; Aspen Basin and Cowles 7.5-minute USGS quads.
Best season:	Late May through October.
Water availability:	Rio Nambe.
Special attractions:	Tremendous 360-degree views of the Sangre de Cristo Mountains; Jemez Mountains; and Rio Grande Valley.

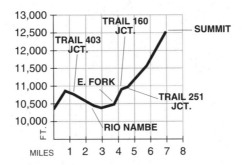

Finding the trailhead: Take NM 475 (Hyde Park Road) from Santa Fe about 15 miles to the parking area just below the ski area. Signs indicate the trailhead.

The hike: Santa Fe Baldy is one of a line of high peaks along the divide between the Rio Grande and Pecos River drainages. At 12,622 feet, the peak rises well above timberline. Its rounded, "bald" appearance probably led to its name. The prominent summit gives one of the best views possible of the 223,000-acre Pecos Wilderness. The wilderness and the surrounding Santa Fe National Forest, divided between the Sangre de Cristo and Jemez Mountains, have about 1,000 miles of mapped trails.

The Winsor Trail (254) is well marked at the parking area just below the Santa Fe Ski Basin. The wide, popular trail climbs steeply for the first 0.5 mile to the Pecos Wilderness Boundary. From the boundary, on a ridge top, the trail descends slightly through lush Douglas-fir, spruce, and aspen to the Rio Nambe at about 2.5 miles. A short distance past the wilderness boundary, you will pass the lightly used Trail 403 forking to the left. The Rio Nambe is the best source of water along the route. An informal side trail follows the river up a steep climb to Nambe Lake.

From the Rio Nambe, the trail climbs gradually again, crossing the east fork of the river at about 4 miles. This is the last reliable water source. The

Santa Fe Baldy

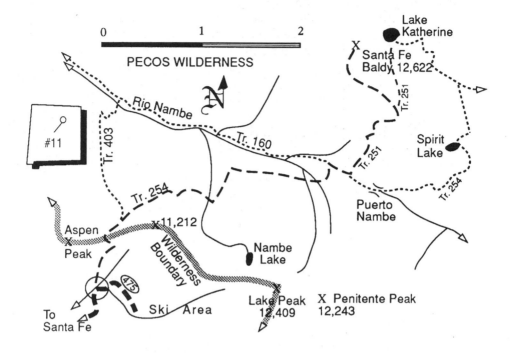

forest begins to thin in this stretch of trail, offering good views of Baldy above to the north and the Rio Grande Valley to the west. About 0.5 mile beyond the river, the Rio Nambe Trail 160 joins from the left. The area around the east fork of the river and the Trail 160 junction makes an ideal camping area on overnight trips.

Just beyond the Rio Nambe Trail junction, Trail 254 switches back from northwest to southeast. About 0.25 mile from the Trail 160 junction, turn left onto Trail 251 to Lake Katherine. Trail 251 climbs steadily up to the crest of the ridge, reaching an elevation of about 11,600 feet. Leave the trail at the top and climb the crest of the ridge to the left (north). Stay on the crest of the ridge until you reach the summit in about 1 mile. This is the steepest part of the hike, with a gain of about 1,000 feet.

From the summit, virtually the entire wilderness area can be seen to the north and east. The Sandia Mountains are visible far to the south and the Jemez Mountains lie across the Rio Grande Valley to the west. On clear days, peaks in Colorado are visible.

Much of the climb from the pass is above timberline and exposed. Be sure to carry rain gear and warm clothes even in summer. Whether you camp below the peak or do the trip as a day hike, try to get an early enough start to reach the summit by noon. Thunderstorms can develop with astonishing speed, especially in late summer afternoons. Getting caught in a lightning storm above timberline is an experience you will never forget.

The return follows the same route. A more extended backpack can be made by continuing down the east side of the pass to Lake Katherine, Spirit Lake, or many of the other lakes and streams of the Pecos River drainage. The hiking season varies depending on the amount of snow received during the winter.

12 Tesuque Creek

General description:	An easy day hike to a rushing mountain stream within minutes of Santa Fe.
General location:	About 10 miles northeast of Santa Fe.
Length:	About 4 miles round trip.
Elevation:	8,880–8,240 feet.
Maps:	Pecos Wilderness; Santa Fe National Forest; Aspen Basin and McClure Reservoir 7.5-minute USGS quads.
Best season:	May through November.
Water availability:	Tesuque Creek.
Special attractions:	Mountain stream; dense forest.

Finding the trailhead: From Santa Fe, take NM 475 up toward the ski area. On the left, just past Hyde State Park, lies the paved parking area for the trailhead. Signs mark it as the trailhead for Borrego Trail 150.

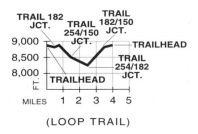

The hike: This hike's proximity to Santa Fe is part of its attraction. Within 20 minutes of leaving the Plaza, you will be strolling through Douglas-fir, spruce, and aspen. The hike touches only a tiny fraction of the Santa Fe National Forest and its 1,000 miles of trails. Many of the other hikes in this book are in the Santa Fe National Forest.

From the parking lot, the well used trail drops down into a wooded, dry creek bottom. It follows the creek down for about 0.5 mile to a junction. Go right at the junction, staying on Trail 150. The trail climbs up a small tributary to a low saddle, before dropping down again. After a fairly steep descent into another tributary, the trail reaches Tesuque Creek, announced in advance by the roar of rushing water. Be sure to purify any water taken from the stream.

At the creek, Trail 150 merges into Trail 254, the Winsor Trail, about 1.5

Tesuque Creek

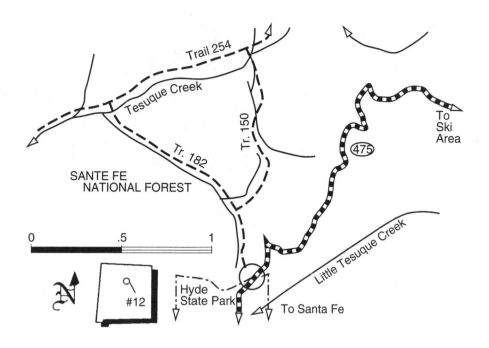

miles from the trailhead. To the right, the Winsor Trail climbs up to the ski area and miles beyond into the Pecos Wilderness. Go left, following Trail 254 down Tesuque Creek for about 1 mile to the junction with Trail 182 on the left.

Follow Trail 182 up a dry tributary for about 1 mile to its junction with Trail 150. The loop is now completed. Turn right and retrace your route up Trail 150 to the parking lot. The hike makes an ideal quick escape from Santa Fe. My wife and I did the hike late one summer afternoon after a long tiring drive up to Santa Fe from Texas.

13 Lake Katherine

General description:	A strenuous day hike or overnight trip to a high alpine lake at the base of Santa Fe Baldy.
General location:	About 40 miles northeast of Santa Fe.
Length:	About 16 miles round trip.
Elevation:	8,440–11,742 feet.
Maps:	Pecos Wilderness; Santa Fe National Forest; Cowles and Aspen Basin 7.5-minute USGS quads.
Best season:	June through October.
Water availability:	Winsor Creek; Lake Katherine.
Special attractions:	Large alpine lake in a glacial cirque.

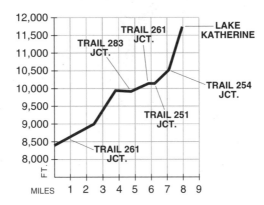

Finding the trailhead: From Pecos, drive about 20 miles north on paved NM 63 to the summer home area at Cowles. In Cowles turn left, crossing the Pecos River, to the marked Winsor Creek Trailhead on FR 121. Drive 1.3 miles to the trailhead at the end of the road. Contrary to what some maps still show, Winsor Creek is no longer a campground; it is only a trailhead.

The hike: Lake Katherine is a popular destination for hikers in the Santa Fe area. The large, crystal-clear lake nestles in the bottom of a valley at the eastern foot of Santa Fe Baldy. The glacial valley, or cirque, was carved out of the bedrock by glaciers in recent ice ages. The rock removed by the flowing ice was deposited in a long narrow mound, or moraine, at the bottom end of the glacier. The massive pile of rubble created a natural dam at the mouth of the cirque and the lake was born.

The lake lies at timberline, with the cliffs and slopes rising above mostly either bare or covered with fragile tundra. The lake lies at a high elevation and requires a climb of more than 3,000 feet to reach. Be sure that you are in good condition before attempting the hike. Take warm clothes and rain gear any time of year. Thunderstorms rise quickly, especially in late summer.

Lake Katherine • Stewart Lake • Cave Creek
Holy Ghost Creek

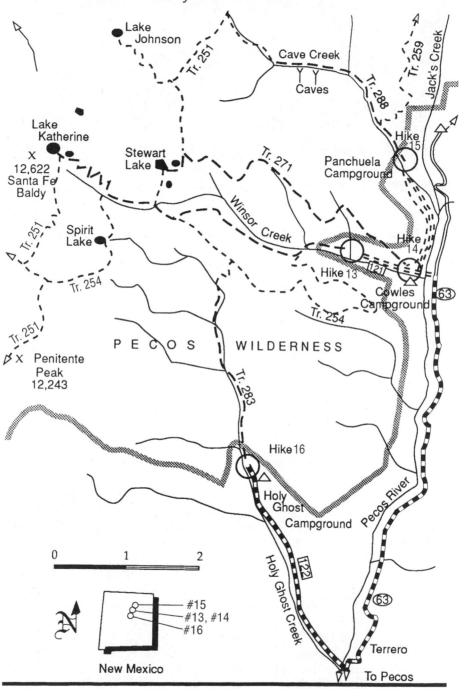

Lake Johnson

Tr. 251

Cave Creek

Caves

Tr. 288

Tr. 259

Jack's Creek

Lake Katherine

X
12,622
Santa Fe
Baldy

Stewart Lake

Tr. 271

Hike 15

Panchuela Campground

Tr. 251

Spirit Lake

Winsor Creek

Hike 14

Hike 13

121

Cowles Campground

63

Tr. 254

Tr. 254

Tr. 251

P E C O S   W I L D E R N E S S

X Penitente Peak
12,243

Tr. 283

Hike 16

Holy Ghost Campground

Pecos River

0   1   2

N

#15
#13, #14
#16

New Mexico

Holy Ghost Creek

122

63

Terrero

To Pecos

Formed by glaciers, spectacular Lake Katherine lies at the foot of Santa Fe Baldy.

From the trailhead at the end of the road, Trail 254 follows lush Winsor Creek upstream on the right bank. A little less than 1 mile up, the trail crosses the creek to the south bank. You may notice an unmarked fork just across the creek. The right fork, former Trail 261, is abandoned and no longer maintained by the Forest Service. Continue up Trail 254, climbing steadily out of Winsor Creek. Eventually the grade moderates some. Stay on Trail 254 to the junction with Trail 251. You hit Winsor Creek again at the junction. Go left, upstream, on combined Trail 254 and 251, following the sign to Lake Katherine. Trail 251 to the right goes to Stewart Lake (see the Stewart Lake hike).

From the Stewart Lake junction, the trail begins to climb a little more steeply again. After another mile or so, Trail 254 splits off to the left to Spirit Lake. Go right on Trail 251 to Lake Katherine, as directed by the sign. The trail now begins to climb and switchback in earnest as the air gets thinner. Spirit Lake is a considerably easier and faster hike from here than Lake Katherine. Some potential campsites can be found in the area of the junction.

As you climb toward Lake Katherine, the dense forest begins to thin along with the air and the trees become smaller. After a long, arduous climb with views opening up to the south and east, the trail reaches a very small lake tucked into a deep valley. One last grunt up the steep slope above the small lake brings you to Lake Katherine at about 8 total miles.

Sheer cliffs rise above the large, clear lake. Boulders and rubble spill down the slopes from the base of the cliffs. Snow and ice persist through the summer in drifts and sheltered crevices. A few hardy spruce trees lie scattered around the shores. Pikas chirp warnings from their hideouts in the rocky talus slopes, while marmots looking for an easy lunch approach hikers.

Santa Fe Baldy towers above the lake, poking high into the deep blue sky. The keen-eyed may observe a few hikers on the summit (see the Santa Fe Baldy hike). If you still have any energy left, the peak can be approached from the lake by continuing up Trail 251 to the crest and, from there, following the crest up to the top.

If you camp at Lake Katherine, be sure to set up on slopes below the lake, outside of the drainage basin. Use care in sanitation. The vegetation at that altitude is very fragile, so try to camp and walk only on bare areas. Be sure to bring warm clothes and sleeping bags.

14 Stewart Lake

See Map on Page 53

General description:	A moderate day hike or overnight trip to a beautiful lake in the Pecos Wilderness.
General location:	About 40 miles northeast of Santa Fe.
Length:	About 10 miles round trip.
Elevation:	8,180–10,232 feet.
Maps:	Pecos Wilderness; Santa Fe National Forest; Cowles 7.5-minute USGS quad.
Best season:	June through October.
Water availability:	Stewart Lake.
Special attractions:	A natural mountain lake.

Finding the trailhead: Follow the same directions to Cowles as the Lake Katherine hike. After turning left onto FR 121, stop right away at the Cowles Campground on the left, rather than following the road to its end at the Winsor Creek trailhead.

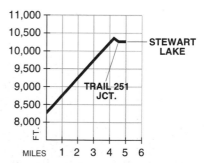

The hike: Stewart Lake is a beautiful small lake created by glaciers during recent ice ages. A small earthen dam enlarges the natural lake somewhat. Unlike the much higher Lake Katherine (see the Lake Katherine hike), Stewart Lake is surrounded by heavy forest. Although the lake requires moderate effort to reach, it is one of the easiest alpine lakes to hike to in the Pecos Wilderness. Thus it is a popular hike, especially on summer weekends.

The trail starts across the road from Cowles Campground. It climbs up the hill a short distance to Trail 271. To the right, Trail 271 goes to Panchuela Trailhead. Go left and start the long steady climb to the west. The trail slowly climbs higher with few switchbacks. The grade is steady, but relatively easy for almost the entire hike. As the trail climbs high above Winsor Creek, better and better views open up to the south and east. The trail passes through a lush forest of Douglas-fir, aspen, and other trees.

Finally, at about 4.5 miles, your trail intersects Trail 251 after a very short descent. Go left on Trail 251 to Stewart Lake. The last 0.5 mile to Stewart Lake is relatively level. Along the way, you will pass a pond on the right, set in an enormous, flat, marshy meadow.

If possible, try to camp for a couple of nights at Stewart Lake. Relax, fish, or day hike up to Lake Katherine, Spirit Lake, or Lake Johnson (see the Lake Katherine hike). Stewart Lake is fairly heavily used, so be sure to camp well away from the lake on bare ground out of the lake's drainage basin. Be careful with sanitation.

The same route can be followed back down or you can continue along Trail 251 about 0.5 mile to the junction with Trail 254. Follow Trail 254 down to Winsor Creek as described in the Lake Katherine hike. Then walk down FR 121 about 1.25 miles to the trailhead. The Trail 254 route is longer but adds some variety.

15 Cave Creek

See Map on Page 53

General description:	An easy Pecos Wilderness day hike through lush forest to a series of caves.
General location:	About 40 miles northeast of Santa Fe.
Length:	About 6 miles round trip.
Elevation:	8,320–9,100 feet.
Maps:	Pecos Wilderness; Santa Fe National Forest; Cowles 7.5-minute USGS quad.
Best season:	Late May into early November.
Water availability:	Hike follows permanent stream.
Special attractions:	Lush forest; trout stream; caves.

Finding the trailhead: From Pecos (about 20 miles east of Santa Fe), drive up the Pecos River Valley on paved NM 63 to the summer home area of Cowles. Drive slowly in Pecos itself; the town is a speed trap. Turn left at the small fishing lake in Cowles and cross the Pecos River, following the signs to Winsor Creek and Panchuela trailheads. Immediately after crossing the river,

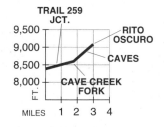

turn right on the Panchuela road. After driving through a guest ranch, you will reach the Panchuela trailhead, picnic area, and wilderness parking area at the end of the road.

The permanent Pecos Wilderness stream of Cave Creek flows through a cave for part of its length.

The hike: The Sangre de Cristo Mountains are the largest and highest mountains in New Mexico. Rising from foothills east of Santa Fe and west of Las Vegas, the mountains continue north for over 200 miles, well into Colorado. According to legend, the mountains were named for the "blood of Christ" by a dying Spanish priest during the Pueblo Revolt of 1680 when the mountains turned red at sunset.

The Santa Fe National Forest, the second oldest national forest in the United States, was created by President Harrison in 1892 as the Pecos River Forest Reserve. Part of the forest was protected as the 223,000-acre Pecos Wilderness in 1933. The wilderness contains over 150 miles of streams, many alpine lakes, and several glacier-sculpted peaks over 13,000 feet high.

Some maps still show Panchuela as a campground. However, fears of lead contamination in road fill obtained from the Terrero Mine caused the Forest Service to close its use to campers. Start the hike by walking from the wilderness parking area into the Panchuela picnic area. The trail (288) leads out of the center of the picnic area by crossing the creek to the north, or right, bank. The trail follows rushing Panchuela Creek upstream for about 1.5 miles. At times the trail lies next to the creek; at others it climbs 50 or 100 feet above. A short distance upstream from the picnic area, Trail 259 forks off to the right and climbs out of Panchuela Creek. Stay left on the trail following the creek. Another trail merges from the left from the direction of the picnic area. It is simply an alternate route back to the trailhead.

The trail passes through lush forests of Douglas-fir, aspen, and blue spruce. Willows and other deciduous shrubs and trees line the banks of the clear, rushing stream. Trout flit out of sight under rocks and banks at your approach.

After about 1.5 miles, the trail turns west along a tributary, Cave Creek, while Panchuela Creek continues north. As you continue up Cave Creek, you will suddenly notice the silence. The roar of rushing water, present for the entire hike, is missing. Except during times of heavy runoff, the stream is dry.

Continue up the trail, watching the creek on your left closely. Soon the sound of running water reappears and a cave mouth appears on the left bank of the creek. The stream disappears into the cave and flows underground for some distance, drying up the normal creek bed. Continue upstream along the trail a short distance farther to two even larger cave entrances taking the bulk of the creek flow. The caves can easily be entered here. Be sure not to enter alone and to wear hard hats and have three sources of light for each person. Use care; the caves are cold and wet with slippery rock and steep drops. Whether you enter the caves or not, the hike is a beautiful introduction to the Pecos Wilderness.

From the caves, follow the trail a short distance further upstream to the confluence of Cave Creek and Rito Oscuro. Ferns flourish among the aspens in a small parklike area at the fork in the creek. Return to the trailhead via the same route. Time and energy allowing, the trail can be followed much farther to such destinations as Horsethief Meadow and alpine Lake Johnson and Stewart Lake.

16 Holy Ghost Creek

See Map on Page 53

General description:	An easy day hike up a rushing trout stream through the lush forest of the Pecos Wilderness.
General location:	About 40 miles northeast of Santa Fe.
Length:	About 6 miles round trip.
Elevation:	8,200–9,180 feet.
Maps:	Pecos Wilderness; Santa Fe National Forest; Cowles 7.5-minute USGS quad.
Best season:	May through November.
Water availability:	Holy Ghost Creek.
Special attractions:	Tumbling mountain stream; beautiful forest.

Finding the trailhead: From Pecos, go about 14 miles north up the Pecos River Valley on NM 63 to the marked Holy Ghost Campground turnoff. Turn left onto the narrow paved road (FR 122) and follow it about 3 miles to the end at the campground.

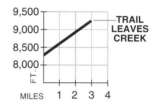

The hike: Holy Ghost Creek provides a pleasant, easy introduction to the Pecos Wilderness. Although this hike is not especially long or difficult, it gives a good feel for the many permanent streams that flow out of the Sangre de Cristo Mountains.

Trail 283 starts by the information board across from the trailhead parking area at the lower end of the campground. The last stretch of road goes through the main campground and upper group campground; parking along it is for fee-paying campground users only. After leaving the campground, the trail follows the stream through lush forests of aspen, Douglas-fir, ponderosa pine, and other trees, crossing the creek occasionally. At about 1.5 miles, a large tributary joins the creek on the left and the trail makes a short, steep climb up onto the left bank. At about 2 miles it rejoins the creek at another left-hand tributary.

The trail again makes a short, steep climb up the left bank and then rejoins the creek another 0.5 mile further at the end of the hike. Beyond this point the trail then crosses to the right bank and begins to climb completely out of the creek drainage, eventually joining Trail 254 on the ridge top. For the energetic, Trail 254 can be followed all the way to Lake Katherine, Santa Fe Baldy, Stewart Lake, and many other destinations. See the Santa Fe Baldy, Lake Katherine, and Stewart Lake hikes.

17 Beatty's Cabin

General description:	A moderate day hike or backpack through forest and lush meadows into the heart of the Pecos Wilderness.
General location:	About 40 miles northeast of Santa Fe.
Length:	About 11 miles round trip.
Elevation:	9,350–10,120 feet.
Maps:	Pecos Wilderness; Santa Fe National Forest; Pecos Falls and Elk Mountain 7.5-minute USGS quads.
Best season:	June through October.
Water availability:	Pecos River at Beatty's Cabin.
Special attractions:	Pecos River headwaters; lush alpine forest and meadows; views; fall color; fishing.

Finding the trailhead: From Pecos (east of Santa Fe, just off I-25), drive north on paved NM 63 about 17.8 miles. Past Terrero, the pavement gets narrower and rougher. Turn right onto the marked fork for Iron Gate Campground (FR 223). Follow it about 4.3 miles to its end at the campground and trailhead. This dirt road is rough and narrow, and is only margin-

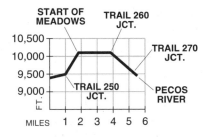

ally passable by sedans, especially when wet. A high-clearance vehicle is better.

The hike: This trail makes a great day hike or, even better, an overnight trip into the heart of the Pecos Wilderness. The 223,000-acre wilderness is the second largest in the state and contains many of the highest peaks and a large concentration of alpine lakes and streams.

The trail climbs from Iron Gate Campground through conifer forest up onto Hamilton Mesa, a beautiful area of meadows with panoramic views of the 12,000- and 13,000-foot peaks of the Pecos Wilderness. It then descends to the clear, rushing, trout-bearing waters of the Pecos River at Beatty's Cabin.

Start the hike at the trailhead at the back of the campground. Trail 249 climbs up into the forest at a moderate grade. In about 1 mile, at the fork with Trail 250, go left and stay on Trail 249 and continue climbing toward Hamilton Mesa. In another 0.5 mile or so, you hit the start of the large ridge-top meadows that blanket the top of Hamilton Mesa. The high point of the hike is at the top of the first meadow. For the next 1.5 to 2.0 miles, the grade levels out as the trail traverses the expansive grassy slopes. Views open up in all directions of the Truchas Peaks, Santa Fe Baldy, and other summits. Be sure not to get caught in these high meadows during a lightning storm.

Beatty's Cabin

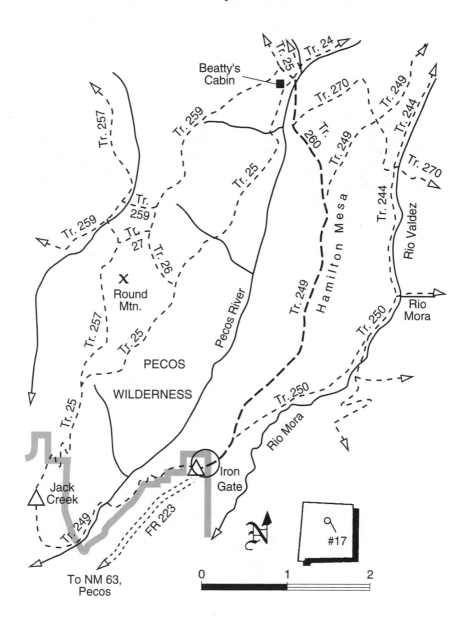

Beatty's Cabin

Tr. 25
Tr. 24
Tr. 270
Tr. 249
Tr. 244
Tr. 259
Tr. 257
Tr. 260
Tr. 249
Tr. 25
Tr. 270
Tr. 259
Tr. 259
Tr. 244
Rio Valdez
Tr. 27
Tr. 26
X Round Mtn.
Pecos River
Tr. 249
Hamilton Mesa
Tr. 257
Tr. 25
Rio Mora
Tr. 250
PECOS

WILDERNESS
Tr. 250
Rio Mora
Tr. 25
Iron Gate
Jack Creek
Tr. 249
FR 223
To NM 63, Pecos

N

#17

0   1   2

Hamilton Mesa offers views of the Truchas Peaks.

At about 4 miles into the hike, you reach the junction with Trail 260 in one of the meadows. Go left on Trail 260 toward Beatty's Cabin. The trail descends about 1.5 miles through the woods to the Pecos River at Beatty's. Ignore Trail 270 where it forks off to the right just before the river.

The trail crosses the rushing waters of the river on a footbridge and enters a large meadow with the cabin on the slope above. A number of trails take off from this area, making Beatty's a good base camp for backpackers. Many day trips to other parts of the wilderness, from lakes to alpine peaks, are possible from here. Be sure to check with the Forest Service; camping may be restricted in the immediate vicinity of the cabin.

The shortest return to the trailhead requires retracing your steps. However, a wilderness map will indicate two other possible return routes. One goes via Trail 25 and Jacks Creek Campground, the other takes Trails 270, 224, and 250 along the Rio Valdez and Mora River.

18 Hermit Peak

General description:	A strenuous day hike to the rocky summit of a prominent Pecos Wilderness peak.
General location:	About 20 miles northwest of Las Vegas.
Length:	About 8 miles round trip.
Elevation:	7,500–10,212 feet.
Maps:	Pecos Wilderness; Santa Fe National Forest; El Porvenir 7.5-minute USGS quad.
Best season:	May through November.
Water availability:	Trailhead; Hermit Spring.
Special attractions:	Views.

Finding the trailhead: From the center of Las Vegas, take NM 65 west. The route is poorly marked; ask for directions if you have trouble finding it. After you pass the Armand Hammer World College, the road, while still paved, becomes narrow, windy, and mountainous. Be careful on the many blind curves. The road passes through the villages of Gallinas and El Porvenir. At about 14.5 miles, the road splits. Go right to El Porvenir Campground, as marked. Park in the parking lot at the entrance of the campground at about 17 miles.

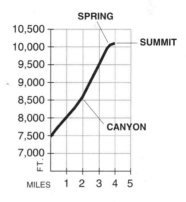

The hike: Hermit Peak anchors the far southeastern arm of the Pecos Wilderness. Although the summit has a broad, flat top, towering cliffs dominate its eastern escarpment. The sheer walls give the peak a notable appearance, making it recognizable miles away out on the high eastern plains. The peak was named for a hermit who supposedly lived in a cave near the summit.

If you parked in the lot at the entrance of the campground, the marked Trail 219 will be right across the road. It follows a beautiful, easy route far up El Porvenir Canyon. To find the Hermit Peak trail, walk along the road across the bridge into the campground. Across from the self-service pay station, a sign marks Trail 223 to Hermit Peak.

The trail immediately climbs out of the canyon onto a bench that slopes up toward Hermit Peak. The trail is well used and easy to follow the entire way. At about 0.25 mile, the faint, but marked, Dispensas Trail forks to the right. Stay left toward Hermit Peak, as directed by the sign. At a little more than 0.5 mile, two old roads join the trail from the right, one after another. Stay left. About 100 feet after joining the roads, the marked trail to the peak climbs off to the right, leaving the roads.

Hermit Peak

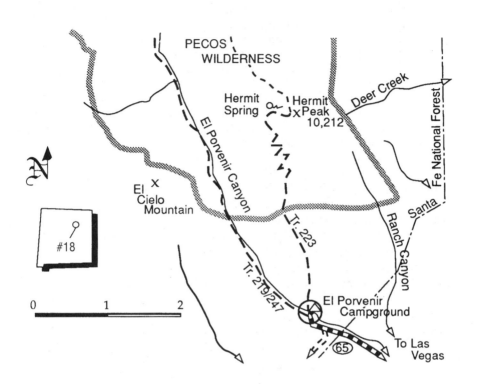

The rocky trail climbs steadily, getting steeper as you progress. It crosses a small stream a couple of times in the first 2 miles. The next 1.5 miles switchback up a narrow canyon hemmed in by the peak's towering cliffs. This steep and rocky stretch is the hardest part of the hike. By the time that you hit the switchbacks, you have crossed the unmarked wilderness boundary.

Just as the steep switchbacks become interminable, you pop out onto a ridge at about 3.5 miles. The view is impressive. Right after reaching the top, the trail makes an unmarked fork. Take either fork; they quickly rejoin. A short distance up the trail lies Hermit Spring, enclosed in a steel and concrete box. A sign marks the water source. Blessedly, the last 0.5 mile to the summit from the spring is on a much more level grade. The large wooded and relatively level summit that you will be crossing has numerous possible campsites. Wooden crosses have been erected along the way by a religious group.

At about 4 miles, a sign on the flat summit marks the continuation of Trail 223 to the left. It continues on to Lone Pine Mesa and Beaver Creek.

About 100 yards straight ahead, visible from the sign, is the sheer eastern escarpment. Soak up the views far to the east; try to imagine the wagons of the Santa Fe Trail traversing the plains at the base of the mountains. Below you, the cliffs fall away hundreds of feet, producing vertigo in all but the least acrophobic.

Naturally, I arrived on the summit when it was wreathed in fog. It took some time for me to get much of a view. A sign near the rim marks the short trail to Hermit's Cave to the right (south). If you camp on the top, be sure to get up for the sunrise. A 14-mile loop can be made by continuing on Trail 223 and by turning left at every succeeding trail junction. Ultimately, you follow El Porvenir Canyon back down to the trailhead on combined Trail 219/247. The loop is best done as an overnight trip. El Porvenir Campground makes a beautiful base camp before or after your hike. It is usually quite busy on summer weekends.

19 Trampas Lakes

General description:	A moderately strenuous day hike or overnight trip to two alpine lakes in the Pecos Wilderness.
General location:	About 40 miles south of Taos.
Length:	About 12 miles round trip.
Elevation:	8,940–11,410 feet.
Maps:	Pecos Wilderness; Carson National Forest; Truchas Peak and El Valle 7.5-minute USGS quads.
Best season:	June through October.
Water availability:	Rio de las Trampas; Trampas Lakes.
Special attractions:	High natural alpine lakes; rugged mountains.

Finding the trailhead: Turn south onto NM 518 from NM 68 on the south side of Taos. Go about 15 miles to the NM 75 junction. Turn right on NM 75 and go about 6.7 miles to the NM 76 junction. Go left on NM 76 4.4 miles to FR 207. The unmarked FR 207 junction is on the left. If you are coming north on NM 76 from Santa Fe and Chimayo, the FR 207 turnoff is 1.1 miles north of the little village of Trampas. Follow FR 207, a good all-weather gravel road, all the way to its end at the Trampas Trailhead Campground at 8.2 miles.

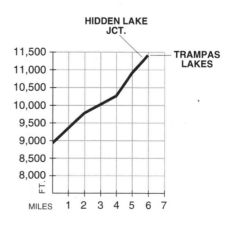

Trampas Lakes • San Leonardo Lakes

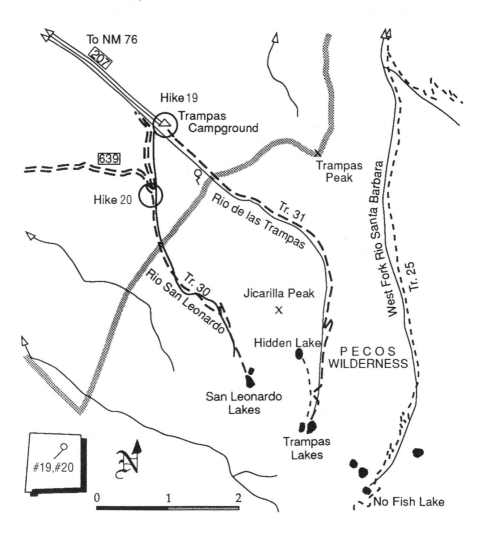

To NM 76

207

Hike 19
Trampas
Campground

639

Hike 20

Rio de las Trampas

Tr. 31

Trampas
Peak

Tr. 30

Rio San Leonardo

Jicarilla Peak
X

West Fork Rio Santa Barbara

Tr. 25

Hidden Lake

PECOS
WILDERNESS

San Leonardo
Lakes

Trampas
Lakes

No Fish Lake

N

#19,#20

0   1   2

Cascades tumble down the Trampas River in the Pecos Wilderness.

The hike: The northern end of the Pecos Wilderness is much less heavily visited than the areas around Santa Fe and the Pecos River drainage. When I did this hike on an August weekday I encountered only two other small groups. On summer weekends, the trail is probably moderately busy.

The two natural Trampas Lakes, and a third another mile up the trail, were formed when glaciers carved out basins in the rock and deposited rock dams, or moraines at the downstream ends of the basins. The lakes are tucked into forest just below timber line. Above tower sheer canyon walls and the 13,000-foot Truchas Peaks, the second highest in New Mexico.

The trailhead campground consists basically of a pit toilet and a sign but still makes a good camp before or after the hike. No water taps or tables are present. Creek water can be treated for use.

Trail 31, marked by a sign, climbs up the hill on the backside of the campground. The trail is one of the best designed and maintained that I have seen in the New Mexico mountains. Except for the last mile, the trail follows a very steady, moderate grade for the entire route up the Rio de las Trampas. Few rocks and roots lie on the smooth trail. Although the elevation gain and distance are considerable, the excellent trail makes the hike easier than it otherwise would be.

The trail follows the river the entire way, with a few easy crossings. An avalanche chute or two remind you that these are serious mountains. The best campsites are probably at about the 3-mile point and at the lakes. The last mile does steepen considerably, with some rocky and muddy areas. At about 6 miles the trail forks. As marked by the sign, the Trampas Lakes are to the left and Hidden Lake is to the right. Go left toward the Trampas Lakes. Just a few feet up the left fork, a sign points the directions to the Upper and Lower Trampas Lakes. The upper lake is less than 100 yards to the right; the lower is a little farther to the left. The lower lake is larger, but both are beautiful. If you have time, be sure to hike the easy additional mile to Hidden Lake.

The lake shores have seen a lot of wear from hikers and campers. Camp well away from the lakes to try to minimize additional damage. Likewise, use good sanitation practices. Walk on already bare areas; try not to trample the fragile alpine vegetation.

20 San Leonardo Lakes

See Map on Page 66

General description:	A strenuous day hike or overnight trip to a pair of natural alpine lakes in the Pecos Wilderness.
General location:	About 40 miles south of Taos.
Length:	About 8 miles round trip.
Elevation:	9,340–11,360 feet.
Maps:	Pecos Wilderness; Carson National Forest; El Valle 7.5-minute USGS quad.
Best season:	June through October.
Water availability:	San Leonardo Creek and Lakes.
Special attractions:	High alpine lakes.

Finding the trailhead: Follow the same directions as those for the Trampas Lakes hike. Instead of driving 8.2 miles up FR 207 to its end, go only 7.8 miles to the FR 639 turnoff. Go right, across the creek, on FR 639 for 1.3 miles. The trailhead, marked by a Trail 30 sign, is on the left where a small side road turns off. Unless you have a 4-wheel drive, do not attempt to drive up FR 639 if it is wet or rain is threatening. Several spots can get very muddy and treacherous. Otherwise, with care, most vehicles should be able to make it up the road.

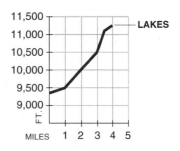

The hike: Although some maps show the lakes as only one lake, in reality there are two adjacent to each other. The northern end of the Pecos Wilderness is less visited than most of the wilderness in the Santa Fe area. Although these lakes are probably among the least visited in the wilderness, they are no less scenic. Like the nearby Trampas Lakes (see the Trampas Lakes hike), they lie in a glacial cirque at timberline surrounded by towering peaks.

From the sign at the side of FR 639, walk up the rough side road into the canyon formed by San Leonardo Creek. The little road can be driven for 0.3 mile by a high clearance vehicle if it is dry. At 0.3 mile the road is blocked and you must walk. The old road ends only another 0.1 mile or so along the way. From there, the remainder of the route is trail. Although the hike to the lakes is only about 4 miles, the trail is very steep and rocky, with numerous stream crossings. Even though the nearby Trampas Lakes Trail is longer and gains more altitude, this hike seemed harder to me. However, by being more difficult and a little more out of the way, this trail is only lightly used.

At a little more than 0.5 mile up from FR 639, you cross the marked Pecos Wilderness boundary. The trail follows the stream for the entire route.

Rain gear proves its value as clouds descend on Upper San Leonardo Lake in the Pecos Wilderness.

The crossings can be done with dry feet, but are tricky with a large pack. The trail passes through lush spruce and fir forest. The source of the stream is passed in a particularly steep stretch about 3 miles up. The water gushes out of a large spring right next to the trail.

The trail finally levels out some for the last 0.25 mile before the lakes. As the trail crosses the little ridges left by the glaciers, it fades in and out. Just keep walking up toward the back of the valley, obvious now with its towering walls. You will pass the smaller lower lake on the left and hit the second right afterwards at the very back of the valley.

The upper lake is a good-sized alpine lake, nestled into the steep slopes and cliffs of the cirque. A few patches of snow usually last through the summer at the base of the cliffs. Dead tree trunks ring the shoreline, carried into the lake by a 1973 landslide.

As with all alpine lakes, please do not camp on or near the shoreline and use good sanitary practices. The high elevation vegetation is very fragile. Unless you have to, it is best not to build campfires because of the shortage of firewood at the lakes' timberline location.

Be sure to take warm clothes and rain gear. It started raining on me within minutes of arriving at the lake and was still pouring two hours later when I got back to my car. I then slipped and slid back down FR 639, narrowly avoiding getting my car stuck.

21 Serpent Lake

General description:	A strenuous hike to an alpine lake and high peak on the northern edge of the Pecos Wilderness.
General location:	About 38 miles south of Taos.
Length:	About 9.5 miles round trip.
Elevation:	10,720–12,828 feet.
Maps:	Pecos Wilderness; Santa Fe National Forest; Jicarita Peak and Holman 7.5-minute USGS quads.
Best season:	June through October.
Water availability:	Serpent Lake, sometimes at spring along Trail 19 between Serpent Lake and crest.
Special attractions:	Alpine lake; high peaks; tundra; lush forest; views.

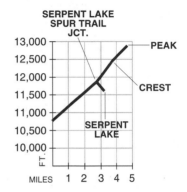

Finding the trailhead: From Ranchos de Taos on the south side of Taos, take NM 518 south toward Mora for about 29.4 miles to the junction with FR 161. Or, from the junction of NM 518 and NM 75 near Placitas, follow NM 518 toward Mora for 13.7 miles to the FR 161 junction. Or, from Mora, head north on NM 518 for 13.9 miles to the junction. Follow FR 161, a good gravel road, 4.5 miles to its end at the trailhead.

The hike: This hike leads into a very scenic, but less traveled part of the Pecos Wilderness. It offers a nearly pristine alpine lake, fields of tundra, and high peaks with views of the wilderness and a vast expanse of northern New Mexico.

Because the upper part of this hike is very high and exposed, be sure to take plenty of warm clothes and rain gear any time of year. Start early to avoid getting caught by storms and lightning on exposed ridges and peaks. The hike to the lake is moderate; up to the peaks above it is strenuous.

Initially, Trail 19 is effectively a continuation of the road. Two other trails start at the trailhead; one goes up the mountainside, the other down. The maps are a bit confusing here; just follow Trail 19, the old road. It is steep and rocky. In less than 0.5 mile, you hit a marked junction. Go left, uphill naturally, on Trail 19 toward Serpent Lake. Soon after, you get to do a balancing act crossing an irrigation ditch on a log.

The old road ends at the ditch, but the trail continues climbing steeply through thick spruce and fir forest. After about 2.5 miles, you cross the Pecos Wilderness boundary. Soon afterwards, you reach a marked junction in a small saddle. To get to Serpent Lake, go right on a spur trail and drop a

Serpent Lake is in a lightly visited part of the Pecos Wilderness.

Serpent Lake

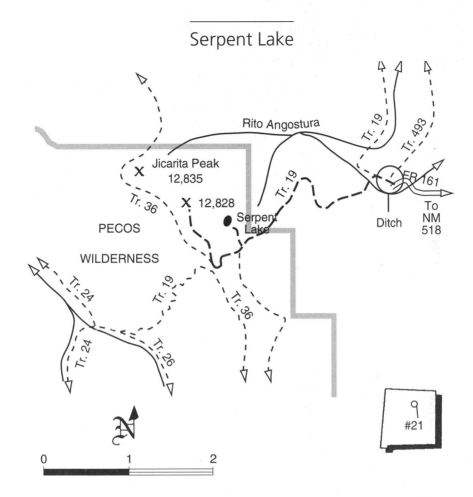

short distance down to the small, jewel-like lake centered in a grassy meadow. Because this trail is far less popular than those to other lakes in the wilderness, such as Lake Katherine, the lake shore is still grassy and covered with flowers. Please try to keep it that way by not walking or camping on or near the lake shore. There are good campsites by the trail junction in the saddle.

If you are tired, head on back down the mountain. If you feel strong or masochistic, take a look at the ridge and peak high above the lake. It looks close, but it is not. This hike continues up to there.

From the lake, climb back up to the junction in the saddle. Turn right and continue up Trail 19 toward the crest and ultimately the Santa Barbara River trails. The trail switchbacks steeply as you rise above timber line. Views stretch for miles to the north and east. Serpent Lake and another adjacent smaller lake become visible below.

At the crest, views open up of the high peaks of the Pecos Wilderness to the southwest. There is a junction here. Trail 36 follows the mountain crest to the right and left across the tundra. Trail 19 drops down to the East Fork of the Santa Barbara River far below. Rather than follow these trails, turn right and follow the highest point of the crest to the northwest, above Serpent Lake. After almost 1 mile of gradual climbing across the tundra, you reach an unnamed summit more than 12,800 feet above sea level. Unless a thunderstorm is bearing down on you, enjoy the view before heading down to more oxygen.

If this peak is not enough to satisfy you, it is only a short distance across a saddle to the summit of slightly higher (7 feet!) Jicarita Peak to the northwest. If you want to climb Jicarita Peak and skip the first peak, it is probably easiest to follow Trail 36 most of the way (see the wilderness or topo maps). For backpackers, there are many possible routes from here, particularly if a car shuttle can be arranged at another trailhead.

22 Wheeler Peak

General description:	A very strenuous day hike or moderately strenuous two- or three-day trip to the summit of New Mexico's highest peak.
General location:	About 20 miles northeast of Taos.
Length:	About 15 miles round trip.
Elevation:	9,390–13,161 feet.
Maps:	Carson National Forest; Wheeler Peak 7.5-minute USGS quad.
Best season:	June through October.
Water availability:	Taos Ski Valley by the trailhead; stream below summit ridge at about the 5-mile point.
Special attractions:	Alpine terrain; tremendous views from New Mexico's highest peak.

Finding the trailhead: Drive about 3.9 miles north of the center of Taos on NM 522 and turn right on NM 150. Follow this road about 15 miles to Taos Ski Valley. Park in the upper gravel parking ramp at the end of the road across from the base of the ski area. Large Wheeler Peak Wilderness signs mark the trailhead.

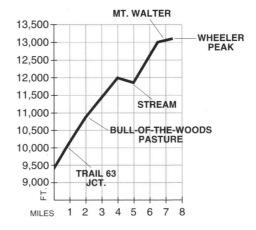

The hike: Wheeler Peak lies in the center of the small 19,000-acre Wheeler Peak Wilderness. Several

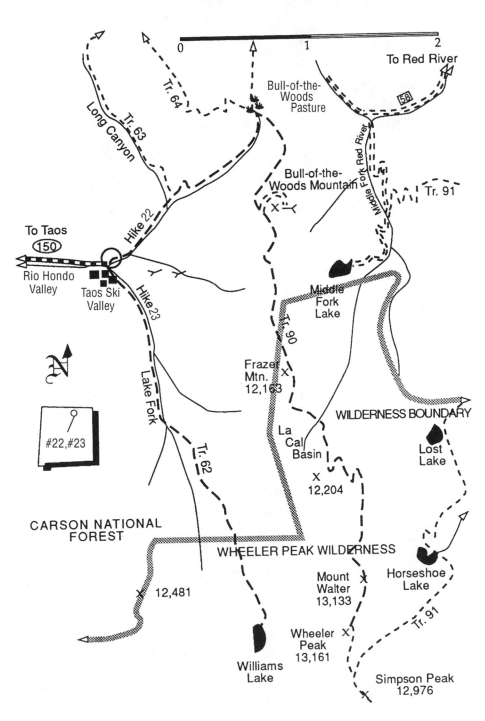

Marmots inhabit alpine areas of the Sangre de Cristo Mountains, such as this spot by Williams Lake.

other of New Mexico's highest peaks lie in and around the wilderness. The peaks and ridges are one of the few areas in New Mexico with extensive amounts of alpine tundra vegetation. The glacial cirques on the slopes of the peaks contain many natural alpine lakes. Snowfields remain year round.

Be sure to get a very early start on this hike. To minimize problems with storms, you ideally want to be on the summit before noon. Snow flurries are possible even in mid-summer. Be sure to take rain gear and extra warm clothing. Lightning and hypothermia are real threats on Wheeler Peak and the exposed summit ridge.

The heavily-used trail leads out of the parking area behind the trail signs and immediately begins climbing up the valley trending northeast. The first mile of the hike is extremely steep and rocky and, in my opinion, the hardest part of the entire hike. The first 2 miles to Bull-of-the-Woods Pasture are somewhat confusing. A maze of old roads and trails criss-cross with inadequate trail markings. However, the proper route is the most heavily worn and is easy to find. On a summer weekend, there will be plenty of people to follow. You will not get lost if you persist in following the valley northeast to Bull-of-the-Woods Pasture. The route stays fairly close to the stream in the valley bottom for the entire 2 miles.

At just short of 1 mile you will pass marked Trail 63, the Long Canyon Trail to Gold Hill, coming in from the left. Ignore it and continue climbing up the northeast-trending valley. Just past the trail junction, the trail hits an old road. Turn left onto the road and follow it the rest of the way up the valley. About 1 mile past Long Canyon the route levels out at Bull-of-the-Woods Pasture. The road forks at the edge of the level area. Turn right, following the sign toward Wheeler Peak.

The road quickly resumes climbing. The old road climbs up around the west side of Bull-of-the-Woods Mountain. A couple of old mines on the side and top of the peak are the destination of the old road. At about 3 miles the route leaves the old road and turns into an obvious trail. From here the trail is easy to follow all the way to the summit.

From this point on, most of the trail traverses the tundra above timberline. It follows the ridge south all the way to Wheeler Peak. If storms are building, do not venture beyond Bull-of-the-Woods Mountain, because the rest of the trail is very exposed to lightning. On my first attempt to climb Wheeler Peak, I was chased down the ridge from just short of the summit by a hair-raising lightning storm.

At about 5 miles, the trail drops slightly into a small, forested valley, probably the only good camping area on the route, other than Bull-of-the-Woods Pasture. A small stream provides water in the valley bottom.

At about 7 miles, you reach the 13,133-foot summit of Mt. Walter (and you thought it was Wheeler Peak!). Do not despair, Wheeler Peak is less than 0.5 mile further. One hiker wrote in the register on Wheeler Peak:

"Thought it was Wheeler,
And did not falter,
Was quite saddened,
To find it was Walter."

Enjoy the splendid views from the top of New Mexico. Ranks of snow-capped peaks line the horizon in Colorado. Alpine lakes fill the cirques at the base of the peak. Marmots look for handouts while the pikas harvest alpine grasses to last them through the long winter.

Unless you got a very early start, do not dawdle too long on the summit. Keep an eye out for storms, especially after lunch. They can build within minutes, threatening hikers with lightning, hail, rain, and cold. Remember, you have 4 miles of exposed ridge to cross on the way down. If the weather is particularly serious, consider dropping straight down the steep west side of the summit to Williams Lake. However, because hikers create serious erosion on the steep slope, I do not recommend the route except in emergencies.

23 Williams Lake

See Map on Page 75

General description: A moderate hike to an alpine lake at the base of Wheeler Peak.

General location: About 20 miles northeast of Taos.

Length: About 8 miles round trip.

Elevation: 9,390–11,120 feet.

Maps: Carson National Forest; Wheeler Peak 7.5-minute USGS quad.

Best season: Late May through October.

Water availability: Lake Fork of Rio Hondo; stream feeding Williams Lake.

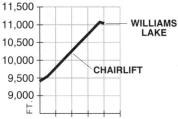

Special attractions: Natural alpine lake; lush forest.

Finding the trailhead: Follow same directions as those for the Wheeler Peak hike.

The hike: Williams Lake nestles in a large glacial cirque at the western base of Wheeler Peak. The level of the small lake fluctuates somewhat depending on precipitation. It does not support fish, possibly because the entire lake freezes some years due to its shallowness. High craggy peaks encircle the lake, providing a stunning setting.

Since the lake is easier to reach than most of the alpine lakes in New Mexico, the hike is popular on summer weekends. From the gravel ski area parking lot, cross the Rio Hondo on either the footbridge or road bridge into the heart of the ski village. Walk toward the two parallel chair lifts ascending the mountain behind the village. The first part of this hike is on private land, so please be courteous.

Climb up the hill underneath the two lifts a very short distance to the first ski trail that goes off into the woods to the left. Follow the ski trail for about 1.5 miles upstream, above the Lake Fork of the Rio Hondo, to the base of the Kachina Chairlift and the Phoenix restaurant. Cross the creek on the trail to the east side when you reach the lift and restaurant. Follow the dirt road up along the creek past the restaurant. The road forks about 100 yards upstream. The main road crosses the stream and climbs up the ski mountain. Stay left and follow the old road up the east side of the canyon. A sign at the road fork points the way to the lake.

The old road narrows to a trail in about 0.25 mile or so. The trail crosses the marked Wheeler Peak Wilderness boundary fairly soon afterwards. The trail climbs relatively steeply for the rest of the 4 miles to the large glacial basin containing Williams Lake. Along the way, you will pass a couple of

Williams Lake lies at the base of Wheeler Peak, New Mexico's highest point.

swaths with flattened trees cut through the forest. Even in New Mexico, avalanches come blasting down from the high ridges in winter.

As with all alpine lakes, the vegetation around Williams Lake is very fragile. Since the lake is fairly heavily visited, camp well away from the shoreline and streams, ideally outside of the lake basin. Use a camp stove for cooking instead of the scarce firewood. Return to the trailhead via the same route.

24 Gold Hill

General description: A strenuous day or overnight hike to a high peak above Red River and Taos Ski Valley.
General location: About 20 miles northeast of Taos.
Length: About 11 miles round trip.
Elevation: 9,390–12,711 feet.
Maps: Carson National Forest; Wheeler Peak and Red River 7.5-minute USGS quads.
Best season: June through October.
Water availability: Long Canyon; Rio Hondo fork.
Special attractions: Spectacular views; tundra; bristlecone pines.

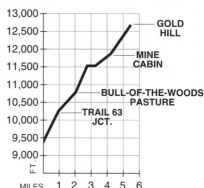

Finding the trailhead: Follow the same directions as those for the Wheeler Peak hike.

The hike: The name Gold Hill is somewhat misleading, since the peak is one of the highest summits in northern New Mexico. Since the peak is separated by several miles from any other summits of comparable height, Gold Hill commands tremendous views of the northern New Mexico mountains. The peak provides views almost as spectacular as Wheeler Peak, New Mexico's highest, but has far fewer people. If you arrive at the trailhead parking lot and find a traffic jam, consider climbing Gold Hill rather than Wheeler Peak (see the Wheeler Peak hike).

Be sure to get an early start on this hike. To avoid thunderstorms, you want to be on the summit before noon. Snow flurries are possible even in mid-summer. Be sure to take rain gear and extra warm clothing. Lightning and hypothermia are real threats on the summit and areas above timberline.

The first 2 miles follow the same route as the Wheeler Peak Trail. The heavily used trail leads out of the parking area behind the trail signs and immediately begins climbing up a valley trending northeast. The first mile of the hike is extremely steep and rocky and, in my opinion, about the hardest part of the entire trip. The first 2 miles to Bull-of-the-Woods Pasture are somewhat confusing. A maze of old roads and trails criss-cross with inadequate trail markings. However, the proper route is the most heavily worn and is easy to find. On a summer weekend, there will be plenty of people to follow. You will not get lost if you persist in following the valley

Gold Hill

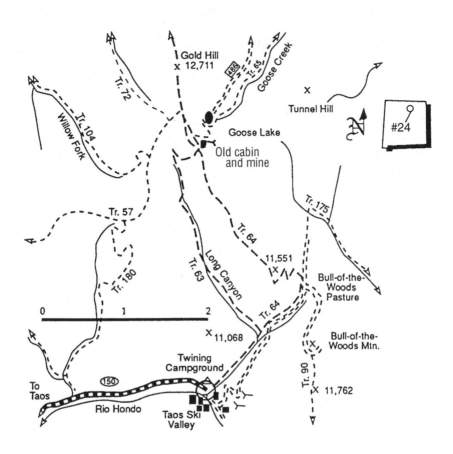

northeast to Bull-of-the-Woods Pasture. The route stays fairly close to the Rio Hondo in the valley bottom for the entire 2 miles.

At just short of 1 mile you will pass marked Trail 63, the Long Canyon Trail to Gold Hill, coming in from the left. This will be your return route coming down from Gold Hill. Ignore it for now and continue climbing up the northeast-trending valley. Just past the trail junction, the trail hits an old road. Turn left onto the road and follow it the rest of the way up the valley. About 1 mile past Long Canyon the route levels out at Bull-of-the-Woods Pasture.

The area is well named. Sure enough, I ran into a large bull and a herd of cows on the old road just short of the pasture. Fortunately, they were more interested in grazing than in me. The road forks at the edge of the pasture. Turn left at the fork, off of the Wheeler Peak route, go about 50 feet along the old road, and turn left again off the road onto the Gold Hill trail. A sign marks the turnoff.

The trail climbs steeply up onto a wooded ridge above the pasture. The trail levels out and even goes slightly downhill for about 0.5 mile, giving a good breather after the steep first half of the hike. The trail then pops out of the dense spruce forest onto a bare area that gives great views of Taos Ski Valley to the south. The breather ends and the trail resumes climbing.

At a little more than 4 miles, at timberline, the trail encounters an old mine and ruined cabin. Actually, the official trail to Gold Hill forks left just before the cabin, but it is easy to miss. So just go on up to the cabin and climb to the summit from there.

By now you should be puffing and panting in the thin air. Relax and enjoy the views from the cabin before the final push. While you are resting, look carefully about 100 yards across the meadow to the west and you will see a sign marking the Long Canyon trail. Note carefully where it is in relation to the cabin, since that will be your return route. The trail gets somewhat faint on the flower-covered tundra above timberline. The trail to Long Canyon is generally easier to find on the way down.

From the cabin, follow a faint trail up onto the top of the bare ridge just above. At this point the trail fades out. However, just walk up the ridge to the left to the obvious summit. Part way up the ridge the official trail reappears from the left. Goose Lake will be visible far below to your right. Ignore the steep Goose Lake Trail 65 that drops down to it. Follow the last stretch of trail up to the rounded summit, passing the marked turnoff to Lobo Peak that goes downhill to the left.

Relax and enjoy the incredible views. Numerous 13,000- and 14,000-foot peaks line the horizon to the north in Colorado. The closer Latir Peaks of New Mexico lie across the Red River Canyon to the north. Several miles to the south towers Wheeler Peak. Keep an eye out for storms building. Be ready to flee at the first sign.

The trail continues on down the other side of the summit, eventually winding up in either Columbine Campground or the town of Red River. A car shuttle would make such a hike feasible. If you have time and the weather permits, consider hiking out along the alpine ridges on the Lobo Peak Trail.

For the return, try the Long Canyon Trail. It is similar in length and difficulty. Retrace your route back down the summit ridge to the Lobo Peak sign. The trail gets faint here, but keep going the same direction downwards through the open tundra to the Goose Lake junction sign. Pass that sign and keep going the same direction downwards. The trail is faint but visible. In a few hundred yards you will hit the Long Canyon sign, the same sign that you saw from the old miner's cabin 100 yards away. The Long Canyon trail goes straight southwest from the sign, as indicated by the arrow, to the edge of Long Canyon a couple of hundred yards distant. Some wood posts and rock cairns mark the route. At the canyon rim, the trail becomes well worn and obvious for the rest of the return. If you have trouble finding the route to Long Canyon, just go back to the miner's cabin and return via the way you came up.

A lot of gnarled bristlecone pines line the first few hundred yards of the trail as you drop down into Long Canyon. I also saw large patches of Colorado blue columbine on the slope. The trail drops steadily down the canyon, encountering the creek after a while. It finally rejoins the trail to Bull-of-the-Woods Pasture. Turn right and walk down the last steep mile to the trailhead.

The best campsites are probably at Bull-of-the-Woods Pasture, the level ridge top above the pasture, in the scattered forest just below the miner's cabin, and in upper Long Canyon.

25 East Fork Red River

General description:	A relatively easy hike to the edge of the Wheeler Peak Wilderness.
General location:	About 7 miles south of Red River.
Length:	About 7 miles round trip.
Elevation:	9,640–10,800 feet.
Maps:	Carson National Forest; Wheeler Peak 7.5-minute USGS quad.
Best season:	Mid-May through October.
Water availability:	East Fork Red River; Sawmill Creek.
Special attractions:	Lush forest; mountain streams.

Finding the trailhead: From Red River, take NM 578 south 6.2 miles to the marked turnoff to the East Fork of the Red River. Go left across the bridge at the end of the pavement, as directed by the sign. The road splits several ways after crossing the bridge. Turn right, following the broad, rocky road up the hill. Ignore the driveways on the right. Follow the road south 1.25 miles to the marked trailhead, past numerous summer homes. The road is marked FR 58 on the ground, FR 58A on the old Carson National Forest map, and FR 54A on the new map, so take your pick. When dry, the rocky road should be passable to most vehicles if care is used. When wet, a muddy spot about halfway along can be treacherous to vehicles other than those with four-wheel drive. Walking part of the road will not add much distance to the hike.

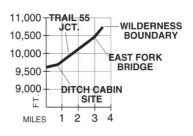

The hike: The mountains around the Taos and Red River area are the highest in the state, with many high peaks and alpine lakes. The high elevations create some of the most spectacular hikes in this book but require a considerable amount of climbing, making them moderate to strenuous in diffi-

The trail up the east Fork of the Red River crosses into the Wheeler Peak Wilderness.

culty. This trail, up the lush East Fork of the Red River, is a relatively easy hike through dense forest to the edge of the Wheeler Peak Wilderness. The Red River is a major Rio Grande tributary.

From the marked trailhead at the end of the road, hike up the hill behind the trail signs and follow the old road, now made impassable to vehicles. Trail 56 climbs through thick spruce and fir, reaching a clearing at the Ditch Cabin Site in a little less than 0.75 mile. The old road ends at the site and the trail continues onward, crossing Sawmill Creek. The trail climbs upstream, high on the wooded slope above the East Fork. At about 1.25 miles, you reach the old Elizabethtown Ditch. The 41-mile-long ditch carried water from the East Fork to gold mines in the Moreno Valley. The abandoned ditch was built in 1868 by Lucien Maxwell. With some bushwhacking, the ditch can be followed for miles.

At about 1.5 miles, the Sawmill Park Trail 55 climbs up to the left. Stay right, following the sign to Lost Lake. At about 3 miles, the trail crosses to the right, or west, side of the East Fork on a sturdy wooden bridge. A 0.5 mile climb up the west bank from the river brings you to the marked Wheeler Peak Wilderness boundary, just after crossing a small side creek.

Return to the trailhead by the same route, or continue as far as energy and desire take you. Horseshoe and Lost Lakes are about 3 miles farther up the trail. A 14-mile loop can be done by following Trail 91 past Lost Lake and down the Middle Fork of the Red River to FR 58. Go down FR 58 to NM 578 and walk the 1.25 miles back up FR 58A to the trailhead.

East Fork Red River

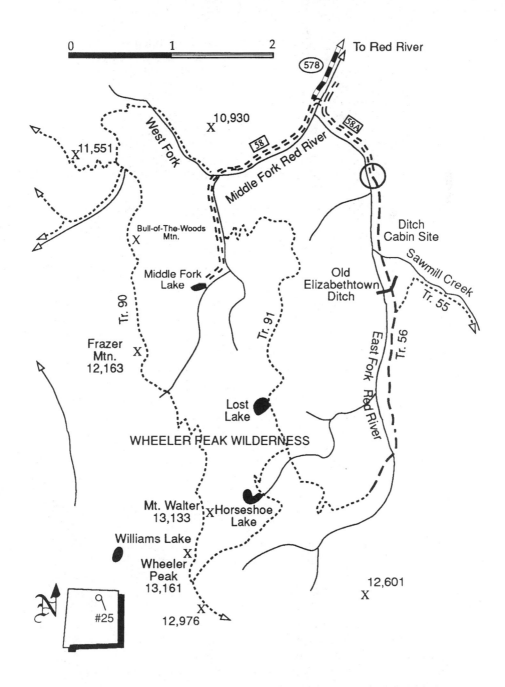

To Red River

578

X 10,930

West Fork

X 11,551

58

Middle Fork Red River

58A

Ditch
Cabin Site

Sawmill Creek

Bull-of-The-Woods
Mtn.
X

Middle Fork
Lake

Old
Elizabethtown
Ditch

Tr. 55

Tr. 90

Tr. 91

East Fork Red River

Tr. 56

Frazer
Mtn.
12,163
X

Lost
Lake

WHEELER PEAK WILDERNESS

Mt. Walter
13,133
X Horseshoe
Lake

Williams Lake
X
Wheeler
Peak
13,161

X 12,601

N
#25

X
12,976

0   1   2

26 Rio Grande Gorge

General description:	A relatively easy hike down into the rocky canyon of the Rio Grande Wild and Scenic River.
General location:	About 35 miles northwest of Taos.
Length:	About 7 miles round trip.
Elevation:	7,450–6,560 feet.
Maps:	Wild Rivers Recreation Area BLM brochure; Guadalupe Mountain 7.5-minute USGS quad.
Best season:	Year round.
Water availability:	Trailhead; Big and Little Arsenic Springs.
Special attractions:	Rugged canyon of the Rio Grande.

Finding the trailhead: From the center of Questa (about 20 miles north of Taos), drive north on NM 522 about 2.6 miles to the marked turnoff to the Rio Grande Wild and Scenic River (NM 378). Turn left (west) and drive 11.7 miles on the paved road to the marked Big Arsenic Springs Campground entrance. Drive into the campground, taking either of the two forks encountered just after leaving NM 378. The marked trailhead is located at the back of the campground on the canyon rim. Unless you pay the overnight camping fee, be sure not to park at a campsite. The campground, along with several others along the canyon rim, makes an excellent place to spend the night. The campsites, with water, tables, and pit toilets, rarely fill up, even in summer.

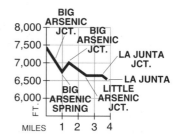

The hike: The rugged canyon of the Rio Grande, from the Colorado border south for 48 miles, was protected by Congress as a National Wild and Scenic River. The protected area includes the Red River from its confluence to a point 4 miles upstream.

Over millions of years, the Rio Grande has carved a deep canyon through the relatively flat plains on the west side of the Sangre de Cristo Mountains. The canyon rim falls off abruptly in a series of sheer basalt cliffs. The narrow canyon is more than 800 feet deep in the area of the hike.

The canyon is suitable for hiking all year. Summers can be quite hot, making the climb out of the canyon fairly strenuous. The occasional winter snows usually melt off fairly quickly. Although nearby Taos and Red River may be crowded with tourists in summer and skiers in winter, the Wild Rivers Recreation Area is surprisingly undiscovered. The campgrounds along the rim were only half full when I last visited on a summer Friday evening. Most trails in northern New Mexico are mountain hikes. This trail makes an interesting change.

From the trailhead on the rim, the trail drops steeply down well main-

Rio Grande Gorge

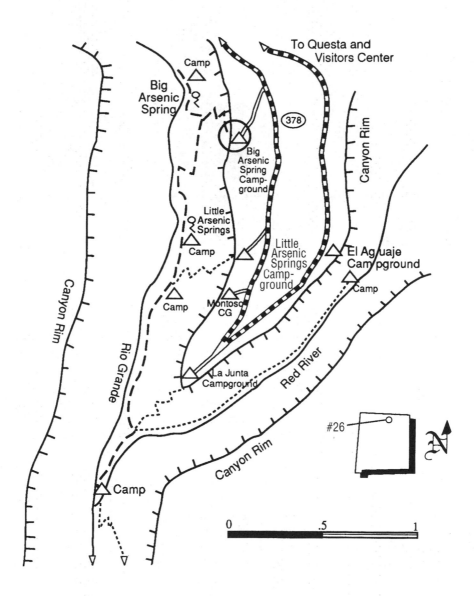

Scattered ponderosa pines line the rocky gorge of the Rio Grande.

tained switchbacks into the canyon. The rim is wooded with pinyon pine and juniper. As you descend into the canyon, you encounter ponderosa pine on the slopes and along the river. Usually ponderosa pine grows at higher elevations than pinyon and juniper, but apparently the canyon walls provide enough extra protection for ponderosa pine to grow.

At about 0.6 mile, the trail forks. Go right, toward Big Arsenic Springs, as marked. The trail goes 0.4 mile, passing several three-sided metal camping shelters along the river. The large springs gush out of the base of a talus slope and pass under the trail before flowing into the river. The Rio Grande here is not the slow muddy river of most of New Mexico. It roars and tumbles downstream, around boulders and over cascades.

The shelters make excellent sites for an overnight stay. (There is a fee.) They rarely fill up because of the hike required to reach them. Fishermen sometimes use them as camps. Retrace the 0.4 mile back up to the trail junction and continue downstream along the river, toward La Junta. About 1 mile down the river from the junction, the trail passes the smaller Little Arsenic Springs and a camp shelter. A little less than 0.25 mile further is another junction. The left fork climbs 0.8 mile back up to the rim at Little Arsenic Springs Campground. Stay right, down the river toward La Junta. Just past the junction lie several more camping shelters tucked into a stand of ponderosa pine.

About 2.1 miles from the first junction (at Big Arsenic Springs), the trail hits the third fork. The left fork climbs up to La Junta Campground on the rim. Go downstream to the right, to La Junta at the confluence of the Red River and Rio Grande. More camping shelters provide fine campsites. From here several options are possible for the return trip, all of relatively similar length and difficulty. You can retrace the same trail all the way back or climb out the trails to Little Arsenic Springs or La Junta campgrounds. From the two campgrounds, just follow the road back to the trailhead at Big Arsenic Springs Campground.

The hike can be lengthened 1 mile by crossing the Red River footbridge next to the shelters at La Junta. The trail follows down the river and then climbs up to Cebolla Mesa Campground on the rim. Another option involves following the unmaintained trail upstream on the bank of the Red River for about 2 miles to the formal trail that comes down from El Aguaje Campground on the rim. Several other shorter loops are possible using different combinations of the trails.

27 Capulin Volcano

General description: A very easy day hike with spectacular views from the crater rim of a recent volcano.
General location: About 30 miles east of Raton.
Length: 1 mile round trip.
Elevation: 7,880–8,182 feet.
Maps: Park brochure; Folsom 7.5-minute USGS quad.
Best season: Spring through fall.
Water availability: None.
Special attractions: Large, symmetrical volcanic crater; tremendous views.

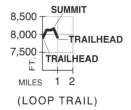

Finding the trailhead: From park headquarters at Capulin Volcano National Monument, take the 2-mile road that spirals up to the parking lot on the crater rim.

The hike: About 60,000 years ago, Capulin Volcano was built up over 1,000 feet above the surrounding plain by fountains of ash and lava. Scores of other surrounding peaks and hills were built during the same period of volcanism. Because Capulin's three lava flows erupted from vents at the base of the mountain, the peak retained a very symmetrical cone shape. In the center of the cone lies the original crater.

The loop trail begins and ends at the parking lot. The climb is less steep if you start on the south side. The trail follows the circular rim of the crater. Vegetation has gained a good foothold on the steep, cinder-covered mountain. The trail passes through windswept stands of pinyon pine and juniper. Mountain mahogany, squaw bush, gambel oak, and chokecherry form shrubby thickets. Open areas are heavily vegetated by grasses.

The trail affords continuous 360-degree views of the surrounding plains and mountains. Scattered volcanic hills and mountains break up the endless expanse of lush grasslands. Ten miles to the southeast lies Sierra Grande, the largest of the volcanoes. To the west tower the snow-capped peaks of the Sangre de Cristo Mountains. On a clear day you can see the highest point in Oklahoma, Black Mesa, far to the east.

28 Cruces Basin

General description:	A moderate day hike in the beautiful, high mountain country of the Cruces Basin Wilderness.
General location:	About 42 miles northwest of Tres Piedras.
Length:	About 7 miles round trip.
Elevation:	9,820–8,500 feet.
Maps:	Carson National Forest; Toltec Mesa 7.5-minute USGS quad.
Best season:	Mid-May through October.
Water availability:	Beaver Creek.
Special attractions:	Lush mountain meadows and forest; trout streams; solitude.

Finding the trailhead: Drive about 15 miles west of Tres Piedras on US 64. Turn right on marked FR 133. A sign here indicates Lagunitas is 29 miles away. The trailhead is a few miles short of Lagunitas. FR 133 is a good gravel road suitable for most vehicles. However, use care when wet; some of these forest roads can get slick. Follow FR 133 for roughly 12 to 13 miles past several well marked junctions. When FR 133 ends at the junction with FR 87, turn left onto FR 87. (For an alternate return route to Tres Piedras, follow FR 87 to the right for about 10 miles to US 285 north of Tres Piedras.) Follow FR 87 west for about 12 miles to the junction

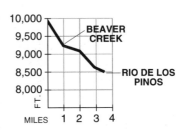

with FR 87A. (FR 87A is another good alternate return route. It eventually ends up in Antonito, Colorado.) From the FR 87/FR 87A junction, continue west on FR 87 for 0.9 mile to the junction with FR 572 on the right. It is marked with a sign for the Cruces Basin Wilderness. FR 572 descends 1.7 miles into the Cruces Basin and ends in a large somewhat marshy meadow with scattered aspens. It is considerably rougher than the rest of the roads. With great care, a sedan can sometimes be driven on FR 572, but a high-clearance vehicle is recommended.

Cruces Basin

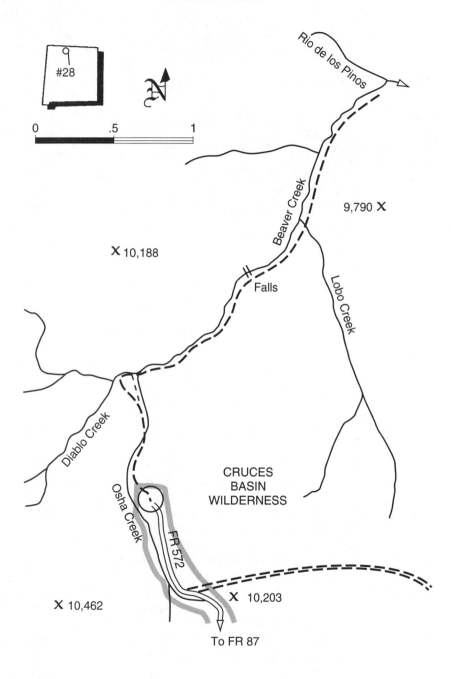

#28

N

0   .5   1

Rio de los Pinos

Beaver Creek

9,790 X

X 10,188

Falls

Lobo Creek

Diablo Creek

Osha Creek

CRUCES
BASIN
WILDERNESS

FR 572

X 10,462

X 10,203

To FR 87

Hikers cross Diablo Creek in the Cruces Basin Wilderness.

The hike: This hike lies in a beautiful high mountain area that is one of the least visited in northern New Mexico. The long, dirt-road drive necessary to reach the area discourages many people. The two small campgrounds at Lagunitas just a few miles beyond the FR 572 junction often do not even fill up on Fourth of July weekend. The campgrounds are named for a number of small ponds.

Cruces Basin is a large basin in the mountains carved by several creeks that feed into the Rio de los Pinos. Some of the area burned many years ago, creating a mix of vast open meadows dotted with groves of spruce, fir, and aspen. Much of the area lies above 10,000 feet, making for cool weather and short summers. Come prepared with warm clothing even in the peak of summer. The mountains here are an extension of the San Juan Mountains of Colorado to the north. The Cumbres and Toltec Scenic Railroad travels through the mountains across the canyon of the Rio de los Pinos near the end of this hike. The train can sometimes be heard and even seen from some areas along the hike.

This is a lightly visited area and trails tend to be primitive or nonexistent. For those experienced with a map and compass, the vast open meadows offer great opportunities for multi-day trips of relatively easy cross-country hiking. It is even possible (with advance planning with the railroad and a car shuttle) to hike to the Cumbres and Toltec and ride the train out.

The first mile of this hike has a trail that is quite easy to follow, even for less experienced hikers. Follow the trail behind the sign at the trailhead down into the Osha Creek drainage. It is steep initially, but the grade lessens after a while. Parts of it follow an old road. In about 1 mile, the trail splits. Both drop down to Beaver Creek in a very short distance. Take the left fork, staying at the same level and then dropping down a hill to Beaver Creek at its junction with Diablo Creek. Here the choices open up, just like the landscape. Both crystal-clear creeks tumble down broad, meadow-lined valleys. It is tempting to hike up either valley—and why not? Beaver Creek, the more northerly fork, splits into Beaver and Cruces creeks a short distance upstream, giving you yet another choice. Formal trails disappear here, so be sure to have enough experience before venturing any farther.

For this hike, rather than going upstream, I arbitrarily hiked downstream along Beaver Creek. Very soon, you pass the other trail fork on the right leading back to the trailhead. Be sure to note where the two return trails are so that you can find them on your return. Remember, these are primitive hiking routes. The informal trail continues down the canyon for about 2.5 miles to Beaver Creek's confluence with the Rio de los Pinos. The trail comes and goes along Beaver Creek as you progress. It generally gets fainter as you go. At times it will be necessary to either wade the creek or bushwhack up onto the canyon slopes to keep your feet dry. If you want to wade (which is probably easier), wear boots that you do not mind getting wet, or bring extra sandals or tennis shoes for the crossings. The cold water will wake you up. You pass a side canyon or two along the way, so be sure you walk back up the correct canyon on your return.

About 1 mile or so below Osha Creek, the canyon carved by Beaver Creek narrows and drops about 400 feet or so in a fairly short distance. Waterfalls here are quite scenic, but it does make progress a little tricky. Bushwhack your way around the falls as necessary. Backtracking a bit and climbing up high on the right side may be the easiest route. A topo map is helpful here. According to a forest ranger, an old road climbs up off the right (east) side of Osha Creek and eventually descends to the falls. However, I did not try the route and cannot attest to it.

You leave the wilderness at the Rio de los Pinos. Much of the land along the river is private, so respect owners' privacy. The river's flow is often too high to cross safely. The Cumbres and Toltec Railroad follows a route high up on the other side of the river canyon. If you time your hike right, maybe you will hear or see the steam train chugging its way through the mountains.

29 Angel Peak

General description:	A moderate day hike into the badlands below Angel Peak.
General location:	About 34 miles southeast of Farmington.
Length:	About 2 miles round trip.
Elevation:	6,680–6,250 feet.
Maps:	East Fork Kutz Canyon and Huerfanito Peak 7.5-minute USGS quads.
Best season:	Year round.
Water availability:	None.
Special attractions:	Colorful eroded badlands.

Finding the trailhead: From the intersection of US 64 and NM 44 in Bloomfield, drive south about 15 miles on NM 44. Turn left, northeast, onto a gravel road marked with a BLM Angel Peak Recreation Area sign. The road is good, but has some washboard. Initially the road crosses sagebrush flats, but quickly reaches the steep rim of the canyons below. Be sure to stop at some of the overlooks. Park at Angel Peak Campground at the end of the main gravel road, a little less than 6.5 miles from NM 44.

The hike: The route leads down into the badlands below the canyon rim on the north side of the campground. There are no formal trails. Since the route is steep and several sandstone ledges must be worked around, the hike is not recommended for inexperienced hikers or children alone.

The colorful badlands were cut by drainages flowing into the San Juan River about 10 or 15 miles north. Angel Peak is the prominent peak about 1 mile north of the campground. The clay and sandstone beds exposed in the badlands are but a small part of the huge sedimentary San Juan Basin. Deeply buried sandstone layers form one of the largest natural gas fields in the United States. Widely scattered gas wells, visible from the hike, reduce the area's wildness, but do not seriously harm the badlands' scenic beauty.

Follow the canyon rim on the northeast side of the campground to the northeast about 0.25 mile until you reach a long ridge sloping downward to the west. Hike down the ridgetop into the badlands, scrambling down the occasional sandstone ledges. In about 0.5 mile the ridge peters out into a broad sandy wash at the bottom. A short walk farther down the wash brings you to the oil field road that goes down the middle of the canyon. Picnic shelters of the campground will visible on the rim above for the entire hike. Return via the same route or bushwhack up one of the other many ridges that climb up to the rim.

The Angel Peak area can be very cold in winter and hot in summer, but generally the hike is good any time of year. Right after a heavy rain or snow,

Angel Peak

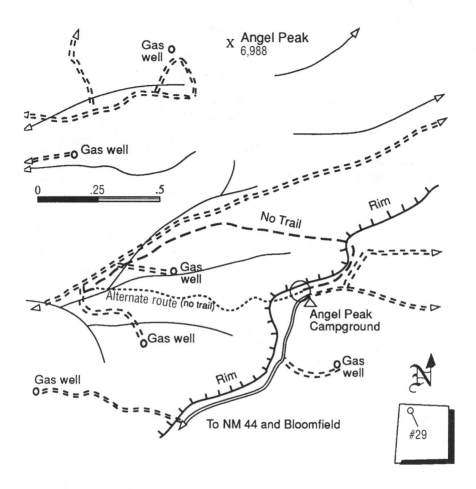

the clay soil gets very slick and muddy, making the hike difficult. The BLM campground, set among the gnarled junipers clinging to the canyon rim, has pit toilets, picnic tables, and shelters. Be sure to stay at least until dark to watch the last rays of the sun turn the badlands flaming shades of red and gold.

30 Bisti Badlands

General description:	An easy day hike into the tortured badlands of the Bisti Wilderness.
General location:	About 38 miles south of Farmington.
Length:	About 4 miles round trip.
Elevation:	5,770–5,850 feet.
Maps:	Bisti Trading Post and Alamo Mesa West 7.5-minute USGS quads.
Best season:	Spring and fall.
Water availability:	None.
Special attractions:	Colorful eroded badlands with pinnacles, mushroom rocks, and many other features.

Finding the trailhead: Drive about 36.5 miles south of Farmington on NM 371 (from where NM 371 crosses the San Juan River on the southwest side of downtown Farmington). Turn left onto a good gravel road marked with a sign. Be sure not to turn left at the NM Highway Department sign. Follow

Bisti Badlands

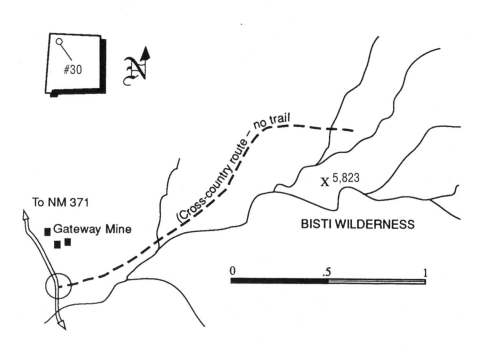

Shiprock is a prominent landmark northwest of the Bisti Badlands.

the gravel road about 2 miles to the parking area on the right side of the road. The parking lot is well marked with a BLM wilderness sign.

The hike: The Bisti/De-Na-Zin Wilderness contains a maze of eroded clay beds and sandstone remnants. The clay beds, colored many shades of gray, with highlights of red and yellow, are very soft and erode easily. Little vegetation grows on the poor, unstable soil. Remnants of a harder sandstone caprock protect the softer underlying clay beds, producing many fanciful forms, from mushroom-shaped formations to pinnacles and small arches. The soft sedimentary beds also contain many seams of coal, obvious as black bands on eroded hillsides. Many coal seams are thick enough to make mining economical all over the Farmington area. The Bisti/De-Na-Zin Wilderness contains considerable coal, but fortunately the area was preserved as wilderness because of its unique badlands. Until 1996, the Bisti and De-Na-Zin were separate wildernesses, but legislation added connecting land between the two areas, creating one large wilderness.

This trail description is meant only as an introduction to the Bisti Badlands. No trails really exist in the wilderness. The badlands can seem maze-like to the inexperienced hiker, making it easy to get lost. However, if you are a beginner, do not be afraid to at least walk into the edge of the badlands. To go farther, take a map and compass and go with experienced hikers.

From the parking lot, a faint, broad trail leads east along the fence marking the boundary of the Gateway Mine to the north. The trail fades out at about 0.5 mile. Continue to follow the coal mine fence until it turns north in about another 0.25 mile. From the fence corner, continue east-northeast up the broad, low-relief wash. Mushroom rocks and hoodoos will be encountered soon after leaving the mine area. Keeping the mine in view will help prevent getting lost. I show the hike as going another 1.25 miles past the mine, but there really is no defined length. Wander at will among the weird rock formations, but be careful to keep track of direction. If you get lost, just hike west until you hit the mine, the gravel road, or NM 371.

The Bisti is good for hiking anytime of year. Summers can be very hot, however, with little shade. Rain or snow can make the bare clay soils very muddy and slick. Winters are generally good, but the occasional snow storm can make for a frigid hike. A friend and I hiked in the Bisti in February on a day with a low, threatening sky. About 1 mile from the car, a snow squall hit, instantly cutting visibility to a few hundred feet. We hustled back before we got lost. By next morning the badlands had received 6 inches of snow.

31 Pueblo Alto

General description:	An easy day hike to several ancestral Pueblo (Anasazi) ruins in Chaco Culture National Historical Park.
General location:	About 70 miles south of Farmington.
Length:	About 5.4 miles round trip.
Elevation:	6,140–6,440 feet.
Maps:	National Park Service map and brochure; Pueblo Bonito 7.5-minute USGS quad.
Best season:	All year.
Water availability:	None.
Special attractions:	Isolation; Chaco great house ruins and stairs.

Finding the trailhead: Follow the same directions as for the Penasco Blanco hike. Obtain a free permit and orientation at the Visitor Center. Drive past the Visitor Center on the paved loop road and park at the Pueblo del Arroyo parking area. The trailhead begins here. Walk to Kin Kletso and locate the Pueblo Alto Trail behind the site.

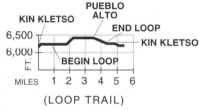

Kin Kletso ruin lies covered with snow at the start of the Pueblo Alto Trail.

Pueblo Alto

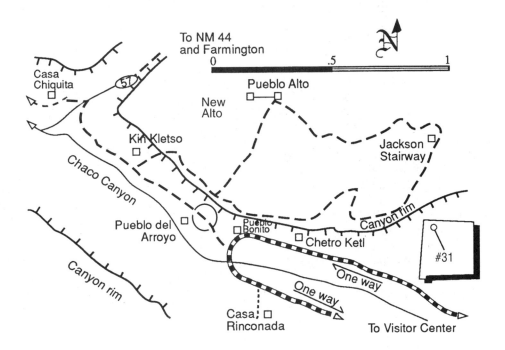

The hike: The many ruins in and surrounding Chaco Canyon were the center of the Chacoan culture in northwestern New Mexico. From about the mid-900s to the mid-1100s AD, towns and villages flourished. Today only the crumbling walls remain, abandoned for uncertain reasons. Archaeologists suspect that the political, ceremonial, and trade network shifted to other areas, like Aztec Ruins and Mesa Verde. Also, local natural resources were probably deleted.

Be sure to walk around Kin Kletso before starting up the trail. The large but compact site had about 100 rooms and may have risen three stories. The Pueblo Alto trail starts from the back side of Kin Kletso and immediately scrambles up through a narrow cleft in the canyon wall. The trail winds to the southeast along the canyon rim, giving excellent views of Kin Kletso and Pueblo del Arroyo below. The trail often crosses bare slickrock, but is well marked with rock cairns. At a little less than 1 mile from the start, the trail forks. At the fork, be sure to walk out onto the sandstone promontory to look down at massive Pueblo Bonito below. With 600 rooms and 40 kivas, the 4-story structure is the largest in the park and was the center of Chacoan culture.

Farther along the rim, the trail overlooks 500-room Chetro Ketl ruin. Beyond Chetro Ketl, the trail contours around a side canyon, at one point following a section of prehistoric road. The trail then gradually climbs northeast toward the crest of the mesa. Near the top of the mesa, the trail overlooks an Anasazi stairway, the Jackson Stairs, climbing out of a side canyon. From the stairs, the trail follows the mesa top west for about 1 mile to Pueblo Alto, overlooking ancient farming terraces on the way.

Pueblo Alto, at the very crest of the mesa, is divided into two sections. The trail reaches the larger ruin, Old Alto, first. Old Alto has deteriorated more than its sister ruin, New Alto, located a few hundred yards farther west. Enjoy the view from the ruins. For miles and miles in every direction stretch nothing but empty sagebrush flats, cut by the occasional canyon. The vast country dwarfs even the elaborate ruins of Chaco Canyon.

From Pueblo Alto, the trail slowly drops back down toward Chaco Canyon to the southwest. The loop trail ends at the junction at the Pueblo Bonito overlook. From there, follow the same trail back to Kin Kletso and the trailhead. For those with limited time, follow the left fork at the overlook straight up to Pueblo Alto. The round trip is reduced to about 3 miles by cutting off the loop.

32 Peñasco Blanco

General description: An easy day hike to a major Chacoan great house in Chaco Culture National Historical Park.
General location: About 70 miles south of Farmington.
Length: About 6.4 miles round trip.
Elevation: 6,050–6,270 feet.
Maps: National Park Service map and brochure; Pueblo Bonito and Kin Klizhin 7.5-minute USGS quads.
Best season: All year.
Water availability: None.
Special attractions: Large Chacoan great house; petroglyphs; isolation.

Finding the trailhead: Drive south of Bloomfield on NM 44. 3 miles south of the Nageezi Trading Post, turn right (southwest) onto CR 7900 (paved for 5 miles). Then turn right onto CR 7950 (16 miles of graded dirt road, impassable in bad weather) and follow

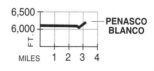

signs to the park. Call ahead for current road conditions (505-786-7014). After passing the campground, go to the Visitor Center for free hiking permits and orientation. The South entrance road from Crownpoint is unmaintained and not recommended.

The hike: Chaco Canyon was a major center for the widespread Chaco (Anasazi) culture of the Southwest. Extensive masonry buildings dot the canyon floors and surrounding mesas. The largest, Pueblo Bonito, had 600 rooms and 40 kivas. Chaco thrived for 300 years, but was abandoned in the late 1100s AD as new centers emerged in the north, south, and west at Aztec Ruins, Mesa Verde, and other areas. Today, only the lonesome wind inhabits the tumbling sandstone walls.

From the parking lot at Pueblo del Arroyo, the trail follows an abandoned dirt road northwest down the broad, sandy Chaco Canyon floor. After passing Casa Chiquita, keep an eye on the nearby north wall of the canyon. In several spots, ancient petroglyphs adorn the buff-colored sandstone. Unfortunately, more recent visitors have sometimes added their graffiti. Before crossing Chaco wash, a side trail takes off to the right. It goes a few hundred yards to visit some pictographs painted on the walls and roof of an overhang. One painting, on the roof of the overhang, is thought to represent the supernova of 1054 AD.

The main trail winds its way up the sandstone ledges of the south wall to Penasco Blanco ruin, perched on a point of the mesa that forms the canyon wall. The site is not as well preserved as some of the sites in the canyon, but many walls still stand. Please do not climb on the fragile walls or collect artifacts.

From the ruin, you can see far up and down the canyon. Few people make the hike, so you will probably have the ruin to yourself. I visited Penasco Blanco in February after a heavy snowfall. I reached the great house shortly before sunset, after breaking trail through the snow. The mercury was falling fast as the sun sank in the west. Combined with a wind howling out of the northwest across the treeless mesas, my sense of cold and isolation was extreme. It was hard to picture the buildings ever being inhabited.

Peñasco Blanco

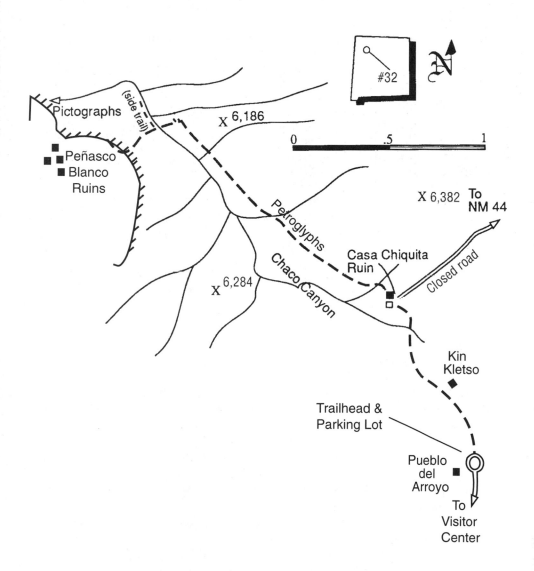

Pictographs

(side trail)

X 6,186

#32

N

0 .5 1

Peñasco
Blanco
Ruins

Petroglyphs

X 6,382 **To
NM 44**

Casa Chiquita
Ruin

Closed road

Chaco Canyon

X 6,284

Kin
Kletso

Trailhead &
Parking Lot

Pueblo
del
Arroyo

To
Visitor
Center

33 Mount Taylor

General description:	A moderately strenuous day hike to the summit of an extinct volcano.
General location:	About 20 miles northeast of Grants.
Length:	About 6 miles round trip.
Elevation:	9,280–11,301 feet.
Maps:	Cibola National Forest—Mt. Taylor Ranger District; Mount Taylor and Lobo Springs 7.5-minute USGS quads.
Best season:	May through October.
Water availability:	Gooseberry Spring—see text.
Special attractions:	Views; solitude.

Finding the trailhead: From the center of Grants, take NM 547 northeast toward the mountain. The route out of town is well marked with Mount Taylor and route signs. Follow NM 547 for 13.3 miles to the FR 193 turnoff at the end of the pavement. Turn right on improved gravel road FR 193 and go 5.1 miles to the trailhead (only about 0.1 mile short of the FR 501 turnoff). The trailhead, on the left side of the road, is marked by Trail 77 signs.

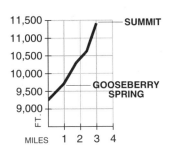

The hike: Several million years ago Mount Taylor erupted, creating a large volcano in the midst of an extensive plateau capped by several hundred feet of basalt. Numerous volcanic necks and cinder cones surround the main volcano. To the south, at El Malpais National Monument, lava flowed as recently as 2,000 years ago. Today, dense forests of pine, fir, aspen, and spruce cloak the old volcano's slopes. The solitary, towering peak, snowcapped much of the year, forms one of the most prominent landmarks of northwestern New Mexico.

Unfortunately, even though Mount Taylor is such a major peak, the trail to the summit appears to be the only significant developed hiking trail in the entire mountain range. The trail starts in mixed ponderosa pine and aspen forest, and begins climbing at an easy to moderate grade immediately. The first part of the trail is relatively new and has been rerouted from the old trailhead.

At a little over .05 mile, the trail drops down into the draw that it has been paralleling from the start. An old road (probably the old trail) joins the draw from the other side. A sign with motor vehicle restrictions marks the spot. A small, seasonal spring sometimes flows here. Walk up the broad, open draw past the sign. The trail up the draw is basically a faint, old road. At a little over 1 mile, the road passes a metal stock watering tank. The tank

Mount Taylor

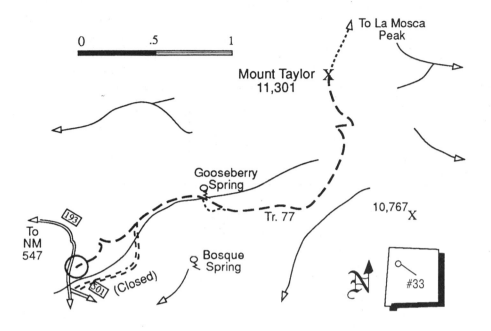

is probably fed by Gooseberry Spring, but I did not see any water on my visit. Check with the Forest Service about the spring's status ahead of time.

Just past the tank, another sign restricts motor vehicles. Just past the sign, the obvious trail climbs straight up the right bank of the draw. Follow the steep route and turn left onto the trail just short of the top. The trail quickly leaves the forest and comes out onto the steep grassy slopes of the mountain. The summit is visible above and to the left. Although you are not above timberline, most of the rest of the hike is on open, treeless slopes. Try to get an early start to avoid afternoon thunderstorms in summer. If thunderstorms form, quickly retreat back down into trees in a low area.

Several parallel trails climb steeply straight up the slope to the ridge top. Follow them up to the ridge. The 0.5-mile climb is probably the hardest part of the hike. The views to the south and west get better with every step. At the crest of the ridge, the trail improves and moderates its grade somewhat. It turns left and climbs north toward the summit on the back side of the ridge. At about 2.25 miles the trail crosses a ridge saddle back to the southwest-facing slope. A couple of long switchbacks bring you to the final approach. The trail passes through a fence gate a little before the top, and reaches the summit at about 3 miles.

Enjoy the incredible views. Mount Taylor is the highest peak for many miles in every direction. Unlike the bare grassy southwest slopes, the north and east slopes of the peak are densely forested with spruce, fir, and aspen. A grove of trees on the northwest side of the summit offers camping possibilities. A mile-long trail goes down the north ridge of Mount Taylor to the La Mosca Lookout road. A forest of radio towers decorates the summit of nearby La Mosca Peak. Even though Mount Taylor is close and accessible to Albuquerque and I-40, it is surprising how few people use this trail. The bare, grassy slopes of the peak would probably make excellent cross-country ski routes in winter. Remember to keep an eye on the weather. Lightning and hail sent me scurrying for cover on my climb.

34 El Morro

General description:	An easy day hike to historic rock inscriptions and ancient Indian pueblo ruins.
General location:	About 42 miles southwest of Grants.
Length:	About 2.3 miles round trip.
Elevation:	7,220–7,450 feet (no elevation graph).
Maps:	El Morro National Monument brochure; El Morro 7.5-minute USGS quad.
Best season:	All year.
Water availability:	Visitor center.
Special attractions:	Prehistoric carvings and historic rock inscriptions; Indian pueblo ruins; views.

Inscription Rock has been visited for centuries by many different groups of people.

El Morro

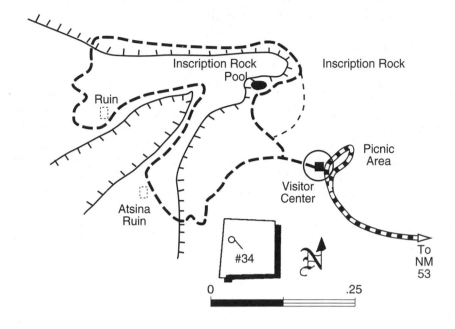

Inscription Rock

Inscription Rock
Pool

Ruin

Picnic
Area

Visitor
Center

Atsina
Ruin

#34

To
NM
53

0   .25

Finding the trailhead: Take NM 53 south from I-40 on the west side of Grants. Follow it about 42 miles to El Morro National Monument and park at the visitor center.

The hike: People have been attracted to El Morro for thousands of years because of a permanent waterhole at the base of a prominent sandstone bluff. Early Indian groups carved petroglyphs into the soft rock by the waterhole. Spanish explorers, American soldiers, emigrants, and others visited the waterhole in succeeding years and left inscriptions that marked their passage. This hike visits the carvings, along with pueblo ruins.

Consider borrowing a copy of the trail booklet at the visitor center. It gives a very detailed description of the entire hike. The paved loop trail starts right behind the visitor center. Part of the route is wheelchair accessible. The trail climbs gently up to the towering sandstone bluff of El Morro through pinyon pine-juniper woodland. Stay right when you reach the return leg of the loop trail.

The trail soon reaches the large pool, tucked into an alcove in the cliff wall. The deep pool, filled with runoff from the cliffs above, was a powerful draw in the dry country. Begin looking at the walls around the pool for the carvings. Carvings here range from ancient petroglyphs to inscriptions dating from 1605 to the turn of this century. Be sure not to touch the inscriptions. The rock is soft and repeated touching will wear the carvings away.

As the trail follows along the bluff, many more carvings are passed. Watch for the oldest and most famous inscription, that of Don Juan de Oñate. He led the first permanent settlers into New Mexico and became governor. His carving was done in 1605. One of the most impressive inscriptions is the ornate one done by E. Pen Long in the mid-1800s. The trail booklet gives details about many of the carvings.

Here and there, you pass tall ponderosa pines on the north side of the bluff. After the inscriptions, the trail climbs up onto the top of the bluff. Views open up of the Zuni Mountains to the north and other sights. The trail crosses the rocky top of the bluff, passing an unexcavated Indian pueblo ruin and then curving around a small box canyon. Be sure to stay on the trail; the cliffs are high.

The trail then passes Atsina, a partly excavated pueblo. The large ruin is about 200 by 300 feet in size. It was occupied during the thirteenth and fourteenth centuries and abandoned for uncertain reasons. Possibly the growing season was too short at this elevation, drought made crops difficult to produce, or resources were depleted by overuse. After Atsina, the trail descends back to the visitor center.

35 Zuni-Acoma Trail

General description:	A moderately difficult day hike or overnight trip across the main lava flows at El Malpais National Monument.
General location:	About 16 miles south of Grants.
Length:	About 14 miles round trip.
Elevation:	6,920–6,880 feet (no elevation graph).
Maps:	El Malpais brochure; National Park Service trail brochure; Arrosa Ranch and Los Pilares 7.5-minute USGS quads.
Best season:	All year.
Water availability:	None.
Special attractions:	Rugged lava features; the trail is part of an ancient Indian trail; solitude.

Finding the trailhead: From the intersection of I-40 and NM 53 on the west side of Grants, drive about 16 miles south on NM 53. The parking area for the trail is on the left (south) side of the highway. To follow the hike in reverse, from the east trailhead, drive east of Grants about 5 miles on I-40. At the NM 117 junction, go south on NM 117 about 15 miles to the east trailhead on the right side of the highway.

The hike: The trail is part of an old Indian trail that connected the villages of Zuni and Acoma. It crosses five different lava flows, the most recent

Zuni-Acoma Trail

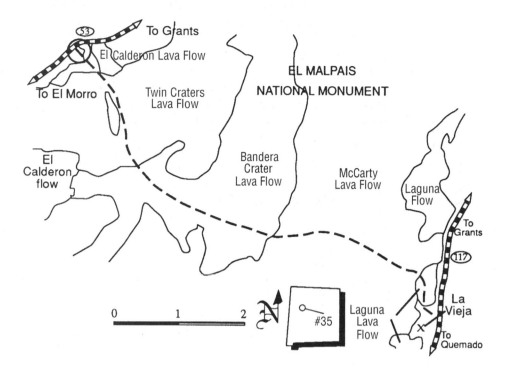

To Grants
El Calderon Lava Flow
To El Morro
Twin Craters Lava Flow
El Calderon flow
EL MALPAIS
NATIONAL MONUMENT
Bandera Crater Lava Flow
McCarty Lava Flow
Laguna Flow
To Grants
Laguna Lava Flow
La Vieja
To Quemado
#35
0   1   2

being only 2,000 years old.

Be sure to wear sturdy boots, since most of the trail surface consists of rough lava. Because the trail often lies on bare rock, it can be relatively faint. Rock cairns, some hundreds of years old, mark the route.

Traveling from west to east, the trail loses a small amount of elevation, but has a considerable number of small ups and downs as it crosses the lava flows.

The first lava flow at the start of the trail is the oldest in the valley. Although you walk on it for only a short time, it underlies many of the other flows that the trail crosses. Gnarled ponderosa pines, pinyon pines, and junipers dot the lava for much of the hike.

The second lava flow, that issued from Twin Craters to the northwest, is younger and less vegetated. Rough and chunky aa lava make up this flow. At about 2.5 miles the trail crosses onto the even younger Bandera Flow. This flow, coming from Bandera Crater to the northwest, contains extensive systems of lava tubes.

The fourth and youngest flow, the McCarty Flow, is only about 2,000 years old. This lava, called pahoehoe, has a ropy, frozen molasses-like texture and is reached at about 3.5 miles. It flowed north from a vent about 8 miles southwest. Finally, just before reaching the trail's end at NM 117, you cross onto the older Laguna Flow. It erupted from the Hoya de Cibola Volcano about 14 miles west.

The trail ends at NM 117 at the base of the sandstone cliffs marking the east side of the broad lava-filled valley. By using a car shuttle, the trail distance can be halved to 7 miles. Generally the trail can be hiked year-round. Occasional winter snows will make crossing difficult (and even dangerous) for a few days until it melts. The area can be very cold in winter, but also quite hot in summer, so prepare accordingly. The slight elevation change and moderate distance (especially when hiked one-way with a car shuttle) make the hike appear easy, but the rough lava and many small ups and downs are tiring.

36 Big Skylight Cave

General description:	An easy day hike to an extensive lava tube cave system.
General location:	About 35 miles southwest of Grants.
Length:	1 mile round trip to tube.
Elevation:	7,580–7,600 feet (no elevation graph).
Maps:	El Malpais brochure; National Park Service "Big Tubes Area" brochure; Ice Caves 7.5-minute USGS quad.
Best season:	All year when roads are dry.
Water availability:	None.
Special attractions:	Large lava tube caves.

Finding the trailhead: From Grants, take NM 53 south from I-40 about 27 miles to County Road 42. Follow the dirt county road about 6.5 miles to a small dirt road heading east through a gate. A high clearance vehicle is mandatory for the next 3.8 miles to the parking area. Be sure that your tires are in good condition and you have a spare; the lava rocks are jagged. Do not attempt after a heavy rain or snow; even a four-wheel-drive vehicle will have difficulty (I have gotten stuck here in one). Leave all gates as you find them. Several roads fork off to the right; bear left at the junctions. The parking area is marked with a "Big Lava Tubes" sign.

The hike: From the National Park Service "Big Lava Tubes" sign at the parking area, look for rock cairns heading east. Follow the cairns out onto the black lava flow. Watch carefully, so that you do not lose the cairns. You are entering a rolling sea of lava that is fairly heavily wooded with ponderosa pine, alligator juniper, and pinyon pine. It is easy to get lost if you lose the route. The trail is not worn into the lava flow; only the cairns mark the way. Be sure to take a compass and a topo map.

Big Skylight Cave

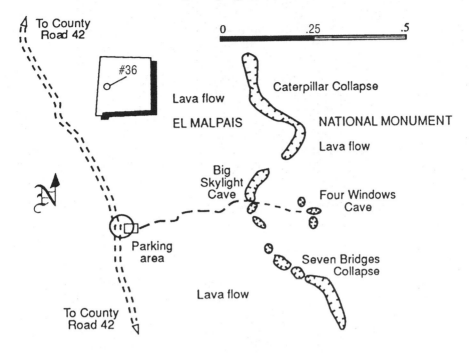

The marked route reaches the lava tube in about 0.5 mile. Just before you get to the tube, the cairns seem to go in two directions. Do not worry; they just go to different sections of the continuous tube.

The huge area of volcanoes and lava flows in El Malpais National Monument was formed over the past 3 million years in a series of many eruptions. The lava flows are new enough to be rough and jagged to hike over, but the area has been calm long enough for much of the area to become wooded with trees and shrubs. Lava tubes formed when the crust on the surface of the flow hardened, but the still-molten lava flowed out from underneath.

Big Skylight and Four Windows caves, at the end of the trail, are just two openings into a lava tube over 17 miles long, including collapsed sections. By following the tube, many other entrances can be found. Some of the entrances, such as Big Skylight, are deep pits. However, you can find easy places to scramble down into the tubes at many of the entrances. The floors of the tubes are commonly boulder piles of loose shifting rock. Use extreme caution. To go beyond daylight in the tubes, be sure that each member of your party has a hard hat and three good sources of light. (The Park Service discourages lanterns with flames, candles, or other fire sources.) The dark colored rock and ceilings as high as 40 feet easily soak up small sources of light. If you exit the tube from an entrance different from the one you entered, be careful not to become lost on the surface.

111

37 Sandstone Bluffs/La Ventana Arch

See Maps on Pages 113 and 116

General description:	A very easy day hike to the second largest arch in New Mexico and a dramatic rocky bluff.
General location:	About 23 miles south of Grants.
Length:	About 0.5 mile round trip for La Ventana Arch, about 1.0 to 5.5 miles round trip depending on route for the Sandstone Bluffs.
Elevation:	Arch: 6,950–7,100 feet; Bluffs: 7,000–6,700 feet (no elevation graph).
Maps:	El Malpais National Monument brochure; North Pasture (for Arch) and Los Pilares (for Bluffs) 7.5-minute USGS quads.
Best season:	All year.
Water availability:	None.
Special attractions:	Large sandstone arch; views.

Finding the trailhead: To get to the Sandstone Bluffs, one part of this hike, drive about 5 miles east of Grants on I-40 and then exit onto NM 117. Follow it south 10 miles to the marked turnoff on the right for the Sandstone Bluffs. Follow the good gravel road 1.5 miles to the parking lot at the end of the road. To get to La Ventana Arch, follow NM 117 an additional 8 miles south past the Sandstone Bluffs turnoff to a large, marked parking area on the left.

The hike: This hike is composed of two easy hikes, one on a short trail, the other an easy cross-country route. Both visit features along a line of dramatic cliffs that mark the eastern edge of an ancient lava flow.

The first hike, at La Ventana Arch (see map for Hike 38), starts from the large paved parking lot along NM 117. The massive stone arch, the second largest in New Mexico, is obvious in the cliffs above the parking area. It lies in a designated wilderness, part of the El Malpais National Conservation Area managed by the Bureau of Land Management. The topographic map does not show the arch in quite the right spot, but you do not need that map for this hike anyway.

The trail leads past pit toilets toward the arch. In a short distance it splits. The right fork, as marked, goes maybe 50 yards to a good view of the arch. The left fork switchbacks up a steep slope covered with pinyon pines and junipers and reaches the arch not much more than 0.25 mile from the parking lot. Kick back in the cool shade and enjoy the view of the massive ocher sandstone span towering over you.

For the other hike, backtrack down NM 117 toward Grants to the Sandstone Bluffs turnoff. Park in the lot at the end of the gravel side road. The bluffs are a long, sheer north-south escarpment of sandstone that rises high

Sandstone Bluffs

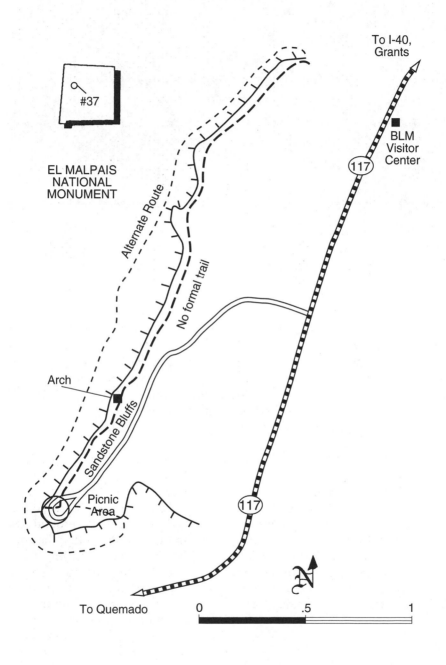

#37

EL MALPAIS
NATIONAL
MONUMENT

To I-40,
Grants

BLM
Visitor
Center

117

Alternate Route

No formal trail

Arch

Sandstone Bluffs

Picnic
Area

117

To Quemado

N

0   .5   1

Lightning strikes just north of the Sandstone Bluffs. Leave exposed areas when storms threaten.

above the black lava flows of El Malpais National Monument. There is no formal trail here; rather, you can walk along the bluffs for about 2.75 miles to the north, following the edge of the cliffs and exploring rocky promontories that extend out toward the lava. Views are tremendous, from the Zuni Mountains to the west, to the lofty summit of Mount Taylor to the north. If you watch closely, you will find another stone arch along the way. The bluffs slowly decline in height and eventually end. If you look carefully, you may find some petroglyphs pecked into the rock at the base of the bluffs near the north end. As with all historical items, please do not touch or disturb them.

From the north end of the bluffs, return via the same route along the cliff tops or follow an old trail back along the base of the bluffs. When you reach the south end, you are below the parking lot. Hunt around and you can find several ways to scramble back up through the cliffs. The easiest route is probably all the way around on the south end of the bluffs.

Since there is no formal trail, be sure to watch your route so you will have no trouble finding your way back. Be careful near the edges of cliffs and expect thunderstorms and lightning, particularly on summer afternoons. In summer, these hikes can be quite hot in the middle of the day. Start early or late.

38 The Narrows

General description: A relatively easy day hike that overlooks the vast lava flows of El Malpais National Monument and La Ventana Arch, the second largest stone arch in New Mexico.

General location: About 27 miles south of Grants.

Length: About 7 miles round trip.

Elevation: 7,080–7,500 feet.

Maps: El Malpais National Monument/El Malpais National Conservation Area brochure; North Pasture 7.5-minute USGS quad.

Best season: All year.

Water availability: None.

Special attractions: La Ventana Arch; El Malpais lava flows; views.

Finding the trailhead: To get to the Narrows trailhead, drive about 5 miles east of Grants on I-40 and then exit onto NM 117. Follow it south 22 miles to the marked turnoff on the left for South Narrows. Turn left onto a short gravel road that leads to several picnic tables. The marked trailhead is on the right almost immediately after turning off the highway.

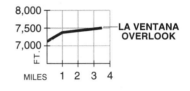

The hike: This hike climbs slowly up onto the high cliffs that line the east side of El Malpais National Monument. The area is called the Narrows because NM 117 is squeezed into a narrow corridor between the black lava flows of El Malpais and the towering sandstone cliffs that mark the west edge of Cebollita Mesa. The hike follows the edge of the cliffs as they rise to the north and culminates at an overlook of La Ventana Arch, a massive arch carved from sandstone by erosion.

The hike lies just within the Cebolla Wilderness, a large undeveloped tract of land that is part of El Malpais National Conservation Area. The BLM administers the conservation area in cooperation with adjoining El Malpais National Monument.

From the trailhead, the path scrambles up a short distance to the top of the mesa. Here the mesa is low and the cliffs not very high. The sandy trail winds its way north through pinyon-juniper woodland near the brink of the cliffs. Occasional ponderosa pines rise above the smaller trees. The mesa steadily rises and the cliffs become quite imposing, especially to the vertigo-prone. Because of increasing elevation and the high cliffs, the views become grand as you travel north. Directly below is the highway, while the lava flows of El Malpais stretch for miles to the west. To the north towers 11,301-foot Mount Taylor, to the northwest, the smaller Zuni Mountains.

The Narrows/La Ventana Arch

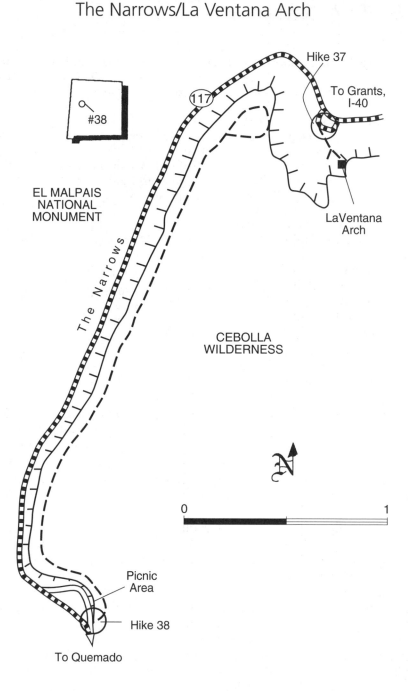

Hike 37

To Grants, I-40

117

#38

EL MALPAIS
NATIONAL
MONUMENT

The Narrows

LaVentana
Arch

CEBOLLA
WILDERNESS

N

0   1

Picnic
Area

Hike 38

To Quemado

The trail ends in a short loop that overlooks La Ventana Arch. The massive sandstone span was carved by thousands of years of water and wind erosion. A separate short trail, described in the Sandstone Bluffs/La Ventana Arch hike in this guide, leads to the base of the arch. Return to the trailhead by the same route. If this lightly used trail was appealing and you are an experienced hiker, consider trying some primitive routes in the little-visited Cebolla Wilderness.

39 La Luz Trail

General description:	A strenuous day hike or overnight trip through the Sandia Wilderness to the crest of the Sandia Mountains.
General location:	The northeast side of Albuquerque.
Length:	About 15 miles round trip.
Elevation:	7,060–10,678 feet.
Maps:	Sandia Mountain Wilderness; Cibola National Forest—Sandia-Mountainair Ranger Districts; Sandia Crest 7.5-minute USGS quad.
Best season:	April through November.
Water availability:	See text.
Special attractions:	Views; passage through several life zones.

Finding the trailhead: From I-40 on the east side of Albuquerque, take the Tramway Boulevard exit and follow it north 9.8 miles to paved FR 333. Follow FR 333 for 2.5 miles to the La Luz trailhead at the upper end of the Juan Tabo Picnic Ground. Lead-in signs direct you through the picnic area. Tramway Boulevard can also be reached from I-25 and much of the rest of the city.

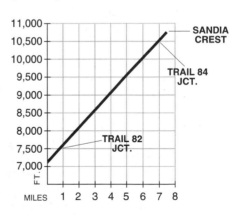

The hike: Even though more than a half-million people sprawl across the Rio Grande Valley at the base of the Sandias, much of the rugged west face of the mountains has remained wild. In 1978, Congress protected much of the area as the Sandia Mountain Wilderness, now 37,232 acres.

Tremendous faulting tilted the mountains high above the Rio Grande Valley. The steep and rugged west side exposes the bare bones of the earth's crust as enormous cliffs and pinnacles, while the east side slopes much more gently, with a softening coat of forest. Precambrian granite makes up

The upper tramway terminal at the end of the La Luz Trail makes a loop trip possible.

most of the west face through which the trail climbs. A layer of Pennsylvanian limestone caps the crest.

Because of the large elevation gain on the trail, you will pass through several of the West's major life zones as you go. The increased moisture and lower temperatures found at higher elevations creates different habitats. The trail starts in the Upper Sonoran Zone, characterized by semi-arid grasslands and scrubby forests of pinyon and juniper. Ponderosa pine typifies the Transition Zone, the next one up, although pinyon grows in the lower levels and Douglas-fir grows in the upper levels. As the trail approaches the crest it moves into the Canadian Life Zone. Common trees here are Douglas-fir, aspen, and blue spruce. Finally, on the crest, lies the Hudsonian Zone, with Engelmann spruce, sub-alpine fir, and other hardy trees.

Because of the proximity to Albuquerque, the trail is probably one of the most popular in the state, even though it is strenuous. Footraces are even held on the trail. Summer weekends are the busiest, naturally. The continuously changing views still make the trail a rewarding hike. Just relax and enjoy the camaraderie of other hikers. Some of the other trails in this book are so unused, you will probably be happy to see people for a change.

In summer, try to get an early start, since the bottom half of the trail can be very hot and exposed. Also take some warm clothes and rain gear because of the frequent summer thunderstorms on the crest. Looking up at the mountain from the parking lot, you will wonder how the trail ever gets through the towering cliffs above. From the trailhead, the La Luz Trail 137 immediately begins to climb at a moderate grade and never lets up. Another

La Luz Trail

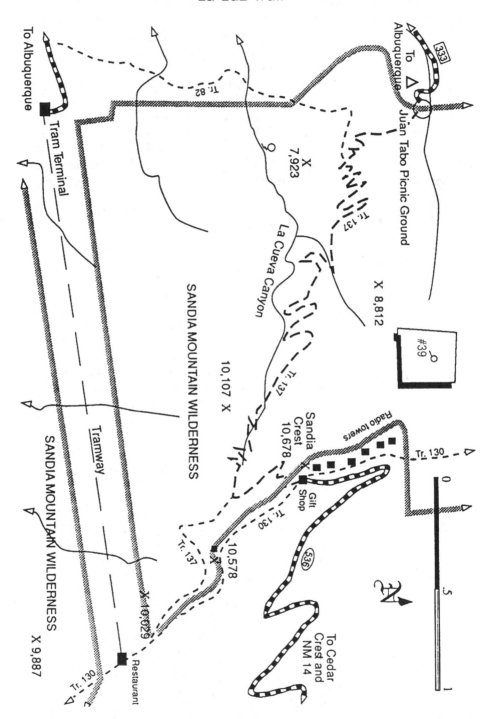

trail, the Piedra Lisa Trail also starts from the same trailhead. A little less than 1 mile up, Tramway Trail 82 turns off to the right. Stay with the La Luz Trail to Sandia Crest. Switchbacks start in earnest after the junction. Please do not shortcut the switchbacks, as it erodes the hillside.

At close to 3 miles up, the trail crosses a canyon that usually has some running water. Check with the Forest Service ahead of time before depending on it. In a pinch, water can be obtained at the gift shop on Sandia Crest. However, since they have to truck their water up the mountain, do not expect to get large quantities. Buying a soft drink or other item would be a nice gesture if you must ask for water.

No official junctions are encountered for the next 6 miles. However, here and there trails lead off the main route, usually to rock climbing destinations. The main trail is well maintained and heavily used, so you should not have any trouble staying with it. The trail slowly goes higher, finally climbing up a steep canyon through towering cliffs of reddish granite. Cooler temperatures and more trees make the second half of the climb more pleasant in summer. If you are lucky, you may see a bighorn climbing on the crags above the trail.

Finally, at about 7 miles, you will reach the junction with Trail 84, the Crest Spur Trail. Turn left on it toward Sandia Crest. After struggling up the steep 0.5 mile of Trail 84, you reach the summit, with its gift shop, radio towers, and crowds. If desired, a car shuttle can be arranged ahead of time to get back down by driving up the back side of the mountains on NM 536. Alternately, rather than turning left onto the Crest Spur Trail, stay on the La Luz Trail for an additional 1 mile to the top of the tramway. Ride the tramway back down and hike the 2 miles back to your car on Trail 82, the Tramway Trail, mentioned at the start of the trail description.

40 10-K Trail

General description:	An easy loop day hike into the northern section of the Sandia Mountain Wilderness.
General location:	About 30 miles northwest of Albuquerque.
Length:	About 6.5 miles round trip.
Elevation:	9,600–10,678 feet.
Maps:	Sandia Mountain Wilderness; Cibola National Forest—Sandia-Mountainair Districts; Sandia Crest 7.5-minute USGS quad.
Best season:	Mid-May through October.
Water availability:	Media Spring.
Special attractions:	Views; lush forest; excellent marked winter cross-country ski route.

Finding the trailhead: Go east out of the center of Albuquerque on I-40 about 15 miles to the turnoff to Cedar Crest on NM 14. Go left on NM 14 about 6 miles to the turnoff to Sandia Crest on NM 536. Follow paved NM 536 11.6 miles to the trailhead about 2 miles short of the crest. The 10-K Trail is marked by signs on both sides of the road in a huge grassy swath cleared through the forest. Park in the rough parking lot in the cleared area on the right, or north, side of the highway.

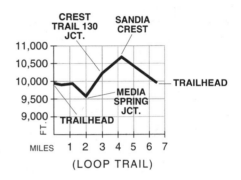

The hike: The 10-K Trail got its name because it roughly follows the 10,000-foot elevation contour along the east side of the Sandias. The huge cleared strip was the initial work of a large scenic highway that was planned to run along much of Sandia Crest. Fortunately the plan was killed before it was completed, even though the builders had already cleared an ugly swath several miles long through the forest.

The first part of the hike passes through dense forests of aspen, spruce, and Douglas-fir. Most of the return loop follows the crest, with spectacular views of the Rio Grande Valley and beyond. From the parking area, look for the trail leading up into the woods from the uphill side of the cleared area right next to the highway. Do not follow the rough dirt road that heads down the cleared strip.

Once you get on the well maintained trail, it is easy to follow. Blue plastic diamonds nailed to the trees mark the route for skiers in winter. At about 0.5 miles, the trail splits. Take either route; the forks quickly rejoin. Overall,

Views stretch for miles from Sandia Crest.

the trail descends slightly for its first 2 miles. At almost 2 miles, a sign marks the Sandia Mountain Wilderness boundary. Just beyond, the trail forks. A short hike down to the right lies Media Spring. Check with the Forest Service ahead of time to find out its status.

Go left at the junction on the 10-K Trail and begin the short, but moderately steep climb to the crest. Less than 0.25 mile up, the trail crosses the ugly cleared strip. A few hundred yards up from the strip, a cross-country ski trail cuts in sharply from the left. Stay right on the 10-K trail. The 10-K Trail soon ends at about 2.5 miles at Crest Trail 130. Enjoy the incredible views from the rugged crest. The Jemez Mountains loom to the north, while Mt. Taylor is usually visible far to the west.

Go left on the Crest Trail toward Sandia Crest, climbing some as you go. The trail breaks in and out of the forest, mixing great views with lush forest. The trail passes a virtual forest of radio towers on the right for the last 0.5 mile to Sandia Crest. The Crest, at the end of the highway, is the highest point on the hike and in the Sandias. A gift shop and crowds decorate the summit. Return to the trailhead by walking 2.2 miles back down NM 536 to your car. Experienced hikers, armed with the topo map or wilderness map, can cut across the highway switchbacks and shorten the return by bushwhacking through the forest. A similar, alternate loop can be done by following the 10-K Trail south to the crest and returning by the Crest Trail.

10-K Trail

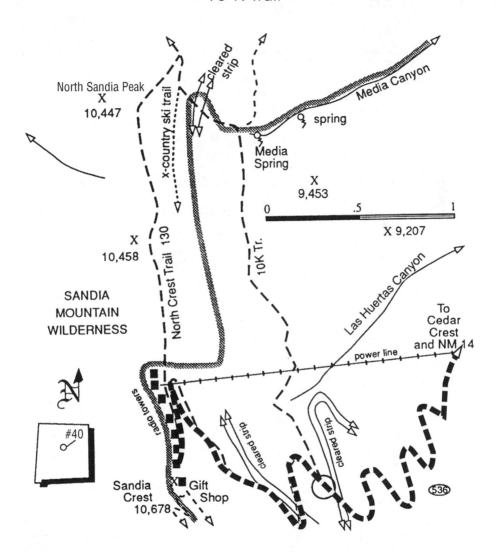

41 Tree Spring Trail

General description:	A moderate day hike to the top of the Sandia Peak Tramway.
General location:	About 25 miles east of Albuquerque.
Length:	About 6 miles round trip.
Elevation:	8,460–10,290 feet.
Maps:	Cibola National Forest—Sandia-Mountainair Ranger Districts; Sandia Mountain Wilderness; Sandia Crest 7.5-minute USGS quad.
Best season:	Mid-May to November.
Water availability:	Restaurant and visitor center at top of tramway, when open.
Special attractions:	Views; lush forest.

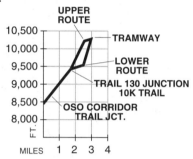

Finding the trailhead: Go west about 15 miles from the center of Albuquerque on I-40 to the NM 14/Cedar Crest exit. Exit and turn left, or north, on NM 14. Go about 5.9 miles on NM 14 to the NM 536 fork on the left. Follow NM 536 toward Sandia Crest. At about 5.7 miles, park at the well marked Tree Spring Trail 147 trailhead on the left.

The hike: Most of the trails to the crest in the Sandia Mountains are fairly long and strenuous. The Tree Spring Trail is the easiest route to the crest (other than driving up NM 536 or taking the tramway). It reaches the crest a little more than halfway up this hike after gaining only about 1,000 feet. The trail is well maintained and follows a steady moderate grade to the crest. Because of its proximity to Albuquerque, do not expect to have it to yourself.

The trailhead has a paved parking area and even a bathroom. Be sure that your valuables are out of sight or carried with you; a temporary sign says "Experiencing break-ins—protect your valuables."

The trailhead signs are slightly off in their mileages. The trail starts climbing through lush Douglas-fir, and reaches the marked Oso Corridor Trail forking off to the left about 0.3 mile up. The trail does not appear on many maps. Stay right, toward the Crest Trail.

At a little less than 2 miles, you hit the marked Sandia Mountain Wilderness boundary at a four-way intersection. To the left, Crest Trail 130 goes 13 miles all the way to Canyon Estates. It makes a great backpack with a car shuttle or ride at the end. Straight ahead, Trail 130 goes up to the tramway about 1 mile away (the sign distance of 0.5 mile is wrong). This will be your return route. Turn right on the 10-K Trail. The 10-K Trail is marked with blue plastic diamonds for cross-country ski use in winter.

Tree Spring Trail

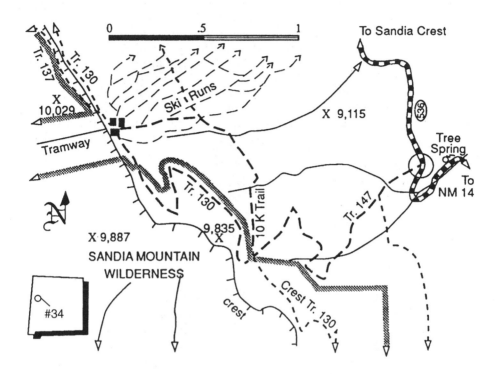

Go a little less than 0.75 mile along the relatively level 10 K Trail to an unmarked fork. Take either fork; they quickly rejoin when they hit the downhill ski trails of the Sandia ski area. Turn left at the ski runs and follow the runs up the mountain to the crest at the top of the ski area. The 0.5 mile climb up the grassy ski run is steep and the air is getting thin, so take your time.

At the top, views open up in all directions. A visitor center crowns the crest at the top terminal of the tramway that comes up from Albuquerque, below to the west. The Cibola National Forest visitor center has interesting exhibits about the Sandia Mountains. Since the summit is not exactly a wilderness anyway, why not join the crowd and enjoy lunch at the High Finance Restaurant before hiking back down?

To return, follow Trail 130 down the crest to the south, away from the summit buildings. In about 0.25 mile you re-enter the wilderness. The trail descends at a moderate grade through dense forest to the same four-way junction described earlier. Go straight ahead, back down Tree Spring Trail 147. If you wish to avoid the steep climb up the ski run on your way up, just follow Trail 130 to the tramway, rather than the 10-K Trail and the ski run.

42 North Sandia Crest

General description:	A moderate one-way day hike (or strenuous round-trip overnight trip) along the crest of the northern section of the Sandia Mountains.
General location:	The east side of Albuquerque.
Length:	About 13.5 miles one-way (27 miles round trip).
Elevation:	10,678–6,380 feet.
Maps:	Sandia Mountain Wilderness; Cibola National Forest—Sandia-Mountainair Ranger Districts; Sandia Crest and Placitas 7.5-minute USGS quads.
Best season:	May through October.
Water availability:	Both trailheads and Sandia Crest.
Special attractions:	Great views; lush forest.

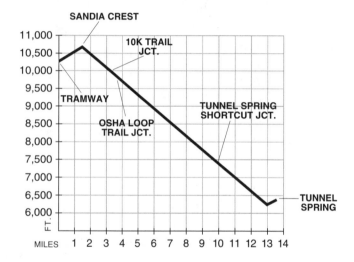

Finding the trailhead: From the east side of Albuquerque, take Tramway Boulevard north from I-40 to the Sandia Peak Tramway. From the north side of the city, take Tramway Road east from I-25 to the Sandia Peak Tramway. Take the tram to the top of the mountains and the south trailhead. The north trailhead is reached by following I-25 north from Albuquerque to the Placitas/Bernalillo exit. Turn right, toward the mountains, and follow NM 165 about 5 miles to Tunnel Spring Road/FR 231 on the right. Follow the gravel road about 1.5 miles, past a number of houses, to Tunnel Spring at the end of the road. The road is a little rough, but is passable with a sedan if care is used.

The hike: The Sandia Mountains tower over Albuquerque, rising abruptly from the east side of the city. A trail follows the dramatic crest of the mountains from the south end of the range in Tijeras Canyon to near the village of Placitas on the north side. This hike follows the northern section of the trail.

North Sandia Crest

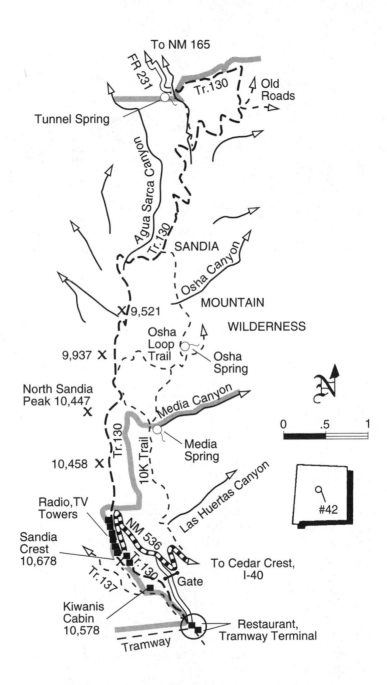

To NM 165

FR 231

Tr.130

Old Roads

Tunnel Spring

Agua Sarca Canyon

Tr.130

SANDIA

Osha Canyon

MOUNTAIN

WILDERNESS

X 9,521

Osha Loop Trail

Osha Spring

9,937 X

North Sandia Peak 10,447 X

Media Canyon

Tr.130

10K Trail

Media Spring

10,458 X

Las Huertas Canyon

Radio,TV Towers

NM 536

Sandia Crest 10,678 X

Tr.130

To Cedar Crest, I-40

Tr.137

Gate

Kiwanis Cabin 10,578

Restaurant, Tramway Terminal

Tramway

0   .5   1

#42

A hiker relaxes at the north end of the Sandia Mountains.

To add an interesting twist, I started the hike with a ride up the tramway to the crest of the mountains. The trail is most easily done with a car shuttle. It is far easier to start the hike at the top of the tramway and hike north, mostly downhill, than to start at Tunnel Spring and hike up. If you do not want to take the tram, drive up the back side of the mountains all the way to the top at Sandia Crest. (Follow the trailhead directions for the Tree Spring or 10-K hikes in this guide and continue all the way up NM 536 to the road's end at Sandia Crest.)

Be sure to start early to avoid thunderstorms, especially in late summer during the monsoon season. Quite a bit of the hike crosses exposed ridges and meadows.

From the tram terminal on the top of the mountains, head north past the restaurant on Trail 130. You can see the radio towers on Sandia Crest some distance ahead. The initial 1.5 miles to Sandia Crest climb gradually about 400 feet. Generally the trail stays in lush forest of Engelmann spruce and subalpine fir just below the crest. Initially, the trail is part of a nature trail, with interpretive signs along the way. The La Luz Trail, described in this guide, joins the trail right after you begin. You pass several junctions with bike and ski trails along the route to Sandia Crest, but stay on the main trail, Trail 130. Most maps still show the trail as following the crest to and past the Kiwanis Cabin. However, it was recently routed away from part of the crest to protect wildlife.

The trail returns to the crest and a great overlook just before the Sandia Crest parking lot. Views from the many overlooks along this trail are tremendous. They stretch from the city below to the distant summit of Mount Taylor far to the west.

Cross the large parking lot at Sandia Crest and find the continuation of Trail 130 on the north side, below a forest of radio and television towers. The trail re-enters the woods and soon leaves the towers and crowds behind. From here, the trail generally goes downhill for almost the entire remainder of the hike. Fortunately, it is not very steep, so your knees should withstand the 4,300-foot descent without too much difficulty.

As before, the trail passes through deep forest, with occasional viewpoints on the crest. The first nice viewpoint along this section lies about 2 miles from the parking lot, just past where the 10-K Trail joins Trail 130 from the right. A whole mountainside of aspens here catches fire with color in early October.

Soon, the Osha Loop Trail joins from the right. Stay with Trail 130 as always. As it descends, the trail passes through different life zones and the lush spruce-fir forest gives way to ponderosa pine and then pinyon-juniper forest. One stretch of trail passes through a dense thicket of scrub oak that seems determined to scratch your legs. The scrub oak ends near the marked junction with the Peñasco Blanco Trail, a new route not shown on some maps. Stay left on Trail 130.

The trail enters relatively continuous pinyon-juniper forest after the junction and steadily descends with large, gradual switchbacks. The path finally reaches the head of a canyon with a view of Tunnel Spring and the northern trailhead below. It seems close, but is really still quite some distance away. A trail forks down steeply to the left here and follows the canyon down to the trailhead. Although it is shorter, it is steep and rocky. I prefer the longer right fork.

The right fork traverses across a long, west-facing slope high above Tunnel Spring and then turns away onto a more gradual slope. It carves a long, curving path east, then north, and finally back west to the trailhead. Along the way, it passes some old, abandoned Jeep roads, but Trail 130 is obvious. To make you earn your dinner, the last bit of trail climbs gradually to the Tunnel Spring. Enjoy the shady cottonwoods and cool water at the spring, site of a former fish hatchery.

43 Manzano Peak

General description:	A moderate day hike to the highest point in the Manzano Mountains.
General location:	About 65 miles southeast of Albuquerque.
Length:	About 7.25 miles round trip.
Elevation:	8,080–10,098 feet.
Maps:	Manzano Mountain Wilderness; Cibola National Forest—Sandia-Mountainair Ranger Districts; Manzano Peak 7.5-minute USGS quad.
Best season:	Late April through November.
Water availability:	Unreliable—see text.
Special attractions:	Views; lush forest; solitude.

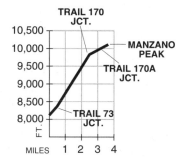

Finding the trailhead: Drive about 12 miles north of Mountainair on NM 55 to Manzano. Turn left on gravel FR 253 and drive 5 miles to the marked FR 422 turnoff. Go left on gravel FR 422 for 3.8 miles to its junction with FR 275 and park.

The hike: The 40-mile long Manzano Mountains are an extension of the fault block that raised the Sandia Mountains to the north. The mountains appear deceptively small and uninteresting from a distance. However, the mountains' long crest maintains an altitude of 9,000-10,000 feet. Lush forest covers the slopes and several canyons have small streams. The 36,970-acre Manzano Mountain Wilderness protects the heart of the range.

The word *manzano* means apple in Spanish. In the 1700s, explorers found very old apple trees growing in a village on the eastern side of the mountains. Since apples are not native to North America, the visitors were unable to determine how the apple trees appeared. Most probably, the apples were brought in by early Spanish explorers and settlers.

The area surrounding the Manzano Mountains was one of the first places settled in the United States. Spaniards established missions at Quarai, Abo, and other sites at the foot of the mountains in the early 1600s. If you have time, be sure to visit the ruins, protected in Salinas Pueblo Missions National Monument. One site is included in the Quarai hike in this guide.

From the FR 422 and FR 275 junction, turn right (west) and walk up the rough extension of FR 275. The trail begins in heavily logged new-growth ponderosa pine. High clearance vehicles can usually make it up to the road's end about 0.6 mile toward the mountains. About 0.5 mile up, marked Trail 73 forks off to the left. Continue a short distance up the road to its end in a little clearing.

Trail 80, the Kayser Mill Trail, climbs up out of the left side of the clear-

Manzano Peak

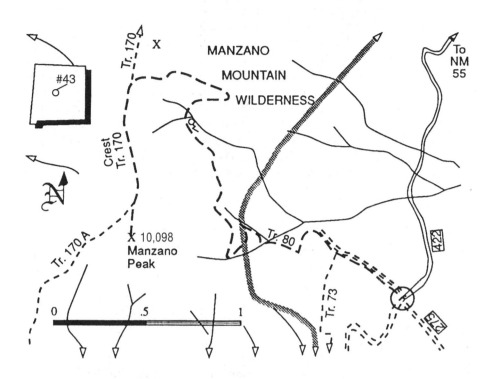

ing back toward the valley. A sign marks its start. The trail quickly turns back toward the mountains and begins climbing. The excellent trail climbs steadily for the entire 2.25 miles to the crest. About 0.5 mile beyond the end of the road, a sign marks the wilderness boundary.

The trail travels through lush forests of Douglas-fir, white fir, aspen, and spruce for most of the climb. Right before the trail crosses a large rockslide near the crest, it contours around the head of a small drainage in a clearing. An unreliable spring is visible just below the trail in the creek bottom. Check with the Forest Service about its status before you start. When it is flowing, it helps overnight campers immensely because it is close to the crest.

The trail reaches the crest in a large meadow on a saddle at almost 3 total miles. Go straight up the 9,800-foot elevation meadow to signs marking the Crest Trail 170. The saddle and rest of the crest make excellent camping areas. Most of the rest of the hike is not level enough for camping. Be careful about lightning on the crest. The views from the saddle are impressive, but the vista from Manzano Peak easily tops them.

From the saddle, go left (south) and follow the Crest Trail to the summit of Manzano Peak. A little more than 0.5 mile along the crest, Trail 170A forks downward to the right. Stay left for the last 0.25 mile to the summit.

After the long hike through the densely wooded mountains, the bare, rocky peak is a pleasant surprise. With few trees, the views are unbeatable. The mountains fall away abruptly to the east, south, and west. On clear days, mountains as far away as Sierra Blanca Peak, the San Mateos, Mount Taylor, and the Sangre de Cristos can be seen rising prominently on the horizon. Oddly enough, tiny cacti cover the bare summit. A mailbox that someone placed on the summit adds a comic touch. Do not worry about crowds. The register inside the box indicates light visitation. I climbed the peak in mid-June and the most recent signature I found was made two weeks earlier.

An alternate but considerably longer route turns the hike into a loop trip if desired. Take Trail 170A down off the peak to FR 422. Go left up FR 422 about 0.5 mile to Trail 73 on the left. Follow Trail 73 to FR 275 and the trailhead. The alternate route is about 4 miles longer and involves some climbing on Trail 73.

44 Red Canyon

General description:	A moderate day hike through heavy forest to the wilderness crest of the Manzano Mountains.
General location:	About 60 miles southeast of Albuquerque.
Length:	About 7.5 miles round trip.
Elevation:	8,000–9,960 feet.
Maps:	Manzano Mountain Wilderness; Cibola National Forest—Sandia-Mountainair Ranger Districts; Capilla Peak and Manzano Peak 7.5 minute USGS quads.
Best season:	Late April through November.
Water availability:	Spruce Spring; Red Canyon.
Special attractions:	Views; lush forest; small waterfalls.

Finding the trailhead: Drive north of Mountainair about 12 miles on NM 55 to Manzano. Turn left on gravel FR 253 and drive 5.9 miles to the Red Canyon Campground. Signs mark the way.

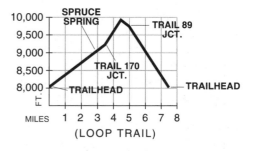

The hike: The Manzano Mountains are an unassuming range with hidden surprises. This hike provides great views, lush forest, and even two small waterfalls. The campground at the trailhead lies in dense forest and is a pleasant place to camp either before or after your hike. At the time of my last visit, however, potable water was not available. However, a good spring by the creek in the campground could be used, along with purification.

Red Canyon

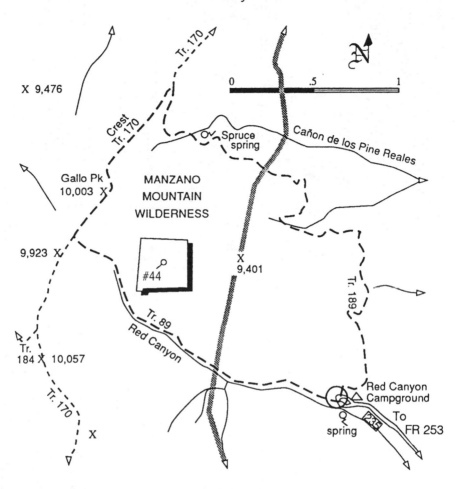

The trail starts at the upper end of the campground loop. Follow the signs for Spruce Trail 189 up out of the campground. The trail winds its way to the crest at a very mild grade through ponderosa pine, aspen, Douglas-fir, spruce, and other trees. About 3 miles up the trail, a sign marks Spruce Spring on the right. A 300-foot side trail leads down to the spring. The trail reaches the crest soon after, at almost 3.5 miles, and intersects with Crest Trail 170. The crest is open and grassy at the junction, providing great views to the east and west. Level areas along the crest near the junction provide the best campsites on this hike.

Turn left (south) on the Crest Trail and follow it as it climbs up toward Gallo Peak. The crest is exposed to lightning, so be aware of developing thunderstorms. At close to 1 mile up Trail 170, the route hits its high point

Cornhusk lilies grow at Spruce Spring in the Manzano Mountains.

when it crests an east-trending ridge. A short off-trail scramble up the ridge to the right will take you to the summit of 10,003–foot Gallo Peak. A short descent from the ridge brings Trail 170 to another grassy saddle with views to the east and west. The saddle area, at almost 5 miles, provides the other good camping area along the hike.

From the grassy saddle, turn left onto Trail 89 to return to the Red Canyon Campground. Trail 89 drops more steeply than the Spruce Trail and is more heavily used. About 1 mile down, the trail reaches the bottom of Red Canyon. The trail follows the canyon the rest of the way, accompanied by a small running stream in all but the driest years. The canyon becomes lush, wet, narrow, and rocky. Two small waterfalls drop off ledges along the way. The trail ends at the campground at about 7.5 miles.

45 Fourth of July

General description:	A moderate day hike to the crest of the Manzano Mountains through some of the best fall color in the Southwest.
General location:	About 55 miles southeast of Albuquerque.
Length:	About 6.25 miles round trip.
Elevation:	7,520–8,660 feet.
Maps:	Manzano Mountain Wilderness; Cibola National Forest—Sandia-Mountainair District; Bosque Peak 7.5-minute USGS quad.
Best season:	Late April through November.
Water availability:	Upper Fourth of July Spring; Big Spring.
Special attractions:	Bigtooth maples; views; lush forest.

Finding the trailhead: Follow the same directions as for the Albuquerque Trail hike, except drive 0.5 mile further up FR 55 to Fourth of July Campground. Drive 0.4 mile to the upper end of the campground and park.

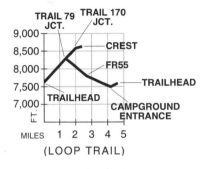

The hike: The Manzano Mountains area around the upper ends of Tajique and Torreon canyons boasts one of the best stands of bigtooth maples in the Southwest. The trees turn rich shades of scarlet and gold in the fall. The campground itself is well wooded with maples. Because of the fall color, the trails around the campground are very popular on fall weekends. The excellent trail traverses miles of beautiful forest, making it a worthwhile hike any time of year. On a summer weekday, only one other vehicle shared the campground with me and I saw only one couple on the trail.

The marked trailhead for Trail 173 is at the upper end of the campground. The trail follows the canyon bottom up into the mountains. A stream usually flows partway down, fed by Upper Fourth of July Spring. You soon pass the spring, obvious with its small tank used by livestock. Just past it is the Manzano Mountain Wilderness boundary. A fairly new trail that connects with the Albuquerque Trail comes in from the right (see the Albuquerque Trail hike). Continue up the canyon on Trail 173 to the junction with Trail 79 at almost 1.5 miles. Turn right and follow the signs uphill toward the Crest Trail.

Maples almost solidly forest the next 0.5 mile. At about 2 miles, turn right onto Crest Trail 170 at the intersection. The mileages on the different signs do not quite agree with each other. The trail levels out for the next 0.25 miles to a saddle in the crest. Enjoy the tremendous views of the Rio

Fourth of July • Albuquerque Trail

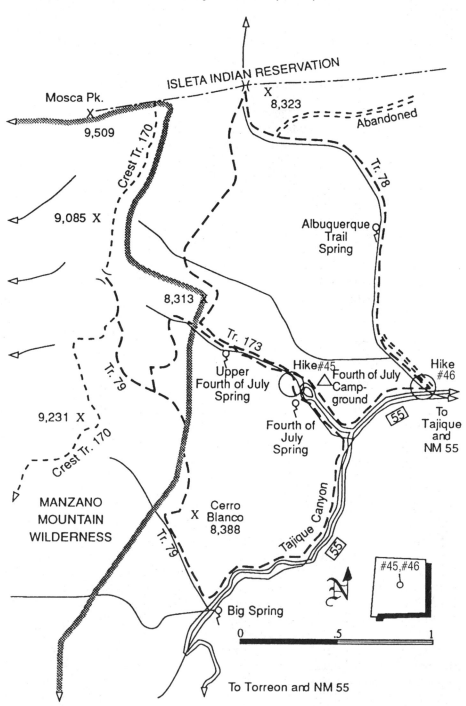

ISLETA INDIAN RESERVATION

Mosca Pk.
X
9,509

X
8,323

Abandoned

Crest Tr. 170

Tr. 78

9,085 X

Albuquerque
Trail
Spring

8,313

Tr. 173

Tr. 79

Upper
Fourth of July
Spring

Hike#45

Fourth of July
Camp-
ground

Hike
#46

9,231 X

Crest Tr. 170

Fourth of
July
Spring

55

To
Tajique
and
NM 55

MANZANO
MOUNTAIN
WILDERNESS

Tr. 79

Cerro
X Blanco
8,388

Tajique Canyon

55

#45, #46

N

Big Spring

0   .5   1

To Torreon and NM 55

Grande and Estancia Valleys. Just above the saddle to the north rises a subsummit of Mosca Peak. Farther away, to the north-northwest, rises Guadalupe Peak. Be careful not to get confused at the saddle. Several informal trails wind through the oak scrub.

Retrace your route back to Trail 79. Follow Trail 79 all the way down the mountain, instead of turning off on Trail 173. The descent down Trail 79 is relatively mild, except for a short, steep stretch about halfway down where it drops into a canyon. Maples forest much of the canyon bottom. A small stream usually comes and goes. An unmarked trail joins the main trail on the right just before reaching FR 55. At about 4.25 miles you reach FR 55. Big Spring lies right across the road from Trail 79. Go left on FR 55 about 1.4 miles to the Fourth of July Campground entrance. The road is a pleasant downhill walk along a permanent stream lined with maples.

The loop can be extended considerably by continuing south on the Crest Trail 170 to Trail 174. Go left and down on Trail 174 to FR 55. Follow FR 55 left back to the campground. Alternately, Trails 79, 170, and 174 make a good loop day hike, when combined with a short stretch of FR 55.

46 Albuquerque Trail

General description:	An easy day hike into an area of bigtooth maples noted for their fall color.
General location:	About 55 miles southeast of Albuquerque.
Length:	About 5.25 miles round trip.
Elevation:	7,420–8,250 feet.
Maps:	Manzano Mountain Wilderness; Cibola National Forest— Sandia-Mountainair Ranger Districts; Tajique and Bosque Peak 7.5-minute USGS quads.
Best season:	April through November.
Water availability:	Albuquerque Trail Spring; Upper Fourth of July Spring.
Special attractions:	Bigtooth maples.

Finding the trailhead: Go east on I-40 about 15 miles from the center of Albuquerque to NM 337. Turn right and follow NM 337 about 30 miles to NM 55. Turn right and follow NM 55 about 3 miles into Tajique. Turn right on gravel FR 55, marked with a Fourth of July Campground sign, and follow it west into the mountains. At 6.9 miles, park along the road at the Albuquerque Trail 78 sign (just short of the campground entrance).

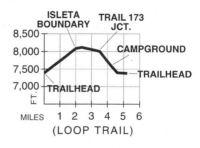

Black bears, such as this one in the Manzano Mountains, make frequent campground raids in New Mexico mountains. Keep your food out of reach.

The hike: The northern end of the Manzano Mountains is noted for its impressive stands of bigtooth maples. The maples provide some of the best fall color in the southwest. This loop trail climbs at an easy grade up through conifer forest to some dense stands of the trees.

The first 0.4 mile of the trail follows a rough dirt road. Unless it is wet, a high clearance vehicle can make it. At 0.4 mile, the Forest Service has gated the old logging road and converted the road to a trail. A very small stream usually flows down the creek bottom. The old road used to follow much of the bottom and was wet and muddy in places. The Forest Service has raised the new trail slightly out of the bottom. Initially, the forest you pass through has signs of fairly recent logging, but the trail eventually leaves it behind. The most common conifers are ponderosa pine and Douglas-fir.

A short distance up the trail, you pass the spring that creates the stream, Albuquerque Trail Spring. On this short hike, I recommend that you carry water, rather than bother to purify the spring water. After you get about 1 mile up the trail, maples begin to appear. At a little more than 1.5 miles, a faint abandoned road comes in from the right. Stay left, following the signs marking Trail 78 up the canyon bottom. The next 0.5 mile is particularly nice, with dense stands of maples. Often they even arch over the trail. Try to come on fall weekdays, because the area is popular on the weekends.

The trail appears to end at a fence at about 2 miles. The fence marks the boundary of the Isleta Indian Reservation. Do not cross it without permission. A few years ago the Forest Service completed an extension of Trail 78 from the end of the trail. It is not shown yet on some maps. From the fence, the new trail cuts left up the hillside. It traverses the mountain slopes to Trail 173 above Fourth of July Campground at about 3.5 miles. The trail intersects Trail 173 at the wilderness boundary just above Upper Fourth of July Spring. Turn left and follow Trail 173 downhill into the campground at about 4.25 miles, walk down through the campground to FR 55, and go left on the road about 0.5 mile to your car at the trailhead. Trail 173 is the start of another route in this book, the Fourth of July hike.

On quiet days, keep an eye out for bears in the Manzano Mountains. I surprised a young bear (and myself!) on this trail one summer afternoon.

47 Quarai

General description:	An easy day hike around one of the historic Spanish missions of Salinas Pueblo Missions National Monument.
General location:	About 10 miles northwest of Mountainair.
Length:	About 1.5 miles round trip.
Elevation:	6,610–6,650 feet (no elevation graph).
Maps:	Quarai Trail Guide; Punta de Agua 7.5-minute USGS quad.
Best season:	All year.
Water availability:	Trailhead (Visitor Center).
Special attractions:	Historic Spanish mission ruins.

Finding the trailhead: Drive about 9 miles north of Mountainair on NM 55 to Punta de Agua. Follow the signs for Salinas Pueblos Missions National Monument and turn left onto a paved, potholed road. Follow it 1 mile to the Quarai visitor center and parking lot.

The hike: Quarai was a thriving Indian pueblo when the Spaniards first visited the Salinas Valley in 1581. Don Juan de Onate approached it in 1598 to obtain an oath of allegiance to Spain. In the early 1600s, Spanish priests arrived at Quarai and other nearby pueblos to establish missions. Large stone churches were built and efforts were made to convert the Indians to Christianity and create self-sufficient communities. Tensions between the priests and the Spanish civil authorities, plus attempts to suppress the Indians' native religion led to serious strains at the missions. Warfare with the Apaches, plus drought and famine in the 1660s and 1670s led to abandonment of the missions and pueblos in the 1670s.

This easy trail winds through the ruins of the mission church and the surrounding Indian pueblo and onto a hill overlooking Quarai. First, stop in at the visitor center to see the exhibits and get more information. The Quarai Trail Guide is particularly helpful in describing the ruins. It matches

The old Spanish mission church still resists the element at Quarai.

numbered markers along the trail.

The hike can be hot in midday in summer, but there is some shade along the way. Winters can be cold, but snows are usually short-lived.

The trail heads out of the back side of the visitor center straight toward the stone church ruins. Mounds along the trail with sections of wall exposed are collapsed ruins of the old pueblos. A stone foundation on the left marks the site of a church begun in 1829, long after the mission was abandoned, but never finished. You then reach the walls of the church of Nuestra Senora de la Purisima Concepcion de Cuarac. Although its roof and plaster are long gone, the red sandstone walls still rise 40 feet from massive 6-foot-thick bases. An immense amount of labor went into its construction. The massive building would have been very impressive in the 1600s when compared to the tiny pueblo rooms.

The trail winds through the church and adjoining convent and then past the mission gardens and other ruins. It continues toward the small valley stream and begins to curve back toward the visitor center. At a junction, turn left onto the Spanish Corral Trail, a side loop off the mission loop. Cross the creek on a wooden bridge. The trail soon splits at the start of the loop. Go right and follow the narrow, more primitive trail as it winds up onto a low ridge dotted with pinyon and juniper trees. There are frequent views of the mission ruins in the valley below. At a bench, the trail passes the old rock Spanish corral.

The trail then winds back down to the creek with its lush cottonwoods, cattails, and willows. A bench offers tempting shade under some large cottonwoods. The trail then follows the creek upstream to the end of the Spanish Corral Trail loop. Turn right, cross the footbridge, and go left to return to the visitor center.

Quarai

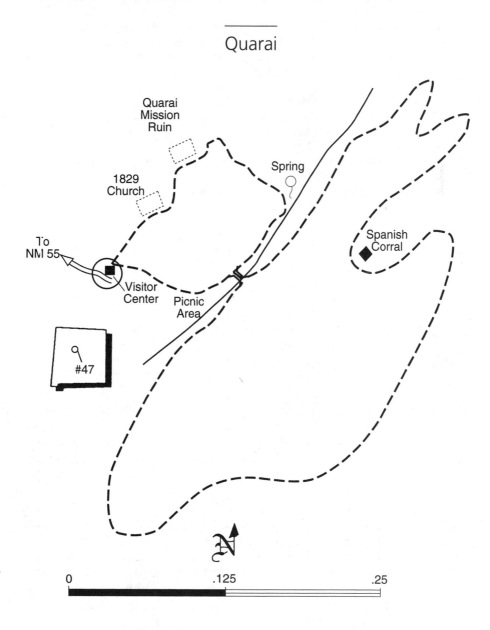

48 Trigo Canyon

General description:	A fairly strenuous day hike up a rugged canyon to the lush crest of the Manzano Mountains
General location:	About 55 miles southeast of Albuquerque.
Length:	About 7.5 miles round trip.
Elevation:	6,240–8,780 feet.
Maps:	Manzano Mountain Wilderness; Cibola National Forest—Sandia-Mountainair Ranger Districts; Capilla Peak 7.5-minute USGS quad.
Best season:	May through November.
Water availability:	The creek often has some water between about mile 1 and mile 2.5.
Special attractions:	Small waterfall; rugged and spectacular canyon; views; forest.

Finding the trailhead: In Belen, start at the junction of NM 47 and NM 304 on the east side of the river (it lies just south of where NM 309 crosses the river). From the junction, go south on NM 47 about 1.9 miles to North Navajo Road, a dirt road on the left marked by the dilapidated walls of a failed subdivision development. Follow North Navajo Road about 8.3 miles toward the mountains. It is a little sandy and washboarded, but should not be a problem for most vehicles. Turn left on Trigo Springs Road (another reasonably good dirt road) and follow it north about 3.2 miles. Turn right onto FR 33 and follow it toward the mountains about 7 miles to John F. Kennedy Campground. The last mile or two of this road can be a bit rough; use care. The trailhead is at the back side of the campground at the end of the road.

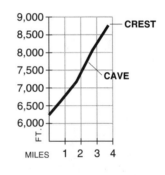

The hike: This hike climbs to the crest of the Manzano Mountains from the lower and drier west side of the range. From a distance, the Manzano Mountains appear as a somewhat small, boring, and dry range. The reality becomes apparent when you drive or hike into the mountains. They reach an altitude of more than 10,000 feet and are thickly forested with pine, spruce, and fir. Much of the range, including this hike, lies within the 36,970-acre Manzano Mountain Wilderness. Canyons such as Trigo that seem insignificant from a distance become, deep, rugged defiles upon approach.

This trail climbs from dry, sparse pinyon-juniper forest at the base of the mountains up Trigo Canyon to the lush conifer forest of the mountain crest. The lower parts of the trail can be hot in summer, so be sure to start early at

Trigo Canyon

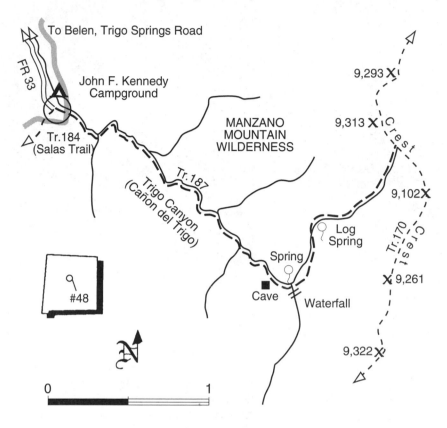

that time of year. Plan to carry water unless the Forest Service tells you that water is available in the creek.

The trail starts on the back side of the John F. Kennedy Campground. Unfortunately, the campground has been heavily vandalized and marred with graffiti, probably because of its proximity to Albuquerque and Belen. It also suffers serious erosion and could use some maintenance work. I would recommend not leaving any valuables in your vehicle and locking everything else out of sight.

Two trails start at the back side of the campground by a steel gate. One, the Salas Trail, climbs up the hill to the right. The Trigo Canyon Trail goes through the gate and up the canyon. It enters the wilderness immediately. The first 0.5 mile of the trail was once an old road and is quite wide. The canyon slowly narrows and the old road ends. Vegetation becomes more lush and a trickle of water is often present in the creek bottom. The trail climbs through an area burned relatively recently. Although brush and many

A cave is a popular campsite in Trigo Canyon.

small trees perished, most large ponderosa pines survived. At the upper end of the burned area, the trail passes under a large, sheer cliff. This is a popular cliff with local rock climbers.

After the cliff, the canyon narrows into a scenic, rocky gorge for a short distance. Beyond, the canyon widens and narrows several times. As the trail gains altitude, the terrain gets increasingly lush. Firs and pines line the canyon bottom. At about 2.5 miles, the trail enters a particularly scenic section with cliffs towering above a narrow canyon bottom wooded with Douglas-fir. A cave on the right side has been heavily used for camping. A short distance beyond is a small 25-foot waterfall with a flow that varies considerably with precipitation. Often only a trickle dribbles down.

The waterfall and cave make a good stopping point for a day hike, but I recommend climbing at least a short distance above them for some tremendous views. Although the trail has been climbing at a moderate grade already, it begins climbing in earnest after the waterfall. It works its way onto the top of the cliffs that tower over the canyon bottom. Views stretch down the canyon and far out across the Rio Grande Valley. Vertigo can be quite impressive, too, if you come too close to the edge.

The grade lessens somewhat as the trail works its way along the cliff tops and into a shady tributary canyon. The path here is much less heavily traveled; most people probably stop at the cave and waterfall. From here, the trail continues up the small canyon and finally climbs out onto the crest of the Manzano Mountains at the junction with Crest Trail 170.

From here, retrace your steps to the trailhead or consider a much longer loop return. Strong hikers with an early start and plenty of water can follow the Crest Trail south for several miles and then descend back to the trailhead on the Salas Trail 184. With a shuttle, it is possible to hike down to another trailhead on the eastern side of the mountains. A relatively easy alternative is to arrange a shuttle where the Crest Trail meets FR 245 near Capilla Peak about 2 miles north.

49 North Baldy

General description:	A moderate day hike along the crest of the Magdalena Mountains.
General location:	About 30 miles west of Socorro.
Length:	About 11 miles round trip.
Elevation:	10,420–9,320 feet.
Maps:	Cibola National Forest—Magdalena Ranger District; Magdalena and South Baldy 7.5-minute USGS quads.
Best season:	May to November.
Water availability:	None.
Special attractions:	Solitude; views; lush forest.

Finding the trailhead: From Socorro, take US 60 15.6 miles west toward Magdalena to the Water Canyon turnoff. Turn left and follow the paved road, FR 235, for 12.6 miles to the marked North Baldy trailhead. The pavement ends at 4.8 miles at the attractive Water Canyon Campground. The remaining 7.8 miles of improved dirt road are usually passable by any vehicle during the warm months. Check with the Forest Service office in Magdalena first. Drive the narrow, windy road slowly and carefully, watching for rocks. The first couple of miles past the campground were the worst during my September visit.

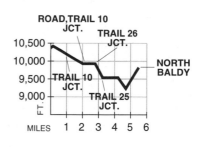

The hike: The North Baldy Trail was the last hike that I did for the first edition of this guidebook. The Magdalena Mountains are beautiful; although time did not allow me to add another trail or two here in the second edition, I highly recommend spending some time in these mountains.

The Magdalena Mountains are a fairly small range in area, but with a top elevation of 10,783 feet are the third highest range in southern New Mexico. The mountains rise abruptly from the surrounding grassy plains. Numerous old mines, most long abandoned, lie scattered throughout the mountains.

The old ghost town of Kelly, on the north side of the range, boomed and died intermittently until the last few mines closed in the 1950s.

FR 235 goes only a short distance beyond the trailhead before being blocked by a gate. Just beyond the gate lies the astronomical and atmospheric research facilities of the Langmuir Research Site. Langmuir Laboratory, operated by New Mexico Tech, specializes in lightning and thunderstorm studies.

The trail starts at the sign on the right side of the road. It climbs steeply uphill to the left from the parking area. The trail is lightly used and tends to fade out in open grassy areas such as the slope above the trailhead. Follow the marker arrow on the sign just up the slope from the trailhead. Rock cairns help mark the way. Do not let the short, steep, thin-air climb above the trailhead discourage you; most of the rest of the trail is easier. At the crest of the ridge, still in view of your car, you hit the highest point of the hike. From the ridge, the now clearly visible trail drops down the other side into lush spruce and fir forest. The trail soon pops out onto a meadow on the long north-south crest of the range.

The rest of the trail follows the crest all the way to North Baldy. Beware of lightning on this exposed hike, especially on summer afternoons. Most of the trail consists of long, level stretches with occasional downhill sections to the low point at the saddle below North Baldy. The little-used trail tends to fade out in the occasional open grassy saddles and hilltops. Just keep following the crest and sooner or later you will find the trail again. Rock cairns and tree blazes will help.

When you first hit the crest, in an open meadow, the trail makes a switchback down the west slope before continuing north through the woods just below the crest. It is easy to miss the faint switchback; if you do, just follow the faint trail on the very top of the crest that was made by other people who missed the proper trail. At about 1 mile, the two routes rejoin in a large grassy saddle. A sign marks Trail 10 forking down off the crest to the right. Continue north through the grass along the crest, watching carefully for cairns until the trail re-enters the forest. At about 2 miles, the trail hits a relatively new-looking mine road that crosses over a saddle in the crest. The road does not show on most maps. Follow the road to the right (east) for 100 feet or so, just over the top of the crest. Look closely below the edge of the road on the left. The trail and a sign will be visible, about 50 feet below the crest on the east slope.

Scramble down the road embankment to the trail and continue north. At a little less than 3 miles, Trail 26 forks off left. Stay right, on the crest on Trail 8. Just a bit further along, Trail 25 also forks off to the left. Again, stay right, on the crest. At a little over 4 miles, the trail begins its descent to a saddle, the lowest point of the hike.

The last 0.75 mile of the hike climbs 500 feet from the saddle to the 9,858-foot summit of North Baldy and the old four-wheel-drive mine road that climbs up over the peak. Much of the last climb crosses a treeless slope.

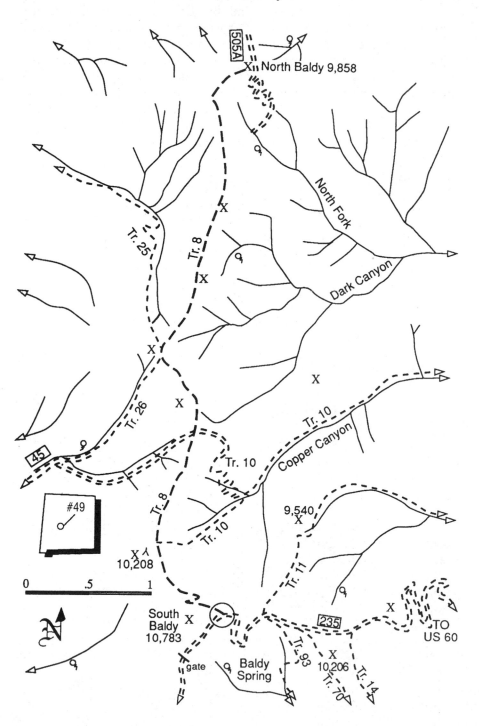

505A

X North Baldy 9,858

North Fork

Dark Canyon

Tr. 25

Tr. 8

X

X

X

Tr. 26

X

Tr. 10

Copper Canyon

45

Tr. 10

Tr. 8

Tr. 10

9,540
X

#49

X
10,208

Tr. 11

0   .5   1

N

South
Baldy
10,783

X

235

X

TO
US 60

gate

Baldy
Spring

Tr. 93

X
10,206

Tr. 70

Tr. 14

The view from the top, and much of the trail along the crest, is spectacular, with views from the Sandia Mountains to the San Mateos.

No water sources lie along the trail, but backpackers armed with topo maps should be able to find water in springs below the crest. Check with the Forest Service about their status. Come visit the empty Magdalena Mountains and give the overused Sandia Mountains and Pecos Wilderness a rest. The Magdalenas are only a two-hour drive from Albuquerque. Trails 11, 70, and 93 are also accessible from FR 235 and promise to be beautiful routes. A strenuous, but spectacular, loop backpack is possible using trails 11, 15, 12, and 14.

50 Mount Withington

General description:	A strenuous overnight hike through the remote Withington Wilderness.
General location:	About 35 miles southwest of Magdalena.
Length:	About 14 miles round trip.
Elevation:	6,720–10,119 feet.
Maps:	Cibola National Forest—Magdalena Ranger District; Mount Withington and Grassy Lookout 7.5-minute USGS quads.
Best season:	Late April through November.
Water availability:	See text.
Special attractions:	Solitude; seasonal waterfall; views; forest.

Finding the trailhead: From Magdalena, drive 12.3 miles west on US 60 to the marked turnoff on the left to Mount Withington (FR 549). Follow FR 549 about 8.6 miles south to the marked FR 52 turnoff on the left. FR 549 is an excellent gravel road, although it may get a little muddy in spots with rain. Follow FR 52 for about 10.8 miles to the marked FR 56 turnoff on the right. Follow FR 56 down into Big Rosa Canyon for

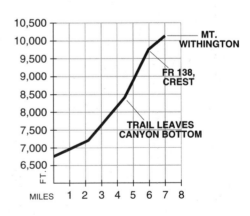

about 2.8 miles to the trailhead, marked with a Potato Canyon Trail 38 sign. FR 52 and FR 56 are usually in good condition and passable with any vehicle if care is used. Call the Forest Service in Magdalena for current conditions.

Mount Withington

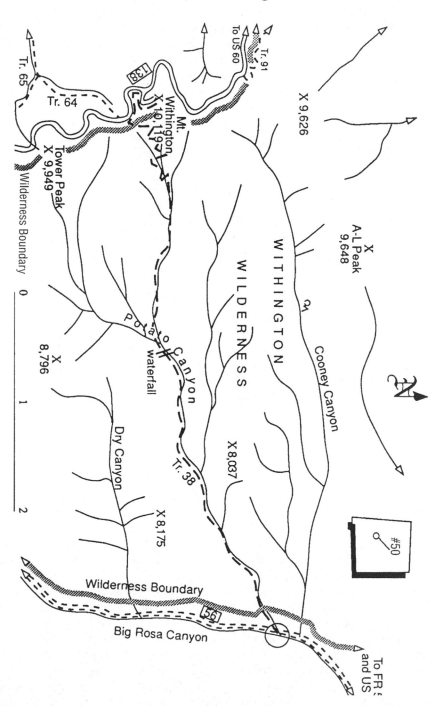

The hike: The San Mateo Range is one of the least visited in New Mexico. One beautiful September day, my mother and I spent several hours driving 80 miles of improved dirt roads in the north end of the mountains around Mount Withington and saw only one pickup. Two wilderness areas lie in the mountains, the Apache Kid in the south (see the San Mateo Peak hike) and the Withington in the north. Only two trails pass through the Withington Wilderness, the longer of which is described in this hike. The Withington Wilderness is very possibly the least visited Forest Service wilderness in the state.

Potato Canyon Trail 38 is very strenuous if hiked in its entirety as a round trip. However, the first 4 miles make an easy to moderate hike, since most of the climb is in the last 3 miles. A car shuttle can also be run to the top of the hike, halving the distance.

This trail is the place where you go to escape your in-laws and the IRS. The trail is so little-used that it is hard to follow in places. Except for the top around Mount Withington, you will probably not see anyone on this trail.

The second half of the hike should be done only if an expert hiker is with your party. A topographic map and a compass are necessities. Although the route is a relatively straightforward hike up a canyon to the mountain crest, it is easy to lose the trail.

The first 4.5 miles follow the canyon bottom, much of the way with no visible trail. Tree blazes mark the route fairly well, but you must look for them. From the trailhead, an old road leads about 0.3 mile up the canyon to the marked wilderness boundary. Continue upstream on the flat canyon floor, keeping an eye out for tree blazes. For the first 3 miles it is not especially important to stay with the marked route, since it just follows the canyon bottom. The blazes just serve as reassurance that you are on the proper route.

Walking in some canyon bottoms can be a nightmare, with either soft, mushy sand and gravel or ankle-turning cobbles and boulders. The alluvial sediment in Potato Canyon, however, is composed of flat, light-colored, shaly-looking rock and gravel that makes a smooth and firm walking surface. The gravel must occasionally wash down in tremendous floods because it has buried tree trunks several feet deep in places, creating an odd looking canyon floor. Some blazes were visible at ankle-height, instead of eye-level.

The canyon bottom starts in scattered pinyon-juniper forest with occasional ponderosa pines. As it climbs, the ponderosa pines and deciduous trees thicken, eventually grading into Douglas-fir.

Overall, with a few exceptions, the canyon narrows as it climbs. At about 1.8 miles the canyon makes a major fork. Go left, following the blazes. Most other forks are minor; stay with the main canyon and the blazes. A spring with a trough is at about 2.25 miles in a narrow part of the canyon. The spring is seasonal, so check with the Forest Service ahead of time about its status. An old ruined cabin will be encountered on the right at almost 3 miles. When the canyon narrows into a small gorge, the trail bypasses it by climbing the left wall. It is actually easier just to stay in the canyon bottom.

A small stream often flows in this stretch. After surmounting a few boulders, you will encounter a small waterfall at about 3.25 miles, beautiful if it is flowing.

Scramble around the waterfall and continue up the little gorge. Be sure to get water here if you need it; it is the last chance. Remember, this stream is seasonal. The gorge quickly ends and the official trail drops back into the canyon bottom from the left wall. The trees in the canyon bottom are now much thicker. Many excellent campsites lie just above the gorge. Do not camp in the bottom; find a site up on the benches in case of floods. The buried trees serve as a warning.

The canyon forks again just above the gorge. Stay in the right fork, following the blazes. From here on, make an effort to follow the tree blazes. The trail frequently lies on the benches, slightly up out of the creek bottom. The canyon will start to get a little steeper and rockier, making travel on the benches easier. The trail crosses back and forth from bank to bank.

If you lose the blazes, backtrack and look carefully. The route is fairly well marked. At about 4.5 miles, the canyon leaves the stream bottom for good and begins switchbacking up to the crest. Watch carefully; you do not want to miss this point. The last 1.5 miles to the crest climb through lush Douglas-firs and other trees, with views to the east. The trail is faint, but generally visible. Some deadfalls will probably lie across the little-maintained route. The trail switchbacks up with a steep, but steady, grade all the way to the top. If you lose the trail, backtrack a bit. You probably missed a faint switchback.

The trail reaches the top and FR 138 in a forested saddle on the crest. A water cache could be hidden here ahead of time for multi-day backpackers. Signs mark the trailhead on FR 138, for those wishing to do the hike in reverse. Camping is possible on level areas along the crest. Views open up to the west. From here, follow the road to the right (north) toward Mount Withington. At about 0.6 mile, turn right onto FR 138B, and climb the last 0.2 mile to the lookout tower on the summit. If you want to avoid the road, just follow the crest uphill to the right from the saddle and you will reach the peak. Tremendous views in every direction spread out below the grassy summit.

Come visit the Withington Wilderness. Give the heavily-used Sandia, Jemez, and Sangre de Cristo Mountains a rest. If at least a few people do not use these trails, the Forest Service will probably abandon them altogether. Do not worry about getting lost on the first half of the hike. Even if you lose the trail, provided that you never leave the canyon bottom, all you have to do to find your car is follow the canyon back downstream to the road. An excellent two- or three-day backpacking loop would take Trail 38 to FR 138 on the crest, traveling south (left) on FR 138 about 2 miles to Trail 37 on the left, descending Trail 37 down Water Canyon to FR 56, and following FR 56 down Big Rosa Canyon to the Trail 38 trailhead.

51 San Mateo Peak

General description:	A strenuous day hike or overnight trip to a high peak in the heart of the Apache Kid Wilderness.
General location:	About 40 miles northwest of Truth or Consequences.
Length:	About 8 miles round trip.
Elevation:	7,360–10,139 feet.
Maps:	Cibola National Forest—Magdalena Ranger District; Vicks Peak 7.5-minute USGS quad.
Best season:	Mid-April through November.
Water availability:	San Mateo Spring—see text.
Special attractions:	Views; solitude; dense forest.

Finding the trailhead: From the north side of Truth or Consequences, take I-25 north a little more than 20 miles to Exit 100. Leave the freeway and get onto the old highway paralleling the interstate on the west side. Turn right, or north, on the old highway and follow it for about 4.8 miles to the FR 225 turnoff to Springtime Campground. Turn left on gravel FR 225 and follow it about 13.4 miles to the Springtime Campground entrance, FR 225A. Turn right onto the campground road and drive to the campground, about 0.5 mile.

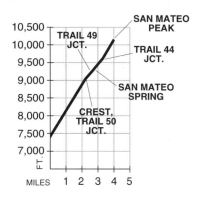

For an alternate and very scenic route to take when you leave, drive south on the continuation of FR 225 to FR 139, Monticello, and ultimately I-25. The Cibola National Forest map shows the route. With care, improved FR 225 is usually quite good and passable with any vehicle. The southern approach, through Monticello, is usually rougher. Call about road status ahead of time.

From Socorro, follow I-25 south to Exit 115. Get onto the old highway paralleling the freeway and follow it south to FR 225, the Springtime Campground turnoff described above.

The hike: The 45-mile long San Mateo Mountains stretch from the high Plains of San Agustin to the Rio Grande Valley above Elephant Butte Lake. The mountains surrounding Mount Taylor (see the Mount Taylor hike) have the same name, but are a completely different range. The mountains form a long chain of steep, forested peaks. Vicks Peak, just south of San Mateo Peak, was named for the Apache chief Victorio, who used these mountains as hunting grounds and as a refuge. A few old mines, scattered around Vicks Peak and Rosedale Canyon, never produced much.

San Mateo Peak

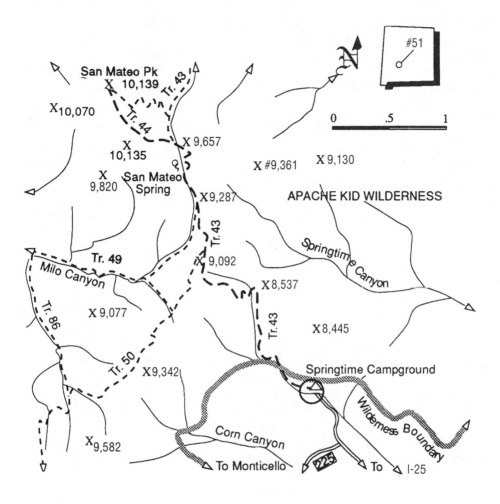

The heart of the south end of the range lies in the Apache Kid Wilderness, while part of the northern end lies in the Withington Wilderness (see the Mount Withington hike). The Apache Kid Wilderness contains 44,650 acres and is named after the Apache Kid, an Indian who was killed and buried near Blue Mountain. A little-used trail system of 68 miles criss-crosses the wilderness.

The trail to San Mateo Peak, described here, is the most popular in the mountains, which does not mean much. The San Mateos are one of the least visited mountain ranges in New Mexico. What little visitation occurs is usually restricted to the roads and campgrounds. Even on summer weekends and during deer season, you will probably see few people on this trail. Other trails are even more likely to be deserted. Come to the San Mateos for solitude.

Well-marked Trail 43 starts at the sign in Springtime Campground. The campground is a small, beautiful, and quiet place with shelters, picnic tables, and pit toilets. The trail starts up the canyon above the campground through ponderosa pine. At about 0.25 mile you pass the marked wilderness boundary. The stream flows part of the year. The trail is well maintained and easy to follow. The trail quickly leaves the canyon bottom and begins a steep 2-mile climb, gaining something like 1,700 feet. Finally, sweating and puffing, you will reach the crest at about 2.25 miles. If you can make it this far, you are home free. The crest is level enough for camping.

The grade levels out and the trail intersects with Trail 50 just over the crest. A chewed-up sign marks the fork. Stay right, toward San Mateo Peak and Lookout. The next 0.5 mile to the junction with Trail 49 is easy. Stay right toward San Mateo Peak and begin climbing again at a moderate grade. Just past the junction, you pass the ruins of an old cabin and then you hit San Mateo Spring. The spring has a concrete and stone horse trough fed by a pipe. The spring dries up during dry spells and sometimes in early summer. Do not count on it without checking with the Forest Service in Magdalena first. Two other springs lie along Trail 50 to the south.

The trail switchbacks fairly steeply up from the spring to the well marked junction with Trail 44 at about 3.25 miles. Plenty of level campsites lie around the junction. The right-hand fork to Blue Mountain is the continuation of Trail 43. Turn left on more heavily traveled Cowboy Trail 44 to the peak and lookout. The trail enters a dense stand of aspen and climbs the last 0.75 mile through lush forest at a moderate grade.

The large flat summit contains a lookout tower and Forest Service cabin. Please do not disturb the facilities. The 60-foot tower is missing the lower part of its ladder and is dangerous to climb. The forest opens up on the north side of the summit, giving a good view of Blue Mountain. Camping is possible on the summit and about 0.25 mile back down the trail in a fairly level area of woods.

Since you have to make quite an effort to get up to the top, bring a backpack and plan to stay a few days. Trail 43 can be followed along the crest for miles to the north and Trail 50 can be followed south. A good two- or three-day loop involves following Trail 43 north to Trail 48. Follow Trail 48 down Indian Creek to FR 225 and walk back up FR 225 to Springtime Campground.

A fire lookout crowns San Mateo Peak in the Apache Kid Wilderness.

52 Datil Well

General description:	An easy day hike through pinyon-juniper woodland in a remote mountain area of the state.
General location:	About 1 mile west of Datil.
Length:	About 2.7 miles round trip.
Elevation:	7,440–7,690 feet (no elevation graph).
Maps:	Datil Well Campground brochure; Datil 7.5-minute USGS quad.
Best season:	All year.
Water availability:	Campground at trailhead.
Special attractions:	Views.

Finding the trailhead: Start in Datil, a small village in the southwestern part of the state. From the junction of US 60 and NM 12, go west on US 60 0.8 mile. Turn left onto a well marked gravel road on the left for Datil Well Campground. Follow it 0.4 mile to the campground. The marked trailhead starts by campsite 10. To avoid the campground fee, you may want to drive just past the campground entrance. Watch carefully and you will see where the trail crosses the gravel road.

The trail at Datil Well is an easy woodland walk.

Datil Well

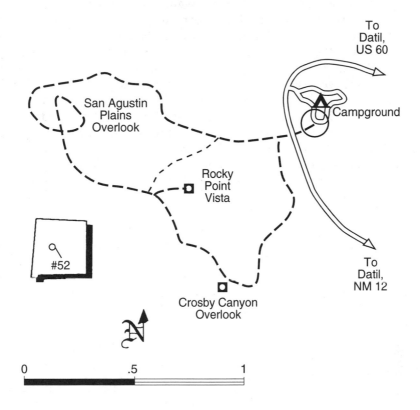

To
Datil,
US 60

San Agustin
Plains
Overlook

Campground

Rocky
Point
Vista

#52

Crosby Canyon
Overlook

To
Datil,
NM 12

N

0   .5   1

The hike: This is an easy hike just outside of the village of Datil in one of the least populated parts of the state. The trail is not spectacular, but is a pleasant hike through pinyon-juniper woodland to several viewpoints in an area with a dearth of developed trails.

The trail starts at the campground, a good spot to spend the night before or after doing the hike. The campground is the site of 1 of 15 water wells spaced about every 10 miles along the Magdalena Livestock Driveway. The 132-mile driveway, often called the Beefsteak Trail, was used to drive live-stock to the former railhead in Magdalena. One fork went to Springerville, Arizona; the other went to Horse Springs, southwest of Datil. Use of the trail began in 1885 and peaked in 1919 with 21,000 cattle and 150,000 sheep. Its use declined with the coming of highways and trucks, but part of the driveway was used as late as 1971, making it the last regularly used cattle trail in the United States.

The hiking trail starts in the campground and makes a 2.7-mile loop count-ing the spurs to the overlooks. As is obvious on the map, a connecting trail makes two shorter loops possible. The trail is easy to follow and well marked.

Soon after the start, the trail crosses the gravel road. It then forks. Go right and follow the large loop counterclockwise. In a little more than 0.25 mile, the trail forks again. Go right unless you want to do a shorter loop.

The trail crosses a dry drainage and then climbs slowly up onto a ridge. The next junction is a very short side loop that climbs up to the highest point on the trail, the San Agustin Plains Overlook. It offers a good view of part of the plains, a vast, relatively level valley surrounded by remote mountains. After the overlook side loop, the trail follows the ridge about 0.3 mile to another junction. Stay right, unless you want to cut the hike short. Just beyond that junction is yet another. A very short spur here leads to the Rocky Point Overlook. The next overlook, Crosby Canyon, lies along the main trail about 0.25 mile past the Rocky Point spur.

After the last overlook, the trail continues along the ridge top for some distance to the southeast. It then turns north and drops off the ridge top. At the next junction at the start of the loop, turn right to return to the campground.

Although this area of the state has few developed trails, it also has very few people, great if you want solitude. Experienced hikers may want to explore off-trail routes in the nearby Datil and Sawtooth Mountains. Interesting sites include the Enchanted Tower rock climbing area in Thompson Canyon, Davenport Lookout, and the rugged peaks of the Sawtooth Mountains.

53 Pueblo Park

General description:	An easy day hike into the little-known Blue Range Wilderness.
General location:	About 95 miles northwest of Silver City.
Length:	About 4 miles round trip.
Elevation:	6,150–5,920 feet (no elevation graph).
Maps:	Gila National Forest; Saliz Pass 7.5-minute USGS quad.
Best season:	All year.
Water availability:	Pueblo Park Spring (seasonal).
Special attractions:	Solitude; bytownite crystals.

Finding the trailhead: From Silver City, drive about 65 miles north on US 180 to Glenwood. From Glenwood, continue north on US 180 for about 26.5 miles to the junction with FR 232. Turn left onto FR 232, marked with a Pueblo Park Campground sign. Follow the good gravel road 6.2 miles to the Pueblo Park Campground.

The hike: Pueblo Park is actually located in the Apache National Forest, but shows up on the Gila National Forest map. The 29,304-acre Blue Range

Pueblo Park

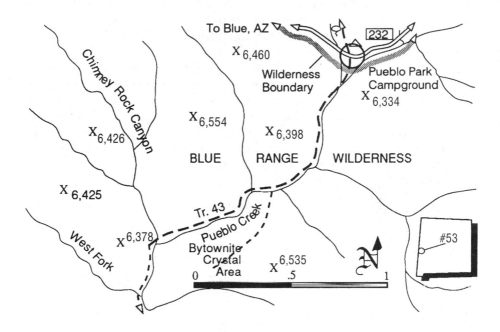

Wilderness was created out of the New Mexico portion of the Blue Range Primitive Area. It adjoins the much larger Blue Range Primitive Area in Arizona. The rugged, mountainous area is probably one of the least visited areas in either state. Trails do not even penetrate large sections of the wilderness and primitive areas. The eastern end of the famous Mogollon Rim of Arizona begins here.

W.S. Mountain Trail 43 starts right across the road from the campground. The campground is set in a peaceful park-like area, wooded with large ponderosa pine. Except in very dry years, a spring supplies a water source at the campground.

The hike is an easy walk down a scenic canyon, usually with some running water. The well-marked trailhead goes through a fence and immediately enters the wilderness. It quickly drops down off the bench into a rocky canyon bottom.

The trail is not obvious because floods periodically wash it out where it crosses the bottom. However, just follow the canyon bottom downstream and you will pick it up again. Rock cairns and blazes occasionally help you find the way. Be sure to note where the trail first drops into the creek bottom so that you will not have trouble finding it on the way back.

The canyon quickly narrows and the walls steepen as the trail goes downstream. The trail crosses back and forth from side to side and travels on the narrow benches whenever possible. Do not worry if you lose the trail; it stays with the canyon for several miles. Generally, it is easier walking to follow the trail on the benches when possible. Ponderosa pines, alligator junipers, and cherry trees canopy much of the route. Below about the 1-mile point, the stream usually runs with at least a small trickle.

Between about 1 and 1.5 miles, a faint trail climbs steeply several hundred feet up the left canyon wall onto a mesa top. Part of the mesa top is known for the occurrence of semi-precious bytownite crystals. The clear, hard, pale yellow crystals are of good enough quality to cut and facet for jewelry. The small crystals lie loose on the ground, visible to the keen eye. If you can't find the side trail, don't worry. I have even found a few crystals simply by scrambling around on the left wall of the canyon after hiking a little more than a mile downstream from the trailhead.

At almost 2 miles, the canyon widens again where Chimney Rock Canyon flows in from the west. The large wooded bench at the confluence makes an excellent camp area at the end of the hike.

The easy trail continues almost 3 miles further down Pueblo Creek, before turning west up a major tributary, Bear Canyon. It continues for miles further, ultimately traveling far into Arizona. As with all warm weather hikes below 9,000 feet or so in elevation, keep an eye open for rattlesnakes, especially at dusk. An upset blacktail rattler that we did not see in the dimness of twilight startled us as we neared the campground at the end of this hike. We gave him a wide berth and let him continue his evening hunt.

54 Whitewater Creek

General description:	A moderate day hike into the Gila Wilderness via a spectacular rocky gorge.
General location:	About 70 miles northwest of Silver City.
Length:	About 6 miles round trip.
Elevation:	5,150–6,200 feet.
Maps:	Gila Wilderness; Gila National Forest; Holt Mountain and Mogollon 7.5-minute USGS quads.
Best season:	March through November.
Water availability:	Whitewater Creek.
Special attractions:	The "Catwalk;" fall maples; permanent stream.

Finding the trailhead: From Silver City, drive northwest about 65 miles on US 180 to Glenwood. On the north side of the little village, turn right (east) on the marked turnoff (NM 174) to the Catwalk. Drive about 5 miles to the paved road's end at the Whitewater Picnic Ground.

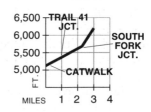

Whitewater Creek

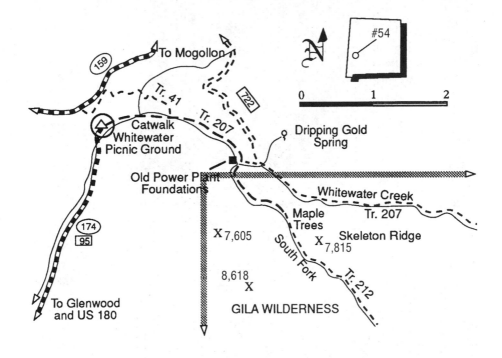

The hike: The picnic area is located at the old townsite of Graham. The town was established in the late 1800s to mill ore taken from mines high in the mountains. Floods have destroyed all but the mill foundations on the hillside above.

From the picnic ground, well-developed Trail 207 quickly enters a narrow, rocky gorge. Parts of the trail follow steel catwalks suspended from the walls, with the rushing stream filling the canyon bottom below. Numerous bridges, large and small, criss-cross the creek. Here and there, the rusted remains of large pipes, iron bolts, and concrete foundations mark the old waterline used to feed the town and mill at Graham. The pipeline, built in 1893 and enlarged in 1897, was suspended high above the canyon bottom to avoid washouts, similar to the trail today. The narrow walkway on top of the pipe formed the first "catwalk" for repairmen.

The highly developed Catwalk Trail ends under a large overhang above a waterfall. Trail 207 turns off to the left at the lower end of the suspension bridge right before the end of the developed trail. Look for the small "207" sign bolted to the rock at the bridge. The trail climbs about 0.25 mile steeply upstream on the north side of the canyon to the junction with Trail 41, the Gold Dust Trail. Trail 41 forks sharply uphill to the left and goes to NM 159.

Steel catwalks suspend the trail above Whitewater Creek.

It is used largely for Whitewater Creek access by horses; they can't use the Catwalk Trail.

The trail stays on the north side of the canyon all the way to the junction with the South Fork. Originally the trail followed the creek bottom, requiring several stream crossings and was subject to washouts. Unfortunately, the newer trail was poorly designed when it was relocated on the north wall to avoid flood damage. Rather than following a continuous mild grade, the trail climbs steeply up the hillside and then drops down to the creek multiple times in the next mile. Although the overall elevation gain for the hike is not excessive, the continuous ups and downs add greatly to the effort required.

Although the absolute elevation of the hike is relatively low, the deep canyon cuts into the heart of the massive Mogollon Range, where peaks reach almost 11,000 feet. Because of their height and size, the mountains receive generous precipitation and the creek is well wooded with ponderosa pine, Douglas-fir, sycamore, and other trees. At about 2.25 miles, the South Fork of the creek joins the main canyon from the right. Turn right at the sign, and take South Fork Trail 212 across the creek and into the South Fork. At the junction are the foundations of the old power plant used to generate electricity for the mines at the ghost town of Mogollon. The wooded, level area at the junction provides several good campsites.

From the junction, the trail climbs steadily along the creek in the bottom of a narrower canyon. The tiring up and down of Trail 207 is left behind. At about 0.5 mile from the junction, the trail passes a large bench ideal for camping. Just beyond the bench, the trail enters a very narrow inner gorge where the trail and creek both try to occupy the same space. Just the other side of the short, mossy-walled gorge, the trail reaches the first good stands of bigtooth maples. The trail passes through the maples for some distance, before continuing miles further into the high wilderness country. Try to do the hike in mid-to late October when the maples turn glorious shades of gold and scarlet.

55 Mogollon Baldy

General description:	A moderate two- to three-day backpack to a remote mountaintop fire lookout in the heart of the Gila Wilderness.
General location:	About 85 miles northwest of Silver City.
Length:	About 24 miles round trip
Elevation:	9,132–10,770 feet.
Maps:	Gila Wilderness; Gila National Forest; Grouse Mountain and Mogollon Baldy Peak 7.5-minute USGS quads.
Best season:	Mid-May through October.
Water availability:	Bead; Hummingbird; Apache; Hobo; Little Hobo; and Blacktail Springs.
Special attractions:	Lush high mountain forest; spectacular views; isolation.

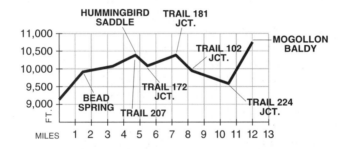

Finding the trailhead: From Silver City, drive about 65 miles northwest on US 180 to Glenwood. From Glenwood, drive about 3.7 miles north on US 180 to the junction with paved NM 159. Turn right and follow the steep, winding mountain road to the old mining ghost town of Mogollon. A few escapees from civilization are bringing new life to the picturesque village. The pavement ends in Mogollon, but a good, all-weather, gravel surface continues to and past the trailhead. After the first snows, the road is closed beyond Mogollon until late spring. From Mogollon, the road continues to climb up into forest thickly wooded with Douglas-fir, ponderosa pine, and aspen. Stop at the marked Sandy Point Trailhead, approximately 18.2 miles from the turnoff at US 180.

The hike: This hike follows the crest of the Mogollon Range, the highest range in not only the Gila Wilderness, but all of southern New Mexico except Sierra Blanca many miles east. Most of the trail lies above 10,000 feet, so prepare to do a little heavy breathing. The Sandy Point Trailhead is probably the most commonly used access point to the high country, but is rarely crowded.

Mogollon Baldy

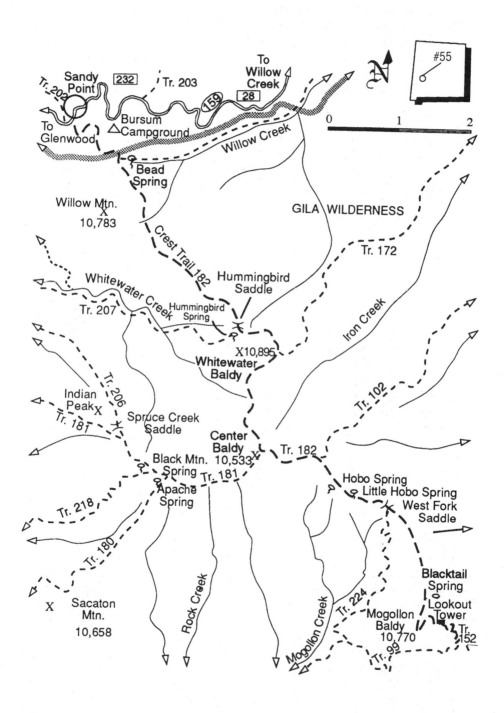

The Gila Wilderness contains 558,065 acres, making it the largest in New Mexico. The wilderness lies in the heart of a rugged mountainous area that covers several million acres of southwestern New Mexico and stretches far into Arizona. The Gila forms the oldest wilderness area in the United States, having been set aside in 1924. Congress made the designation permanent in 1964 for the Gila Wilderness and many other areas. The headwaters of much of the Gila River start high in the Mogollon Range. The large mountain area supports healthy populations of deer, elk, bear, mountain lion, and other wildlife.

Be sure to take warm clothes and rain gear, especially in late summer when the rainy season is in full swing. Since the trail follows the crest of the range, it does not go near any creeks. Fortunately, however, the trail does pass several springs, making it unnecessary to carry large quantities of water. Before driving up the mountain from Glenwood, check at the Forest Service ranger station there about the status of the various springs along the route. I last did the hike at the end of an extended drought, and Bead, Hummingbird, and Apache springs were still all flowing well. Hobo and Little Hobo were very low, however, with only a small quantity of somewhat stagnant water. I did not visit Blacktail Spring. Be sure to treat your water before using.

The well-marked, well-maintained Trail 182 is easy to follow. It immediately begins climbing at a moderate grade from Sandy Point, passing some of the largest Douglas-firs I have seen in the Southwest. At about 1.5 miles the trail's grade lessens and it crosses into the wilderness.

Shortly afterwards, the marked side trail to Bead Spring goes downhill to the left. The reliable, strongly flowing spring is only about 500 feet down the trail. Be careful not to trample the lush ferns, mosses, and other delicate vegetation at the spring. Huge aspens are mixed in with the spruce at the spring. After Bead Spring, most of the rest of the hike consists of relatively small ups and downs along the crest.

The trail maintains a very easy grade for the next 1.5 miles. Then a short, moderate climb brings the trail to a high point before dropping down slightly to Hummingbird Saddle. At about 4 miles out, the forest opens up for a short distance, giving a great view of the Whitewater Creek drainage below and far out into Arizona. Hummingbird Saddle, at about 4.75 miles, is a popular camping area because of many possible level sites and nearby Hummingbird Spring. It also makes a good destination for day hikers. The spring is a few hundred yards down below the saddle to the right (west). A marked trail leads to it. The trail, 207, continues on past the spring to Redstone Park and all the way down Whitewater Creek (see the Whitewater Creek hike). Whitewater Baldy, the highest point in the Mogollon Range, rises right above the south side of the saddle. A faint, unofficial trail follows the crest from the saddle up to the summit. A bare area on its south side offers great views.

At all the trail junctions, just follow the signs to Mogollon Baldy. Usually the distances shown are not exactly right, but they are close enough. The Forest Service has not generally marked the trail numbers on the signs, but

166

Trail 182 is the route all the way to Mogollon Baldy.

From Hummingbird Saddle, Trail 182 drops slightly for the next mile or so. At about 5.5 miles (about 0.75 miles from the saddle), marked Trail 172 forks off to the left, to Iron Creek Lake (see the Iron Creek hike). Stay right, towards Baldy. In another 0.75 mile or so, the trail reaches another saddle on the crest. The level area makes an ideal campsite, although there is no close water source. The trail then climbs back up some, reaching the junction with Trail 181 at about 7.25 miles. Plentiful campsites exist in the crest area around the junction. The marked right-hand trail goes to Spruce Creek Saddle and many other destinations. Apache Spring and possible campsites lie about 1.5 miles out on Trail 181. To continue on to Baldy, follow the sign onto the left-hand fork.

The trail begins to descend a short distance beyond the Trail 181 junction. At a little more than 8 miles, marked Trail 102 climbs steeply off to the left to Turkeyfeather Pass. Bear right to Baldy. Hobo Spring is next to the trail on the right about 0.5 mile beyond the Turkeyfeather Pass junction. A small area has been leveled out for camping near the spring. Check with the Forest Service about the spring's status before you start your hike. Little Hobo Spring is on the left side of the trail another 0.5 mile down the way.

At about 10 miles, the trail reaches West Fork Saddle. At about 9,600 feet, it is the lowest point on the hike other than the start of the trail at Sandy Point. The saddle has several excellent, level campsites. Trail 224 to Mogollon Creek forks down to the right from the saddle. The last 2 miles (1.5 miles according to the sign) to Baldy make up the longest sustained climb of the hike, gaining over 1,100 feet. Blacktail Spring is to the left of the trail a little below the summit.

The summit commands tremendous views of not only the Gila Wilderness, but of mountains over much of southern New Mexico and Arizona. So much of the hike passes through dense woods that the views from the treeless summit are breathtaking in contrast. Such a large area surrounding the peak is undeveloped that virtually no sign of man is visible as far as the eye can see. The Forest Service, being aware of the peak's prominent summit, long ago built a fire lookout and ranger cabin on the summit. The lookout is manned from May through August. The facilities are for Forest Service use only, but the rangers usually enjoy visiting with hikers.

Camping is allowed on the summit, but not in the immediate vicinity of the tower and cabin. Be sure to pick up water on the way up; the rangers' supply on the summit is extremely limited. Please do not disturb the Forest Service facilities if the rangers are not in residence. Believe it or not, even here vandals have struck.

Lightning is a threat along most of the crest trail, but is particularly dangerous on the bare summit of Mogollon Baldy. Thunderstorms can build within minutes in the mountains, especially in late summer afternoons. If you get wet, hypothermia is also a danger. While early summer is usually the driest time of year for hiking in the Mogollons, the mountains look their lush green best in August. Even here in southern New Mexico, patches of snow can cover the trail as late as early June in good snow years. I day-hiked up Whitewater Baldy on Memorial Day weekend one year and had to push through drifts for much of the last half of the hike. Check with the Forest Service for current conditions.

56 Iron Creek

General description:	An easy day hike to one of many permanent streams in the Gila Wilderness.
General location:	About 95 miles northwest of Silver City.
Length:	About 5 miles round trip.
Elevation:	7,880–8,330 feet.
Maps:	Gila Wilderness; Gila National Forest; Negrito Mountain 7.5-minute USGS quad.
Best season:	May through November.
Water availability:	Iron Creek.
Special attractions:	Trout stream; lush forest.

Finding the trailhead: Follow the same directions as those for the Mogollon Baldy hike. However, take NM 159 for 27.2 miles from US 180, instead of the 18.2 miles described in the Mogollon Baldy hike.

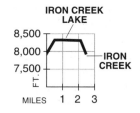

This road is usually closed from the first snow to late spring. The trailhead is usually accessible for a somewhat longer season by using FR 141 from Reserve. At 27.2 miles turn right onto FR 507, the Willow Creek Campground turnoff.

Go 0.2 mile down FR 507 to a small dirt road on the left marked with a Forest Trail 151 sign (just past the campground entrance). Turn onto it and cross Willow Creek (if beaver dams have not flooded the crossing—a common occurrence here). Go left in about 0.1 mile at an unmarked fork. The road ends at the trailhead in about 100 yards.

The hike: Trail 151 is one of the more heavily used trailheads in the enormous Gila Wilderness. However, as with most of the Gila area, "heavily used" does not usually signify great numbers of people. The area is just too remote to receive large numbers of visitors. The nearest cities of any size, Albuquerque and El Paso, are more than 200 miles away.

Even Silver City, with fewer than 20,000 people, is almost 100 miles away. Catron County, in which much of the wilderness is located, is the largest county in New Mexico with about 8,000 square miles, but has fewer than 3,000 people. This hike is an introduction to the heavily forested, middle-elevation area of the wilderness. Many of the trails in the Willow Creek

Iron Creek

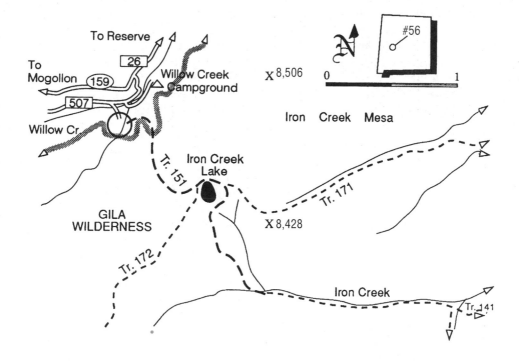

area are characteristically long, but easy, with only moderate elevation changes.

From the marked trailhead, the well maintained route goes about 150 yards up a small tributary of Willow Creek, before turning left and crossing the little stream. A short fork to the right goes only to a corral and storage shed. Just across the creek, signs mark the trail and wilderness boundary. The trail climbs up the hillside, overlooking the Willow Creek valley. It then turns southerly up a small drainage and away from Willow Creek.

The trail passes through lush stands of Douglas-fir and other conifers as it climbs up the small drainage to the top of a relatively flat mesa. The trail passes through heavy ponderosa pine until it meets the junction with Trail 172 on the right at Iron Creek Lake. Trail 172 climbs up to Whitewater Baldy and Hummingbird Saddle (see the Mogollon Baldy hike). Stay left on Trail 151 as it goes around the lake, a shallow, marshy pond with water levels dependent on precipitation. Just past the lake, Trail 171 splits off to the left, going to the Middle Fork of the Gila River and Snow Lake. Trail 171, combined with Trail 157, makes a long, but not too difficult loop back to Willow Creek. However, for this hike, stay right on Trail 151 to Iron Creek.

From the junction, the trail stays relatively level for some distance before dropping down into a small drainage that leads into Iron Creek. At about 2.5 miles from the start, the trail reaches Iron Creek and turns downstream. The permanent stream tumbles down from the high crest of the Mogollon Range through lush forest. As with most of the permanent streams of the Gila Wilderness, trout thrive in the cold mountain waters.

The hike can easily be extended by following Trail 151 further downstream. A large overnight loop can be created by following 151 to Trail 141. Go left on 141, then left again on 175 at its intersection. Finally return to Willow Creek by going left on either Trail 171 or 157 from Trail 175.

57 Gila Cliff Dwellings

General description:	A very easy day hike up to the ancient ruins of Gila Cliff Dwellings National Monument.
General location:	About 45 miles north of Silver City.
Length:	About 1 mile round trip.
Elevation:	5,700–5,880 feet (no elevation graph).
Maps:	Gila Cliff Dwellings brochure; Little Turkey Park 7.5-minute USGS quad.
Best season:	All year.
Water availability:	Trailhead.
Special attractions:	Ancient Indian dwellings.

Finding the trailhead: Take NM 15 from Silver City about 45 miles north to the end of the road at Gila Cliff Dwellings National Monument.

The hike: The easy hike climbs up to a series of seven natural caves, five of which contain the ruins of cliff dwellings. The buildings were constructed sometime after 1000 AD, along with other pueblos built in the open on terraces above the Gila River's West Fork. The Pueblo people who lived here farmed the flood plain and mesa tops, raising corn, beans, and squash. Hunting and gathering supplemented their diet. Sometime in the early 1300s, they abandoned their homes and left. Archaeologists have not been able to determine why with any certainty.

The caves protected the ruins from the elements, leaving them much better preserved than those built in the open. About 40 rooms were built in the caves using stone and timber. All of the wood remaining in the dwellings are original.

From the parking lot at the end of NM 15, the trail crosses a bridge over the West Fork and enters a small, narrow canyon. The trail criss-crosses the wooded canyon's usually permanent small stream, before climbing 180 feet up to the dwellings. At the ruins, the trail goes in and out of the caves,

Caves have protected the dwellings at Gila Cliff Dwellings from erosion.

Gila Cliff Dwellings

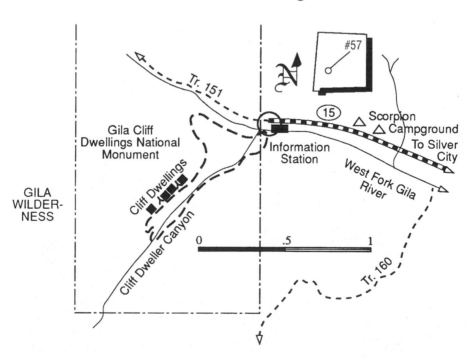

through the old buildings. The loop trail then descends back to the trailhead by a different route.

The ruins trail is open all year except Christmas and New Year's Day. The hours vary seasonally, so call ahead for current times. NM 15 from Silver City is narrow, steep, and winding; allow two hours to drive it.

58 Gila West Fork

General description:	An easy day hike up the West Fork of the Gila River into the Gila Wilderness.
General location:	About 45 miles north of Silver City.
Length:	About 6 miles round trip.
Elevation:	5,700–5,790 feet (no elevation graph).
Maps:	Gila Wilderness; Gila National Forest; Little Turkey Park 7.5-minute USGS quad.
Best season:	All year.
Water availability:	Gila River.
Special attractions:	Rugged gorge; beaver dams; cliff dwelling.

Finding the trailhead: Take NM 15 from Silver City about 45 miles north to the end of the road at Gila Cliff Dwellings National Monument.

The hike: The Gila River, especially the west and middle forks, drains large areas of the immense Gila Wilderness. With over 0.5 million acres, the wilderness is by far the largest in New Mexico. The long, winding drive to the Gila Cliff Dwellings gives some idea of the size of the unpopulated mountainous area. Even though the road is paved, allow two hours to traverse the steep, narrow highway.

The trail starts at the Gila Cliff Dwellings parking lot at the end of the road. The trailhead is one of the most popular entry points into the Gila Wilderness but is still rarely crowded. The size of the wilderness and the multitude of possible trails quickly dilutes the density of hikers. This hike is an easy day hike up the river, serving as an introduction to the lower part of the wilderness. This trail and others can be easily followed 30 miles or more without hitting another road.

The trail starts up the north side of the broad river bottom. Cottonwoods, willows, and ash trees cover the floodplain. Even though the elevation is relatively low, the surrounding mountains attract more rain than is typical for this elevation in New Mexico. Thus, ponderosa pines, mixed with pinyon and juniper, grow on the hillsides. However, it is still dry country, as you will see. Some of the forest traversed by this hike burned in the mid-1990s.

The river is a permanent, broad stream that can be difficult to ford with dry feet even at its lowest levels. During spring snow melt and late summer rains, the river is often high enough to make dry crossings, and at times any

Gila West Fork

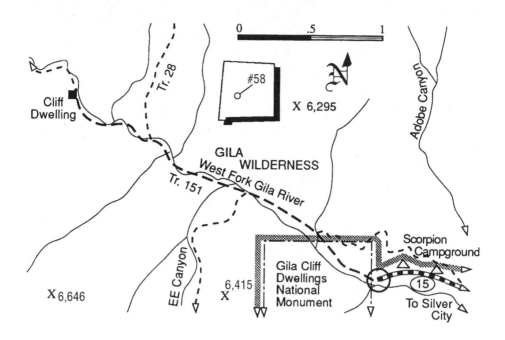

crossings, impossible. Because of the multiple river crossings, I recommend that you carry an extra pair of old tennis shoes, especially on overnight trips. Be aware of the weather, even miles away. The Gila occasionally has severe floods.

After passing some beaver dams, the trail crosses into the wilderness at about 0.5 mile. About 0.5 mile further, the trail makes its first crossing to the south bank and climbs onto a low bench. The level, ponderosa pine-covered bench is ideal for camping. On the bench a marked trail forks off to the left to Little Creek. Stay right, along the river to Hells Hole. The river valley begins to narrow into a rocky canyon.

About 0.75 mile from the trail junction, the trail drops off the bench and crosses back to the north side of the river. Just across the river, the trail forks again. The marked trail to the Meadows goes right and climbs out of the canyon. Bear left and stay with the river trail toward Hells Hole.

After the trail junction, the river trail gets rocky, somewhat overgrown, and hard to follow for a couple of hundred yards. Just follow the river and you will find it again. The canyon begins to really narrow and deepen, with sheer rocky walls. The trail starts to criss-cross the river frequently, with one stretch climbing well up the south bank. At a sharp bend in the river, a little less than 3 miles from the trailhead, the canyon becomes a spectacular rocky chasm. High on the walls are arches and caves. On the left wall an ancient cliff dwelling rests in a small cave. It is best not to try to climb up to it. The route is a dangerous scramble above a cliff, and erosion created by visitation is causing the ruin's walls to collapse. Enjoy the rocky gorge just beyond the cliff dwelling before returning the same way.

59 Signal Peak

General description:	A moderate day hike to the summit of one the highest peaks in the Pinos Altos Range.
General location:	About 15 miles north of Silver City.
Length:	About 5 miles round trip.
Elevation:	7,260–9,001 feet.
Maps:	Gila National Forest; Twin Sisters 7.5-minute USGS quad.
Best season:	April through November.
Water availability:	None.
Special attractions:	Tremendous views of Gila Wilderness and as far as the Chiricahua and Pinaleno Mountains of Arizona; thick conifer forest.

Finding the trailhead: Take NM 15 north from Silver City through the village of Pinos Altos. About 4 miles past Pinos Altos, the road passes the Ben Lilly Memorial and then enters Cherry Creek Canyon. The highway soon passes Cherry Creek and then McMillan Forest campgrounds. The marked trail (742) takes off from the right side of the road about 1.5 miles past McMillan Campground. The Signal Peak road (154) turns off to the right only a couple of hundred yards further.

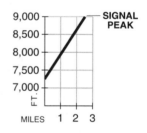

The hike: The Pinos Altos Range is the southernmost mountain range of the Gila Wilderness, the largest wilderness in New Mexico. Although this hike does not enter the wilderness area, great views of the wilderness greet hikers from the trail and the summit.

From its start on NM 15, the trail crosses a meadow before starting its climb up into the forest covering the flanks of Signal Peak. Initially the trail passes through thick stands of Douglas-fir on the moister north slopes of the mountain. As it climbs, it curves around onto the sunnier, drier, south-facing slopes of the peak and ponderosa pine becomes more common. While most of the hike travels through dense forest, regular breaks in the trees give increasingly dramatic views, especially to the south and southwest.

A fresh winter snow blankets Signal Peak.

Signal Peak

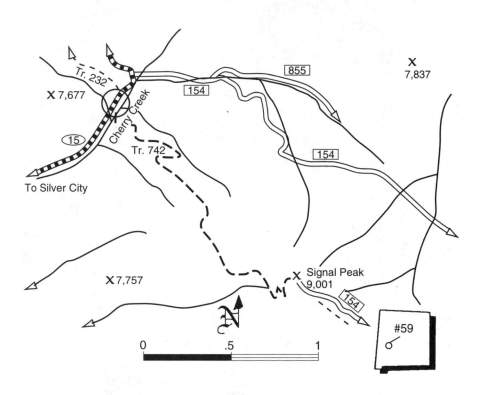

From the summit, with its fire lookout tower, you can see 360 degrees. To the east, north, and west lie the endless mountain ranges of the 3.3 million-acre Gila National Forest.

To the south and southwest, desert basin and range country stretches far into Arizona and Mexico. Below lies sleepy Pinos Altos, site of a gold mining boom begun in 1859. Little mining continues today in Pinos Altos, but other large mines near Silver City and Santa Rita still produce enormous amounts of copper and other metals every year.

The Gila National Forest covers a large unpopulated area of high country consisting of many interconnected mountain ranges. The Continental Divide meanders though the national forest for 170 miles and crosses the Pinos Altos Range only about 1 mile southeast of the summit of Signal Peak. The Continental Divide Trail is being developed in New Mexico as part of a route planned from Canada to Mexico. Much of it will traverse the Gila National Forest.

You can return to the trailhead via the lookout tower road, but at 7 miles, it is considerably longer than the trail.

60 Tadpole Ridge

General description:	A moderate day hike (with shuttle) or strenuous overnight trip (without) along the crest of the Pinos Altos Range.
General location:	About 15 miles north of Silver City (to east trailhead).
Length:	About 16.5 miles round trip (8.25 miles with shuttle).
Elevation:	7,150–8,610 feet.
Maps:	Gila National Forest; Twin Sisters and Reading Mountain 7.5-minute USGS quads.
Best season:	May through November.
Water availability:	Tadpole Lake—see text.
Special attractions:	Great views; forest.

[Elevation profile chart showing the route from SHEEP CORRAL TRAILHEAD (about 7,150 ft) rising past TRAIL 234 JCT. and TADPOLE LAKE (about 8,610 ft), then descending past OLD ROAD to NM 15 TRAILHEAD. Y-axis labeled FT. from 7,000 to 9,000; X-axis labeled MILES 1 through 9.]

Finding the trailhead: Take paved NM 15 north from Silver City about 6.6 miles to the mountain village of Pinos Altos. Continue along NM 15 almost an additional 8 miles to the marked eastern trailhead for Tadpole Ridge Trail 232 on the left. It lies just across the road from the Signal Peak trailhead and a couple of hundred yards before the obvious junction with the Signal Peak Road, FR 154. To get to the western trailhead, continue along NM 15 another 3.1 miles to the Sheep Corral Canyon Road, FR 282, on the left. Follow the narrow, but good gravel road for 6.8 miles to the marked trailhead in the bottom of a canyon by a corral and water tank. There are several road junctions along FR 282; stay on the better, main road (which is FR 282) to get to the trailhead.

The hike: Tadpole Ridge is a long, narrow ridge that runs roughly northwest to southeast and forms the crest of part of the Pinos Altos Range. The mountains are one of many ranges that lie within the massive Gila National Forest. Part of the Pinos Altos Range is in the Gila Wilderness, but not the section traversed by this trail.

This hike is an easy escape into the cool pines from nearby Silver City. Although parts of Tadpole Ridge burned during dry years in the mid-1990s, most of the hike is still shaded by pines and firs. Because most of the maintained trail follows the crest of the ridge, views are excellent. Water is usu-

Tadpole Lake is only a small pond on Tadpole Ridge.

ally available at Tadpole Lake; however, check with the Forest Service about its status ahead of time. It is really just a large stock tank with murky water, so unless you are backpacking, plan to carry enough.

The hike is most easily done as a one-way hike with a shuttle. Drop one vehicle at the eastern trailhead and start your hike at the western trailhead. This description describes the hike by starting on the west side.

Marked Trail 232 starts at the road by a corral and water tank. From the road, start up the hill past the rusty water tank. Look carefully for a big cairn and follow the trail past it up a narrow canyon bottom. Ponderosa pines and Douglas-firs shade the trail here and along much of the route. The first part of the trail was once an old road.

You will soon pass burned forest areas, but here and along much of the route the fire generally cleared underbrush and did only minor harm to the larger trees. After a little less than 1 mile, the trail steepens abruptly and switchbacks out of the canyon. Views of the Mogollon Range to the northwest open up. The path reaches a saddle and marked trail junction at about 1.25 miles. The faint, lightly traveled Sycamore Canyon Trail 234 turns off to the right and drops down off the other side of the saddle.

The trail sign at the junction indicates a distance of 7 miles to the eastern trailhead on NM 15, giving a total hike length of 8.25 miles as written above. However, another source shows a total distance of 9.5 miles. Take your pick; I used the shorter distance here.

Tadpole Ridge

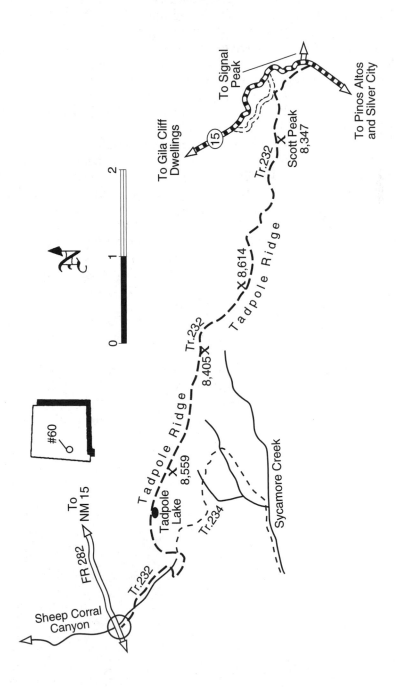

To Gila Cliff Dwellings

To Signal Peak

To Pinos Altos and Silver City

15

Scott Peak
X 8,347

Tr.232

X 8,614

Tadpole Ridge

Tr.232

8,405 X

Tadpole Ridge

#60

To NM 15

FR 282

Tr.232

Sheep Corral Canyon

Tadpole Lake

X 8,559

Tr.234

Sycamore Creek

0 1 2

From the saddle, continue hiking up Tadpole Ridge on Trail 232. The trail climbs through a short, but heavily burned section, and then levels off some on the ridge top in 0.5 mile or so. It soon passes Tadpole Lake in the middle of a level area that would be good for camping. After Tadpole Lake, the trail follows the ridge top for most of the rest of the hike. Fortunately, at times it contours along the north slope of the ridge, rather than climb over every small summit along the crest. Even so, it does cross numerous saddles. Although no single saddle requires a lot of elevation loss and gain, the many saddles add quite a bit of climbing in addition to the initial climb up onto the ridge top. Generally, the western half of the trail has more ups and downs and is rockier that the eastern half.

Views stretch in every direction from many points along the trail. To the northwest lie the Mogollon and Diablo ranges in the heart of the Gila Wilderness. To the east lies the Black Range, high north-south trending mountains. On clear days, the Chiricahua and Pinaleno mountains of Arizona can be seen far to the southwest. Notice that the south side of Tadpole Ridge is much less lush than the north side because of greater sun exposure. On early or late season hikes, you may have to walk through patches of snow where the trail crosses shady north slopes.

After roughly the midpoint of the hike, the trail becomes smoother and follows a long stretch of mostly level ground through thick, relatively unburned ponderosa pine forest. From here on, the trail is relatively level or downhill trending. It really begins to descend when it reaches a heavily burned area. Here the trees are quite dead and hazardous to be under in strong winds.

Signal Peak is visible across Cherry Creek Canyon to the southeast. Soon after leaving the heavily burned area, the trail drops down the north side and off of the ridgetop for good. After a couple of switchbacks, the trail becomes a rough, unofficial woodcutter's road. Turn right (east) and follow the road a short distance downhill until it turns back into a trail. Continue downhill along the trail. Soon paved NM 15 is visible below to the left. Stay on the trail another 0.25 mile or so to the trailhead—it is shorter than following the highway.

61 Fort Bayard Champion Tree

General description:	An easy day hike to an enormous alligator juniper, a New Mexico record-sized tree.
General location:	About 12 miles northeast of Silver City.
Length:	About 5.5 miles round trip.
Elevation:	6,400–6,850 feet.
Maps:	Gila National Forest; Fort Bayard 7.5-minute USGS quad.
Best season:	All year.
Water availability:	None; see text.
Special attractions:	Record-sized alligator juniper; very large cottonwoods.

Finding the trailhead: Start at the well-marked Fort Bayard turnoff on US 180 in the village of Central, about 7 miles east of Silver City. Drive north from US 180 to the fort, now a hospital. Follow signs for the Gila National Forest and FR 536 through the grounds. After passing the fort, the paved road turns to a good gravel surface and becomes FR 536. It enters the

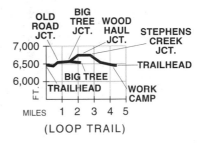

national forest about 1.6 miles from US 180. Ignore FR 775 splitting off to the right; stay on FR 536. The road reaches a forest service work camp at 4.5 miles. Go left at the entrance to the camp and follow the sign for the National Recreation Trails. Stop at the large, marked parking area on the right in less than 0.25 mile.

The hike: Alligator junipers thrive in the lower elevations of the mountains around Silver City. They usually grow in mixed stands with pinyon pines and oaks. They are easily recognized because their deeply checkered bark resembles alligator skin. Older junipers usually have a thick, gnarled trunk, but rarely get more than 30 or 40 feet tall. This hike leads to a mammoth, thick-trunked tree that towers more than 60 feet into the sky. It also makes an easy loop through the foothills of the Pinos Altos Range.

The trail is good any time of year. In summer it can be hot, so plan to start early. In winter snow usually melts off within a few days. Water is sometimes available in Cameron Creek behind the Big Tree, the massive alligator juniper, but do not count on it. It can also sometimes be found by taking a side trip to Comanche Springs about halfway around the loop. However, with this short a hike, it is better just to carry enough.

The national forest map is somewhat confusing for this hike. The topo map or the map with this guidebook is better.

The parking area is the starting point for three trails. A color-coded sign

The Fort Bayard tree may be the largest alligator juniper you will ever see.

Fort Bayard Champion Tree

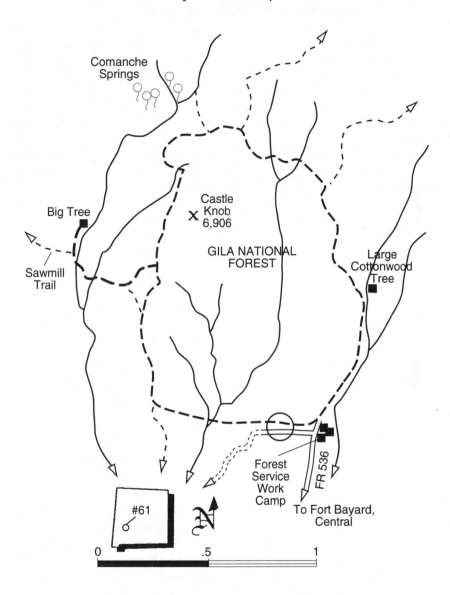

Comanche Springs

Big Tree

Sawmill Trail

Castle Knob 6,906

GILA NATIONAL FOREST

Large Cottonwood Tree

#61

N

Forest Service Work Camp

FR 536

To Fort Bayard, Central

0   .5   1

at the trailhead shows red for the Big Tree Trail, green for the Sawmill Trail, and pale blue for the Wood Haul Trail. All three trails share the same route initially. The trail cuts through the fence and then follows it west, crossing a small canyon in about 0.25 mile. A short distance after climbing out of the canyon, the trail goes through a gate and then hits an old, unused road. As directed by the trail sign, turn right and follow the road uphill to the north.

After about 0.7 miles you will come to a marked junction with another old road. (You may notice a small, unmarked trail turning off to the left a bit before the junction. It is just a small shortcut to the Big Tree Trail.) Turn left onto the Big Tree/Sawmill Trail at the marked junction. You will return here after visiting the tree.

The trail soon drops into a broad, grassy valley bottom dotted here and there with cottonwoods. The trail crosses the valley to the junction with the Sawmill Trail. The Sawmill Trail can be followed using a topo map to Pinos Altos, a good day hike if a shuttle or pick-up is arranged ahead of time. Stay right at the junction and go only another 0.1 mile or so to the Big Tree. The tree is so massive that it is hard to believe that it is a juniper. A short distance behind the tree, along sometimes flowing Cameron Creek, is a very large cottonwood.

From the Big Tree, retrace your route back to the junction of the two old roads. Go left on the Wood Haul Trail and climb north further into the foothills. The trail was once a wagon road used by historic Fort Bayard for gathering firewood and harvesting construction timber. It climbs at a moderate grade through a few ponderosa pines onto a low mesa, and then levels off. The old road forks in front of a gate. The left fork goes downhill to Cameron Creek and Comanche Springs. Take the right fork and go through the gate. In less than 0.25 mile, the marked Wood Haul Trail forks to the left and ascends a ridge. It makes an excellent side trip off of the main loop of this hike. It climbs up and over the main ridge of the Pinos Altos Range and goes to the Mimbres Valley, the Signal Peak Road, and other destinations. Along the way, it passes deep ruts cut into the rock by wagon wheels. However, for this hike stay right and continue hiking along the old road on a relatively level bench.

In about 0.5 mile, a little-used, unmarked trail goes left to the upper part of Stephens Creek. Stay straight on the main route. The trail soon begins to descend, offering good views to the south. The massive open pit copper mine at Santa Rita is partly visible. The descent is the only really rocky part of the entire hike; the rest of the trail is quite smooth. The trail drops into another broad, grassy valley with a huge, solitary cottonwood. Be sure to walk over to the tree; it is impressive.

From the cottonwood, the old road continues south down the valley to the Forest Service work camp. Go through three gates in quick succession and turn right on the road that leads to the starting trailhead visible only a short distance away.

62 Mimbres River

General description: A moderate day hike or overnight trip along the Mimbres River in the Aldo Leopold Wilderness.

General location: About 50 miles northeast of Silver City.

Length: About 13 miles round trip.

Elevation: 6,940–7,675 feet.

Maps: Gila National Forest; Aldo Leopold Wilderness; Hay Mesa 7.5-minute USGS quad.

Best season: April through December.

Water availability: Mimbres River.

Special attractions: Mountain stream; forest; solitude.

Finding the trailhead: From Silver City, drive about 8 miles east on US 180 to Central. Turn left on NM 152 and drive about 14.4 miles east to NM 35. Turn left and follow NM 35 about 15.2 miles north to NM 61, the Wall Lake turnoff. Turn right on gravel NM 61. If

you had any doubt that you were entering a remote area, read the sign: "Road Ahead Restricted—Four-Wheel-Drive and High-Axle Vehicle." This is a state highway? Another sign says: "No Food, Lodging, or Gasoline Next 120 Miles." Don't worry; you are stopping short of the bad stretch of road.

Follow NM 61/FR 150, a good all-weather gravel road, for about 7.3 miles to the marked FR 150A turnoff to Cooney and the Mimbres River on the right. The road crosses North Star Mesa, where the forest has been practically clearcut by firewood cutters. The dry, slow-growing southwestern forests used for firewood cutting are not a renewable resource with the current large human population. Turn right onto FR 150A.

The first 0.7 mile is very good and the next 0.7 mile down to the river is steep, but usually passable by any vehicle.

Cross the river and continue up the canyon to the end of the road at a ranch house at 2.8 miles. Park outside the fence surrounding the ranch house.

The hike: The Black Range is long, stretching almost 100 miles from north to south along a high crest. Several peaks along the crest top out at over 10,000 feet. The mountains make up a major component of the enormous 3.3-million-acre Gila National Forest. Most of the mountains are accessible only by horse or foot, with the heart protected by the 202,000-acre Aldo Leopold Wilderness. The heavily forested range is criss-crossed with several hundred miles of trails, most little, if ever, used. The very long trails are ideal for multi-day backpacking trips.

Mimbres River • Mimbres Lake

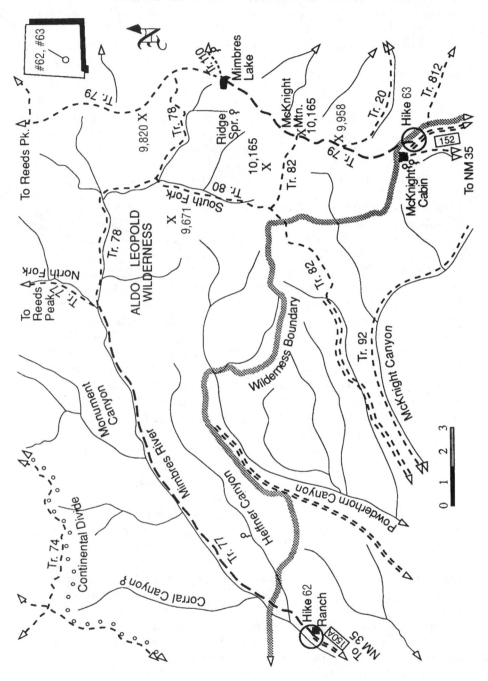

The almost undiscovered mountains make a great place to lose yourself, far from civilization. This trail was chosen because it is usually accessible by any vehicle and it follows along one of the range's permanent streams. It is one of the most popular entry points into the Aldo Leopold Wilderness, but don't worry, it is all relative. You still probably won't see but a handful of people on the trail at most.

From the parking area in front of the ranch house, hike up the rough road to the right along the fence and around the house. Do not cut through the yard; it is private property.

Trail 77 goes upstream, skirting the ranch on the slopes above, before rejoining the river. A sign marks the trailhead in front of the house, but it was in bad shape when I last visited. It says that Mimbres Lake is 11.75 miles and Reeds Peak is 12.25 miles.

The trail is excellent, smooth, and well maintained. The hiking is easy; I gave this hike a moderate rating only because of its length. Most of the first part of the hike is in open ponderosa pine and cottonwood forest. The trail enters the wilderness area a bit less than 1 mile up the canyon. Shortly afterward you hit the first of many stream crossings. The Mimbres River is really more of a stream than a river, except in flood. However, it is still large enough to be a nuisance to cross. In early spring and late summer, plan on getting your feet wet and do not worry about trying to find a dry crossing point. Take an extra pair of shoes if you are backpacking. Many beautiful campsites lie all along the hike. Camp well away from the stream and trail.

At about 3 miles, in a park-like area of ponderosa pine in a broad part of the canyon, you will pass an old corral. Shortly afterward, you will hit lush patches of Douglas-fir and aspen mixed in with the ponderosa pine. At about 5 miles, another even more deteriorated corral is passed. At about 6.5 miles, at the end of this hike, the trail forks. To the left, according to the sign, lies Reeds Peak 5.75 miles away on Trail 77 and to the right lies Mimbres Lake 5.25 miles away on Trail 78. The Mimbres River also forks, with Trail 77 following the North Fork and Trail 78 following the Middle Fork.

For a tremendous 3-day backpacking trip, follow Trail 78 up to Mimbres Lake (see the Mimbres Lake hike), take Crest Trail 79 north to Reeds Peak, and return via Trail 77 to the fork at the end of this hike.

63 Mimbres Lake

See Map on Page 186

General description:	A moderate day hike to a small, marshy, natural pond in the Aldo Leopold Wilderness.
General location:	About 50 miles northeast of Silver City.
Length:	About 7 miles round trip.
Elevation:	9,560–10,165 feet.
Maps:	Gila National Forest; Aldo Leopold Wilderness; Victoria Park 7.5-minute USGS quad.
Best season:	May through November.
Water availability:	See text—Mimbres Lake; Ridge Spring; North Seco Spring; McKnight Cabin Spring.
Special attractions:	Small pond; lush forest; views; solitude.

Finding the trailhead: From Silver City, take US 180 about 8 miles east to Central. Turn left onto NM 152 and continue east about 14.4 miles to NM 35. Turn left and go north on NM 35 about 12.3 miles to the marked McKnight Road (FR 152). Follow FR 152 about 17.4 miles up onto the crest of the Black Range. Park at the Trail 79 sign. The end of the road is only

0.3 mile further at the McKnight Cabin. FR 152 is an excellent gravel road for about the first 9 miles to the junction of FR 537. After this point a high-clearance vehicle is recommended to negotiate the rocks and ruts. I made it to the top in a sedan, but I would recommend it only for short wheelbase sedans with very able drivers. Check with the Forest Service in advance.

The hike: This trail starts on the crest of the Black Range and is one of the most scenic hikes in the mountains. Much of the heart of the range is protected by the enormous Aldo Leopold Wilderness. This trail enters the wilderness area almost immediately. Most of the mountains have never had much impact from the activities of man. Even today, the extensive mountain range is relatively undiscovered, making it unlikely that you will see many people. Most people who actually make it to this corner of New Mexico head for the better-known Gila Wilderness.

The hike can easily be done as a day hike, but begs to be done as a 2- or 3-day trip. If you are doing more than a day hike, be sure to check on the status of the springs and lake before starting. Usually water can be found in at least some of the sources, but you need to know ahead of time. Water is usually available at McKnight Cabin Spring by the corral just below the cabin at the end of the road.

The trail starts out by heading straight into an aspen grove. The sign at the trailhead, saying "Mimbres Lake 4.5″ miles, is wrong; it is about 3.5

Mimbres Lake is a small marshy natural lake in the Aldo Leopold Wilderness.

miles. The trail is somewhat more difficult than the elevations and length indicate because it climbs up over a couple of mountains before reaching the lake, which lies at almost the same elevation as the trailhead. The trail quickly begins climbing. At about 0.3 mile, an unmarked trail forks downhill to the left, going to the cabin. The trail then climbs steeply to the top of a flat-topped, unnamed summit.

The trail then drops down to a saddle in the crest, passing in and out of young aspen stands. The next 1.5 miles follow the narrow crest, giving great views both east and west. The young aspens and frequent views are the result of the 40,000-acre McKnight fire in the 1950s. The maps show Trail 20 as forking off to the right, but I did not see it. Many Black Range trails are disappearing from lack of use.

At about 1.5 miles, the trail begins the steep climb up McKnight Mountain, gaining about 500 feet. The top is reached at about 2 miles. A 50-yard, marked side trail on the right takes you to the rocky summit. Be sure to climb up and enjoy the 360-degree views from the highest point in the Black Range. You will see endless miles of mountains with almost no sign of man.

Just past the summit, marked Trail 82 forks uphill to the left to FR 151. Go downhill to the right toward Mimbres Lake.

The observant will notice that the rest of the trail appears to follow what was a four-wheel drive road many years ago. The trail leaves the old burned area and descends steeply for a short distance off of the peak. The trail now passes through dense fir and spruce forest on a broader, flatter portion of the crest. At about 3 miles, a drainage is passed on the left, down which lies

Ridge Spring. I did not visit the spring, although a faint trail appeared to lead down the drainage toward it.

Just before reaching the lake, hikers will notice an enormous Douglas-fir on the right side of the trail. The tree is probably the largest tree of its kind that I have seen in New Mexico. It appeared to be about 7 feet in diameter at chest height and towered high up in the canopy.

The shallow, marshy Mimbres Lake lies in a beautiful level clearing, surrounded by a dense forest of spruce, fir, and aspen. I day-hiked to the lake and regretted not being able to camp. Be sure to find a site well away from the lake to avoid polluting it or scaring away wildlife. Innumerable campsites exist in the large, level mountaintop area around the lake. The area would make a great base camp for day hikes along the Crest Trail and side trails. Marked Trail 110 forks off of Trail 79 at the lake. Although I did not visit it, the map indicates North Seco Spring as lying about 0.5 mile down Trail 110. Ridge Spring or North Seco Spring would probably make better water sources than the marshy lake. If all are dry, try walking down the Mimbres River on Trail 78 until the stream appears (see map).

A tremendous three-day backpack could be done by following Trail 79 to Reeds Peak and looping back to the lake via Trails 77 and 78. See the map and the description of the Mimbres River hike for ideas.

64 Hillsboro Peak

General description:	A moderate day hike to a lookout tower on one of the high peaks of the Black Range.
General location:	About 40 miles east of Silver City.
Length:	About 10 miles round trip.
Elevation:	8,166–10,011 feet.
Maps:	Gila National Forest; Aldo Leopold Wilderness; Hillsboro Peak 7.5-minute USGS quad.
Best season:	May through November.
Water availability:	Hillsboro

Spring—see text.

Special attractions: Views; forest.

Finding the trailhead: From Silver City, drive about 8 miles east on US 180 to Central. Turn left onto NM 152 and continue east about 32 miles to the trailhead at the top of Emory Pass. From I-25 to the east, drive west on NM 152 past Hillsboro and Kingston to Emory Pass at the top of the Black Range.

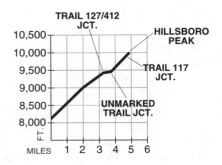

Hillsboro Peak

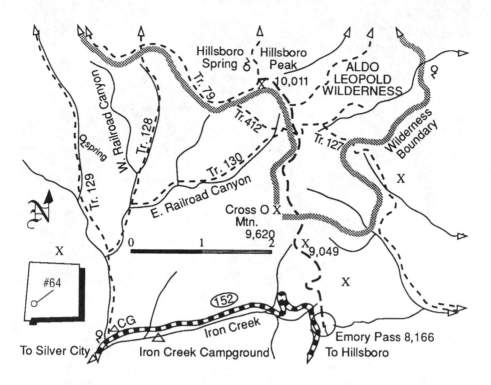

The hike: The Black Range stretches almost 100 miles from north to south, west of the Rio Grande Valley. The Continental Divide follows the crest along the north end of the range. The rugged mountains have fewer people in them now than at the turn of the century. Mining towns in the foothills boomed in the 1880s: Kingston; Hillsboro; and Lake Valley on the southeast side below Hillsboro Peak and Winston and Chloride on the northeast. Lake Valley had one of the most famous mining discoveries in the West. A single underground room, the "Bridal Chamber," contained over $3 million of pure silver. The metal was so easy to mine that it was loaded directly onto railroad cars without any smelting. Today, the mines have closed and the saloons have disappeared, leaving the communities to slumber peacefully in the New Mexico sun. The mountains towering over the towns now contain one of New Mexico's largest wildernesses and are almost forgotten.

When you do this hike, be sure to spend a little time in Kingston and Hillsboro, just down NM 152 from the trailhead. The sleepy little villages, with their old buildings and apple orchards, invite exploration. Paved NM 152 winds over the crest of the southern end of the mountains and provides the easiest access to Black Range trails. The trails leading from the pass are probably the most popular in the mountains, but are still relatively lightly

191

A fire lookout tower caps the flat summit of Hillsboro Peak.

used. You will probably see people only on summer weekends. Several nice campgrounds lie along NM 152, just down the west side of the pass.

Park at Emory Pass Vista, located just off the highway at the pass. Well marked Trail 79 starts about 200 feet up the short, paved side road that leads to the vista parking lot.

The well maintained trail immediately begins climbing to the north from the road. Just up the way, you hit a dirt road. The short road just leads from the highway to some Forest Service facilities. Turn right and follow it uphill a short distance, passing a building, heliport, and radio tower. Go through a gate and follow an old, unused road, now the trail.

About 200 yards past the gate, the old road is blocked off. The trail drops below and parallel to the abandoned road before rejoining it in about 0.25 mile.

The trail passes through Douglas-fir and ponderosa pine, alternating with patches of oak scrub that have grown up after an old fire. Open areas provide great views as you follow the crest north. At about 2 miles, you hit the Aldo Leopold Wilderness boundary, marked by a small sign. The rest of the trail roughly follows the edge of the wilderness. At a little over 3 miles, the trail hits a well marked four-way intersection. A large sign formally announces the wilderness. To the right, little-used Trail 127 descends 6 miles to Kingston, a nice hike with a car shuttle. To the left goes the more popular Hillsboro Peak Bypass Trail 412. Trail 412 makes a good cutoff for early season hikers wanting to continue north along the crest. Trail 79, up on the north side of the peak, retains snow until later in the spring.

Continue straight ahead, uphill, on Trail 79 to the summit. An unmarked trail forks off to the right, descending into Mineral Creek, about 0.5 mile up Trail 79 from the intersection. Like many Black Range trails, it is faint and almost unused. You probably will not even notice it. Another unmarked, but much more obvious intersection is reached just short of the summit. The right fork is Trail 117. Stay left and climb the last 50 yards or so onto the large, flat summit at just less than 5 miles. A tall lookout tower and some Forest Service buildings are clustered at one side of the summit. The tower is occupied in the fire season of late spring and early summer. Please do not disturb any of the facilities. The views from the summit, and especially the tower, are tremendous. On a clear day, the view stretches from Sierra Blanca in southeastern New Mexico to mountains in southeastern Arizona.

Since much of the trail, the summit in particular, is exposed to lightning, start your hike early in the day. Good campsites can be found on several saddles along the way and on the summit (but not too close to the buildings). Hillsboro Spring lies below the summit to the northwest off of Trail 117. I did not visit the spring, so ask the Forest Service ahead of time about its status and exact location. For a long one-day or good two-day hike with a car shuttle, continue north on Trail 79 to Trail 128. Turn left on Trail 128 and follow it down Railroad Canyon to Trail 129 in Gallinas Canyon. Continue down Trail 129 to NM 152. The hike can be expanded by continuing further along Trail 79 to Trail 129 and following it all the way down Gallinas Canyon to NM 152. The Black Range has miles and miles of empty trails to explore. Use this hike as an introduction. If more people do not use some of these trails, the Forest Service will probably abandon them.

65 Sawyers Peak

General description:	A moderate day hike to a southern peak of the Black Range.
General location:	About 40 miles east of Silver City.
Length:	About 8 miles round trip.
Elevation:	8,166–9,668 feet.
Maps:	Gila National Forest; Hillsboro Peak and Maverick Mountain 7.5-minute USGS quads.
Best season:	May through November.
Water availability:	None.
Special attractions:	Views; lush forest; solitude.

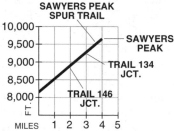

Finding the trailhead: Follow the same directions as those for the Hillsboro Peak hike. Park in the gravel lot right on the highway at the pass, rather than in the Emory Pass Vista parking area.

The hike: Like the Hillsboro Peak hike, the Sawyers Peak trail is easily accessible from NM 152 at Emory Pass. The trail is one of the more popular trails in the Black Range, but "popular" is relative. Some trails near Santa Fe and Albuquerque probably get more visitors on a summer weekend than Sawyers Peak gets all year. This trail follows the crest of the Black Range south from NM 152. The bulk of the mountains lie to the north of the highway, but the smaller southern section is very scenic and little-visited. The southern end does not lie in a formal wilderness, unlike much of the central and northern parts, but still has all the trappings.

Trail 79 climbs southwest from the gravel parking lot. A trail sign marks the start. The well maintained trail climbs at a moderate grade on or near the crest for most of the hike. Unlike Hillsboro or McKnight peaks, the area around Sawyers Peak has not had any forest fires for many years. Because of the lack of fires and the trail's location on shady north-facing slopes for much of the way, lush forest lines almost the entire route. Broad views open up occasionally, but for the most part the trail winds through dense fir, spruce, aspen, and pine.

At a little over 2 miles, little-used Silver Creek Trail 146 forks off to the right. Stay left on Trail 79 and continue climbing. At about 3 miles, even less-used Trail 134 forks left down Trujillo Canyon. Continue to the right on Trail 79 to Sawyers Peak. Finally, about 0.75 mile further on, you reach the base of the peak on the southeast side. At this point, Trail 79 begins to descend to the south, following the lowering crest of the mountains. Views start to open up to the south. The summit is reached by climbing back to the northwest on a short side trail up the crest through the trees. The rounded

Sawyers Peak

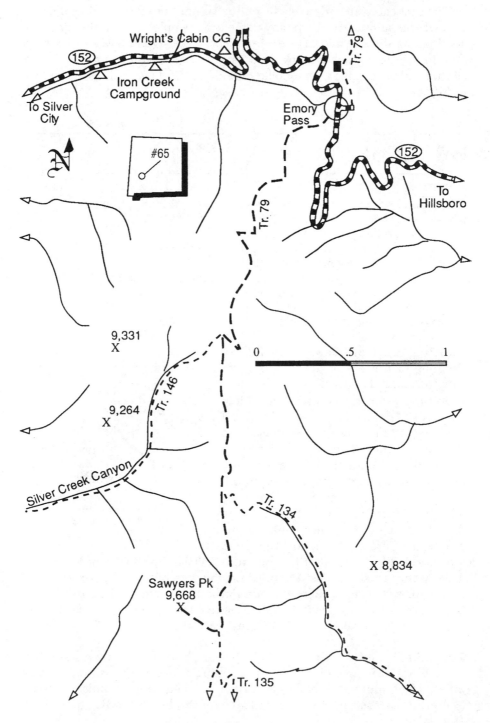

Wright's Cabin CG

Iron Creek Campground

152

To Silver City

Emory Pass

Tr. 79

152

To Hillsboro

#65

N

9,331
X

Tr. 146

9,264
X

Silver Creek Canyon

Tr. 134

X 8,834

Sawyers Pk
9,668
X

Tr. 135

0   .5   1

peak is heavily wooded, allowing few clear views. Better views lie just to the south of the peak along Trail 79.

The best campsites probably lie on the summit or along Trail 79 near the base of the summit. To leave any remaining people behind, just continue south along the Crest Trail. Very few people go beyond Sawyers Peak. Be sure to take topographic maps, since the trail gets faint in places. If a car shuttle can be arranged, an excellent hike would follow Trail 79 all the way to FR 886.

66 Cooks Peak

General description:	A strenuous day hike to the craggy summit of Cooks Peak.
General location:	About 25 miles north of Deming.
Length:	About 11.5 miles round trip.
Elevation:	5,380–8,408 feet.
Maps:	OK Canyon 7.5-minute USGS quad.
Best season:	Spring and fall.
Water availability:	Riley Spring—see text.
Special attractions:	Ghost town; views; solitude.

Finding the trailhead: From I-25 in Deming, turn north on US 180 to Silver City. At about 1 mile, turn right on NM 26 toward Hatch. Go northeast on NM 26 for about 14.6 miles to an unmarked gravel road on the left. A lone ranch house is on the corner and a large old water tank is on the right. Follow the excellent county dirt road to the northwest toward prominent Cooks Peak. At about 5.1 miles, ignore the Hyatt Ranch road forking off to the left. At about 9.8 miles, the road hits a large, dry desert wash. Ignore the rough road forking off to the left just before the wash. To this point the road is usually very good. The last 1.2 miles are rougher, but usually passable with a sedan if care is used. Recent storms usually determine the road's condition. Carefully cross the wash, and drive to a locked gate at about 11 miles. A corral, a cottonwood, and BLM signs mark the spot.

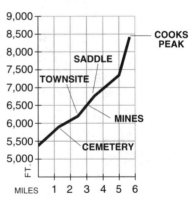

The hike: Cooks (or Cookes) Peak towers above the southwestern New Mexico desert in splendid isolation, forming a landmark visible for many miles. The granite peak makes a distinctive rocky crag reminiscent of the Matterhorn. A series of low foothills connects the Cooks Range with the

Cooks Peak

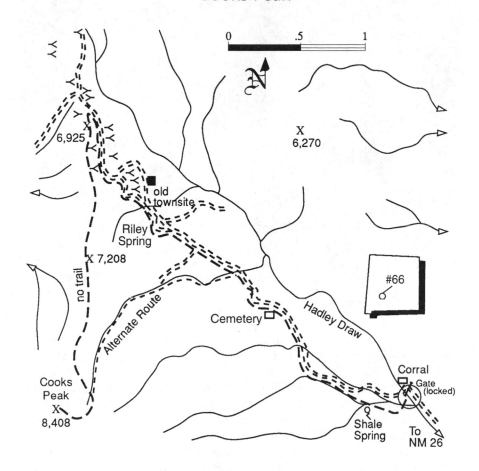

larger Black Range to the north. For centuries, the Apaches used the peak as a lookout. In the 1850s, the Butterfield Stage was routed by the peak to get water at several springs.

Frequent Indian raids led to the establishment of Fort Cummings at Cooks Spring in 1863. Lead-silver ore was discovered at the base of the peak in the 1870s and a small town was established along the route of the hike. The mines have long since played out and little remains of the town.

This hike initially follows an old road, but then climbs cross-country to the summit. The route is steep and strenuous and requires some scrambling up bare rock. Only expert hikers in good condition should attempt it. Except right after heavy snows, this hike can be done any time of year. However, since this is mostly a desert hike, summers can be very hot. Winters are unpredictable. I climbed the peak in late December in a T-shirt, but colder weather is more normal. A topographic map and compass should be taken

Distant Cooks Peak rises above City of Rocks State Park.

for this hike. Be sure to carry enough water; the springs may not be reliable.

Except for a few inholdings, most of the land around the peak is state- or BLM-owned. The fence at the locked gate says "No trespassing" because the road runs through a small inholding. The BLM has established legal right of road access to the gate, but not beyond. Originally the landowner, Tom Hyatt, did not lock the gate. However, he probably suffered vandalism or other problems from inconsiderate visitors.

Please respect private property. By calling Mr. Hyatt ahead of time, you might be able to obtain permission to drive through the gate, cutting 2 miles from the hike. However, the last 2 miles of road often require at least a high clearance vehicle for one of the wash crossings.

Assuming that you do not have permission to cross Hyatt's land, walk left (south) along the fence line to the large dry wash that you drove across a mile back down the road. Follow the wash upstream until you hit the road again in a short distance. Along the way, you will pass fairly close to Shale Spring. Rejoin the road and follow it up the broad canyon. A little more than 1 mile up, you will pass a windmill and the weathered, leaning crosses of the old cemetery on the left. At about 2.5 miles you will find the old townsite. Not much remains, other than scattered junk and an old rusting car. A couple of frame buildings still stand on the slope above, but probably not for much longer. At night, when the wind whistles and moans, you can almost hear the clink of whiskey bottles and the pounding of the stamp mills. Please do not disturb or remove what little is left. Riley Spring, if you can find it, is near the townsite.

Continue to follow the old road northwest up the slope toward the mine workings and the ridge top. Be careful around the old mines. Open shafts are scattered across the ridge and the tunnels are unstable. At about 3.5 miles, the road reaches a saddle along the top of the ridge. Leave the road and cut back south, cross-country, toward the peak along the ridge top.

The first 1.5 miles along the ridge are not too difficult. The ridge does not climb too much and is relatively flat. You will encounter a few pinyons and junipers that provide welcome shade. At about 4.5 miles, you will be at the base of the peak, although still about 1,200 feet below the summit.

Sheer cliffs crown most of the peak, so you must circle around the base to the east side as you climb. The last mile is by far the hardest part of the hike. Work your way southeast around the base into the upper end of the canyon below you to the left (east). Do not climb too high before you get to the upper end of the canyon, or you will find yourself having to cross several steep talus slopes below the cliffs. Do not venture onto the talus slopes. They are composed of larger rocks and boulders on a very unstable slope. Climb south up and out of the drainage to the ridge top. Follow the ridgetop west to the summit. Pick your route carefully; although you will have to scramble up some rock at the end, there is no need to climb any cliffs.

If you achieve the summit, congratulations. Few people ever climb it. Chances are, you and the ghosts will have the entire mountain range to yourselves. Relax and enjoy one of the best views in New Mexico. You can descend the same way, or go all the way down the steep canyon that you climbed up near the top. Another way to shorten the distance is to cut straight down off the long approach ridge to the townsite, rather than following it all the way north back to the road. Or, for a completely different route to Cooks Peak, follow OK Canyon (see the topo map).

67 Blackwater Hole

General description:	An easy day hike in the remote Peloncillo Mountains of far southwestern New Mexico.
General location:	About 40 miles south of Animas in the Coronado National Forest.
Length:	About 5 miles round trip.
Elevation:	5,450–6,000 feet.
Maps:	Coronado National Forest; Clanton Draw; Skeleton Canyon; and Guadalupe Spring 7.5-minute USGS quads.
Best season:	All year.
Water availability:	Seasonal at Blackwater Hole.
Special attractions:	Chihuahua pines; birds; solitude.

Finding the trailhead: Take NM 338 south from Animas about 30 miles (pavement ends after 20 miles) and turn at the marked junction to Douglas, Arizona. Follow the unpaved Douglas road west without turning at any junctions to the Coronado National Forest boundary. Go 2 miles further to a small left fork that climbs up the bank. Drive up the fork 50 yards to an open area and park. The fork is rough; those without a high-clearance vehicle may want to park along the main road. The rest of the dirt roads are good, except during and after heavy rains, which usually occur in late summer.

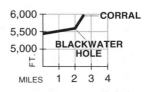

The hike: The far southwestern corner of New Mexico, the "Bootheel," is one of the least visited areas of the state. At the nearby Port of Entry on the Mexican border at Antelope Wells, only four vehicles per day enter the United States. To the surprise of first-time visitors, the southern part of the Bootheel consists of lush grasslands and partially wooded mountains.

The Peloncillo Mountains straddle the Arizona-New Mexico line, continuing south into Mexico. Successive ranges farther south lead into the remote Sierra Madre. The Peloncillos consist of low rounded hills, covered with grass and scattered oaks, pinyon pines, and junipers, leading into a more rugged crest with peaks reaching 6,500 feet in elevation.

The hike follows up a fork of Clanton Draw to a relatively permanent pool called Blackwater Hole and up to the site of an old corral. Clanton Draw was named for the hideout of the Clanton Gang, notorious for their shootout at the OK Corral in Tombstone, Arizona. The Clantons used the hideout, only 1 mile or so from the trailhead, to raid Mexican smuggler parties in the 1880s. Nearby Skeleton Canyon was named for the many bones left after two particularly brutal raids in 1881.

The first part of the hike follows an old Jeep trail up the canyon for about

Blackwater Hole

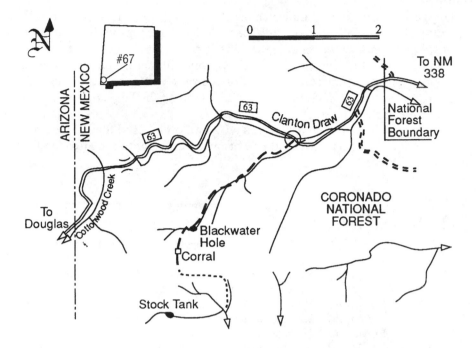

0.5 mile. The canyon sometimes flows in late summer and fall after the rainy season. After the road disappears, the trail becomes very faint from disuse. You can follow the canyon bottom the rest of the way, but the remnants of the old trail cross the dry creek bottom back and forth to the benches lining the creek. If you can stay with the old trail, it is generally easier to walk on the benches. Several small side canyons will join the canyon. Stay in the main canyon which, although it winds some, trends southwest the entire route to Blackwater Hole.

As you hike, you will pass through small groves of Chihuahua pines. The only place that the tree grows in the United States is in a few of the mountain ranges of New Mexico's Bootheel and adjoining areas of Arizona. It looks similar to the ponderosa pine, but with shorter needles and darker colored bark.

You reach Blackwater Hole, a pond created by a small concrete dam, at about 2 miles. Because the pond is basically a cattle tank, carrying your own water is recommended. About 200 to 300 yards upstream from the pond, a small drainage climbs steeply to the left. The faint trail climbs up out of the main canyon on the west side of the small draw. Shortly after you climb out of the canyon, you reach the end of the hike at a large grassy meadow, site of an old corral. The meadow, dotted with junipers, makes a good campsite.

A short walk up the hill to the south of the meadow gives great views of the Animas Mountains to the east and the San Luis Mountains of Mexico to the southeast.

The Forest Service map indicates a trail leading south from the corral, but it is difficult to follow. Following the rounded ridge tops with a map and compass is the easiest way to lengthen the trip.

Keep an eye out for birds on the hike. The mountains are famous among birders, especially at the southern end of the range in Guadalupe Canyon. The proximity to Mexico gives the Peloncillos one of the largest numbers of bird species in the United States.

Be sure to take maps and a compass with you on hikes in the Peloncillos. Trails are faint to nonexistent and you are very unlikely to see anyone else during your hikes.

68 Ice Canyon

General description:	An easy day hike into a sheltered canyon on the west side of the Organ Mountains.
General location:	About 10 miles east of Las Cruces.
Length:	About 3 miles round trip.
Elevation:	5,650–6,150 feet.
Maps:	BLM brochure; Organ Peak 7.5-minute USGS quad.
Best season:	Year round.
Water availability:	Dripping Springs.
Special attractions:	Sheltered steep-walled canyon; historic buildings.

Finding the trailhead: In Las Cruces, take the University exit off of I-25 and turn east, up toward the mountains. The pavement quickly turns into a washboard gravel surface. At about 4 miles, the pavement returns for about 1 mile. When the pavement ends again, bear straight ahead back onto the gravel road. Do not turn right and follow the pavement.

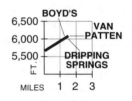

Follow the BLM Dripping Springs signs. Continue east-northeast. At about 10.5 miles, park at road's end at the A. B. Cox Visitor Center.

The hike: In the 1870s, Colonel Eugene Van Patten built a mountain resort at Dripping Springs. The resort was a popular escape from the heat of the Rio Grande Valley at the turn of the century. In 1917 the resort went bankrupt and was sold to Dr. Nathan Boyd, who converted it into a tuberculosis sanatorium. He built additional structures in the canyon to house his patients. Eventually the sanatorium closed and the buildings fell into disrepair.

A few years ago The Nature Conservancy bought part of the property to

Ice Canyon

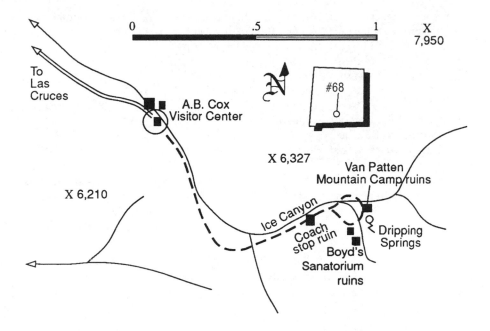

help protect endangered species found in the canyon, particularly the Organ Mountain primrose. The land was turned over to the BLM, but is jointly managed by volunteers from both organizations. The visitor center and canyon are open for day use only. Since the canyon is closed on certain weekdays, be sure to call either the visitor center or the BLM office in Las Cruces before making the drive up to the canyon.

From the visitor center, follow the trail signs up the old road. The road goes up the broad, mostly desert canyon floor. At the ruined buildings of the old coach stop, the canyon starts to narrow, and oak, juniper, and hackberry woodlands start to appear. The sheer canyon walls pull in closer and closer as the trail continues up. Near the end, the trail splits into a small loop. Go right and up to some of the old buildings erected as part of Boyd's Sanatorium. Just around the loop from the sanatorium, the water of Dripping Springs drips off of cliffs above. In a pinch, water can be obtained here, but it must be purified. Also, the spring is very small; use by many people would deplete it. For this short of a walk, it is better to carry what you need.

A bit further along the loop lie the ruins of Van Patten's mountain camp. The ruins of the large buildings are tucked into the base of the canyon wall. Be sure not to climb on the fragile and dangerous ruins. The loop continues back to the same fork. Behind the mountain camp ruins are oak-shaded picnic tables, ideal resting places on a hot summer day.

69 Baylor Pass

General description:	An easy day hike to a pass in the Organ Mountains.
General location:	About 20 miles northeast of Las Cruces.
Length:	About 4 miles round trip.
Elevation:	5,680–6,390 feet.
Maps:	Organ, Organ Peak NW, and Organ Peak 7.5-minute USGS quads.
Best season:	Year round.
Water availability:	None.
Special attractions:	Views.

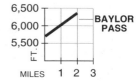

Finding the trailhead: Drive about 15 miles northeast of I-25 in Las Cruces on US 70-82. Just after driving over San Augustin Pass, turn right (south) onto the well marked Aguirre Springs Recreation Area road. Follow the paved road 5.9 miles to the marked trailhead just before the campground entrance.

The hike: The Organ Mountains are noted for the tall spires that, with their resemblance to organ pipes, give the mountains their name. The mountains rise over 5,000 feet above the Rio Grande Valley to the west. Rock climbers

The rock needles of the Organ Mountains rise precipitously from the surrounding plains.

Baylor Pass • Pine Tree Trail

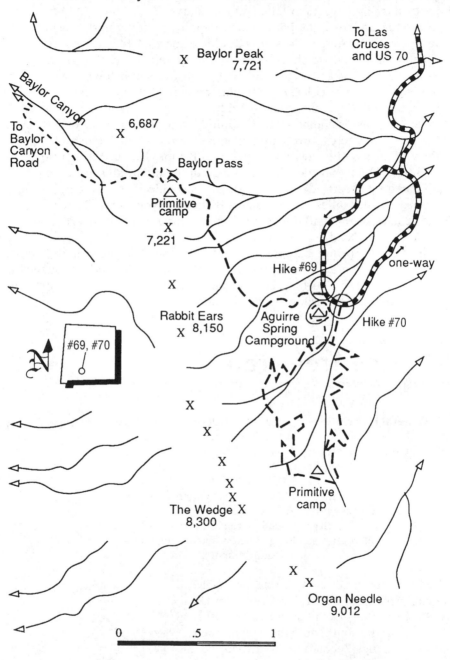

To Las
Cruces
and US 70

x Baylor Peak
7,721

Baylor Canyon

To
Baylor
Canyon
Road

x 6,687

Baylor Pass

Primitive
camp
x
7,221

Hike #69

one-way

x

Rabbit Ears
x 8,150

Aguirre
Spring
Campground

Hike #70

N #69, #70

x

x

x

x
x

The Wedge x
8,300

Primitive
camp

x
x

Organ Needle
9,012

0   .5   1

regularly scale the sheer peaks, but without good training and plenty of experience, do not attempt to climb any of the summits. A number of people have died over the years in falls and rockslides.

From the trailhead, the path climbs steadily, trending northwest overall. The trail winds through occasional boulders and rock formations. Scattered oaks and junipers offer shade along the route. As you climb, views to the east and northeast get better and better. To the south tower the igneous crags of the Organ Needles. A particularly good viewpoint is reached shortly before the end of the hike at about 1.5 miles. Baylor Pass is reached at about 2 miles. The pass is named after the Confederate general who went through the pass in 1861 to capture Union troops located at San Augustin Springs.

From the pass, the view looks down on Baylor Canyon and a little of the Rio Grande Valley beyond. The west side of the mountains are much more dominated by desert vegetation than the east side. The trail can be easily followed about 4 miles farther, down Baylor Canyon to the Baylor Canyon Road. The west trailhead is located about 1.9 miles south of US 70-82 on the Baylor Canyon Road.

The Aguirre Springs Campground at the trailhead is an excellent place to spend the night before or after the hike. There are tables and pit toilets, but no running water. The hike is good all year, but can be hot in summer. Spring winds can be strong, especially at the pass.

70 Pine Tree Trail

See Map on Page 205

General description:	An easy to moderate day hike below the rugged crags of the Organ Needles.
General location:	About 20 miles northeast of Las Cruces.
Length:	About 4.5 miles round trip.
Elevation:	5,700–6,880 feet.
Maps:	BLM brochure; Organ Peak 7.5-minute USGS quad.
Best season:	Year round.
Water availability:	Usually a reliable stream—see text.
Special attractions:	Rugged peaks above trail; views; enormous alligator junipers.

Finding the trailhead: Drive about 15 miles northeast of I-25 in Las Cruces on US 70-82. Just after driving over San Augustin Pass, turn right (south) onto the well marked Aguirre Springs Recreation Area road. Follow the paved road 6.1 miles to the marked trailhead just past the campground entrance.

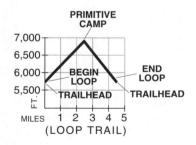

The hike: The Organ Mountains were originally named the Mountains of Solitude by the Spaniards. Later settlers renamed the mountains because of the resemblance of the rock spires to the pipes in an organ. The sheer spires or needles of the central peaks are made of monzonite uplifted in a fault block and eroded into the present jagged form.

The trail follows a broad loop around a drainage basin at the base of Rabbit Ears and several of the other Needles. From the trailhead, the well-constructed trail climbs steadily uphill through patchy oak-juniper woodland. Within less than 0.25 mile, the trail hits the loop. Go right. Within 50 yards a trail forks off to the right and drops back down to another trailhead in the campground. Continue to climb to the left up a steady grade.

The trail winds through boulders tumbled from the heights above and passes by ponderosa pines scattered along the creek bottoms. Some of the largest, most gnarled alligator junipers I have ever seen lie along the trail. Some of the trunks are four or five feet in diameter.

At close to halfway along the loop, the trail traverses around a hillside, reaching a prominent point with tremendous views of the Tularosa Valley, the San Andres Mountains, and even the distant 12,000-foot peak of Sierra Blanca in the Sacramento Mountains. A short climb further and the trail reaches the formal primitive campground, tucked onto a bench wooded with scattered oak, alligator junipers, and ponderosa pine. The primitive camp is one of the few sites along the hike that is level enough to camp on. A few other sites are possible farther down the return leg of the loop.

The camp is located at both the highest point of the hike and about the halfway point. From there, the trail drops steadily down to the end of the loop. About 0.5 mile past the camp, the trail crosses a small stream that is usually reliable, except in very dry spells. Be sure to purify the water. The trail recrosses the same stream just before reaching the end of the loop. The trail is well built, but has become heavily eroded in places because of shortcutting. Try to resist the temptation.

The Aguirre Springs Campground at the trailhead is an excellent place to spend the night before or after the hike. There are tables and pit toilets but no running water. The hike is good all year but can be hot in summer. The common spring winds do not affect this hike as much as most areas in southern New Mexico. The towering peaks just to the west of the trail provide shelter from the southwesterly winds. The last time I hiked the trail in spring, I could hear a steady roar as the wind howled through the crags above, but no more than a breeze touched me.

71 White Sands

General description: A very easy day hike through sand dunes to a back country campsite.

General location: About 15 miles southwest of Alamogordo.

Length: 0.6 miles round trip.

Elevation: 3,975–4,000 feet (no elevation graph).

Maps: Heart of the Sands and Garton Lake 7.5-minute USGS quads.

Best season: All year.

Water availability: None.

Special attractions: The world's largest gypsum dune field.

Permit: Required for camping; obtain at visitor center.

Finding the trailhead: Drive about 15 miles southwest of Alamogordo on US 70 to the entrance of White Sands National Monument. From the visitor center at the entrance, drive into the monument 4.9 miles along the Heart of the Sands Loop Drive to the marked parking lot for the backcountry campsite.

White Sands

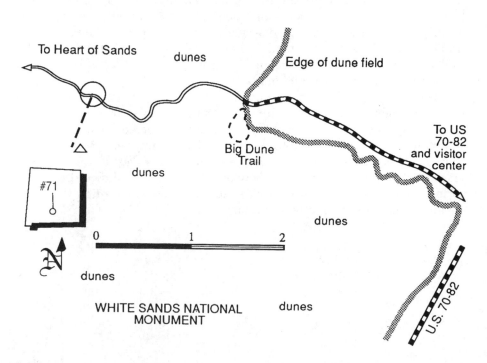

A sea of sand greets hikers at White Sands. PHOTO BY PATRICIA CAPERTON PARENT

The hike: White Sands lies in the center of a large fault-created basin surrounded by high mountains including the Sacramento, Organ, San Andres, and Oscura ranges. For millennia, rain and melting snow have carried dissolved gypsum down into the basin from large deposits in these mountains. The gypsum is carried to Lake Lucero, the lowest point in the basin. The hot desert sun dries the lake waters, leaving a lake bed covered with gypsum crystals. The prevailing southwest wind erodes the crystals into fine grains and sweeps them away to the northeast in endless ranks of dunes.

This hike is an exceptionally easy walk, included because of the uniqueness of White Sands. From the parking area, follow a series of numbered marker posts southwest 0.3 mile to the campsite, marked with a large sign. Markers are used because the wind can obliterate all paths and tracks within hours. The trail climbs over several dunes, but otherwise the route is level and very short. The camping area is in a flat area between the dunes.

Be sure to camp if you have time. On a night with a full moon, the almost snow-white dunes are very bright. Be sure not to take anything that you do not want to get sandy. Since the monument does not open until after sunrise, camping is the only way to see the dunes at sunrise.

Do not let the shortness of the trail prevent you from exploring further. Take day hikes farther out into the dunes and enjoy the endless expanse of sand. Occasional cottonwoods, with many of their roots exposed, break up the sameness of the terrain. Yucca, rabbitbrush, four-wing saltbush, and other shrubs manage a tenuous hold on life in the shifting sands. Be sure to take the Big Dune Trail, a nature trail 2 miles from the visitor center along the Loop Drive, to learn more about the dunes. Another trail, Alkali Flat, is described in this guide.

Be extremely careful when leaving the established roads or trails. Use a compass, maps, and landmarks to avoid becoming lost. Spring is the most likely time for wind and sandstorms.

Wear dark glasses and sunscreen, because the sand is extremely bright. At times the dunes are closed to overnight camping because of military testing at adjacent White Sands Missile Range. You may want to call ahead to determine if any testing is planned.

72 Alkali Flat

General description:	An easy day hike through a large dune field to Alkali Flat, a source of gypsum sand for White Sands National Monument.
General location:	About 18 miles southwest of Alamogordo.
Length:	4.6 miles round trip.
Elevation:	3,950–4,000 feet (no elevation graph).
Maps:	Alkali Flat Trail brochure; Heart of the Sands 7.5-minute USGS quad.
Best season:	October through April.
Water availability:	None.
Special attractions:	Large gypsum sand dunes.

Finding the trailhead: From the White Sands National Monument visitor center, drive into the park on the paved Heart of the Sands Loop drive. The pavement ends at about 4.7 miles; continue into the dunes on a good packed sand road. The loop starts at 6.4 miles; go right another 1.2 miles to the marked parking area on the right at the far end of the loop.

The hike: The Alkali Flat Trail leads through the heart of the dunes at White Sands National Monument. The dunes are large, closely spaced, and

Alkali Flat

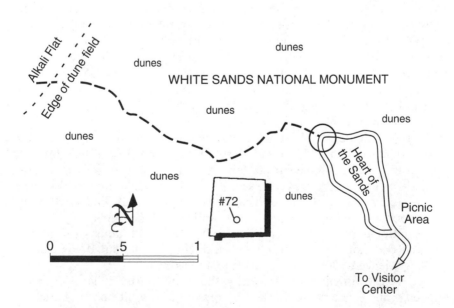

Hikers cross many dunes to reach Alkali Flat.

move with every wind storm, allowing little vegetation to survive. The landscape, with bright white dunes, endless sky, and distant mountain ranges, has a stark appeal.

White Sands has the largest field of gypsum dunes in the world. The Tularosa Valley in which the dunes lie was created when a large fault block dropped, leaving a broad valley with high mountains on either side. The valley does not have an outlet to the sea, so during wetter ice age times, precipitation washed gypsum and other minerals down into a large lake in the valley. When the climate dried, the lake evaporated, leaving a usually dry bed exposed now at Alkali Flat and Lake Lucero. When lake waters dry, gypsum crystals form; the prevailing southwest wind erodes the crystals into sand and blows the grains into dunes. This hike crosses the dune field to the edge of Alkali Flat.

The hike is relatively short and has little net elevation change, but many dunes of soft sand have to be crossed, requiring some effort. The white sand is dazzling in sunshine; be sure to take sunglasses and sunscreen. There is no shade or water, so start very early if you do this hike in warm weather. Be careful if you leave the marked route, especially during bad weather. It is easy to become lost in the many square miles of dune fields.

The national monument is surrounded by the White Sands Missile Range, so debris occasionally falls into the park during flight tests. If you find any wreckage, leave it alone and report it to a park ranger.

Because the dunes move constantly, the route to Alkali Flat is not a constructed trail. It is a route marked by orange and white posts. Be sure to register at the trailhead before you start. The hike is in a day use area, so you must be back by sunset. From the parking area, the route heads west in a small inter-dune flat. Other than a few hardy grasses that manage to grow sparsely in the small flats between dunes, there is little vegetation on most of the hike. A rare exception are the two or three interesting hillocks anchored by clumps of brush.

The route soon begins climbing up and over the first of many dunes. On top of the higher dunes, views stretch for miles across the empty, silent landscape. Only an occasional dust devil or a vulture floating high above brings movement to the stark terrain. After a little more than 2 miles, the dunes end. The trail goes a short distance further into Alkali Flat, a well-named locale. If the wind is still and there are no planes, it is incredibly quiet at the end of the trail. A small missile range facility is visible some miles to the north; otherwise the area seems almost as empty and remote as the moon.

73 Three Rivers Petroglyphs

General description:	An easy day hike along a rocky ridge decorated with thousands of prehistoric petroglyphs.
General location:	About 22 miles north of Tularosa (about 35 miles north of Alamogordo).
Length:	About 1.5 miles round trip for both short trails.
Elevation:	4,980–5,180 feet (no elevation graph).
Maps:	Three Rivers Petroglyph Site brochure; Three Rivers 7.5-minute USGS quad.
Best season:	All year.
Water availability:	Picnic area at trailhead.
Special attractions:	Numerous petroglyphs; ancient village site; views.

Finding the trailhead: From Tularosa, drive north on US 54 about 17.3 miles (or south from Carrizozo about 28 miles). Turn right onto paved County Road B30. The junction is well marked with signs for Three Rivers Petroglyph Site. Follow the road 4.5 miles west to the marked entrance to the petroglyph site on the left. Enter the site, pay the nominal entrance fee, and park at the trailhead on the northwest side of the small picnic area.

The hike: The Three Rivers Petroglyph Site is one of the premier rock art sites in the Southwest, with more than 21,000 rock carvings. These two short easy trails lead to many of the petroglyphs and to a partly excavated village. In summer, the desert here is hot. Hike early or late in the day then, watching out for rattlesnakes.

The petroglyph trail starts behind the shade shelter at the trailhead. It crosses a dry desert wash and then climbs up onto a rocky basalt ridge.

Three Rivers Petroglyphs

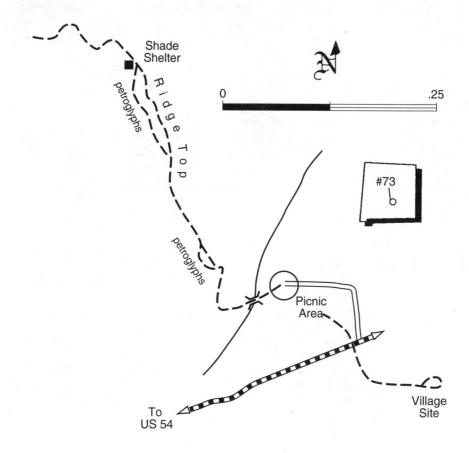

Ancient carvings dot the dark rock, some scratched into the hard stone, others laboriously pecked into place. All along the rocky basalt ridge followed by the trail, prehistoric artists carved geometric patterns, masks, animals, hand prints, and other subjects hundreds of years ago.

Although archaeologists believe that a group of prehistoric Indians known as the Jornada Mogollon carved the petroglyphs, they are uncertain why they were made and what they mean. Researchers believe that the inhabitants of a nearby village on the banks of Three Rivers Creek carved them during the 400 years that the village was occupied.

The Jornada Mogollon farmed here about a thousand years ago. These people lived in southwestern New Mexico, southeastern Arizona, and northern Chihuahua in Mexico. They traded with the Anasazi to the north and Mesoamericans to the south in Mexico.

Thousands of petroglyphs cover the rocks at Three Rivers Petroglyph site. PHOTO BY PATRICIA CAPERTON PARENT

Mysteriously, the Mogollon disappeared from the Southwest, leaving little more than abandoned villages, scattered artifacts, and extensive rock art behind. While researchers cannot be certain, they believe that war, drought, social decay, depletion of natural resources, or some combination of these factors led to the Mogollon people's disappearance.

The trail follows the crest of the ridge almost 0.5 mile to a shade shelter, past numerous petroglyphs. The trail splits and rejoins twice along the way. With many side trails to various rock carvings, it is sometimes hard to determine which trail is the main route. However, just stay on the best looking path close to the ridge crest; it is very difficult to get lost here. Beyond the shade shelter, the trail climbs to a higher section of ridge with a lower concentration of petroglyphs and then peters out.

Unfortunately, as you will see, some of the petroglyphs have been vandalized. To avoid unintentional damage, be sure not to step on or touch the rock art.

A second shorter trail leads to a partly excavated Mogollon village. It starts from the opposite side of the picnic area, crosses the county road, and ends at the remnants of the village.

74 Valley of Fires

General description:	An easy day hike through the rocky terrain of a relatively new lava flow.
General location:	About 4 miles west of Carrizozo.
Length:	About 0.75 mile round trip. A new trail opening in 1998 will be 2 miles round trip.
Elevation:	5,260–5,200 feet (no elevation graph).
Maps:	Valley of Fires brochure; Carrizozo West 7.5-minute USGS quad.
Best season:	All year.
Water availability:	Trailhead.
Special attractions:	Recent lava flow.

Finding the trailhead: Drive west of Carrizozo about 4 miles on US 380 to Valley of Fires Recreation Area on the left. Enter the park and pay the small entrance fee. The marked trailhead is on the right a short distance into the park at a large roofed pavilion.

The hike: Valley of Fires Recreation Area lies in a large lava flow that blankets 125 square miles of the northern part of the Tularosa Valley. It is often called the Malpais, or "bad land" in Spanish. The name comes naturally—try to walk across a section of it. The dark lava has crumbled and folded, splintered and collapsed, creating a very rough surface for travel or any other human activity. The lava flow is still so rough because the hard

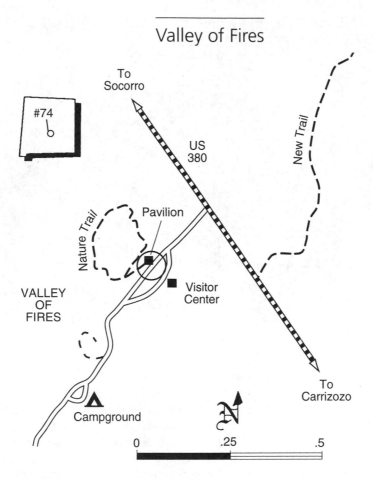

Valley of Fires

To
Socorro

#74

US
380

New Trail

Nature Trail

Pavilion

VALLEY
OF
FIRES

Visitor
Center

To
Carrizozo

Campground

N

0   .25   .5

rock has had little time to weather. Some geologists believe it to be one of the youngest lava flows in the continental United States. The most recent flow may be only 1,500 to 2,000 years old.

The loop nature trail starts at the pavilion on a low ridge and drops down to the flow via numerous annoying switchbacks built to accommodate wheelchairs. The first part of the trail is paved to serve the handicapped. The trail loops out into the twisted and tortured rock of the lava flow past pressure ridges and collapsed lava tubes. A brochure obtainable at the visitor center describes many of the sights along the trail.

Although much of the terrain is nothing but broken, bare rock, a surprising number of plants have managed to gain a foothold in pockets and crevices which have filled with soil. A large 400-year-old juniper along the trail has sent roots down deep into cracks in the lava flow. Several species, six rodent, five lizard, and one snake have developed a darker coloration to blend in with the black rock. Interestingly, these same species have developed an abnormally light color for life on the gypsum dunes of White Sands

Vegetation is gaining a foothold in the lava at Valley of Fires.

National Monument to the south.

At the end of the loop, rejoin the paved trail and climb back up to the pavilion. Part of the reason for including this trail in the guide is the planned addition of another longer, more primitive trail. By the time this book is available, the BLM should have opened a 2-mile round trip trail across US 380. It leads to the site of an old moonshining cabin. Inquire about the trail's status at the visitor center. The recreation area also offers camping and picnicking. The desert area is hot in summer, so hike early or late in the day during that time of year. Keep an eye out for rattlesnakes on warm summer evenings. They come out to hunt then.

75 Capitan Peak

General description:	A strenuous two- or three-day backpack into one of the least visited wildernesses in New Mexico.
General location:	About 50 miles west of Roswell.
Length:	About 20 miles round trip.
Elevation:	6,300–10,083 feet.
Maps:	Lincoln National Forest; Arroyo Serrano West, Kyle Harrison Canyon, and Capitan Peak 7.5-minute USGS quads.
Best season:	Late April through mid-November.
Water availability:	Seasonal in Pine Lodge; Copeland; and Seven Cabins canyons—see text.
Special attractions:	Lush old growth conifer forest; views of much of the southeastern part of the state; solitude.

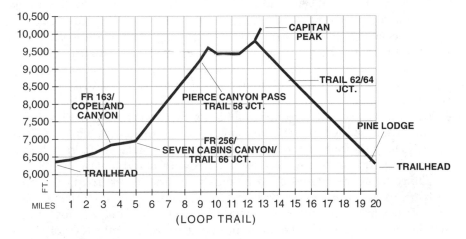

Finding the trailhead: Drive 4 miles north of the center of Roswell on US 285 to the junction with NM NM 246. Turn left and drive west about 50 miles to the junction with the dirt FR 130 (the sign says Boy Scout Mountain). Or from Capitan, follow NM 246 about 32 miles north and east to the junction. Follow FR 130 southeast about 3.9 miles to the large North Base Trail 65 sign and park. With care, the rocky FR 130 can usually be negotiated with passenger cars; however, it would be best to call the Lincoln National Forest ranger station in Capitan or Ruidoso first for current road conditions.

The hike: The Capitan Mountains are one of the few ranges in the United States that run east-west. The steep rugged mountains, rising abruptly from the high plains of southeastern New Mexico, are the first mountains seen by visitors entering New Mexico from much of the eastern part of the state. On clear days, the Capitans can be seen from as far away as the Texas state line.

219

In 1950, a 17,000-acre forest fire raged for several days in the western end of the mountains. A small burned black bear cub was found clinging to a charred tree. After receiving veterinary care, he was flown to the National Zoo in Washington, DC, to become the national symbol of forest fire prevention, Smokey Bear.

The steep, higher elevations of the eastern end of the Capitans were too difficult to enter with logging roads, so they have never been timbered. In recent years, much of the east section has been designated the Capitan Mountain Wilderness. Dense old growth forests of Douglas-fir, spruce, ponderosa pine, and other trees greet hikers willing to make the strenuous climb up into the Capitans.

Even though the popular resort towns of Ruidoso and Cloudcroft are not far to the south, the Capitans are almost completely undiscovered. Except during hunting season, you may well hike the entire 20-mile loop without seeing another person.

The creeks in Pine Lodge, Copeland, and Seven Cabins canyons run much of the year, often even year round. Inquire at the Capitan or Ruidoso ranger office for their current status. On this hike, Seven Cabins Creek is most useful, because it allows hikers to avoid carrying much water for the first 5 miles of the loop. The other two canyons are too close to the trailhead to be of much use. There is no reliable water on the mountain crest, so either carry sufficient water or load up at Seven Cabins Creek. Purify if you use the stream water.

The first section of the route, Trail 65, contours west along the base of the mountains, crossing numerous drainages. Almost the entire hike is in heavy forest. The only part of the hike that can be confusing is the first 5 miles along the North Base Trail because of a network of old logging roads.

The route at the trailhead starts initially as an old dirt road. It immediately drops down into and crosses Pine Lodge Creek. On the other side, the bank is covered with fire rings from hunter camps. Look for the Trail 65 sign at the west side of the area of hunters' campsites (only 100 yards or so from the creek). The trail trends west through a mixed alligator juniper, pinyon pine, oak, and ponderosa pine forest. A little more than 1 mile from the start, you hit a T-shaped junction with a Trail 65 sign. Take the left fork of the T uphill. You are now on a faint old road again. A few hundred yards further, a faint trail goes uphill to the left. Ignore it and stay on the more traveled right-hand route. Ignore another faint left-hand trail another 0.5 mile further and drop down into a creek bottom on the more-travelled trail instead. After crossing the dry creek and climbing out, you reach an old road junction. Take the right-hand fork, marked by a Trail 65 sign, even though in this case it appears to be the less-travelled route. Trail 65 and the rest of the route are well marked by tree blazes. Within 0.5 mile of the junction, the old road ends and reverts to a trail in the bottom of a dry creek.

A trailside sign denotes Red Lick Canyon at about 3 miles. At 3.5 miles the trail hits FR 163 coming up Copeland Canyon. At the junction, signs

Capitan Peak

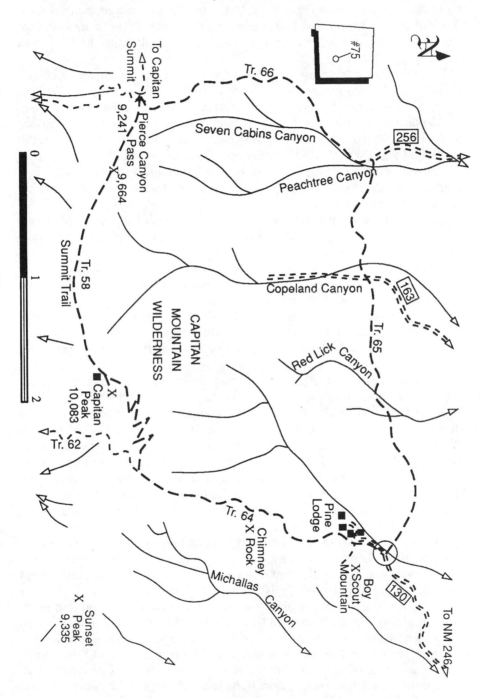

indicate the proper route, up the road to the left (south) for about 0.25 mile. A trail sign marks the turnoff to the right (west again). In about 100 yards the trail crosses the small stream of Copeland Creek, marked with a sign. The trail is faint for a bit just after crossing the creek. It turns downstream and parallels the creek for a short distance before climbing the bank and continuing west again.

At 5 miles, the trail crosses the stream at Seven Cabins Canyon and hits a thicket of trail junction signs. Just downhill to the right is the end of FR 256, but turn left (south) up the canyon on Trail 66. You enter the Capitan Mountain Wilderness within 50 yards. Although the trail is in excellent condition, Trail 66 is the toughest part of the loop because of the 2,300-foot gain in the 4 miles to the crest at Pierce Canyon Pass. The first part of the climb follows the canyon bottom, passing groves of bigtooth maples, beautiful in October. If you need water, be sure to get it here before the trail starts switchbacking up out of the canyon bottom.

Several flat ridge top areas make decent campsites along the climb, but if you have enough energy, the crest is the best area for camping with numerous level, needle-carpeted sites in old growth timber.

At the four-way marked intersection on the crest, turn left (east) on Trail 58, the Summit Trail. The area around the intersection would make a good first night's campsite. The sign indicates a distance of 3 miles to Capitan Peak, but it appears to be more like 3.5 miles. The difficult part of the hike is over. The Summit Trail climbs very gradually east toward the summit of Capitan Peak through lush virgin stands of Douglas-fir, spruce, aspen, and other trees.

At about 12.5 miles the trail climbs into the lower end of a clearing with a sign saying "Capitan Peak, 10,083 feet." A short side trail leads to a Forest Service cabin, visible above in the trees. Please do not disturb it or any of the fire equipment and other gear stored in it. Be sure to take the time to climb up through the clearing above the sign a few hundred yards to the bare summit of Capitan Peak. On clear days, 360-degree views reveal mountains as distant as the Sangre de Cristos above Santa Fe and the Guadalupe Mountains of West Texas. Level areas in the trees just below the peak would make an excellent site for a second night's camp. Watching the sunrise or sunset from the summit is hard to beat.

The descent back to the trailhead is long, dropping almost 4,000 feet in about 7 miles, so take your time and enjoy the almost continuous views. After leaving Capitan Peak, continue east on Trail 58 as it descends about 1.5 miles to the junction of Trails 62 and 64. Along the way you will pass another faint route climbing off to the right to the summit of Capitan Peak. At the junction, turn left on Trail 64 to FR 130. The trail descends through many switchbacks; please do not shortcut. Right after leaving the wilderness near the end of the hike, you will pass by the first cabin of Pine Lodge.

After passing above several more cabins, the trail intersects another trail in the bottom of a dry creek. Ignore it; its left fork goes to the cabins and the right fork climbs up the dry creek. Trail 64 soon hits FR 130 only about 100 yards up from the starting point at the North Base Trailhead.

Trail 64 can be climbed by itself to Capitan Peak as a strenuous day hike. An easier day hike or overnight trip would be to drive to the end of FR 256 in Seven Cabins Canyon and hike up Trail 66 to Pierce Canyon Pass. To avoid the steep climb up to the crest altogether, drive up the very rough FR 56 from Capitan Pass to the start of the Summit Trail at Capitan Summit.

76 Tucson Mountain

General description:	A moderate day hike or easy overnight trip to the top of a subrange of the Sacramento Mountains.
General location:	About 40 miles north of Ruidoso.
Length:	About 10 miles round trip.
Elevation:	6,840–8,333 feet.
Maps:	Lincoln National Forest; White Oaks South 7.5-minute USGS quad.
Best season:	April through November.
Water availability:	Goat Spring.
Special attractions:	Open, park-like stands of ponderosa pine; views.

Finding the trailhead: Drive 12 miles west of Capitan on US 380. Across from the junction with NM 37, turn right (north) onto the excellent gravel Forest Road 441. Ignore the incredible array of "No Trespassing" signs along FR 441; the public has right of way access to the forest boundary. Just past the impressive O-Bar-O Ranch headquarters, you will reach the Lincoln National Forest boundary at about 5.5 miles. After passing through the boundary gate

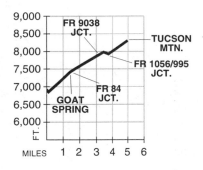

(leave it as you find it), the road gets steeper and rougher. Depending on road conditions, sometimes a passenger car can make it to the trailhead. However, a high clearance vehicle is recommended.

The well marked Tucson Mountain trailhead is only 1 mile up the road from the Forest Service boundary, so park and walk the extra distance if in doubt about the road. The large sign marking the trailhead is on the right side as the road enters a large grassy meadow.

The hike: Tucson Mountain is the highest point in the Vera Cruz Mountains, a small subrange of the Sacramento Mountains.

It connects with the larger Capitan Mountains to the east by a 7,000-foot pass traversed by NM 246 and connects to the west with the Carrizo Mountains by another low pass crossed by FR 441. The trail climbs gradually

Tucson Mountain

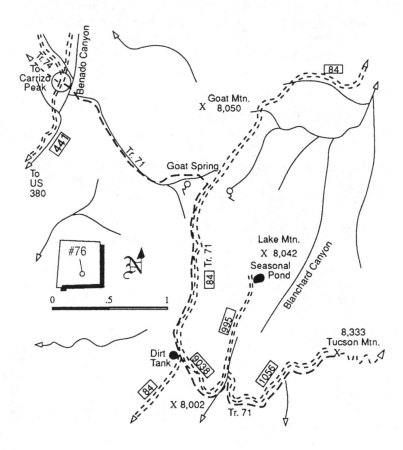

from pinyon-juniper forest to pure stands of ponderosa on the broad summit. The trail is easy to follow, but since several of the junctions are not marked, be sure to follow the directions carefully.

From the trailhead sign, Trail 71 is not obvious. Look east 50 yards away or so for a blaze on a ponderosa pine. From the blazed ponderosa pine, cross the tiny dry creek behind it and then drop into the main dry creek bottom. You should be on a faint old road that ends in the creek a few yards from where you stand. The trail is quite obvious as it crosses the creek to the southeast as an extension of the old road. Shortly after climbing out of the main creek, it drops back down into a southeast-trending dry tributary. The trail follows the creek all the way upstream to Goat Spring at about 1.5 miles. It crosses back and forth from bank to bank. The creek bottom is densely wooded with ponderosa pine, oak, Douglas-fir, and alligator juniper and offers many good campsites. Do not expect to see anyone on this hike, especially the section leading to Goat Spring. Be careful in deer season, however, as the trail does see significant use then.

At about 1.5 miles, water from Goat Spring appears, trickling down the canyon bottom. The trail climbs high up the left (north) bank for a few hundred yards when you reach the water. It rejoins the creek at the small pool at Goat Spring, marked with a sign. If you get water, be sure to purify it.

About 0.25 mile beyond the spring, the trail hits a dirt road, little-used FR 84. Turn right (south) on the road and follow it about 1.5 miles to the junction with FR 9038 at a dirt cattle tank. As you climb, you pass grassy meadows with scattered park-like stands of ponderosa pine. Turn left at the tank and follow FR 9038 up the hill for about 0.5 mile to the junction where FR 9038 splits into FR 1056 and FR 995. The junction occurs in a large meadow.

From FR 9038 onwards, the camping opportunities become more and more inviting. Turn right onto the much fainter fork, FR 1056. From here, wind up the old road through open meadows and stands of ponderosa to the broad, wooded summit of the mountain. About 1 mile past the 1056/995 junction, you will pass a yellow stone aerial marker in a meadow. The summit is a short distance beyond. An old well of some sort, a large rock cairn, and the foundation of what looks to be an old fire lookout crown the summit. From the crest, the best views are to the east and southeast of Capitan and the Capitan Mountains. Move down the crest of the summit to the west a bit for good views of the Carrizo, Patos, and Jicarilla mountains. Return the same way.

Trail 71 continues on down the east side of Tucson Mountain to FR 165. A more difficult, but spectacular, hike is Trail 74 up Johnnie Canyon to the much higher (9,656 feet) Carrizo Peak. Its marked trailhead is just across FR 441 from the Tucson Mountain trailhead.

General description: A strenuous day hike to the summit of the highest mountain in southern New Mexico.

General location: About 20 miles northwest of Ruidoso.

Length: About 9.25 miles round trip.

Elevation: 9,830–11,973 feet.

Maps: White Mountain Wilderness; Lincoln National Forest; Sierra Blanca Peak and Nogal Peak 7.5-minute USGS quads.

Best season: Late May through October.

Water availability: Ice Spring is usually reliable.

Special attractions: Tremendous views; alpine tundra.

Permit: Since the summit itself lies within the Mescalero Apache Reservation, inquire at tribal headquarters in Mescalero to get permission for the hike.

Finding the trailhead: Take NM 48 about 7 miles north of Ruidoso to the well marked junction with NM 532. Turn left (west) and follow it 12 miles all the way up to the end of the road at the ski area. The winding and steep, but paved, road is one of the most spectacular in the state. The trailhead is at the small parking area on the last highway curve just before you enter the main ski area parking lot.

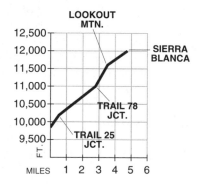

The hike: The USGS designates the entire mountain range from the Jicarillas in the north to just north of north end of the Guadalupes in the south as the Sacramento Mountains. The names of distinct subranges are used for more specific identification. The large part of the range south of US 70, centered around Cloudcroft, is generally known as the Sacramentos. Other subranges include the Capitans, Jicarillas, Patos, Sierra Blanca, Carrizo, and Vera Cruz mountains. Although passes and divides separate the subranges and many were formed from different geological processes, the entire range is high enough to be continuously forested.

The Sierra Blanca Range has the highest point, not only in the Sacramentos, but in the entire state except for the Sangre de Cristo Mountains to the north. The huge extrusive volcanic mountain of Sierra Blanca Peak towers 7,800 feet above the Tularosa Valley for the greatest relief in New Mexico. The peak and surrounding ridges and summits are the only area in southern New Mexico to rise above timberline into alpine tundra vegetation. Small moraines and cirques indicate that the peak was probably glaciated in the Pleistocene. The climb to the summit is popular in summer; try to avoid

Sierra Blanca

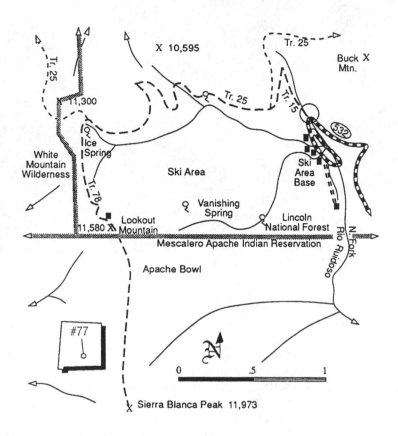

weekends if possible.

Take marked Trail 15 from the parking lot up along a small creek and then up a grassy hillside about 0.6 mile (although the sign says 0.5 mile) to the junction with Crest Trail 25. Go left (west) on Trail 25 toward the Lookout Mountain Trail, about 2 miles away. The trail traverses a heavily wooded hillside across from the ski area. Some of the Douglas-firs in the old growth forest are as large as 5 feet in diameter. At a little more than 0.5 mile beyond the junction, the trail enters a grassy sloping valley with many good campsites possible. Faded orange-painted fence posts mark the trail across the small valley. The trail switchbacks up into dense spruce and fir on a northslope, leaving the ski area behind for a time. This section of trail can have snow well into early summer; check with the Forest Service in Ruidoso before starting early season hikes.

The trail curves back around into sight of the ski area and climbs steadily to the junction with Lookout Mountain Trail 78, about 2.6 miles from the trailhead. Ice Spring lies in the draw just below the junction. Turn left (south)

A late spring snow dusts 12,000-foot Sierra Blanca, the highest peak in southern New Mexico.

onto Trail 78 and climb steadily to the crest of the range. After you reach the crest, you climb above timberline, so, if you are camping, you may want to pick a site before then.

The trail climbs steadily, passing the buildings at the top of the ski area gondola before reaching the summit of Lookout Mountain at 11,580 feet and about 0.8 mile from the Trail 78 junction. The formal trail ends at Lookout Mountain, but Sierra Blanca Peak looms about 1.25 miles south. A well worn route follows the crest down across a divide and back up the last steep climb to the summit. The tundra, covered with flowers in summer, is very fragile, so try to stay on the worn route rather than trampling other areas. The summit gives some of the best views in the state, from the Guadalupe Mountains of west Texas to the Sangre de Cristos above Santa Fe to the Gila Wilderness far to the west. If desired, your return route can follow some of the ski runs back down the mountain, although they can be steep.

Even though the hike is in southern New Mexico, the area above timberline can be very cold and windy even in summer. Take adequate clothes on the hike. Try to start the hike early in the morning, since summer thunderstorms build extremely quickly on the peak, especially in the afternoon. Ideally, you should be starting down the mountain after lunchtime. The area above timberline is not a good place to be caught in a lightning storm.

78 Monjeau Lookout

General description:	A moderate day hike or easy overnight trip (an easy day hike with a car shuttle) along a high ridge of the White Mountain Wilderness.
General location:	About 20 miles northwest of Ruidoso.
Length:	About 11.25 miles round trip.
Elevation:	9,120–10,460 feet.
Maps:	White Mountain Wilderness; Lincoln National Forest;Nogal Peak and Angus 7.5-minute USGS quads.
Best season:	Late May through October, depending on snow.
Water availability:	None.
Special attractions:	Aspens in fall; excellent views of the White Mountain Wilderness.

Finding the trailhead: This hike shares the same trailhead as the Sierra Blanca hike; see the directions there.

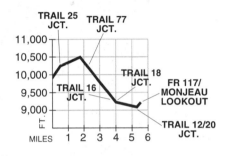

The hike: This hike follows a section of the Crest Trail from the ski area along a long scenic ridge to the access road just below the fire lookout on Monjeau Peak. The enormous stands of aspen along the hike turn the hillsides gold in October.

The trail starts at about 9,830 feet and climbs within the first 2 miles to the high point at about 10,460 feet. For the most part, the rest of the hike is a slow easy descent along the ridge to a low point of about 9,120 feet. The last 0.25 mile climbs about 200 feet up to the lookout access road, FR 117.

From the parking area, take marked Trail 15 up a creek and across a grassy hillside about 0.6 mile (although the sign says 0.5 mile) to the junction with Crest Trail 25. Turn right (north) onto Trail 25 (the Sierra Blanca hike turns left here). In a few hundred yards the trail re-enters the forest in a stand of enormous virgin spruce. It soon returns to an open grassy area and begins climbing. At the upper end of the meadow, about 0.5 mile from the Trail 15 junction, the trail forks at a junction marked only by an old fence post. Take the right (east fork), rather than switchbacking up the hill to the left. In about 50 yards the trail hits the dirt road leading up to the radio towers on Buck Mountain. Follow the road to the right (southeast) for about 50 yards, where the trail leaves the road by climbing uphill to the left. In about 100 yards, the trail hits the road again. Follow the road to the right (southeast) again for about 100 yards until the trail again forks uphill to the left, away from the road. In effect, the trail simply cuts across a large

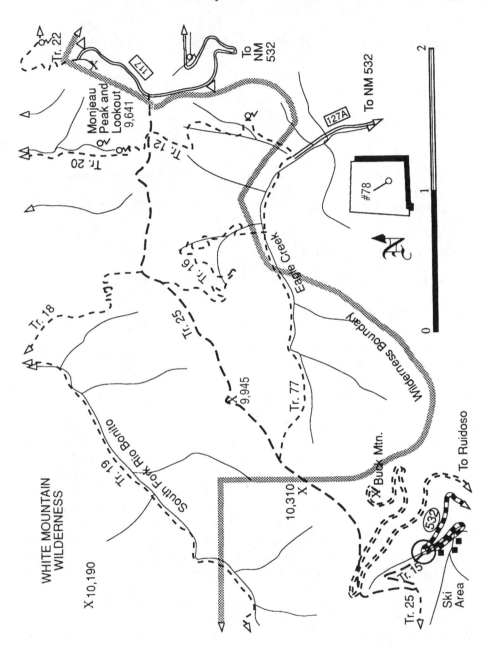

Aspens are common in the White Mountain Wilderness.

switchback in the road. The other fork at the unmarked trail junction just below the road also climbs up to the road, joining it at a different spot.

Within about 200 yards of the road, the trail reaches its high point on a forested hill and then begins the long slow descent along the ridge top to Monjeau Lookout. About 0.5 mile from the high point, the trail reaches a large, bare, windswept section of ridge with a White Mountain Wilderness boundary sign. The views are tremendous, from Nogal Peak across the Rio Bonito drainage to the distant Manzano Mountains far to the northwest.

The rest of the route is visible to the east, as it follows the alternately wooded and bare ridge all the way to the lookout. Campsites abound along the ridge top, although there are no easily accessible springs, unlike much of the rest of the Crest Trail. Since the trail does follow the ridgetop for the most part, be careful about lightning storms.

Junctions for trails 77, 16, 18, 12, and 20 will be passed, but just stay on Trail 25 along the ridgetop. At about 5.5 miles, the trail hits FR 117 after a short climb. If you have set up a car shuttle, your hike is over, otherwise return the same way. If you have time, be sure to walk up to the lookout, less than 1 mile and only a few hundred feet above you. Its 360-degree views are hard to beat.

79 Argentina Canyon

General description:	A moderately easy day hike through the high forest of the White Mountain Wilderness.
General location:	About 25 miles northwest of Ruidoso.
Length:	About 6.5 miles round trip.
Elevation:	7,800–9,100 feet.
Maps:	White Mountain Wilderness; Lincoln National Forest; Nogal Peak 7.5-minute USGS quad.
Best season:	May to mid-November.
Water availability:	Argentina Spring; Spring Cabin Spring.
Special attractions:	Lush virgin forest with running streams; tremendous views.

Finding the trailhead: Drive 10 miles south of Capitan on NM 48 and turn right (west) onto NM 37 or drive about 12 miles north of Ruidoso on NM 48 and turn left (west) onto NM 37. Follow NM 37 about 1.3 miles to the paved and marked Bonito Lake and South Fork Campground turnoff on the left (FR 107). Follow FR 107

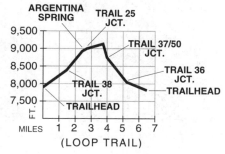

Argentina Canyon

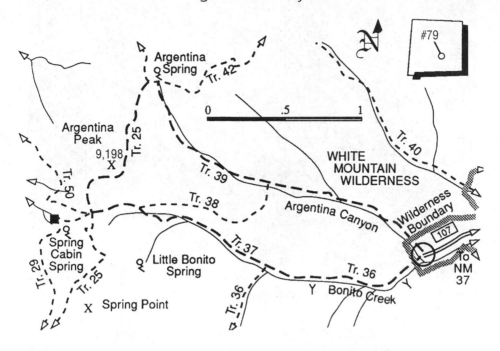

about 9 miles to the end of the road, passing Bonito Lake on the way. The road turns to gravel after the South Fork Campground turnoff. The trail starts from the large parking lot at the end of the road.

The hike: The White Mountain Wilderness is a 49,000-acre tract ranging from 6,000 to 11,500 feet in elevation. For the most part, its boundaries contain the high crest that encircles the Rio Bonito drainage. The wilderness and adjacent Sierra Blanca Peak are the highest mountains in southern New Mexico and have alpine tundra and glaciation scars from recent ice ages. The mountains' height and abrupt rise (7,800 feet of relief) from the Tularosa Valley to the west allow the mountains to trap considerable rain and snow. Thus, the mountains are blessed with many permanent springs and streams. Unlike many New Mexico mountains, quite a few springs occur along the crest of the range, limiting the need for backpackers to carry large amounts of water. This hike follows one of many possible loops along running streams to the crest of the range. The wilderness is a popular area with many hikers, especially on summer weekends.

Follow the signs on the north side of the parking lot to Argentina Canyon Trail 39. The trail climbs steadily up the canyon along a running stream for 2.5 miles to the Crest Trail, passing enormous Douglas-fir trees. In a grassy meadow at about 1.5 miles, a marked trail, Cut Across Trail 38, forks to the left. Should you desire to shorten the hike, you can follow Trail 38 to the

233

Idyllic campsites are easy to find in the White Mountain Wilderness.

Little Bonito Trail 37 and cut off the upper part of the loop. However, if possible, stay with Trail 39 so that you will not miss the tremendous views along the Crest Trail. The trail passes through a large aspen grove at the head of the canyon, beautiful in fall. A short rocky stretch brings you to marked Argentina Spring at the edge of the broad treeless crest. Get water, if necessary, from the plastic pipe at the spring. Purify it. Trail 39 joins Crest Trail 25 about 100 yards west across the grassy meadow. Trail 42 joins Trail 39 from the east at Argentina Spring. Stay with Trail 39 to the Crest Trail. The best camping in this area is probably back down Trail 39 a short distance in the aspen grove.

Turn left (south) on the Crest Trail and follow it for 1.25 miles to the next trail junction. Much of the first part of the Crest Trail is bare, giving tremendous views of the Rio Bonito drainage to the east. To the north and west, the mountains drop off sharply into the Tularosa Valley. Across the valley, with its black Malpais lava flow, lies the Sierra Oscura. Multitudes of other mountain ranges are visible on clear days.

At a grassy saddle the trail hits a well marked five-way junction. The Crest Trail continues south and makes up two of the trails. The Doherty Ridge Trail 50 goes right and drops down into the Tularosa Valley to the west. The trail that you want, 37, angles sharply left (northeast). The well worn fifth trail is the only unmarked trail. If you need water or want a good campsite, follow it southwest of the junction onto the north side of a slight ridge. In about 0.25 mile, passing good campsites as you go, the trail reaches Spring Cabin, a Forest Service cabin. Do not camp right by the cabin. If you need water, follow an unmarked trail trending southeast from the cabin for about 200 yards to Spring Cabin Spring in a draw.

From the five-way junction, Trail 37 descends steeply along flowing Little Bonito Creek for about 1.25 miles to the junction with Bonito Creek. About 0.25 mile down Trail 37, you will pass Trail 38, the Cut Across Trail, on your left.

At the junction with Bonito Creek and Bonito Trail 36, turn left on Trail 36. An easy 1.25-mile walk down Trail 36 along a rushing stream past two old mines brings you back to the trailhead.

The loop can be lengthened considerably by following the Crest Trail farther south from the five-way junction to Trail 36 and following it all the way down Bonito Creek and back to the trailhead. Another considerably longer and more strenuous loop is possible from the South Fork Campground trailhead. Follow Trail 19 to the crest and return via Trail 33. Many other loops are possible; all are beautiful with running streams and great views (see the Bonito Creek hike). A loop involving the entire crest trail would be on the order of 25 miles long.

80 Bonito Creek

General description:	A fairly strenuous day hike or overnight trip through the lush White Mountain Wilderness.
General location:	About 25 miles northwest of Ruidoso.
Length:	About 10 miles round trip.
Elevation:	7,800–10,000 feet.
Maps:	White Mountain Wilderness; Lincoln National Forest; Sierra Blanca Peak and Nogal Peak 7.5-minute USGS quads.
Best season:	May through October.
Water availability:	Bonito Creek; Aspen Canyon Creek.
Special attractions:	Views; lush forest; mountain streams; fall color.

Finding the trailhead: Drive 10 miles south of Capitan on NM 48 and turn

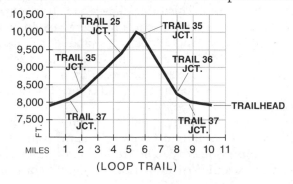

Much of the crest of the White Mountains is covered with grassy meadows.

right (west) onto NM 37 or drive about 12 miles north of Ruidoso on NM 48 and turn left (west) onto NM 37. Follow 37 about 1.3 miles to the paved and marked Bonito Lake and South Fork Campground turnoff on the left (FR 107). Follow FR 107 about 9 miles to the end of the road, passing Bonito Lake on the way. The road turns to gravel after the South Fork Campground turnoff. The trail starts from the large parking lot at the end of the road.

The hike: The White Mountain Wilderness occupies some of the highest terrain in southern New Mexico. It lies in the White Mountains, part of the Sacramentos, a large mountain range that trends north-south across a vast swath of country. The range reaches a high point just outside of the wilderness at 12,000-foot Sierra Blanca. The mountains' great height attracts copious precipitation that supports a lush forest.

Permanent streams rush down from a high, curving crest and join the eastward-flowing Rio Bonito. This hike follows one stream up to the crest, continues along the crest, and then comes back down along another creek. It makes a beautiful loop through thick forest and along rushing streams, with great views as a bonus. The Argentina Canyon hike described in this guide is another similar, but shorter and easier loop. Many of the trails in the wilderness follow streams to the crest and connect with the Crest Trail, making many different loops possible.

From the parking area, take Trail 36, the Big Bonito Trail (do not take Trail 39). The path follows Bonito Creek upstream, sometimes following what was once an old mine road. The trail enters the wilderness almost immediately and crosses the stream periodically. Crossings can usually be

Bonito Creek

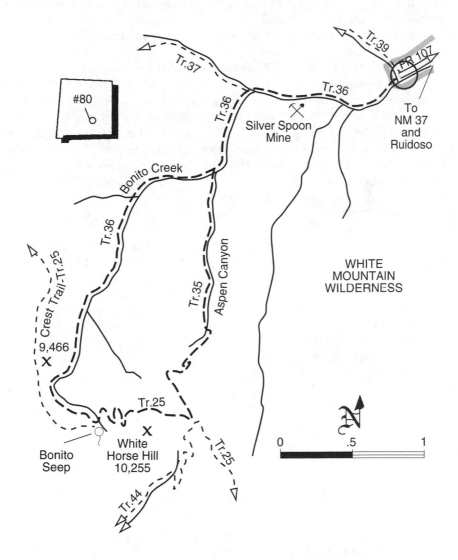

made with dry feet, but rain or snowmelt can raise water levels and make it tricky. Some side trails drop down to creekside campsites.

After about 1 mile, the trail passes the remains of the Silver Spoon Mine. It is small and probably did not put any silver spoons in anyone's mouth. In another 0.25 mile or so, the trail hits the junction with Trail 37, the Little Bonito Trail. Stay left on Trail 36. In another 0.75 mile, the trail hits the junction with Trail 35, the Aspen Trail. This will be the return leg of the loop. For now, stay right on Trail 36. From here it is a slowly steepening climb to the crest 2.75 miles away.

The stream slowly shrinks as you follow it upstream, through thick forest, including some large aspens. About 0.5 mile below the junction with Crest Trail 25, the path breaks out of the woods into a grassy basin at the headwaters of the creek. Probably the last reasonably flat campsite before climbing up onto the crest lies here in a grove of ponderosa pines along the creek.

Trail 36 reaches Crest Trail 25 at the head of the grassy valley. Here the Crest Trail is not quite on the mountain crest. Go left on the Crest Trail and you soon will be. The trail climbs steadily with large switchbacks. Lush grasses and flowers almost hide the path. Nettles sometimes grow here, which can be brutal on bare legs. If necessary, hold a poncho or jacket in front of your legs as you walk to keep from brushing them. Watch carefully for the switchbacks; one unofficial trail continues off the end of a switchback and fades out on a ridge. Without any trees here, the views get better with every step, reaching far to the west, north, and east. The lightning also gets better with every step if you get caught up here on these high, open slopes in a thunderstorm.

The trail curves around White Horse Hill, reaching the hike's high point of about 10,000 feet, and then descends a bit to a trail junction in a large, grassy saddle (with potential campsites). The views are great here. Turn left onto Trail 35, the Aspen Trail, and begin the big descent. Initially the trail crosses open meadows with more views, but it soon drops into forest. Look for a grove of interesting gnarled trees on the right just after you reach the creek. From here, the trail descends down Aspen Canyon Creek and rejoins Trail 36 at the confluence with Bonito Creek. Turn right and retrace your path back to the trailhead. For a similar, but easier loop, see the Argentina Canyon hike.

81 Sacramento Rim

General description:	An easy two- or three-day backpack following the high western rim of the Sacramento Mountains.
General location:	About 2 miles south of the center of Cloudcroft.
Length:	28 miles round trip (14 miles with car shuttle); multiple trailheads allow the hike to be shortened or lengthened as desired.
Elevation:	8,360–9,500 feet.
Maps:	Lincoln National Forest; Sacramento Peak and High Rolls 7.5-minute USGS quads.
Best season:	May through November, depending on snow.
Water availability:	None.
Special attractions:	Lush mountain forest; views.

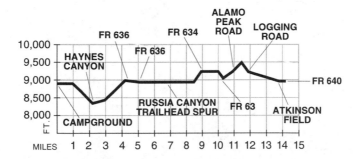

Finding the trailhead: From the center of Cloudcroft, drive 1.9 miles south on NM 130 to the junction with paved highway NM 6563 leading to Sunspot and Timberon. Turn right on it and go about 0.1 miles to Slide Campground. Park in the gravel area along the highway at the campground entrance.

The hike: The mountain range around Cloudcroft has the same name as the entire series of ranges that stretches from the Jicarilla Mountains far north of Ruidoso to a point far south of Cloudcroft. The subrange known as the Sacramento Mountains is the largest, although not highest, range and runs south from Tularosa Canyon, traversed by US 70, to near the Guadalupe Mountains at Piñon. The mountains formed as a huge fault block lifted up sharply from the floor of the Tularosa Valley. On the west, the mountains rise abruptly in two steps, with deep rugged canyons and towering cliffs of Permian and Pennsylvanian limestones. To the east, the mountains slope gradually downwards from lush fir and aspen forest to the desert scrub of the Pecos River Valley.

The crest or rim of the rugged west side lies above 9,000 feet for over 20 miles. The Rim Trail 105 follows the rim for many miles south of Cloudcroft.

Sacramento Rim

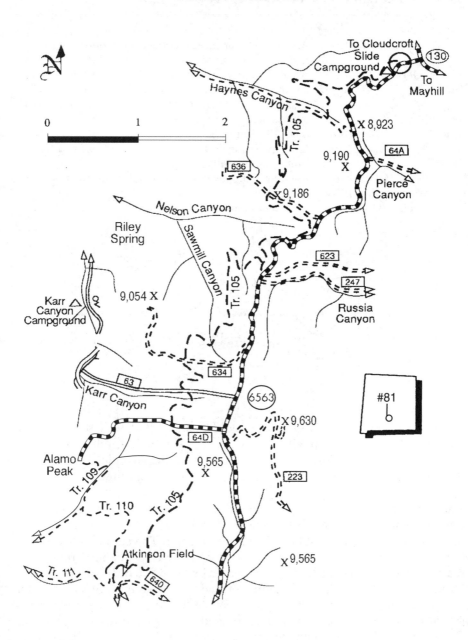

N

0   1   2

To Cloudcroft
Slide
Campground

130
To
Mayhill

Haynes Canyon

Tr. 105

X 8,923

9,190
X

64A

636

Pierce
Canyon

X 9,186

Nelson Canyon

Riley
Spring

Sawmill Canyon

Tr. 105

623

247

Russia
Canyon

Karr
Canyon
Campground

9,054 X

#81

634

63

6563

Karr Canyon

X 9,630

64D

9,565
X

223

Alamo
Peak

Tr. 109

Tr. 110

Tr. 105

Atkinson Field

X 9,565

Tr. 111

640

It was the first national forest trail in New Mexico to be designated a National Recreation Trail. The trail has some ups and downs as it crosses drainages, but in general it is a very easy, but long, trail. No good water sources exist along the route, but water caches can be easily set up in advance because of the trail's multiple access points. The trail generally parallels the highway to Sunspot, but usually lies a considerable distance to the west. Unfortunately motorcycles are permitted on the Rim Trail; weekends, especially in summer, are the most likely times for such activity.

Large signs mark the start of the popular hike at the entrance to the campground. Go left at the large Rim Trail sign, not down the gully to the right into Deer Head Campground. The trail quickly passes Slide Campground, staying not far from the highway for most of the first mile.

Just before the 1-mile point, the trail touches NM 6563, the Sunspot Highway, again, forming an alternate trailhead. After this secondary trailhead, the trail turns sharply west leaving the highway behind. The well-developed trail has mile markers for the entire 14 miles (although some have been vandalized), making it easy to determine your location.

After the 1-mile marker, the trail continues out onto the end of a long ridge, giving some of the best views of the entire hike. The Tularosa Valley stretches for miles 5,000 feet below, with the snow white dunes of White Sands easily visible. To the north, frequently snow-capped 12,000-foot Sierra Blanca towers into the sky. The trail quickly doubles back into the lush Douglas-fir, white fir, ponderosa pine, spruce, and aspen forest of the rim. At about 2.25 miles, the trail crosses the old road going down grassy Haynes Canyon. Between miles 2 and 3, the trail passes through extensive groves of bigtooth maples, known for their brilliant gold and scarlet fall color. In October, this stretch of trail can be 8 inches deep in maple, oak, and aspen leaves.

Just past mile 3, the trail crosses another small canyon with a faint trail going up and down it. The grassy canyon makes an excellent camping area. At about 4.5 miles, the trail crosses well-marked FR 636. The trail joins FR 636 at about 5.5 miles only about 50 yards from the Sunspot Highway. Follow 636 up to the highway. The trail continues on by dropping down below the highway to the right (south) in front of the stop sign. This is another good, easily found trailhead.

At about 6.75 miles the trail hits a junction in a small, open, grassy canyon bottom. Trail 105 is marked as going uphill to the left, but it only goes a short distance up to another marked trailhead on the Sunspot Highway, across from Russia Canyon. Unless you are ending your hike here, continue straight ahead on the Rim Trail, also 105.

At about 7.25 miles, a faint trail joins the main trail from a large meadow on the left, a beautiful camping area. After about the 8 mile point, excellent level campsites become more and more common. At almost 9 miles the trail crosses a well maintained logging road. The trail crosses Karr Canyon Road (FR 63) at about 10.25 miles. The junction is well marked and makes another good trailhead. If necessary, water can be obtained by walking down

Karr Canyon to a series of travertine springs. Just before the 11-mile point, the trail crosses the paved Alamo Peak road, another possible trailhead.

Just after the Alamo Peak road, the trail crosses a combined powerline and logging road. At about 11.25 miles a side trail branches off to the left. Ignore it. The trail crosses an unused old logging road just short of 12 miles. At about 13.75 miles the trail reaches a huge grassy meadow, Atkinson Field. The trail circles the meadow, remaining in the forest, and crosses FR 640 at about 14 miles, the end of this hike.

By going left, FR 640 leads back to the Sunspot Highway in about 1.4 miles. Trail 105 can be followed further, if desired.

82 Osha Trail

General description:	An easy day hike through the lush forest of the Sacramento Mountains.
General location:	About 1 mile northwest of Cloudcroft.
Length:	About 2.6 miles round trip.
Elevation:	8,420–8,740 feet.
Maps:	Osha Trail brochure; Lincoln National Forest; Cloudcroft and High Rolls 7.5-minute USGS quads.
Best season:	May through November, depending on snow.
Water availability:	None.
Special attractions:	Lush forest; views.

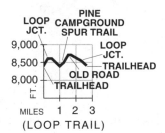

Finding the trailhead: Drive almost 1 mile west of the center of Cloudcroft on US 82 to the trailhead parking area on the right, across from the historic railroad trestle viewpoint.

The hike: The Osha Trail is an easy, popular loop hike very convenient to the high mountain town of Cloudcroft. It passes through lush forest of Douglas-fir, aspen, and pine, and offers views of White Sands and the Tularosa Valley to the west.

Be sure to take a look at the historic Mexican Canyon railroad trestle across the highway from the trailhead. Its history is described in the Cloud Climbing Rail Trail in this guide.

The Osha Trail starts climbing immediately into thick forest. Not to worry, the first 0.25 mile is the only really steep section of the hike. It levels out considerably when it reaches the start of the loop. Go left. The trail curves around a hillside and soon offers views of Cloudcroft and the highway. It then reaches a bench with views of White Sands far below.

From the viewpoint, the trail descends gradually and moves away from the highway. Traffic sounds fade away, and birds and rustling pines and aspens become the dominant noises. Here and there some unvandalized

Lush forest shades the Osha Trail.

Osha Trail

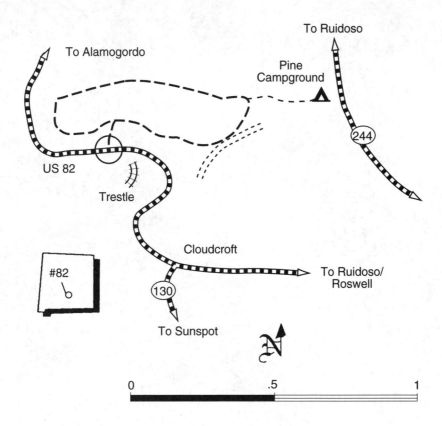

To Ruidoso

To Alamogordo

Pine
Campground

US 82

Trestle

244

Cloudcroft

#82

130

To Ruidoso/
Roswell

To Sunspot

N

0   .5   1

interpretive signs tell about the forest. In fall, maples and aspens add spots of brilliant color. The loop reaches its lowest point about a mile from the viewpoint in a small, lush canyon bottom. It then gradually climbs up the canyon to a junction with a bench. The left fork leads a short distance to Pine Campground. Take the right fork. It climbs out of the canyon bottom at a moderate grade.

The trail levels out when it hits an old dirt road. Go right on the road for about 100 yards and then turn right, as marked, back onto the trail. Cloudcroft is visible again to the left, as is the highway below. The trail slowly descends to the junction at the start of the loop. Go left and retrace your earlier steps to the trailhead.

83 Cloud Climbing Rail Trail

General description:	An easy day hike that goes to two large, historic wooden railroad trestles.
General location:	On the west side of Cloudcroft.
Length:	About 2.2 miles round trip.
Elevation:	8,680–8,320 feet.
Maps:	Trestle Recreation Area brochure; Lincoln National Forest; Cloudcroft and High Rolls 7.5-minute USGS quads.
Best season:	May through November, depending on snow.
Water availability:	Trailhead.
Special attractions:	Historic railroad trestles; views; lush forest.

Finding the trailhead: Go just west of the US 82/ NM 130 junction on the west side of Cloudcroft on US 82 to the marked, paved side road on the left. Drive up the short road to the parking area for the Trestle Recreation Area.

The hike: The Alamogordo and Sacramento Mountain Railway was built at the turn of the century to harvest timber in the heavily forested Sacramento Mountains. To build the railroad up into the mountains from the Tularosa Valley, workers constructed fifty-eight wooden trestles. This hike visits two of the most imposing bridges. Because the railroad climbed from the desert into lush, often rainy and cloudy mountains, it was often called the Cloud Climbing Railroad. The railroad reached 8,700 feet in elevation, at the time the highest standard gauge line in the world. The steep grades and sharp curves made the railroad dangerous. It was not uncommon for engines to lose control on the steep grades, jump the tracks, and plunge over the side.

The railroad did more than just allow harvest of vast amounts of lumber, it also opened up the mountains to people trying to escape the summer heat in nearby desert cities such as El Paso and Alamogordo. The Lodge at Cloudcroft was built soon after the railroad was completed, and the town began its long and continuing life as a small resort community. As taxpayer-funded roads were built and improved into the mountains, trucks began to compete with the railroad. Unable to compete with subsidized highways, the railroad ceased operations in 1947.

The hike starts at the back side of the parking lot, the opposite side from the replica of the old Cloudcroft railroad depot. A sign marked "Village Spur" indicates the start. Follow the trail about 100 feet to a junction. Go right, downhill through the woods. The trail hits the old railroad grade in less than 0.25 mile. Turn right, and follow it downhill as marked. There is a good view of White Sands from a bench by a rock cut called the Devil's

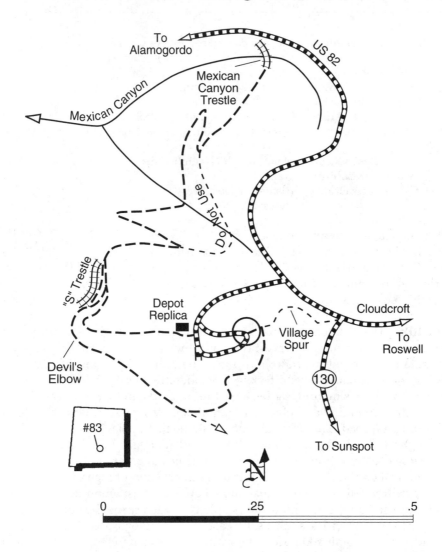

Cloud Climbing Rail Trail

To Alamogordo

US 82

Mexican Canyon Trestle

Mexican Canyon

Mexican Canyon

Do Not Use

"S" Trestle

Depot Replica

Cloudcroft

Village Spur

To Roswell

Devil's Elbow

130

#83

To Sunspot

N

0   .25   .5

Elbow by the railroad crews. It was one of many cuts built with lots of hard physical labor, draft animals, and black powder.

The trail splits just past the cut at the "S" Trestle. It has partially collapsed, but is still impressive. Built in 1899, it was the longest trestle of the railroad, with a length of 338 feet and height of 60 feet. It was unique because of its double curve, an S shape. The two trail forks rejoin in a short distance. The left fork follows the base of the trestle and gives a closer view. If you take the right fork, ignore for now a trail that cuts sharply up the hillside to the right. It will be the return route at the end of the hike.

Snow covers the historic Mexican Canyon railroad trestle.

After the two forks rejoin at the other end of the trestle, continue down the gently sloping railroad grade. Soon the grade runs into a section of private land, so the trail leaves it and descends into a small canyon below. Although the temporary detour from the grade is a nuisance, the trail does lead through a grove of enormous white firs and other trees. Surprisingly, since the logging railroad went right by them, they were not cut even though their large size indicates that they must be old growth trees. After reaching the bottom of the small canyon, the path climbs back up to the railroad grade on the other side. The trail ends soon thereafter at the impressive Mexican Canyon Trestle. Unlike the "S" Trestle, this one is largely intact and rises high above the canyon below. Although it is tempting to climb out onto it, resist the impulse. It is about a hundred years old and not very safe.

From the Mexican Canyon Trestle, retrace your route to the "S" Trestle. Go left at the fork at the trestle and then go left again at the fork mentioned earlier. It climbs steeply up the hill to an overlook of the Devil's Elbow and then ends at the depot replica at the parking lot.

84 Bluff Springs

General description:	An easy day hike along abandoned grades of the historic Cloudcroft logging railroad.
General location:	About 15 miles south of Cloudcroft.
Length:	About 5 miles round trip.
Elevation:	8,070–8,950 feet.
Maps:	Lincoln National Forest; Bluff Springs and Sacramento Peak 7.5-minute USGS quads.
Best season:	Late April through November.
Water availability:	Bluff Springs; small spring at about 1.5 miles.
Special attractions:	Waterfall; historic railroad grade; lush forest.

Finding the trailhead: Go about 1.9 miles south of Cloudcroft on NM 130 to the junction with NM 6563, the Sunspot Highway. Turn right and follow the Sunspot Highway for about 9 miles to the Bluff Springs turnoff on the left, combined FR 164 and County Road C17. Follow FR 164 down the Rio Peñasco 3.9 miles to the marked parking area at Bluff Springs. FR 164 is paved for 2 miles, then turns to gravel at the junction with the Water Canyon road on the right.

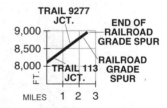

The hike: A railroad was built up into the Sacramento Mountains from the Tularosa Valley in 1898 to haul out timber from the heavily forested mountains. Excursion trains were quickly begun by people seeking to escape the summer heat, leading to the opening of the resort area at Cloudcroft in

Bluff Springs

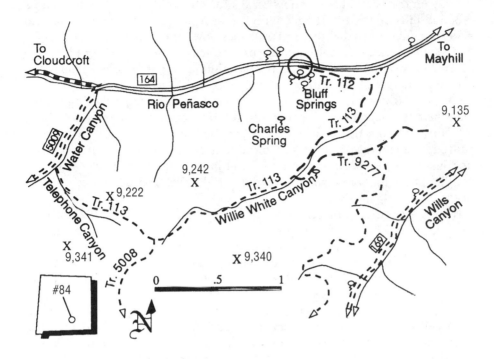

1899. The railroad was abandoned in 1947, leaving wooden trestles and railroad grades scattered across the higher parts of the mountains south of Cloudcroft. One enormous trestle still stands just west of Cloudcroft along US 82. Rotting ties and rusted railroad spikes evoke images of steam engines chugging slowly through the forest, pulling flat cars loaded with logs. The abandoned grades today make excellent trails for both hiking in summer and cross-country skiing in winter. Unfortunately, motorcycles are allowed on some of the grades.

From the parking lot, cross the footbridge over the Rio Peñasco to the railroad grade on the south river bank. The waterfall above you has formed impressive travertine deposits from calcium carbonate dissolved in the water. The main trail climbs the bluff to the top of the waterfall and the spring's source about 0.25 mile away. Be sure to take time to climb up the trail. Obtain and purify water here if you need it. The area around the waterfall is very popular in summer.

The hike, however, turns left at the base of the falls and follows the railroad grade uphill to the east. A large sign indicates the start of the hike up Trail 112, the Willie White Trail Spur. The railroad grade, Trail 112, passes several springs within a few hundred feet of the start. At about 0.25 mile, the trail passes a small, wooden railroad trestle. The railroad grade meets Trail 113 climbing up from the left at about 0.5 mile from the start.

Stay on the railroad grade, now Trail 113. The trail gradually climbs up a wooded hillside until it merges with a grassy canyon bottom at about 1.5 miles. An unmarked, lightly used trail goes down the canyon and back to FR 164. Trail 113 continues up the canyon and leaves the railroad grade.

You, however, should turn sharply back left (east) onto marked Trail 9277, the continuation of the railroad grade.

About 300 yards up Trail 9277, you pass a small spring bubbling up beside the railroad grade. The spring is small, but appears to be reliable. About 0.5 mile up from the Trail 9277/113 junction, an unused and overgrown railroad grade forks sharply back to the right (west). Explore it, if you wish, and leave the people behind. A little less than 1 mile up Trail 9277 from the trail junction, the trail turns sharply back right (west) onto another railroad grade.

Instead, continue east on the same railroad grade for about 0.25 mile to its end. A very faint, old road leads up the hill to the right from the end of the railroad grade. You reach the top of the ridge in 100 yards or so, with level pine needle-covered potential campsites all around. Be very careful once you leave the railroad grades. With no clear landmarks, it is easy to get lost in the dense forest.

Many hikes are possible along the railroad grades. Many spurs lead off of the main lines to old logging camp sites. Trail 9277 can be followed considerably farther. Trail 113 can be followed up over the mountain to the Water Canyon road (FR 5009) and back down FR 164 for an easy 7.2-mile loop.

85 Dog Canyon

General description: A strenuous day hike from the Tularosa Valley up into the Sacramento Mountains.

General location: About 15 miles south of Alamogordo.

Length: About 8.4 miles round trip.

Elevation: 4,400–7,550 feet.

Maps: Lincoln National Forest; Sacramento Peak, Deadman Canyon, and Alamogordo South 7.5-minute USGS quads; Dog Canyon Trail leaflet (Forest Service).

Best season: All year.

Water availability: Dog Canyon stream at 2.4 miles.

Special attractions: Desert stream; rugged canyon; views.

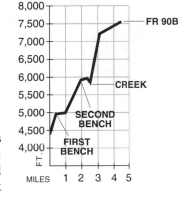

Finding the trailhead: Drive about 10 miles south of Alamogordo on US 54. Turn left (east) on the marked road to Oliver Lee Memorial State Park and drive about 4 miles to the park visitor center.

The hike: Dog Canyon is one of several canyons in the steep western escarpment of the Sacramento Mountains. The rugged west face of the mountains rises more than 5,000 feet within a few miles from the Chihuahuan Desert of the Tularosa Valley to the lush Canadian Zone forest of the crest. The Dog Canyon Trail climbs over 3,100 feet in only 4.2 miles, making it a difficult hike, especially in summer.

Because of the reliable, spring-fed stream in the canyon, the trail has been used for thousands of years as a route from the Tularosa Valley into the Sacramento Mountains. After arrival of the white man, the trail was used as a route of retreat by Apaches fleeing military forces. Many battles were fought in the canyon between Apaches and troops from 1850 to 1881. In 1880, sixty soldiers pursued old Chief Nana and his warriors into the canyon. When the troops were on the "Eyebrow," the steep upper portion of the trail, the Indians rolled rocks onto them, killing and injuring many.

The marked trail (106) starts at the foot of the mountains near the visitor center in the state park. Camping with showers is available in the park. The first 0.4 mile is a steep climb up the mountain slope. The hillside is very susceptible to erosion; try to resist the urge to shortcut the trail. Desert vegetation, such as ocotillo, agave, creosote, and prickly pear, dominate the first 2 miles of trail. Little shade exists.

Dog Canyon

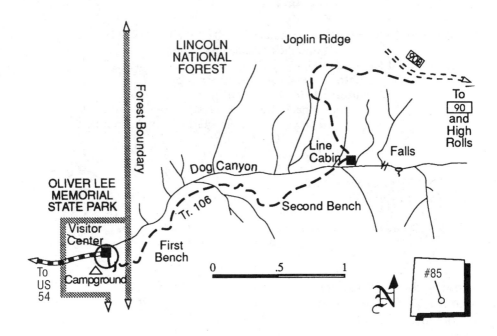

Upon reaching the first bench at about 0.4 mile, the grade moderates somewhat. Sheer walls of limestone, dolomite, and sandstone tower 1,500 feet above the bench. Below the trail on the left, the creek tumbles down in a smaller inner canyon. Views of White Sands open up to the west. The trail climbs steadily, reaching the second bench after about 2 miles.

The vegetation slowly changes. The level second bench is thickly covered with grasses, such as black gramma, sideoats gramma, and tobosa, and a few scattered alligator junipers. The bench makes one of the best camping areas on the hike.

The trail descends a short distance from the end of the bench to the lush riparian zone of the creek. The stream cascades down into pools under the spreading branches of large cottonwoods and willows. A very rough 0.5-mile bushwhack upstream leads the perservering hiker to a high waterfall pouring off the box at the head of the canyon. The old stone line cabin at the creek dates from the turn of the century.

Do not camp near the stream; the area is too small and delicate for such heavy use. Purify any water taken from the creek. At 2.4 miles and an elevation gain of 1,500 feet, the creek makes an excellent destination in itself.

The trail becomes very steep for the next 0.7 mile, gaining about 1,000 feet as it climbs out of the canyon up the "Eyebrow." The views, especially at sunset, from the canyon rim are spectacular. Once out of the canyon, the trail climbs at a more moderate grade the last mile or so through pinyon-juniper woodland to its end at FR 90B. The trail can be done as a one-way hike if a car shuttle is arranged in advance. A high-clearance vehicle is recommended for the forest road.

86 Yucca Canyon

General description: A moderate day hike or easy overnight trip into the Carlsbad Caverns Wilderness with views of rugged Slaughter Canyon.

General location: Carlsbad Caverns National Park.

Length: About 5.5 miles round trip.

Elevation: 4,550–6,000 feet.

Maps: Grapevine Draw and Gunsight Canyon 7.5-minute USGS quads.

Best season: All year.

Water availability: Longview Spring; usually Dog Pen Seep.

Special attractions: Spectacular views; solitude

Permit: Required for camping; obtain at park headquarters.

Finding the trailhead: Follow the same directions as for Hike 87. However, rather than following the directions all the way to the parking lot at the end of the road, stop about 1 mile short at the fenced and marked park boundary (where the pavement ends). Turn left (west) on the small dirt road that follows the fence line just inside the park. You will reach the Yucca Canyon parking lot in about 2 miles at the end of the road. A high clear-

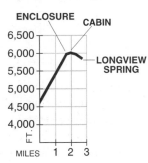

ance vehicle is preferable for this road, but, with care, a sedan can probably make it. Beware the shrubs that try to remove your vehicle's paint.

The hike: The Guadalupe Mountains form a very steep escarpment on the east flank that rises steadily to the south, reaching the highest point, 8,749 feet, in Guadalupe Mountains National Park. Carlsbad Caverns National Park follows the middle section of the escarpment, with escarpment elevations of about 4,000 feet in the northeast section of the park rising to 6,500 feet in the southwest section of the park. At the park visitor center the escarpment rises 800 feet above the valley floor. At Yucca Canyon the relief has increased to 2,000 feet.

Most visitors to the park see only the Chihuahuan desert at Carlsbad Caverns or New Cave. However, the higher southwestern end of the park

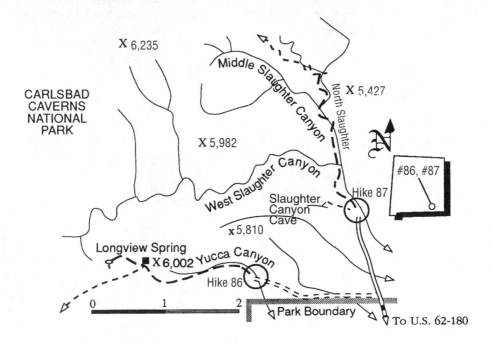

adjoins Lincoln National Forest and is partially wooded with pinyon pine, alligator juniper, Gambel's oak, and even some ponderosa pine and bigtooth maple. Since almost no one hikes into the park's backcountry, you probably will have Yucca Canyon all to yourself.

From the parking lot, the trail follows the canyon bottom with a steady grade all the way to the top of the escarpment. The trail is generally in good condition and easy to follow. For the most part, the trail lies on the south side of the canyon bottom, but occasionally crosses to the north side. As you climb higher, a few junipers and madrones begin to appear, cacti start to give way to grasses.

The trail reaches the top abruptly, giving dramatic views northeast and southwest of the Guadalupe Mountains' steep escarpment. The trail runs into a large, fenced study enclosure, built to study plant growth without deer browsing.

Follow the trail along the south fence of the enclosure to the west corner. Turn right at the corner and follow the trail along the west fence of the enclosure to the ruins of an old cabin. The cabin is about 2 miles from the trailhead. The faint, cairn-marked trail leading west from the fenced enclosure's west corner is a long, but scenic, route up into the Lincoln National Forest.

Gnarled alligator juniper, smooth reddish-barked madrones, and stunted pinyon pines grow in contrast to the desert below. Even a few scattered ponderosa pines eke out a living on the relatively level escarpment crest.

The trail to Longview Spring, marked by rock cairns, runs west from the old cabin. The trail slowly curves right as it drops into a shallow grassy draw. The old walls of a corral mark Dog Pen Seep. Just beyond the walls, on the north side of the draw, water drips over a ledge. Except in dry years, water is usually available here.

The trail continues past the seep down the draw. As the draw gets deeper, the trail moves onto a wide ledge on the south side above the bottom of the draw. Soon you reach the mouth of the draw, where it joins a much larger and deeper canyon. Continue to follow the trail along the ledge as it turns left. Some rusted farm implements signal that the spring is just ahead in a lush green patch of vegetation. Cool water trickles out of a broken pipe and from another terrace below. Longview Spring is nearly always reliable, but in especially dry years ask at park headquarters for an update on its condition.

From the spring, the heart of the Carlsbad Caverns Wilderness is spread out before you. The broad ledges of the spring look out on an incredible view of rugged West Slaughter Canyon more than 1,000 feet below. The sheer cliffs and steep slopes look virtually impassable. Ponderosa pines and bigtooth maples cling to ledges on the moister north-facing slopes underneath you.

If you camp, be sure to obtain a permit at park headquarters beforehand. The areas near the two springs and the patchy woodland around the cabin have many ideal campsites. So that wildlife may drink, be sure to camp at least 100 yards from the springs. Ground fires are not permitted in the park because of the high risk of wildfire.

The hike can be easily done in a day, but plan to stay overnight to allow time to explore the ridgetops overlooking the escarpment and the canyons. Get an early start in summer since it can be hot. Occasional snow storms blow through in winter and spring can be windy, but the hike is enjoyable all year.

87 North Slaughter Canyon

See Map on Page 254

General description:	A moderate day hike into the Carlsbad CavernsWilderness.
General location:	Carlsbad Caverns National Park.
Length:	About 6 miles round trip.
Elevation:	4,200–4,700 feet.
Maps:	Serpentine Bends and Grapevine Draw 7.5-minute USGS quads.
Best season:	Fall through spring.
Water availability:	None.
Special attractions:	Rugged desert canyon; large cave; solitude.

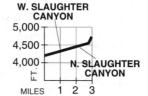

Finding the trailhead: Drive 5 miles south of White's City (25 miles south of Carlsbad) on US 62-180 to the paved turnoff marked by the Park Service as the route to Slaughter Canyon Cave. Turn and follow the Park Service signs 11 more miles to the Slaughter Canyon Cave parking lot in the wide mouth of Slaughter Canyon.

The hike: The Guadalupe Mountains of New Mexico and Texas form one of three exposures of the fossilized Capitan Reef, the world's largest. The other two exposures, also uplifted by faults, are the Apache and Glass Mountains far to the south in West Texas. Slaughter Canyon is the largest drainage contained largely within Carlsbad Caverns National Park. Its rugged defile cuts a 1,400-foot deep gash in the mountains.

Much of the Guadalupe Mountains' fame comes from massive limestone caves, especially Carlsbad Cavern. The Capitan Reef formed as an homogenous mass, rather than in thin layers, allowing the formation of enormous rooms and passages. Thin layers do not have sufficient structural strength to form large roof spans. For years, scientists believed that the Guadalupe caves were formed, as in most areas, by the dissolving action of carbon dioxide dissolved in rainwater (carbonic acid). Recent research, however, indicates that some of the large caves formed instead by the dissolving action of sulfuric acid, created from hydrogen sulfide gas. The gas, which also gives rotten eggs their smell, comes from the natural seepage of oil and gas reservoirs, common in the area.

From the parking lot, follow the signs marked "Middle Slaughter Canyon" up the bottom of the canyon. Do not take the Slaughter Canyon Cave trail. For the first few hundred yards, the trail follows the dry white cobble bottom of the broad canyon floor. Follow the rock cairns when the trail is not obvious. It soon climbs up the left bank onto the remains of an old road. The trail follows the old road for about 0.5 mile.

Chihuahuan Desert vegetation dominates the hike, with lechuguilla, sotol, cholla, and other desert plants common. You are unlikely to see anyone else on your hike.

Just after the old road re-enters the broad canyon wash, a very large tributary, West Slaughter Canyon, joins the main canyon from the left. Continue to follow the rock cairns into the north fork of the canyon, rather than turning left into the west fork. After several hundred yards of crossing the white cobble bottom, the trail climbs back onto a low bench on the left, or west, side of North Slaughter Canyon. About 0.5 mile farther, the trail again crosses the canyon floor to the site of an old homestead on a grassy bench on the east side. Not much more than a few corral posts and rusty tin cans remain.

Continue up the canyon back into the dry wash bottom. A short distance up the wash, the canyon forks again. Take the right fork into North Slaughter Canyon, following the cairns. Right after the fork, the trail climbs up onto the left-hand bench for a short distance, but drops back into the wash again. The trail sometimes climbs back up onto the benches, but, because the north fork is much narrower and more winding, much of the rest of the route stays in the wash bottom. In the narrower canyon, you will begin to see a few oak trees and even an occasional bigtooth maple. The higher and more lush McKittrick Canyon to the south in Guadalupe Mountains National Park is famous for the brilliant fall color of its many maples.

At the next canyon junction, the trail will be on the left-hand, or west bench, as it turns into the left canyon fork. The hike ends here, but if you feel energetic, continue up the trail as it climbs out of the canyon and onto Guadalupe Ridge. The hike can be extended for miles either northeast or southwest along the old road that follows Guadalupe Ridge. To the southwest, the old road climbs higher into the mountains and eventually enters the Lincoln National Forest. To the northeast, the old road heads back toward the main park visitor center. Both are very long, remote hikes, so go prepared with good maps and adequate water and provisions if you attempt them. The rewards are tremendous views of rugged country and lots of solitude.

The return trip follows the same route. Particularly in the wide lower part of the canyon, it is possible to shorten the hike slightly by walking straight down the wash bottom, rather than following the trail on the low benches. However, the benches are much easier to walk on than the rocky, cobbly wash and thus are quicker. The hike can be done in summer, but is very hot, with little shade. Occasional snow storms quickly blow through in winter and spring can be windy, making fall the best season for the hike.

Goat Cave lies a short distance off the route of this hike. The cave is not heavily decorated, but is impressive because of its size. It consists largely of a long, straight passage over 0.25 mile long. Light shines down from a window high in the ceiling. To enter the cave, you must obtain a permit from the Park Service. If you decide to visit the cave, the park will give you directions to it when you get your permit. With only one short side passage, you can't get lost, but be sure that each member of your group takes three sources of light and wears a hard hat. Do not enter the cave alone. Walk lightly in the entrance; it is very dusty.

88 Sitting Bull Falls

General description:	An easy day hike to one of the few flowing streams in the Guadalupe Mountains.
General location:	About 45 miles southwest of Carlsbad.
Length:	About 0.5 mile round trip to falls; about 2.5 miles round trip to spring.
Elevation:	4,650–5,000 feet.
Maps:	Lincoln National Forest—Guadalupe District; Red Bluff Draw and Queen 7.5-minute USGS quads.
Best season:	All year.
Water availability:	Trailhead; Sitting Bull Creek.
Special attractions:	One of the largest waterfalls in New Mexico.

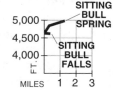

Finding the trailhead: Drive 12 miles north from Carlsbad on US 285 to the junction of NM 137. Turn and follow NM 137 about 25 miles southwest to the marked turnoff (Forest Road 276) to Sitting Bull Falls. Drive 8 miles to the parking lot at the end of the road. The falls are well known and are even shown on many state highway maps.

The hike: Depending on rainfall, you may drive across the running stream a couple of times before you reach the parking lot. A large developed picnic area, with restrooms and running water, flanks the parking area. The area is very popular and crowded on summer and holiday weekends. Try to visit on weekdays, ideally before Memorial Day or after Labor Day. The trails follow the stream but the area receives heavy use, making water purification very necessary. Although there is water at the picnic area, the Forest Service recommends that it be purified before use. It is probably best just to bring some with you.

The water of the 130-foot falls is highly mineralized and has deposited a massive travertine bluff that towers over the picnic ground. The size of the travertine deposit indicates that the falls may have been much bigger in times past.

The hike is split into two parts. Follow the trail southeast through the picnic area a few hundred yards to the falls. The falls pour off of an overhanging travertine bluff high above in a sparkling quicksilver shower. People often swim in the pools at the base of the falls. The permanent water in the

Sitting Bull Falls

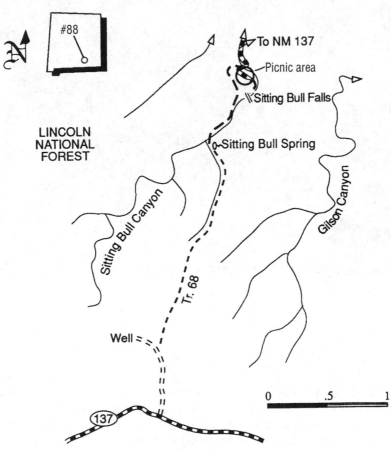

dry semi-desert foothills of the Guadalupe Mountains creates an oasis of ash, sawgrass, walnut, chinkapin oak, madrone, and even ponderosa pine. Maidenhair ferns cling to crevices in the wet travertine and flowers are abundant.

The area has received considerable damage from heavy visitation. Try to avoid additional damage by staying on the trail and off of the delicate vegetation. Even with the heavy use, however, the falls and stream are very beautiful and unlike any other area in New Mexico.

To reach Sitting Bull Spring, take the marked trail (68) from the opposite side of the parking area from the falls trail. The trail quickly climbs the 200 feet up to the small plateau at the top of the falls. The trail reaches the creek in about 0.5 mile. A short side trip downstream to the top of the falls is worthwhile. The creek flows through several deep pools before reaching the falls. Again, please be careful not to damage the delicate vegetation and travertine. The area is already heavily trampled and criss-crossed by trails.

A hiker follows the creek below Sitting Bull Falls.

Be careful at the top of the falls; people have died by falling off the slippery cliff.

Upstream, the trail continues for another 0.75 mile to the spring, enclosed by the Forest Service. Along the way you will pass more lush riparian vegetation and a rushing stream with many deep pools. The trail can be followed for about another 2.5 miles past the spring to the continuation of NM 137, but the most scenic part is between the spring and the falls. One reward for going further, however, will be the lack of people. Less than 1 mile beyond the spring, the trail climbs out onto the canyon rim, giving good views of the surrounding country.

The Forest Service does not allow camping at the falls or picnic area, but does allow it above the falls. Try to resist the temptation to camp along the heavily used stream area and set up camp well away from the watercourse.

89 Guadalupe Ridge

General description: A moderate to strenuous day hike or easy overnight trip along a little-travelled, high ridge of the Guadalupe Mountains.

General location: About 60 miles southwest of Carlsbad.

Length: About 11.5 miles round trip (5.75 miles with car shuttle).

Elevation: 6,780–7,010 feet.

Maps: Lincoln National Forest—Guadalupe District; El Paso Gap and Gunsight Canyon 7.5-minute USGS quads.

Best season: All year.

Water availability: None.

Special attractions: Views; solitude.

Finding the trailhead: Drive about 12 miles northwest of Carlsbad on US 285 to the NM 137 junction. Turn left (southwest) and follow paved NM 137 about 41.5 miles to the well marked junction with FR 540, the Guadalupe Ridge Road. Turn left onto good gravel road FR 540 and follow it about 4.4 miles to the junction with FR 69 at Klondike Gap. Turn left onto FR 69 and follow it 2.3 miles down into Dark Canyon to the junction with FR 69A. FR 69 can get rough where it crosses the (usually) dry wash in the canyon bottom. With care, a sedan can sometimes cross the wash and do the rest of the steep drive to the trailhead. However, a high-clearance vehicle is sometimes necessary. Check with the Forest Service ahead of time for road conditions. Turn right onto FR 69A and climb up out of the canyon 2.3 miles to marked Trail 201 on the right. Parking here is tight—but you probably will not have to fight for it. Be sure not to block Trail 201; it is an old road that is still occasionally used by brave four-wheel-drive enthusiasts.

For a car shuttle (or easier drive if you have a sedan), drive to the other trailhead first and drop a car. Instead of turning onto FR 69 at Klondike Gap, follow FR 540 another 7.3 miles to its end in a large parking area. From the parking area, two primitive roads take off. The proper one is the left-hand (north) one, marked with a FR 70 sign (maps show it as FR 307). The right-hand road is marked with a Trail 201 sign, but it is another section of Trail 201 and not part of this hike.

The hike: This hike follows an old road that is so rough in places only a few sadistic four-wheel-drive owners inflict it upon their vehicles. I did the hike on a summer weekend and saw no one. The only time the route is likely to have even a few people is during deer hunting season.

The hike can be hot in midday in summer and is exposed to lightning on

Guadalupe Ridge

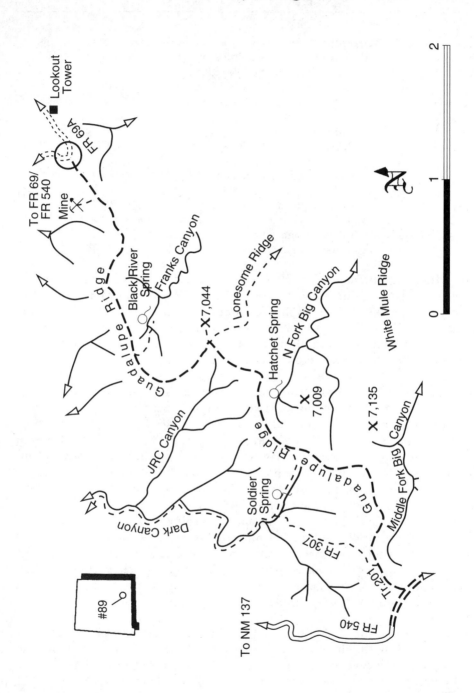

much of its route during storms. Winter storms are relatively uncommon; snow melts off quickly. There are several springs down below and off the trail. However, they can be difficult to find, so plan to carry enough water.

The trail follows part of the backbone of the Guadalupe Mountains from Dark Canyon Lookout to the end of FR 540. Drainages on the right (west) flow into Dark Canyon and eventually into the Pecos River at Carlsbad. Those on the left flow into a number of rugged canyons that cut deeply into the eastern escarpment of the mountains. This hike offers great views and usually lots of solitude. It travels through mostly pinyon-juniper woodland, with some ponderosa pine and even a few Douglas-firs and southwestern white pines. The Guadalupe Mountains are a large, wedge-shaped range with the southern and highest point poking down into Texas at Guadalupe Mountains National Park. The mountains originally formed as a large reef millions of years ago when the area was inundated with a shallow sea. Time, heat, and pressure transformed much of the ocean and reef deposits into limestone, famous today for its caves.

From the trailhead on FR 69A, the trail/old road starts down across a saddle through scattered pinyon-juniper. Ignore the short spur road on the right that goes to an old mine. The main road then climbs gradually back up onto another ridge past some ponderosa pines and even a few bigtooth maples that are beautiful in the fall. The trail tops out in about 1 mile and then reaches a metal cattle tank in another 0.5 mile or so. Another metal tank is visible across the canyon to the south. The old road descends down off the ridge and passes through a fence soon after passing the trail-side tank.

The trail then gently climbs up along another ridge and soon hits an unmarked junction. Go right and remain on Trail 201. According to the topographic map, the left fork drops down to Black River Spring and possibly the water tank visible across the canyon earlier.

The trail continues along ridgetops, following the drainage divide. In a flat, grassy area there are a number of hunter campsites visible, along with two stone rings, or middens. The middens were used by Indians to cook agave hearts. Please do not disturb the sites or remove any artifacts (although it is unlikely that there are any left).

From the campsite area, the trail climbs relatively steadily to an unmarked junction with three possible forks. Go right, onto the least-worn route. One of the others heads out onto Lonesome Ridge and becomes Trail 56. It is a nice detour with great views down into Big and Black canyons and far out onto the plains of eastern New Mexico and West Texas.

The rough right fork descends onto a saddle wooded with ponderosa pines, passes a fallen Trail 201 sign, and then climbs fairly steeply up onto another ridge. The trail continues along the ridgetops with occasional views of deep canyons to the east and FR 540, the Guadalupe Ridge Road, far across wooded upper Dark Canyon to the west. The road stays very rocky and impassible to all but the best four-wheel-drive vehicles and drivers. Somewhere in here a trail forks off to the right to Soldier Spring, but I did not see it.

After reaching a particularly high ridgetop, the trail passes through a recent forest fire that was largely beneficial. It did not kill the majority of trees, just cleared out downed fuel and brush. Another older and much larger fire has been visible off and on to the east. Unfortunately, it was a very hot fire that burned off most of the forest. In these dry mountains it may be centuries before that area recovers, if ever.

The old road finally improves modestly and some evidence appears of occasional use by vehicles. You pass another fallen Trail 201 sign and soon hit the junction with FR 307. Go left, uphill, about 0.25 mile to this hike's end at the end of FR 540.

90 Big Canyon

General description:	An easy day hike onto a promontory overlooking the fork between the three main branches of Big Canyon.
General location:	About 65 miles southwest of Carlsbad.
Length:	About 4 miles round trip.
Elevation:	7,250–6,800 ft.
Maps:	Lincoln National Forest/Guadalupe District; Guadalupe Mountains National Park Trails Illustrated topo map; El Paso Gap 7.5-minute USGS quad.
Best season:	All year.
Water availability:	None.
Special attractions:	Tremendous views of rugged country.

Finding the trailhead: Drive about 12 miles northwest of Carlsbad on US 285 to the NM 137 junction. Turn left (southwest) and follow paved NM 137 about 41.5 miles to the well marked junction with Forest Road 540, the Guadalupe Ridge Road. Turn left onto the good gravel road FR 540 and follow it just over 12 miles to the

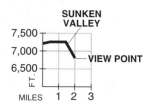

end of the improved gravel surface in a parking area. Two dirt roads depart from the parking lot. Follow the better road to the right (south), marked with a Guadalupe Ridge Trail 201 sign. Ignore the bad road forking to the right at 0.3 mile and drive 0.8 mile further to a fork on the top of a ridge. The fork, marked as an unmaintained primitive road, is the trail. With care, any vehicle should be able to make the last rough 1.1 miles to the fork without any problem.

The hike: The trail ends on a point overlooking one of the deepest and most rugged canyons in the Guadalupe Mountains. The canyon cuts through 1,800 feet of rock at the mouth, including the fossil Capitan Reef. The limestone reef, largest in the world, contains many caves, including the famous Carlsbad

Big Canyon • Camp Wilderness Ridge

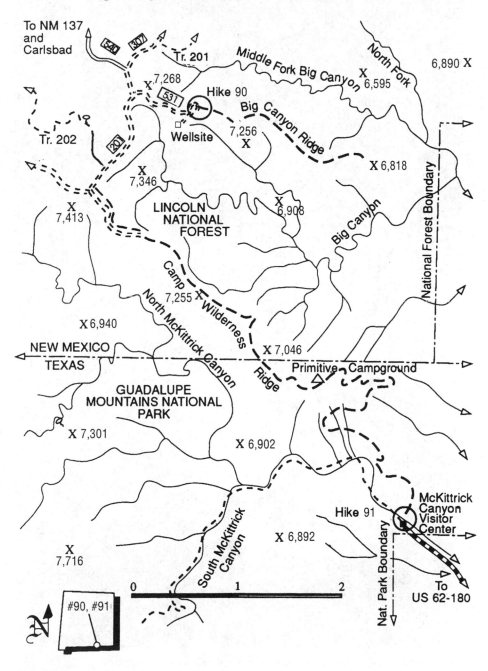

To NM 137 and Carlsbad

340 307

Tr. 201

Middle Fork Big Canyon

North Fork

6,890 X

X 7,268

531

Hike 90

TH

X 6,595

Big Canyon Ridge

Tr. 202

201

Wellsite

7,256 X

X 6,818

X 7,346

LINCOLN NATIONAL FOREST

X 6,908

X 6,818

Big Canyon

National Forest Boundary

X 7,413

Camp Wilderness

7,255 X

NEW MEXICO
TEXAS

X 6,940

North McKittrick Canyon

Ridge

X 7,046

Primitive Campground

GUADALUPE MOUNTAINS NATIONAL PARK

X 7,301

X 6,902

South McKittrick Canyon

Hike 91

McKittrick Canyon Visitor Center

X 6,892

Nat. Park Boundary

X 7,716

0   1   2

To US 62-180

#90, #91

N

Vultures roost before an impending thunderstorm in the Guadalupe Mountains near Big Canyon.

Cavern. The trail follows a wooded ridge with only slight ups and downs along the way. Be sure to be careful with campfires and cigarettes. Several big fires in the early and mid-1990s burned large areas here and in adjoining Guadalupe Mountains National Park. These mountains are very dry and the relict forest barely hangs on to life. Where it has been burned, it may never recover. Although fires have destroyed parts of the forest, hikes in these mountains are still beautiful.

This trail is good any time of year. Snow falls occasionally in winter, but melts quickly. Spring is probably the least desirable season, with frequent strong winds.

The trail starts east along the primitive road in a forest of alligator juniper, pinyon pine, and stunted ponderosa pine. Here and there views open up to the north and south into different forks of Big Canyon. Although there is considerable ponderosa pine on the tops of the Guadalupe Mountains, most of it is stunted by the marginal rainfall. In more sheltered canyons and slopes, the ponderosa pines thrive, along with scattered Douglas-firs and even a few aspens.

The first 0.5 mile or so can be driven by four-wheel drive vehicles, but is very rocky. The primitive road formally ends at a parking area overlooking a southern view into a fork of Big Canyon. Unfortunately, since I first started going there, off-road vehicles have beaten in a rough road for most of the rest of the hike on what used to be the trail. Resist the impulse to drive it yourself. The road has destroyed much of the trees and vegetation and even runs directly over an archaeological site. The Forest Service has not tried to stop the use of the road. Write them and complain.

Even with the road, the hike is still spectacular. Continue down the road through the woods. At about 1.5 miles the road peters out above a beautiful sunken valley cut into the rim of the main canyon below. With a grassy bottom and scattered ponderosa pines, the sheltered valley makes an ideal camping spot. The small narrow valley, with its 20-foot walls, was probably created when an large, long cave collapsed. The floor of Big Canyon lies 1,800 precipitous feet below. Follow a faint trail another 0.5 mile east out to a prominent point overlooking the fork between the three main branches of the canyon. The view, especially at sunrise or sunset, is hard to beat.

91 Camp Wilderness Ridge

See Map on Page 265

General description: A strenuous, but spectacular, overnight hike from Texas into New Mexico.

General location: About 55 miles southwest of Carlsbad.

Length: About 15 miles round trip.

Elevation: 5,000–7,410 feet.

Maps: Guadalupe Mountains National Park Trails Illustrated topo map, Lincoln National Forest—Guadalupe District; El Paso Gap, Guadalupe Peak, and Independence Spring 7.5-minute USGS quads.

Best season: All year.

Water availability: Trailhead.

Special attractions: Rugged canyons; views.

Permit: Required for overnight camping; obtain at Guadalupe Mountains National Park visitor center.

Finding the trailhead: Drive south from Carlsbad on US 62-180 into Texas to the Guadalupe Mountains National Park—McKittrick Canyon turnoff. Turn right onto the paved, well marked road and follow it about 4.5 miles to the parking lot and information station at the end of the road.

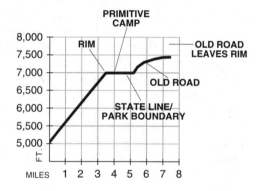

The hike: The trail starts in the mouth of McKittrick Canyon at the Park Service information station. From there, the trail climbs up the north wall of the canyon and crosses into the Lincoln National Forest of New Mexico. McKittrick Canyon is famous for its permanent stream and fall display of bigtooth maples. Be sure to fill up water bottles at the information station because there is no water on the canyon rim.

From the information station, follow the signs for the Permian Reef Geology Trail, rather than those pointing up the canyon. The trail quickly crosses the broad dry wash of the canyon and begins climbing up a bench on the other side. With a series of large switchbacks, the trail steadily climbs the 2,000 feet up to the canyon rim. The trail climbs the south-facing wall of the canyon and is hot in summer. Because of the solar exposure, desert vegetation dominates until the trail reaches the rim at about 7,000 feet.

As the trail climbs, it crosses the limestone heart of the ancient Capitan Reef. Fossils abound in the broken rock along the trail, but since this is a national park be sure to leave them in place. The trail is a favorite of geology students from much of the Southwest.

Upon reaching the rim at about 3.5 miles, the trail abruptly levels out. Tremendous views open up of the rugged McKittrick watershed and of the plains stretching endlessly to the southeast. The rest of the trail consists of only mild ups and downs as it follows the rim of North McKittrick Canyon into New Mexico. The vegetation changes radically at the rim, from prickly pear, sotol, catclaw, and other desert plants to grassy meadows with pinyon and ponderosa pine and alligator juniper.

A little more than 0.5 mile from the rim, the trail reaches the designated Park Service campsite. To camp here you need to have obtained a permit from the Park Service. A short distance further, in the Lincoln National Forest, no permit is necessary. However, if you plan to leave your vehicle overnight in the McKittrick Canyon parking lot, you must inform the Park Service beforehand, since they lock the gate at the highway at night.

About 0.6 mile past the Park Service campsite, the trail crosses a fence into the Lincoln National Forest of New Mexico. The trail follows the canyon rim northwest for about 1.25 miles from the state line, where the trail turns into an extremely rough four-wheel-drive road. Continue along the road for another 1.6 miles to the end of this hike. At this point the road turns north and leaves the canyon rim.

About 50 yards down from the rim, the road splits. The left fork continues across the mountaintop for a short distance before turning into a trail. The right fork leads to another access point as described below.

Taking the trail just up to the rim and back makes a good, although strenuous day hike. To halve the hike, a car shuttle is possible. Follow the directions for finding the Big Canyon hike trailhead. Instead of going 1.1 miles from the gravel parking lot described, go only 0.3 mile to the "bad road" described as forking off to the right. Unless you have a four-wheel-drive vehicle, park at the fork and walk 1.2 miles along the "bad road" to the junction at the canyon rim described in the paragraph above. Ignore the right fork (Forest Road 202) encountered at 0.8 mile. Even with a four-wheel-drive, the road is extremely rocky and difficult to drive on. The stretch of road along the canyon rim becomes almost impassable. Walking is recommended. The hike is much easier to do in reverse, if you have a car shuttle waiting at the McKittrick Canyon parking lot.

Anytime of year is good for hiking in the Guadalupes. Be prepared for occasional snows in winter and thunderstorms in late summer. The Guadalupes are notorious for their winds in spring. I have nearly been blown off the tops of the mountains in April. Fall is probably the ideal season, although the bottom of McKittrick Canyon is very busy with hikers on fall color weekends in late October.

Appendix A: Hiker Checklist

Most hikers realize the importance of a good checklist once they are on the trail: what you have forgotten to pack may turn out to be only an inconvenience, or may pose a serious problem. A good checklist will help you remember the essentials.

The list below is only a suggested list. Use it to create your own, based on the nature of your hike and personal needs. Items will vary depending on whether you are day hiking or backpacking into remote country. If you are carrying supplies on your back, select items judiciously, with weight in mind.

Clothing
- [ ] dependable rain parka
- [ ] wind-resistant jacket
- [ ] wetsuit (for canyon wading in cold weather)
- [ ] thermal underwear
- [ ] shorts
- [ ] long pants
- [ ] cap or hat
- [ ] wool shirt or sweater
- [ ] warm jacket
- [ ] extra socks
- [ ] underwear
- [ ] lightweight shirts
- [ ] T-shirts
- [ ] wool gloves

Footwear
- [ ] comfortable hiking boots
- [ ] lightweight camp shoes
- [ ] aqua shoes or sandals

Bedding
- [ ] sleeping bag
- [ ] foam pad or air mattress
- [ ] pillow (deflating)
- [ ] ground cloth (plastic or nylon)
- [ ] dependable tent

Cooking
- [ ] one quart plastic water containers
- [ ] one gallon collapsible water container
- [ ] backpack stove with extra fuel
- [ ] funnel or pour spout for fuel
- [ ] aluminum foil
- [ ] cooking pot
- [ ] bowl or plate
- [ ] spoon, fork, knife, spatula
- [ ] butane lighter or matches in a waterproof container

APPENDIX B: Additional Information

Government Agencies

Bandelier National Monument
HCR 1, Box 1, Ste. 15
Los Alamos, NM 87544
(505) 672-3861

Bureau of Land Management
1235 La Plata Highway, Suite A
Farmington, NM 87401
(505) 599-8900

Bureau of Land Management
P.O. Box 846
Grants, NM 87020
(505) 287-7911

Bureau of Land Management
1800 Marquess St.
Las Cruces, NM 88005
(505) 525-4300

Bureau of Land Management
2909 W. Second Street
Roswell, NM 88201
(505) 627-0272

Bureau of Land Management
P.O. Box 27115
Santa Fe, NM 87502
(505) 438-7501

Bureau of Land Management
198 Neel Avenue NW
Socorro, NM 87801
(505) 835-0412

Bureau of Land Management
226 Cruz Alta Rd.
Taos, NM 87571
(505) 758-8851

Capulin Volcano National
Monument
P.O. Box 40
Capulin, NM 88414
(505) 278-2201

Carlsbad Caverns National Park
3225 National Parks Highway
Carlsbad, NM 88220
(505) 785-2233

Carson National Forest—

Headquarters
P.O. Box 558
Taos, NM 87571
(505) 758-6200

Camino Real Ranger District
P.O. Box 68
Penasco, NM 87553
(505) 587-2255

Questa Ranger District
P.O. Box 110
Questa, NM 87556
(505) 586-0520

Tres Piedras Ranger District
P.O. Box 38
Tres Piedras, NM 87577
(505) 758-8678

Chaco Culture National
Historical Park
Box 220
Nageezi, NM 87037
(505) 786-7014

Cibola National Forest—

Headquarters
2113 Osuna Road NE, Ste. A
Albuquerque, NM 87112
(505) 761-4650

Magdalena Ranger District
P.O. Box 45
Magdalena, NM 87825
(505) 854-2381

Mountainair Ranger District
P.O. Box E
Mountainair, NM 87036
(505) 847-2990

Mount Taylor Ranger District
1800 Lobo Canyon Road
Grants, NM 87020
(505) 287-8833

Sandia Ranger District
11776 Highway 337
Tijeras, NM 87059
(505) 281-3304

Coronado National Forest—

Headquarters
300 W. Congress
Tucson, AZ 85701
(520) 670-4552

Douglas Ranger District
3081 N. Leslie Canyon Rd.
Douglas, AZ 85607
(520) 364-3468

El Malpais National Monument
P.O. Box 939
Grants, NM 87020
(505) 285-4641

El Morro National Monument
Route 2, Box 43
Ramah, NM 87321
(505) 783-4226

Gila Cliff Dwellings National
Monument, Gila National Forest,
Wilderness District
Route 11, Box 100
Silver City, NM 88061
(505) 536-9461

Gila National Forest—

Headquarters
3005 E. Camino del Bosque
Silver City, NM 88061
(505) 388-8201

Black Range Ranger District
1804 Date St.
Truth or Consequences, NM
87901
(505) 894-6677

Glenwood Ranger District
Box 8
Glenwood, NM 88039
(505) 539-2481

Wilderness Ranger District
Route 11, Box 50
Mimbres, NM 88049
(505) 536-2250

Reserve Ranger District
P.O. Box 170
Reserve, NM 87830
(505) 533-6232

Silver City Ranger District
3005 E. Camino del Bosque
Silver City, NM 88061
(505) 538-2771

Guadalupe Mountains
National Park
HC 60, Box 400
Salt Flat, TX 79847
(915) 828-3251

Lincoln National Forest—

Headquarters, Federal Building
1101 New York Ave.
Alamogordo, NM 88310
(505) 434-7200

Guadalupe Ranger District,
Federal Building
Rm. 159, Carlsbad, NM 88220
(505) 885-4181

Sacramento Ranger District
P.O. Box 288
Cloudcroft, NM 88317
(505) 682-2551

Smokey Bear Ranger District
901 Mechem Dr.
Ruidoso, NM 88345
(505) 257-4095

Map Distribution
U.S. Geological Survey Map Sales
Box 25286
Federal Center, Building 810
Denver, CO 80225
1-800-HELP-MAP

Salinas Pueblo Missions
National Monument
P.O. Box 496
Mountainair, NM 87036
(505) 847-2585

Santa Fe National Forest—

Headquarters
P.O. Box 1689
Santa Fe, NM 87504
(505) 988-6940

Coyote Ranger District
P.O. Box 160
Coyote, NM 87012
(505) 638-5526

Cuba Ranger District
P.O. Box 130
Cuba, NM 87013
(505) 289-3264

Espanola Ranger District
P.O. Box 1364
Espanola, NM 87532
(505) 753-7331

Jemez Ranger District
P.O. Box 150
Jemez Springs, NM 87025
(505) 829-3535

Los Alamos Office
475 20th St., Suite B
Los Alamos, NM 87544
(505) 667-5120

Pecos-Las Vegas Ranger District
P.O. Drawer 429
Pecos, NM 87552
(505) 757-6121

White Sands National Monument
P.O. Box 1086
Holloman AFB, NM 88330
(505) 479-6124

APPENDIX C: Additional Reading

Day Hikes In The Santa Fe Area. The Santa Fe Group of the Sierra Club, Santa Fe, NM, Third Edition 1990.

Evans, Harry. *50 Hikes In New Mexico.* Gem Guides Book Company, Pico Rivera, CA, 1984, revised 1995.

Ganci, Dave. *Hiking The Southwest: Arizona, New Mexico, and West Texas.* Sierra Club Books/Random House, San Francisco, CA, 1983.

Hill, Mike. *Guide to the Hiking Areas of New Mexico.* University of New Mexico Press, Albuquerque, NM, 1995.

Hill, Mike. *Hikers and Climbers Guide To The Sandias.* University of New Mexico Press, Albuquerque, NM, Third Edition 1993.

Hoard, Dorothy. *A Guide To Bandelier National Monument.* Los Alamos Historical Society, Los Alamos, NM, 1989.

Julyan, Bob. *Best Hikes with Children in New Mexico.* Mountaineers Books, Seattle, WA, 1994.

Martin, Craig. *75 Hikes in New Mexico.* Mountaineers Books, Seattle, WA, 1995.

Matthews, Kay. *Day Hikes in the Taos Area.* Acequia Madre Press, NM, 1997.

Matthews, Kay. *Hiking the Mountain Trails of Santa Fe.* Acequia Madre Press, NM, 1995.

Matthews, Kay. *Hiking the Wilderness: A Backpacking Guide to the Wheeler Peak, Pecos & San Pedro Parks Wilderness Areas.* Acequia Madre Press, NM, 1992.

Matthews, Kay. *Hiking Trails of the Sandia and Manzano Mountains.* Acequia Madre Press, NM, 1995.

McDonald, Corry. *Wilderness: A New Mexico Legacy.* Sunstone Press, Santa Fe, NM, 1985.

Murray, John A. *The Gila Wilderness: A Hiking Guide.* University of New Mexico Press, Albuquerque, NM, 1988.

Overhage, Carl. *Six One-Day Walks In The Pecos Wilderness*. Sunstone Press, Santa Fe, NM, revised 1997.

Perry, John and Jane Greverus. *The Sierra Club Guide To The Natural Areas of New Mexico, Arizona, and Nevada*. Sierra Club Books/Random House, San Francisco, CA, 1986.

Robinson, Sherry. *El Malpais, Mt. Taylor, and the Zuni Mountains: A Hiking Guide and History*. University of New Mexico Press, Albuquerque, NM, 1994.

Schneider, Bill. *Hiking Carlsbad Caverns and Guadalupe Mountains National Parks*. Falcon Publishing, Helena, MT, 1996.

Ungnade, Herbert E. *Guide To The New Mexico Mountains*. University of New Mexico Press, Albuquerque, NM, Second Edition 1972.

ABOUT THE AUTHOR

Laurence and Patricia Parent

Laurence Parent was born and raised in New Mexico. After receiving an engineering degree at the University of Texas at Austin, he practiced engineering for six years before becoming a full-time freelance photographer and writer specializing in landscape, travel, and nature subjects. His photos appear in calendars by Sierra Club, Audubon, Kodak, and many other publishers. His article and photo credits include *National Geographic Traveler, Outside, Backpacker, Sierra, Newsweek,* and the *New York Times.* He contributes regularly to regional publications such as *New Mexico Magazine, Arizona Highways, Texas Highways, Texas Monthly,* and *Texas Parks & Wildlife.* Other work includes posters, advertising, museum exhibits, postcards, and brochures.

He has completed more than twenty books, including several for Falcon Publishing: *Hiking Texas; Hiking Big Bend National Park; Scenic Driving Texas; Scenic Driving New Mexico; Scenic Driving Wyoming;* and *Scenic Driving North Carolina.* His work also appears in Falcon's *New Mexico on My Mind* and *Texas on My Mind* books, Falcon Publishing's calendars, and other Falcon products. He makes his home in Austin, Texas, with his wife Patricia.

get
FALCON GUIDED

FalconGuides are available for where-to-go hiking, mountain biking, rock climbing, walking, scenic driving, fishing, rockhounding, paddling, birding, wildlife viewing, and camping. We also have FalconGuides on essential outdoor skills and subjects and field identification. The following titles are currently available, but this list grows every year. For a free catalog with a complete list of titles, call The Globe Pequot Press toll-free at 1–800–243–0495.

HIKING GUIDES

Hiking Alaska
Hiking Alberta
Hiking Arizona
Hiking Arizona's Cactus Country
Hiking the Beartooths
Hiking Big Bend National Park
Hiking Bob Marshall Country
Hiking California
Hiking California's Desert Parks
Hiking Carlsbad Caverns
   and Guadalupe Mtns. National Parks
Hiking Colorado
Hiking the Columbia River Gorge
Hiking Florida
Hiking Georgia
Hiking Glacier & Waterton Lakes National Parks
Hiking Grand Canyon National Park
Hiking Grand Staircase-Escalante/Glen Canyon
Hiking Great Basin National Park
Hiking Hot Springs in the Pacific Northwest
Hiking Idaho
Hiking Maine
Hiking Michigan
Hiking Minnesota
Hiking Montana
Hiker's Guide to Nevada
Hiking New Hampshire
Hiking New Mexico

Hiking New York
Hiking North Cascades
Hiking Northern Arizona
Hiking Olympic National Park
Hiking Oregon
Hiking Oregon's Eagle Cap Wilderness
Hiking Oregon's Mount Hood/Eagle Cap
Hiking Oregon's Three Sisters Country
Hiking Pennsylvania
Hiking Shenandoah National Park
Hiking South Carolina
Hiking South Dakota's Black Hills Country
Hiking Southern New England
Hiking Tennessee
Hiking Texas
Hiking Utah
Hiking Utah's Summits
Hiking Vermont
Hiking Virginia
Hiking Washington
Hiking Wisconsin
Hiking Wyoming
Hiking Wyoming's Wind River Range
Hiking Yellowstone National Park
Hiking Zion & Bryce Canyon National Parks
The Trail Guide to Bob Marshall Country
Wild Montana
Wild Utah

• *To order any of these books, check with your local bookseller or call* The Globe Pequot Press at **1–800–243–0495.**
Visit us on the world wide web at:
www.falcon.com

FALCON®

get
FALCON GUIDED

• *To order any of these books, check with your local bookseller
or call* The Globe Pequot Press *at* **1–800–243–0495.**

FALCON®

Visit us on the world wide web at:
www.falcon.com

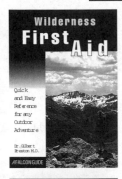

WILDERNESS FIRST AID

By Dr. Gilbert Preston M.D.

Enjoy the outdoors and face the inherent risks with confidence. By reading this easy-to-follow first-aid text, all outdoor enthusiasts can pack a little extra peace of mind on their next adventure. *Wilderness First Aid* offers expert medical advice for dealing with outdoor emergencies beyond the reach of 911. It easily fits in most backcountry first-aid kits.

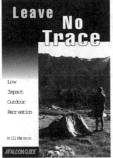

LEAVE NO TRACE

By Will Harmon

The concept of "leave no trace" seems simple, but it actually gets fairly complicated. This handy quick-reference guidebook includes all the newest information on this growing and all-important subject. This book is written to help the outdoor enthusiast make the hundreds of decisions necessary to protect the natural landscape and still have an enjoyable wilderness experience. Part of the proceeds from the sale of this book go to continue leave-no-trace education efforts. The Official Manual of American Hiking Society.

BEAR AWARE

By Bill Schneider

Hiking in bear country can be very safe if hikers follow the guidelines summarized in this small, "packable" book. Extensively reviewed by bear experts, the book contains the latest information on the intriguing science of bear-human interactions. *Bear Aware* can not only make your hike safer, but it can help you avoid the fear of bears that can take the edge off your trip.

MOUNTAIN LION ALERT

By Steve Torres

Recent mountain lion attacks have received national attention. Although infrequent, lion attacks raise concern for public safety. *Mountain Lion Alert* contains helpful advice for mountain bikers, trail runners, horse riders, pet owners, and suburban landowners on how to reduce the chances of mountain lion-human conflicts.

Also Available
• ***Wilderness Survival*** • ***Reading Weather*** • ***Backpacking Tips***
• ***Climbing Safely*** • *Avalanche Aware*

To order check with your local bookseller or
call The Globe Pequot Press at **1-800-243-0495**.

www.falcon.com

**American
Hiking
Society**

American Hiking Society is the only national nonprofit organization dedicated to establishing, protecting and maintaining foot trails in America.

Establishing...

American Hiking Society establishes hiking trails with the AHS National Trails Endowment, providing grants for grassroots organizations to purchase trail lands, construct and maintain trails, and preserve hiking trails' scenic values. The AHS affiliate club program, called the Congress of Hiking Organizations, brings trail clubs together to share information, collaborate on public policy, and advocate legislation and policies that protect hiking trails.

Protecting...

American Hiking Society protects hiking trails through highly focused public policy efforts in the nation's capital. AHS affects federal legislation, shapes public lands policy, collaborates with grassroots trail organizations, and partners with federal land managers to protect the hiking experience. Members become active with letter-writing campaigns and by attending the annual AHS Trails Advocacy Week.

Maintaining...

American Hiking Society maintains hiking trails by sending volunteers to national parks, forests and recreation lands; organizing volunteer teams to help affiliated hiking clubs; and publishing national volunteer directories. AHS members get involved, get dirty and get inspired by participating in AHS programs like National Trails Day, America's largest celebration of the outdoors; and Volunteer Vacations—week-long work trips to beautiful, wild places.

Join American Hiking Society...

Be a part of the organization dedicated to protecting and preserving the nation's footpaths, our footpaths, the ones in our backyards and our backcountry. Visit American Hiking Society's website or call to find out more about membership. When you join, Falcon Publishing will send you a FREE guide as a special thank you for contributing to the efforts of American Hiking Society.

American Hiking Society
1422 Fenwick Lane
Silver Spring, MD 20910
OR CALL: (888) 766-HIKE ext. 1
OR VISIT: www.americanhiking.org

DATE DUE

The curse begins....

"What's this?" Rose Rita had found a little pocket in the cloth wrapper. She pulled out a yellowed packet made of paper. Tucking the scroll beneath her arm, she began to unfold the packet as Lewis looked on with a strange dread.

"What is it?" he asked, his voice a dry croak.

"Some kind of gray powder," Rose Rita said. "There's only a teaspoonful of it—Ouch!" She jerked her hand, dropping the packet. It landed flat without spilling much of the powder.

"What's wrong?" Lewis asked, so frightened he almost dropped his books.

"Paper cut." Rose Rita shook her finger, making a face. She reached down to pick up the packet, and a single bright red drop of blood fell from her finger right into the gray substance. Lewis gasped. The powder began to boil. It hissed and bubbled. A dull brown vapor rose from it, drifting in strange, stringy wisps, like strands of cobwebs. The whole mass sizzled, then it shrank into a dark little ball about the size of a pea. Rose Rita paused. "What is that?" she asked. "It looks like a small black pearl." She reached down for it—

And yanked her hand away with a startled shriek! The black ball sprouted spindly legs and scuttled under one of the bookshelves. Lewis uttered one strangled shout. Somehow, with Rose Rita's drop of blood, the powder had become a living spider....

"[Will] put readers on the edges of their seats."   —*Booklist*

"Great imagination. . . . [M]any students will greatly enjoy the creepy plot, for th. . . . . .ture, and spooky things."   —*VOYA*

Discover the Terrifying World of
John Bellairs!

Johnny Dixon Mysteries
The Bell, the Book, and the Spellbinder
The Chessmen of Doom
The Curse of the Blue Figurine
The Drum, the Doll, and the Zombie
The Eyes of the Killer Robot
The Hand of the Necromancer
The Mummy, the Will, and the Crypt
The Revenge of the Wizard's Ghost
The Secret of the Underground Room
The Spell of the Sorcerer's Skull
The Trolley to Yesterday
The Wrath of the Grinning Ghost

Lewis Barnavelt Mysteries

The Beast Under the Wizard's Bridge

The Doom of the Haunted Opera

The Figure in the Shadows

The Ghost in the Mirror

The House With a Clock in Its Walls

The Letter, the Witch, and the Ring

The Specter from the Magician's Museum

The Tower at the End of the World

The Vengeance of the Witch-Finder

The Whistle, the Grave, and the Ghost

Anthony Monday Mysteries

The Dark Secret of Weatherend

The Lamp from the Warlock's Tomb

The Mansion in the Mist

The Treasure of Alpheus Winterborn

The Specter from the Magician's Museum

A JOHN BELLAIRS MYSTERY
By Brad Strickland

Frontispiece by Edward Gorey

PUFFIN BOOKS

PUFFIN BOOKS
Published by Penguin Group
Penguin Young Readers Group
345 Hudson Street, New York, New York 10014, U.S.A.
Penguin Books Ltd, 80 Strand, London WC2R ORL, England
Penguin Books Australia Ltd, 250 Camberwell Road, Camberwell, Victoria 3124, Australia
Penguin Books Canada Ltd, 10 Alcorn Avenue, Toronto, Ontario, Canada M4V 3B2
Penguin Books (N.Z.) Ltd, 182-190 Wairau Road, Auckland 10, New Zealand

First published in the United States of America by Dial Books for Young Readers,
a member of Penguin Putnam Inc., 1998
Published by Puffin Books, a division of Penguin Putnam Books for Young Readers, 2001
Reissued by Puffin Books, a division of Penguin Young Readers Group, 2004

1 3 5 7 9 10 8 6 4 2

THE LIBRARY OF CONGRESS HAS CATALOGED THE DIAL EDITION AS FOLLOWS:
Strickland, Brad.
The specter from the magician's museum / by Brad Strickland; frontispiece by Edward Gorey.
p. cm.
Summary: When the evil sorceress Belle Frisson ensnares Rose Rita Pottinger in a magic
web in order to steal her life force, Lewis Barnavelt must risk his own life to save a friend.
[1. Witches—Fiction. 2. Magic—Fiction. 3. Supernatural—Fiction.] I. Bellairs, John.
II. Title. III. Title: Specter from the magician's museum.
PZ7. S9166Jo 1998 [Fic]—dc21 97-47167 CIP AC
Puffin Books ISBN 0-14-038652-1

This edition ISBN 0-14-240264-8

Printed in the United States of America

*For Bob and Elaine Lund, whose museum
shows that the secret of magic is people*

The Specter from the
Magician's Museum

CHAPTER ONE

Lewis Barnavelt had been frightened before in his life, but this time he was terrified.

It was a sunny, warm fall day in the 1950s. Lewis stood just outside the junior high school in the small town of New Zebedee, Michigan, and felt his stomach fluttering with a million butterflies. "What am I going to *do*?" he muttered.

Lewis was a chunky blond boy of about thirteen. He had a round, anxious face and a timid way of looking at the world. Now he was waiting for his friend, Rose Rita Pottinger. They were both in the same grade and in the same boat, and Lewis hoped that talking to her would make him feel better.

Lewis stood with his back against the wall, and when Dave Shellenberger and Tom Lutz came running out of

the school, he pressed against the black stones as if he wanted to sink into them and disappear. Dave and Tom had been big wheels all through elementary school, and now they were two of the most popular kids in junior high. Both were great at sports, good-looking, and snappy dressers. By contrast Lewis was clumsy and heavy. Instead of nylon shirts and jeans, he wore flannel shirts and corduroy trousers that went *whip-whip* when he walked. He was not popular either. Sometimes he thought the only people in the world who liked him were his uncle Jonathan Barnavelt, their next-door neighbor Mrs. Zimmermann, and his English pen pal, Bertie Goodring. Plus Rose Rita, of course.

At last Lewis saw her coming out of the school. Rose Rita was sort of like Lewis—another odd duck. She was tall for her age, and skinny, with long, straight, black hair and big, round, black-rimmed spectacles. Lewis knew that Rose Rita regarded herself as an ugly duckling. People thought she was a tomboy too, and she hated the blouses and plaid skirts her mom insisted she wear to school. She felt much more comfortable in sweatshirts, jeans, and sneakers. Rose Rita paused outside the school door, clutching her books to her chest. Then she saw Lewis and gave him a dismal smile. As she came down the steps, she muttered, "It's awful."

Lewis nodded glumly. "What are we going to do?"

Rose Rita rolled her eyes. "I know what I'd *like* to do. I'd like to sail away on a slow boat to China. Or get sick with a disease that would last exactly four weeks!"

"Sure," said Lewis sarcastically. "Or run off and join

the circus, or find a formula to make you the Invisible Girl. Only we can't do any of those things." The two trudged away from the school, heading for Rose Rita's house. Normally Lewis liked to walk down the streets of New Zebedee, at least when no bullies like Woody Mingo were around. New Zebedee was a small town. Its downtown stretched only three blocks long, but the buildings all looked as if they had stories hidden inside them. The old brick shops had high false fronts, and the houses were elaborate Victorian structures with towers, cupolas, and wide, rambling porches. At the west end of Main Street stood a wonderful fountain that spumed a crystal willow tree of water from inside a circle of marble columns. At the east end were the G.A.R. Hall and the Civil War Monument and East End Park. In between were dozens of places that promised excitement and plenty to do.

Except today none of it appealed to Lewis. Because in just four weeks he had to face—

Lewis swallowed. "I don't want to be in any stupid talent show," he complained.

"I'm not thrilled about it myself," snapped Rose Rita. They walked in silence past Heemsoth's Rexall Drug Store, its windows still full of back-to-school items. Lewis and Rose Rita turned off Main Street and plodded up Mansion Street, past the Masonic temple. Rose Rita lived with her dad and mom at 39 Mansion Street, and Lewis waited in the living room while she changed out of her school clothes. After a few minutes she came out again, wearing a ratty old Notre Dame sweatshirt, jeans,

and black P.F. Flyers sneakers. The two of them walked toward High Street in a miserable silence.

Lewis lived at 100 High Street with his uncle Jonathan. Both of Lewis's parents had died in a terrible auto wreck when Lewis was not quite ten. He had moved to New Zebedee soon afterward, and now Uncle Jonathan was his legal guardian. Jonathan Barnavelt was a friendly man with red hair, a bushy red beard streaked here and there with white, and a potbelly. He smiled a lot, laughed easily and loudly, and was rich because he had inherited a pile of money from his grandfather.

Even better, Jonathan Barnavelt was a sorcerer. He could create wonderful illusions, not by trickery, but by real, honest-to-goodness magic. The previous June, to celebrate the end of school, Jonathan had re-created the Battle of Lepanto, the great naval fight between the Christians and the Turks in 1571. The battle had proved a terrific sight, as galleys clashed and a thousand cannon roared. It had delighted both Lewis and Rose Rita, who knew the names of all the different kinds of cannon, from carronades to long nines. In fact, Rose Rita had pointed out that the carronades really didn't belong, because they had not been invented until the eighteenth century.

Remembering the excitement, Lewis grumbled, "Too bad Uncle Jonathan can't help us."

"Maybe he will," said a thoughtful Rose Rita.

Lewis shook his head. "He says I have to do what the school tells me. It's no fair using magic. That's the same as cheating."

"Even in an emergency?" asked Rose Rita. "This is practically a matter of life and death."

They were trudging up the hill toward the summit and Lewis's house. "I should have known this would happen," groaned Lewis. "Every year the elementary-school kids get to see the junior-high talent show. I just never thought about how they got all those junior-high kids to go onstage and make fools of themselves."

"Now you know," said Rose Rita. "They force them."

They reached Lewis's house, a tall old mansion with a tower in front. Fastened to a black wrought-iron fence was the number 100 in red reflecting numerals. Lewis and Rose Rita passed through the gate, across the yard, and up the steps, both still steeped in gloom.

They found Lewis's uncle in the parlor, fiddling with something he had recently bought for the house—a Zenith Stratosphere television. The boxy walnut cabinet looked pretty snazzy. When you opened the front doors of the cabinet, you revealed the television screen, a radio, and a phonograph. The TV screen was perfectly circular, like a porthole. With the spidery antenna that Uncle Jonathan had attached to one of the chimneys, the TV could pick up three channels. The pictures were black and white and so filled with static and snow that sometimes it was hard to tell if you were watching a western adventure or a quiz show.

Uncle Jonathan looked up cheerfully as Lewis and Rose Rita came in. "Hi," he said, thumping the top of the set. As usual, he was wearing tan work pants, a blue shirt, and his red vest. He stepped back from the TV, stuck his

thumbs in the bottom pockets of his vest, tilted his head to one side, and asked, "How's that?"

Rose Rita squinted at the dim picture. "It's hard to say. What's it supposed to be?"

With a snort, Jonathan replied, "That's just the trouble—I can't tell!"

"Then it doesn't matter," said Rose Rita promptly.

Uncle Jonathan threw his head back and laughed. "Good point, Rose Rita!" He switched off the TV, and the picture shrank to a tiny white dot in the center of the blank screen before disappearing.

Lewis asked, "May we have a snack, Uncle Jonathan?"

His uncle pulled out his pocket watch. "Hmm. I suppose so. Just one glass of milk and a couple of cookies apiece. Florence has promised to make dinner for us tonight, and I don't want her thinking we don't appreciate her cooking."

"Great," said Lewis, perking up. Florence Zimmermann, their next-door neighbor, was a fantastic cook. She also happened to be a witch. Not an evil witch, but a friendly, twinkly-eyed, wrinkly-faced good witch whose magical abilities were even greater than Uncle Jonathan's. "Can Rose Rita have dinner with us?"

"Sure," said Uncle Jonathan. "Just call your folks and get permission, Rose Rita. Frizzy Wig and I will cook an extra portion."

Rose Rita called, and her mother cheerfully said Rose Rita could stay. Later that afternoon Rose Rita and Lewis lay on their stomachs in the parlor, watching the TV and wondering what they could possibly do for the school

talent show. Uncle Jonathan and Mrs. Zimmermann were bustling around in the kitchen, rattling pots and pans and producing wonderful aromas. Lewis wasn't really paying much attention to the TV. He and Rose Rita were watching a kids' show, with ancient black-and-white cartoons. Cats chased mice, and pigs sang, and kangaroos boxed. All the animals were drawn as collections of circles, and it was hard to tell the cartoon pigs from cartoon elks or spiny echidnas.

"Maybe you could dance," said Lewis. "You like to dance."

"Huh!" snorted Rose Rita. "There's a big difference between dancing with other people and dancing alone onstage. No thanks."

Lewis sighed and fell silent. The cartoon ended. A clown, dressed in a baggy white outfit, his face covered with white makeup, appeared on the screen. His nose might have been round and red, but it looked like a black bubble on the black-and-white TV. He had painted-on, high, arched eyebrows and a wide smiling mouth. He wore a ruffled collar and a funny hat, shaped like a milk bottle complete with a flat paper lid. "Kids!" said the announcer, who always sounded as if he were on the verge of a heart attack. "Here's your friend and mine, the amazing Creamy the Magical Clown!"

"Thank you," Creamy said in a rumbly voice. The camera pulled back to show that Creamy was standing beside a little girl about seven or eight years old. "I have a helper today!"

Rose Rita said, "She looks scared to death."

Creamy held a microphone down to the little girl and asked her name.

"Edith Arabella Elizabeth Bonny McPeters," she said shyly.

"My goodness!" exclaimed Creamy. "Your parents just didn't know when to stop, did they?"

Edith shook her head and smiled. Lewis saw that she was missing two front teeth.

"Well, Edith Arabella Elizabeth Bonny," said Creamy, "do you like flowers?"

The little girl nodded.

"Good!" said Creamy. Someone handed him a sheet of newspaper. He held it up and turned it so the camera could see both sides. Music began to play—"Saber Dance," a fast number. Creamy shook out the sheet of paper, rolled it up, shaped it into a cone, and gave it to Edith. "Hold this," instructed the clown. The music paused. Creamy turned to the camera. "Now boys and girls, say the magic words!"

The kids in the studio audience all bellowed out, "Twin Oaks milk is the milk for me!"

"Oh!" said Edith, blinking. A bouquet of daisies had sprung up out of the cone of newspapers. The band played a hearty *Tah-dah!*

"You keep those pretty flowers," Creamy rumbled, laughing. The little girl nodded and clutched the bouquet to her chest. Creamy patted her on the head and then looked at the camera. "And now let's hear from our good friends at Twin Oaks Dairy!"

Lewis sprang up and switched off the set. "That's it!" he said with a triumphant grin. "That's the answer to our problem!"

"Twin Oaks milk?" asked Rose Rita, raising her eyebrows. "I don't get it."

"Not milk—magic," replied Lewis. He swept his arms wide and bowed to an imaginary audience. "We'll do a magic act!"

Rose Rita shook her head. "Your uncle would never let you get away with it."

"Not real magic," said Lewis impatiently. "Stage magic, like Creamy the Clown does. Tricks with ropes and rings and stuff. What do you call it—conjuring! I can be the magician, and you can be my beautiful assistant!"

"Hmm." Rose Rita sat up and adjusted her glasses. Her expression became grudgingly thoughtful. "I don't know—maybe. Do you know any magic tricks?"

Lewis sat again, collapsing to the floor like a punctured balloon. "No," he admitted. "Not really."

"We can ask your uncle," suggested Rose Rita. "He entertains at the PTA, and everyone thinks his tricks are just conjuring."

"Maybe some of them are," said Lewis, thinking it over. "I've never really asked him."

Just then Jonathan Barnavelt called from the dining room in a booming voice: "Kids! Dinner's ready! Come and get it, or I'll throw it to the hogs!"

"You will do no such thing, Brush Mush!" said the outraged voice of Mrs. Zimmermann. "Not after I worked so hard over this hot stove, you won't!"

"Come on," said Lewis with a grin, and he and Rose Rita raced to the dining room.

CHAPTER TWO

Even though Lewis knew all about Mrs. Zimmermann's culinary talents, this time he had to admit she had outdone herself. Dinner was a succulent, perfectly browned roast, so tender that it practically melted in Lewis's mouth, together with luscious, buttery whipped potatoes that were just right, not too dry and not too gloopy. Uncle Jonathan used a ladle to make a little well in the top of each mound of mashed potatoes, and he poured in some rich brown gravy. Mrs. Zimmermann had also cooked candied carrots and petite green peas with baby pearl onions, and there was a big apple pie for dessert. "This feast is in honor of school starting again," Mrs. Zimmermann explained, a pleased twinkle in her eye as she saw how much Lewis and Rose Rita liked the food. "I

know how this can be a hard time in life, and I thought a celebration might be in order."

"It's wonderful, Pruny Face," said Jonathan Barnavelt with a chuckle. He patted his stomach. "Still, we'll have to watch it for the rest of the week. I've put on weight since I gave up smoking!"

"Then feast today and fast tomorrow," replied Mrs. Zimmermann tartly. She was a trim, elderly woman with an untidy nest of white hair, and she was wearing a purple floral dress. Florence Zimmermann loved the color purple, and her house was full of purple furnishings—rugs and wallpaper and even the toilet paper. "More carrots, Rose Rita?" she asked.

For a little while Lewis gave all his attention to the wonderful meal. Finally, as he watched his uncle bring in the golden-brown apple pie, Lewis felt Rose Rita kick him under the table. He looked at her in surprise. "Ask him," Rose Rita mouthed.

Lewis cleared his throat. "Uh, Uncle Jonathan," he said, "do you know anything about stage magic? Conjuring?"

Uncle Jonathan raised his red eyebrows as he put a slice of pie on a small plate and passed it to Rose Rita. "Oh, a little," he said. "I can do some nifty card tricks that don't depend on real magic. Why do you ask?"

Lewis explained the problem he and Rose Rita faced. Mrs. Zimmermann shook her head and sighed. "That's one thing I never liked to do when I was teaching school—force a student to get up onstage and perform in

front of others," she said. "Oh, I know it's supposed to give you poise and confidence, but it always seemed cruel to me. Not everyone has the kind of talents that shine out from a stage. Some of us are more quiet and private."

"Hm," said Uncle Jonathan. "I agree with Florence, but it seems to me that we still have a problem. The talent show is an old tradition, and you know how teachers hate to disturb tradition. So your idea is to do a magic show, is it?"

"Yes, but just conjuring tricks, not real magic," Lewis said quickly.

"Good," his uncle replied. "Real magic can get you into a world of trouble—as you know very well. Florence, I think Lewis and Rose Rita ought to consult Mr. Robert Hardwick. What do you say?"

Mrs. Zimmermann's bright blue eyes shone. "That's a wonderful idea, Weird Beard! If anyone in town could help them put an act together, Bob Hardwick is the man!"

"Who's he?" asked Rose Rita. "I never heard of him."

Uncle Jonathan passed a slice of pie to Lewis and laughed. "Bob Hardwick is a retired newspaperman and an amateur conjuror. He can do some amazing tricks with ropes and steel rings. He used to do shows for schools—called himself Marcus the Great. Well, he retired a few months ago and moved from Detroit to New Zebedee. He has a huge collection of magical memorabilia—things like original Houdini posters and a little cannon that the great Blackstone once used in his act—and he's putting these items into a museum that he plans

to open downtown in the old Eugster Brewery building."

Mrs. Zimmermann winked. "Mr. Hardwick thinks your uncle is a conjuror too," she confided. "When you see him, please keep the Capharnaum County Magicians Society a secret. Mr. Hardwick doesn't know there are real sorcerers and witches about."

Lewis nodded. He always kept his uncle's magical hobby to himself. Once, years before, he had asked Uncle Jonathan to show off to impress a friend of his named Tarby Corrigan. Unfortunately, Uncle Jonathan's magical eclipse of the moon had frightened Tarby. Lewis had lost a friend. Except for the other members of the Capharnaum County Magicians Society, now only Rose Rita knew about the real magic that Uncle Jonathan and Mrs. Zimmermann could command. Luckily, Rose Rita liked both of them. She knew better than to talk about their magic.

"Tell you what," Uncle Jonathan said as he served Mrs. Zimmermann's pie. "I'll give Bob a call. Tomorrow's Saturday, so he'll probably be downtown. Maybe we can arrange for you to see what his museum's going to be like. And I'm sure he can help you put together some conjuring tricks."

And so it was all arranged. Early the next morning Lewis and Rose Rita went down to Main Street. The former brewery was a brick building that Lewis liked a lot. The redbrick walls were mossy and battered, and chiseled in the cornerstone was the date 1842 in swirly numerals. One side wall had round windows, like the tops of beer barrels, each one divided into four wedge-shaped

panes. Eugster's Brewery had gone out of business years before. As long as Lewis could remember, the building had been vacant, its front windows papered over from inside, a chain and padlock on its front door.

On Saturday morning, though, the change was obvious. The windows sparkled in the morning light, framed by maroon curtains edged in gold lace. An oblong cardboard sign, inside the window on the right, showed an old-fashioned steel engraving of a top-hatted magician levitating a woman, who lay as stiff as a board in midair. Above the artwork, in ornate circus-poster lettering, were the grand words

The National Museum of Magic

Under the artwork were more words, in a smaller type. Lewis giggled as he read what they had to say:

> ABSOLUTELY the finest collection of memorabilia relating to conjuring, prestidigitation, hocus-pocus, flummery, thimblerigging, sleight of hand, jiggery-pokery, and good-natured foolery known to MAN or BEAST! GUARANTEED thrills, chills, brainteasers, crowd pleasers, mind-bogglers and hornswogglers! YOU will be AMAZED!
>
> ENDORSED by the Pulpit, the Press, and the Lectern as WHOLESOME FAMILY ENTERTAINMENT! If you are OVERCOME by the SHEER GRANDEUR of the show, the Management will provide FREE SMELLING

SALTS to bring you back to FULL CON-
SCIOUSNESS! Come one! Come all!
—Robert W. Hardwick, Prop.

"Whoosh!" commented Rose Rita as she read the plac-
ard. "Mr. Hardwick promises a lot, doesn't he?"

Lewis felt a quiver of anticipation. "I hope he can suggest something for us." He tried the door, and it swung
open, jingling a bell overhead. "Hello?"

Lewis and Rose Rita looked into a long, narrow room,
cluttered with all sorts of weird objects: mummy cases,
steamer trunks with swords thrust into them, a huge
galvanized-steel milk canister with its lid padlocked shut,
shelves full of top hats, canes, wands, and handcuffs,
and on every wall poster after poster advertising magicians and their shows. Lewis saw placards announcing
the Great Rapiri, the Hindoo Fakir; Long Chi, the Chinese Marvel; the Mystic Marquis and His Thousand
Wonders; and many more. It was hard to see anything beyond a few feet from the door, because the
lights were out. Rose Rita said, "Looks like nobody's
home."

Next to the door stood an upright mummy case, six
and a half feet tall. The carved and painted face at the top
was cruel, with frowning eyebrows, a hooked nose, a vi-
cious mouth, and a strange squared-off goatee. But what
caught Lewis's attention were the eyes—the wooden eyelids were opening slowly, and the glaring, dead eyes
stared straight at him! He could only squeak and tug at
Rose Rita's arm, pointing at the thing.

"What is it—Oh!" Rose Rita stiffened as she noticed the mummy case too. Now the lips were moving.

In a grotesque, creaking voice, the mummy case demanded, "Who dares disturb my three-thousand-year slumber? *Who?*"

Lewis gasped.

After a moment the mummy case sighed. "You're supposed to say your names, and then I can tell you to go right upstairs. This is a trick, kids. It's electric motors and a microphone and speaker. I take it you're Lewis and Rose Rita?"

Rose Rita recovered first. "Yes, we are."

"Then come on up." The mummy case's eyelids clicked shut. Then they flicked open again. "The light switch is beside the door on your left. Please close the door before you come upstairs. We're not officially open yet." The eyes clacked closed.

Lewis turned on the lights, and Rose Rita closed the door, its lock clacking loudly. Now they could see the stairway on their right. They climbed up. At the top they saw four men sitting at a table. They had been playing cards, and they all smiled as the kids walked toward them. One man, slim and about sixty, with curly gray hair and glasses, stood. "I'm sorry I startled you," he said, holding up a silvery microphone shaped like a flattened baseball. "I couldn't resist." He put the microphone down and shook hands with Lewis. "Mr. Lewis Barnavelt, I presume?"

"Yes," Lewis answered. "And this is Rose Rita Pottinger."

"Charmed to meet you," replied the man. "I am Robert Hardwick, and with my dear wife, Ellen, I own this establishment. You can call me Bob, if you like. These are my Saturday poker buddies. Allow me to introduce Mr. Clarence Mussenberger, Mr. Thomas Perkins, and Mr. Johnny Stone."

Each of the men stood to shake hands. Mr. Mussenberger was stocky and round faced, with cheerful brown eyes. He looked familiar, somehow. Mr. Perkins was very tall and thin, with distinguished streaks of gray in his black hair. And Mr. Stone was unusually short—even shorter than Lewis—with a mischievous glint in his eye and a double chin. He was almost completely bald, except for a fringe of gray hair.

"Well now," Mr. Hardwick said, bringing over a couple of folding chairs for Lewis and Rose Rita. "Your uncle Jonathan says you need help. Tell him that one of these days I'm going to figure out how he does that trick with the three candles and the ace of spades! But now, what do you need?"

Feeling embarrassed, Lewis stammered out his problem. "So Rose Rita and I thought we might put together a magic act," he finished.

Mr. Mussenberger cleared his throat. "You need about five good, quick tricks," he rumbled.

Rose Rita blinked. "Oh, my gosh! You're Creamy the Magical Clown, from TV!"

The men all laughed, but Mr. Mussenberger beamed. "Pipe down, you mutts," he said to the others. "My dear, you are correct. Five days a week I am Creamy the Mag-

ical Clown, in the service of the Twin Oaks Dairy Company. On weekends, however, I am simply Clare." He nodded to the other men. "Of course, these gentlemen aren't nearly as famous as Creamy, but let me tell you that Mr. Perkins is also known as Lord Puzzlewit, and that he can do amazing things with a deck of cards. When performing, Mr. Stone is Bondini, Escape Artist Extraordinaire. Chains, locks, jail cells, straitjackets—nothing can prevent his getting out!"

"Except his wife, of course," put in Mr. Perkins, with a wink.

"Just for that," said Mr. Stone, "I'm gonna tell the others next time I see you pull a couple of aces out of your sleeve!"

They all laughed again, making Lewis feel more at ease.

"Well, Lewis, you have a number of experts here," said Mr. Hardwick. "So what will it be, gents?"

"The Square Circle," Mr. Mussenberger said at once. "You can't go wrong with that."

Mr. Perkins stroked his long chin thoughtfully. "Hmm. Perhaps the Chinese Rings? Or the Floating Lady? Those both require a lovely assistant."

"The Basket of Torment," added Mr. Stone. "Kids, you'll wow 'em. Miss Rose Rita climbs into the basket, Lewis pierces it with a dozen razor-sharp swords, and when the swords are removed, Rose Rita comes out in a completely different costume!"

Mr. Hardwick held up his hands. "Please, please! Gentlemen, remember that Lewis and Rose Rita have to be

ready in four weeks—and they can't afford fancy props." He got up and opened a door, beckoning Lewis and Rose Rita over. "I'll tell you what. In this room is my collection of books on magic—more than seven thousand of them!" He switched on the light.

Lewis and Rose Rita stepped into a room that was like a library, with shelf after shelf of books. Daylight poured in through two round side windows, and dust motes floated in the slanting sunbeams. Mr. Hardwick pointed to a tall bookcase. "Now, this section has all sorts of books on simple stage-magic tricks," he said. "You two rummage around and find five or six likely books, and I'll let you borrow them—if you promise to take very good care of them!"

"We will," Lewis agreed at once.

"Good." Mr. Hardwick said. "Now I'll get back to fleecing these three marks. I'm already ahead twenty-five cents!" He closed the door as the others protested against being called "marks."

For a couple of minutes Rose Rita and Lewis just stared at all the books. Then they began to look at the intriguing titles—*Chemical Magic with Everyday Ingredients; Close-Up Tricks with Matches, Coins, and String; How to Amaze Your Friends*, and others. Lewis pulled some out, thumbed through them, replaced a few, and kept others. At last he clutched five books under his arm. He looked up and saw that Rose Rita was far off at another shelf. "We can't take those," he said.

"I know," replied Rose Rita. "I was just looking. There are books here by Houdini, the great escape artist. And

here's one by Blackstone—I've seen him on TV. Here's something funny."

Slapping book dust off his clothes, Lewis went over to look. Rose Rita held a scroll—a rolled-up length of parchment. It had a faded cloth wrapper, and some words had been embroidered on the cloth. Rose Rita read them aloud: "Madame Frisson: Her Testament from Beyond the Grave."

Lewis's neck felt prickly. "I don't think we should mess with that," he said uneasily.

"Don't be such a worrywart. I'm not messing with it—I'm just reading it. What's this?" Rose Rita had found a little pocket in the cloth wrapper. She pulled out a yellowed packet made of paper. Tucking the scroll beneath her arm, she began to unfold the packet as Lewis looked on with a strange dread.

"What is it?" he asked, his voice a dry croak.

"Some kind of gray powder," Rose Rita said. "There's only a teaspoonful of it—Ouch!" She jerked her hand, dropping the packet. It landed flat without spilling much of the powder.

"What's wrong?" Lewis asked, so frightened he almost dropped his books.

"Paper cut." Rose Rita shook her finger, making a face. She reached down to pick up the packet, and a single bright red drop of blood fell from her finger right into the gray substance.

Lewis gasped. The powder began to boil. It hissed and bubbled. A dull brown vapor rose from it, drifting in strange, stringy wisps, like strands of cobwebs. The

whole mass sizzled, the reddish-brown bubbles bursting until it became a seething liquid. Then it shrank into a dark little ball about the size of a pea. It was as black and shiny as a round button made of ebony. Rose Rita paused. "What is that?" she asked. "It looks like a small black pearl." She reached down for it—

And yanked her hand away with a startled shriek! The black ball sprouted spindly legs and scuttled under one of the bookshelves. Lewis uttered one strangled shout. Somehow, with Rose Rita's drop of blood, the powder had become a living spider!

CHAPTER THREE

Lewis and Rose Rita backed away toward the door. With his left hand Lewis clutched the books. Reaching behind him with his right, he fumbled for the knob. A horrible thought hit him. What if his hand closed on a cold, squashy, wriggling, round body? Spiders were venomous. He had heard of people dying in agony from the bite of a black widow. The dusty, book-scented air seemed hard to breathe. His throat closed. Lewis gritted his teeth to keep them from chattering. The spider couldn't be there, he told himself. He had seen it run under a shelf all the way across the room, and it was too small to have zipped past them.

More afraid of what he had seen run under the bookshelf than what might be behind him, Lewis grabbed the knob and opened the door. He and Rose Rita stumbled

out. The magicians hardly glanced up from their game. "Find some stuff?" Mr. Hardwick asked in a vague kind of tone as he frowned at his cards. He waved a hand. "Fine! Just let yourselves out, and the door will lock behind you. When you finish with the books, bring them back."

Rose Rita rushed for the stairs, and Lewis followed close at her heels. The two of them clattered down the steps. She unlocked the door, and they plunged out into the morning sunlight. The door slammed shut behind them, the automatic lock clicking. For a second Lewis and Rose Rita just stood there looking at each other with wild eyes and panting to get their breath back.

Then the ordinary Saturday-morning sounds of New Zebedee brought them back to reality. Chevrolets and Fords rolled past. Someone's big brown Labrador dog was barking at a frisky squirrel outside the post office. A kid rode his bike down the street, jangling the bell. Lewis took a long, shaky breath, feeling relief at their escape. Then he stared at what Rose Rita held clenched under her arm. "You've still got it!" he said in a shocked voice.

Rose Rita took the scroll in both hands and swallowed hard. In the sunlight it looked worn and shabby. Lewis saw that the scroll itself was parchment or something like it, creased, dull brown, and badly frayed at the edges. It was on a wooden roller like a spool. The cloth covering was moth-eaten purple velvet, faded to a dull brownish maroon. The embroidered letters were a dull greenish yellow. Maybe they had been gold at one time. "I was so scared, I didn't even drop it," Rose Rita said. She looked

at Lewis with a sick expression. "What should I do?"

"Give it back to Mr. Hardwick," Lewis told her.

Rose Rita bit her lip. She looked from Lewis to the door and then she shook her head. "The door locked behind us. I'd have to knock. He might get mad."

"Why would he get mad?" Lewis asked.

Rose Rita gave him a pained look. "Because he might think I started to swipe it and then lost my nerve. This looks old—it must be valuable."

Lewis took a deep breath. "Maybe we can sneak it back in when we return the books. There's tons of stuff on those shelves. Mr. Hardwick probably won't miss one little scroll for a week or so."

"What if he does?" moaned Rose Rita. "Lewis, this isn't like those books you have. This scroll has some kind of real magic about it. I don't like it."

Lewis nodded unhappily. He didn't like real magic either. Not unless his uncle or Mrs. Zimmermann was firmly in control of it. Real magic could be unpredictable and deadly. "What's wrong?" Lewis asked, noticing Rose Rita staring at her right index finger.

"This is where I cut myself," Rose Rita said, holding her finger up so he could see it. There was a tiny curved white mark on it, like a quarter moon with its points facing downward.

Lewis's flesh crawled. He hated cuts and puncture wounds, and he had a morbid fear of getting a deadly infection or tetanus from one. He asked, "Does it hurt?"

Rose Rita shook her head. "It feels sort of cold. Anyway, it isn't bleeding." She rubbed the scar with her

thumb and made a face. "And it doesn't solve my problem with this scroll."

Lewis thought for a minute. Now that they were safely outside, he began to wonder if they'd really seen what they thought they had. Maybe the spider had just been hiding inside the scroll and had dropped out. Maybe the powder had been just something that fizzed when it got wet, like Bromo-Seltzer. Still, Lewis knew you should never take chances where magic might be concerned. "Look," he said, "why don't you let Mrs. Zimmermann have a look at the scroll? She'd probably know what to do with it."

"And have her think I was poking my nose in where it didn't belong?" asked Rose Rita fiercely. "Mrs. Zimmermann is my best grown-up friend. She'd think I was awful if I told her what I did."

With a sigh Lewis said, "I guess I understand. Maybe you can just put it away until next weekend. We'll try to sneak it back in then. Okay?"

"Okay," Rose Rita said at last. "I don't like it, but I can't think of anything else. Maybe Mr. Hardwick won't miss it. But I still feel like a thief."

"You're not *stealing* it," Lewis pointed out. "You're just borrowing it for a while. And you're not even going to read it."

"You can say that again," Rose Rita told him.

They stopped at Rose Rita's house, and she dashed inside for a few minutes. When she came out, she said, "I hid it in my room. I don't even want to think about it until we

can smuggle it back into the museum. Come on. Let's go to your house and try to concentrate on getting our act ready."

At 100 High Street, Lewis and Rose Rita sat at the study table and leafed through the books. They found some pretty good tricks. Finally they agreed that four of them might be easy enough to work out. One was a way to produce a live rabbit or dove from a crumpled-up sheet of newspaper. Another was a trick that would let Lewis seem to levitate Rose Rita. Covered with a sheet, she would appear to rise and float in the air. Actually, she would be holding a pair of fake legs and feet stretched out in front of her. If they could find a couple of big crates or cardboard boxes, there was another neat trick that would let Rose Rita vanish from one and appear in the other. Finally, with the help of a mirror, a chair, and a sword, they could make Rose Rita's head appear to hover in midair, unattached to her body.

"Can we get all that stuff?" Rose Rita asked.

"I think so," said Lewis. "I don't know about rabbits or doves, but some of the kids live on farms. Maybe I could borrow a baby chick or duckling. That should work just as well. We can make the fake legs from some of your old jeans, some broomsticks, and an old pair of shoes. Uncle Jonathan can probably find us some big boxes. I know he'll let us borrow his grandfather's Civil War sword, and Mrs. Zimmermann has all kinds of mirrors in her house." Lewis thought he might talk his uncle into getting him a special outfit too. A tuxedo, maybe, or perhaps some fancy Chinese or Indian robes. Or he could wear a tur-

ban and call himself Al-Majah, the Mystic Sheik. Rose Rita could wear a costume too. They discussed what would be best—maybe another tuxedo, or an Indian girl's costume with harem pants. "We'll need two pairs," Rose Rita pointed out. "One for me, one for the fake legs."

They worked everything out. By the time Rose Rita left, Lewis was feeling better. The shock of the spider's appearance had worn off, the two of them had solved the problem of the talent show, and things were looking up. Or so he thought.

When Rose Rita headed home, she walked slowly and thoughtfully. She kept rubbing her thumb over the white scar on her finger. It felt cold and numb. The day was cold too, and though a bright sun shone, to Rose Rita it seemed as if a veil had fallen, dimming the clear blue sky, cooling the September sunlight. She had the strangest feeling of not being quite *there*, as if she were only dreaming about walking home. Her mood was dark also. Rose Rita hated junior high. The other girls talked about only one topic: boys, boys, boys. Some of them made fun of her for hanging out with Lewis, who was short, chunky, and no good at sports. Rose Rita knew that the other girls made catty remarks about her. Behind her back they called her "beanpole" or "four-eyes."

It wasn't fair. Just because she had been born with long bones, straight hair, and nearsighted eyes, the others acted as if she weren't as human as they were. Sometimes Rose Rita felt all mixed up. The things she had cared about all her life—history and baseball and her friends—

now seemed childish and unimportant. Other things, like having gorgeous hair and wearing fabulous dresses, seemed more grown-up. Still, Rose Rita thought the girls who spent all their time mooning over movie actors and singers and kids like Dave Shellenberger were drippy.

And as if she didn't have enough on her mind already, the scroll waited in her room at the bottom of her sock drawer. She remembered the sharp pain of the paper cut and the eerie way the spider had come to life. Rose Rita had the uneasy feeling that Lewis was right. She should tell Mrs. Zimmermann about the scroll. Mrs. Zimmermann would understand—

Ugh! Rose Rita stopped dead in her tracks. She had walked into an invisible spiderweb, and it clung to her cheeks. Frantically, she brushed her face to get the sticky strands off. But she couldn't feel anything. Not with her hand, at least.

Yet her mouth felt as if a web had been pulled across it, touching lightly and tickling. Rose Rita began to panic. What if it were some kind of magical web? What if it were connected in some way with the spider? "I won't tell!" she vowed at last, and the feeling eased without quite going away.

Rose Rita hurried the rest of the way home, occasionally swiping at her face with the palm of a hand. She couldn't rub away the sensation. It stayed with her into the evening. After dinner Rose Rita's father, George Pottinger, liked to stretch out in an armchair and listen to a Detroit Tigers baseball game on the radio. Usually Rose

Rita joined him, but on this Saturday night she just dragged herself upstairs to her room.

Rose Rita went to bed early. She lay there feeling weary, but she couldn't sleep. She heard the sounds of her mother and father getting ready for bed, and then the house was quiet. Lying there, Rose Rita felt like screaming. No one understood her. Her mom and dad were kind and well-meaning, but they didn't remember what being young was like. They never gave her good answers to her questions. Mrs. Pottinger fussed and fretted, and Mr. Pottinger always began, "In *my* day we didn't have that problem."

Uncle Jonathan and Lewis were good friends, but they couldn't know what growing up as an ordinary-looking, even plain girl was like. Mrs. Zimmermann always listened sympathetically, but her advice was "Be what you are." That was the problem. Rose Rita wasn't really sure *what* she was, or what she wanted to be. She began to feel sorry for herself. Tears stung her eyes.

Somehow she must have drifted to sleep at last. She had one of those weird dreams in which she knew she was dreaming. It seemed to Rose Rita that she could fly, and she found herself floating along high above New Zebedee. Below her the town spread out like a scale model of itself, from Wilder Park to the quiet neighborhoods to the north. The trees were red, yellow, and orange. Traffic crept along. It looked like an ordinary fall day. She sailed over the junior high and saw a bunch of girls she knew standing outside, laughing and talking.

Mischievously, Rose Rita decided to show off her flying talent. She dropped lower and lower over the girls, thinking that it didn't matter if she scared them. This was only a dream, after all, and nothing she did would really hurt them.

As she slipped lower, Rose Rita could hear the girls giggling and screeching and acting silly, the way they always did. A brown-haired girl named Sue Gottschalk said, "She gives me the creeps, that's all. I think she looks like a long, tall bag of bones!"

"No," said Lauren Muller. "She's not a bone—she's the dog!"

They all roared with laughter. Sue said, "That gives me a great idea. My pop's promised me a puppy for my birthday. If it's a girl, I'm going to name it Rose Rita!"

Rose Rita felt her face turn hot and red. They were talking about her! Rose Rita had always thought that some of the girls, such as Sue, were her friends. Now she wanted to shrivel up and die. She wanted to fly to the moon and never come back.

"No," said a strange, breathy voice, a woman's voice. "Running away is no good, not with your powers. Use your strength. Teach these unworthy ones a lesson."

Rose Rita could not see anyone who might have spoken. Twirling slowly in the air, Rose Rita asked, "Who is that?"

"A friend." Now Rose Rita could tell that the voice was in her mind, and not coming from outside. "Drop down, down, and take one of them. Take Sue. That will show them!"

Rose Rita grinned. Yes, that would show them! She'd snatch Sue right off the ground and scare the daylights out of her. Rose Rita began to drop lower, lower, slowly, and then she stretched out her long, shiny, hairy arms—

Eight of them!

Rose Rita looked down at herself and screamed in terror. She wasn't flying—she was dangling from a spiderweb. Her body had become a huge bloated thing, hairy and blue-black and round as a ball. She opened her mouth to scream, and she found she could make only a hissing noise. Thick green venom drooled out of her mouth.

She had become a giant spider!

CHAPTER FOUR

Rose Rita woke up panting and thrashing. She threw her covers off and jumped out of bed. She turned on the light. Her familiar room looked the same. Her goldfish swam in their tank; the high, black bureau stood against the wall; her math homework lay spread out on her desk. And she was her normal, tall, skinny self. Rose Rita was a sensible girl who did not believe in letting something as unreal as a dream bother her. Still, just remembering the nightmare made her shudder with revulsion. Barefooted, she went to the bathroom and got a drink of water. When she returned to her bedroom, she looked at her bedside clock. It was past two in the morning.

"I should be sleepy," Rose Rita muttered. "But now I'm wide awake." She straightened out her sheets and

cover. Should she read for a little while and see if that made her sleepy? She had just started a novel by C. S. Forrester about a brave naval captain back in the days of the Napoleonic wars. Rose Rita went to her bureau to get it. Then she remembered the scroll. It lay in the top drawer, just a few inches away from her hand. Slowly, as if her hand had a mind of its own, it pulled the drawer open. The scroll was there, along with her miniature Little Duke playing cards, her set of Drueke chessmen, and a little carved wooden farmhouse-and-barn set that Mrs. Zimmermann had bought for her during a trip to Pennsylvania. Rose Rita didn't plan to take the scroll out. She just wanted to look at it, to make sure it was still there.

Somehow, though, Rose Rita found herself back in bed, with pillows propped up behind her. She carefully removed the rolled-up scroll from its cloth wrapper. Like Lewis, Rose Rita had decided that the spider might have just been hiding in the scroll. She didn't want another ugly surprise like that. The parchment felt soft, dusty, and leathery. Rose Rita unrolled it a little. The edges were frayed and worn, but the scroll was not too badly damaged. A peculiar, musty, spicy scent rose from the old parchment. It was not unpleasant, but it seemed a little unsettling. Rose Rita unwound more of the scroll, revealing lettering.

It looked like handwriting. Maybe the ink once had been black and bold, but time had faded it to a dreary, dull brown, almost the color of dried blood. Rose Rita blinked at the strange phrases:

The Last Testament of
Belle Frisson,
The Greatest Sorceress of Her Age

Reading this gave Rose Rita a strange feeling. She remembered Mr. Hardwick's sign in the window of the magicians' museum. The words were obvious exaggerations—they were kind of funny. Mr. Hardwick's sign had the humor of a tall tale. But the heading on the scroll didn't seem funny at all. Whoever Belle Frisson was, Rose Rita thought, she had actually believed herself to be the greatest sorceress of her age. Suddenly the night outside seemed darker. Anything might be waiting out there beyond her closed window. Peering in at her. Watching her.

"Oh, get a grip," Rose Rita told herself. She thrust the scroll back into its cover and under the socks again. Climbing back into bed, she lay wakeful for a long time. Finally she slipped into an uneasy sleep. Vague dreams made her toss and turn, but she did not wake up again until morning.

For the rest of the week Rose Rita and Lewis practiced every day after school. Lewis would be the star of the first trick. And later Rose Rita would take center stage for a trick of her own. Lewis and Rose Rita would come out onstage, and he would introduce them both. Then she would pick up a sheet of newspaper from a low platform on the stage. Rose Rita would display the newspaper, holding it so the audience could see both the front

) 36 (

and the back. Then she would fold it again and hand it to Lewis.

Lewis would take the newspaper and hold it up, open it wide, and say a magic word. Then he would crumple the paper into a ball. He would tear away the paper, like someone peeling an orange, and the live dove—except it would be a chick or duckling—would peep out. At least that was the way the trick was supposed to work. In their rehearsals Lewis had no live animal.

Instead, Lewis practiced until he could successfully produce his stand-in chick, one of his uncle's white socks, stuffed with more socks. Doing the trick really wasn't too hard. As the magic book explained, the key to sleight of hand is misdirection. That meant Lewis had to make the audience suspect the trick was in one part of the presentation, when it really was elsewhere. In this case the audience would be looking closely at the newspaper as Rose Rita paraded back and forth, opening it, showing both sides, even shaking it. The newspaper was not gimmicked, however.

The real trick was that Lewis had made a sort of cloth swing from a handkerchief and some strong black thread. While Rose Rita was showing the paper, Lewis would hook two loops of the black thread around his right thumb. He gently held the handkerchief, in which the stuffed sock rested, against his side with his right elbow. His robe would cover it. When Lewis spread the paper wide, he moved his elbow away from his side, and the sock swung out. The open sheet of paper concealed it from the audience. Lewis crushed the paper carefully

around it. Then, as he held up the ball of newspaper, he slipped his thumb out of the string. When he tore away the paper and took out the imitation chick, he left the handkerchief and the black string in the ball of paper. The audience would be so surprised at the appearance of the living bird that they wouldn't even think about the paper anymore. At least, that was what the book promised.

When Lewis and Rose Rita had practiced several times, they showed their presentation to Uncle Jonathan, who laughed when he saw one of his old socks magically come out of the newspaper. "I guess I'm lucky you didn't decide to produce my underwear!" he said with a grin.

Lewis, who was wearing his bathrobe as a substitute for his costume, snickered. "It's supposed to be a chick," he explained.

"Well, you could certainly have fooled me," said Uncle Jonathan. "Rose Rita, you did a great job of showing off the newspaper. I was sure the trick would be to rig it up somehow."

"Thanks," replied Rose Rita.

Lewis looked at her uneasily. Rose Rita had been acting funny all week, dreamy and lost. Her mind seemed to be miles away. Yet she did just as well at school as she always did, and she certainly didn't mess up the magic act.

On Wednesday they went over to Mrs. Zimmermann's house. Mrs. Zimmermann was sewing their costumes for them. Lewis would wear a silvery turban with a big peacock plume in the front; a short velvet cape, black on the outside and lined with purple; a loose purple tunic; and loose scarlet pants. Mrs. Zimmermann was even sewing

covers for his shoes from the same silvery material as his hat. It would look as if he were wearing Persian slippers with curly toes. Rose Rita would have on a purple outfit that left her arms bare. Baggy harem pants, plus golden slippers, completed the costume. Mrs. Zimmermann was also preparing a headdress for Rose Rita, made up of fake pearls strung on a netting of gold-colored thread. And she would wear a gauzy purple veil too.

"You're going to look like mystics from the fabled East," Mrs. Zimmermann told them with a grin after she had finished measuring and sketching. She was a good artist, and she showed them pictures of the way they would look in the costumes. As a reward for their patience Mrs. Zimmermann had served up some of her wonderful chocolate-chip cookies and milk. Munching a cookie, Lewis asked that the cape be cut a little fuller, so that he could hide his chick under it for the first trick. Rose Rita just looked at the pictures and nodded. She didn't touch her cookies and milk. Mrs. Zimmermann's expression became a little concerned. "Are you feeling all right, Rose Rita?" she asked.

Rose Rita's face flushed. "I wish everybody would stop worrying about me," she snapped. "My mom thinks there's something wrong, Lewis keeps looking at me as if he thinks I'm going to roll over and die, and now you. I'm fine!"

Mrs. Zimmermann stared in astonishment. "Good heavens, Rose Rita! Don't bite my head off."

Rose Rita looked at her feet. "I'm sorry," she mumbled. "I'm tired, that's all."

Later, after Rose Rita had left for home, Lewis asked Mrs. Zimmermann, "Do you think she's sick or something?"

Mrs. Zimmermann began to fold the cloth that she had spread out on the table. She looked thoughtful and tapped her chin with her finger. "I don't know," she said slowly. "Rose Rita certainly doesn't seem to be her usual lively self, but she's at an awkward age for a girl. She's having strange feelings that she never had before. And she's always been very self-conscious. I wouldn't be surprised if the other girls in school are making fun of her."

That upset Lewis. "Why would they do that? She's great!"

Mrs. Zimmermann shrugged and gave Lewis a sad smile. "You know that and I know that, Lewis, but Rose Rita isn't so sure. When you're a little different from all the others, they tend to pick on you. I don't suppose Rose Rita's classmates are intentionally cruel, but some girls can be thoughtless. Rose Rita is lucky to have a good friend like you. I think she'll come through all the stress and strain very well, but you'll have to let her feel sad and mopey every once in a while. Now, then: Do you want silver bells on your Persian slippers, or will they be all right just plain?"

By the following Saturday Lewis had carefully copied all the directions for their four tricks. After breakfast he headed downtown to return the books. It was a cool morning. Autumn was definitely on the way. Lewis wore his windbreaker over a red-plaid flannel shirt, but he still

felt chilly when the wind blew in his face. He hurried down the hill and met Rose Rita at her house. She was wearing a baggy Notre Dame jacket that had belonged to her uncle. "Got it?" asked Lewis.

Rose Rita nodded and unzipped the jacket. Inside she had concealed the scroll. "I'll be glad to get rid of this thing," she murmured.

Lewis could only agree. Rose Rita looked terrible. Her eyes had dark circles under them, and they held a strange, haunted, anxious expression. She looked thinner too. The two friends walked downtown without saying anything to each other.

Their timing was perfect. They met Mr. Hardwick outside the National Museum of Magic just as he fitted his key into the lock. He looked up and smiled. "Lewis and Rose Rita! What a pleasure to see you again. Want me to take those?"

"No," said Lewis quickly. "We'll put them back for you."

Mr. Hardwick opened the door. "In we go! Thanks, Lewis. That's very considerate of you. I hope you found some good tricks."

"We did," replied Lewis. "We're going to have a great act."

Rose Rita, who had not said a word for many minutes, suddenly blurted out, "Mr. Hardwick, who was Belle Frisson?"

Mr. Hardwick switched on the lights, then turned and gave her a quizzical look. "Why, where did you hear that name? I didn't think anyone remembered her."

"Uh," said Lewis, "she was mentioned in one of the old books."

Mr. Hardwick nodded and adjusted his glasses. "Let me see, what do I remember about Belle Frisson?" He clicked his tongue a couple of times. "Hmm. Well, to begin with, her real name was Elizabeth Proctor. Do you two know anything about the Fox sisters?"

When both Lewis and Rose Rita shook their heads, Mr. Hardwick said, "Come on upstairs, and I'll tell you about them." They followed him. He turned on the lights there too and told them to sit down. They sat in the comfortable chairs arranged around the card table. Mr. Hardwick said, "You have to understand that the Fox sisters were quite a sensation a hundred years ago. It began in Hydesville, New York, in 1848. Maggie and Katie Fox were fifteen and twelve years old. They claimed they started to hear strange, thumping noises at night. Do you know what a poltergeist is?"

Again Lewis shook his head, but Rose Rita said, "It's some kind of ghost, isn't it?"

"Absolutely right," said Mr. Hardwick. "The word is German and means 'noisy ghost.' Well, Maggie and Katie said they began to ask this thumping spirit questions, and it answered with one rap for *yes* and two for *no*. Later they worked out an alphabet code too. Their older sister Leah joined in, and the girls began to attract attention as spirit mediums. They would have séances, and the spirits of the dead would supposedly answer their questions. They became world famous. Eventually Elizabeth Proctor saw them perform. She was an unsuccessful ac-

tress at the time. She went back to her hometown of Savannah, Georgia, and put together a magic act that she claimed was based on ancient Egyptian sorcery. It was full of fake poltergeist phenomena. This time she succeeded. From about 1855 to the time she died in 1878, she toured the country as Belle Frisson."

Rose Rita frowned. "She didn't deal with real ghosts?"

Mr. Hardwick guffawed. "Well, neither did the Fox sisters," he said. "In time they confessed it was all trickery. Lots of people believed that Belle Frisson had real magic power, but I'm sure it was all just part of the act. I think I've got a book that has a chapter on her. The writer halfway believed in her powers, so you have to take what he says with a grain of salt." Pausing, Mr. Hardwick looked thoughtful. "You know, you could visit Belle Frisson's grave if you wanted. She's buried only about twenty miles from here, in a cemetery just outside of Cristobal."

"Where's that?" Lewis asked.

"Oh, it's a small farm village southwest of here," Mr. Hardwick said. "That little cemetery is quite unusual. It has half a dozen magicians buried in it." He got up. "Let me find your book, and you can replace the ones you borrowed."

They went into the next room, and Lewis began to put the books back on the shelves. Mr. Hardwick climbed up on a ladder and reached above his head for a volume, and as he did, Rose Rita quickly took the scroll from her jacket and shoved it back into its place, in an open-topped box. She jerked her hand away quickly. Something had popped up from the box as Rose Rita replaced

the scroll. It was a big black spider, its body as large as a grape. It raised its two front legs threateningly, then darted behind the rows of books. Rose Rita looked at Lewis with wide, sick eyes.

"Here we are," Mr. Hardwick said cheerfully, stepping down from the ladder. He held a worn old book, bound in deep olive-green leather. He handed it over to Rose Rita. "Be careful with this," he said. "It was published in Chicago in 1885. It's quite rare."

"I'll be careful," promised Rose Rita. She took the book from Mr. Hardwick and thanked him, and then she and Lewis left. On the sidewalk outside, Rose Rita said, "Whew! I'm glad that's all over."

"So am I," said Lewis. He glanced anxiously at Rose Rita. She still looked tired and drawn, and she had pulled her head down low because of the chilly wind. She held the old volume tight against her chest. Lewis wondered if it really *was* over—if whatever had been bothering Rose Rita was somehow tied in with Belle Frisson, the scroll, and the mysterious spider. He hoped that whatever they had started would end now. Maybe replacing the scroll would break whatever weird chain of events they had accidentally begun.

But he had his doubts.

CHAPTER FIVE

September passed. October began, with cool, crisp days filled with the scent of burning leaves. Rose Rita and Lewis practiced and practiced until they could do all four magic tricks perfectly. There was only one problem. Lewis still had not been able to rehearse the newspaper stunt with a live animal. "Maybe you could produce a bouquet of flowers instead of a chick," suggested Uncle Jonathan a couple of days before the talent show.

Lewis shook his head impatiently. In some ways Lewis was a real perfectionist. Some things had to be done just right, or they were no good at all, and the magic trick was one of them. He said, "Flowers wouldn't be the same. Timmy Lindholm's going to bring a chick in for me. It'll be all right." And he really thought it would. He had become very adept at swinging the stuffed sock into the

newspaper without anyone seeing the move. Even Mrs. Zimmermann, who had sharp eyes for foolery, couldn't quite tell how he produced the sock from the balled-up newspaper.

In fact, Lewis would have been very happy except for his continuing worries about Rose Rita. It was not that she had changed, exactly. She still practiced with him, she tried on the costume that Mrs. Zimmermann had made, and she went to school every day, the same as always. But Rose Rita had become even more withdrawn, silent, and absent recently. She went through their magic routine as if she had only half her mind on what she was doing. At school Rose Rita hardly talked to anyone. She hurried away from the little groups of girls that gathered on the playground or stood outside near the steps. In class she responded when the teachers called on her, but she stopped raising her hand to answer questions.

Lewis found that especially unusual. Rose Rita always waved her hand eagerly when the teacher asked something she knew. He also missed her tall tales. Rose Rita had once told him she wanted to be a famous writer when she grew up, and she certainly had the imagination. Often she would dream up some outrageous or funny story about their teachers or classmates and spin it out for Lewis with a straight face. She might tell how Bill Mackey, an annoying, gangly kid with big feet, had been kidnapped by Martians when he was a baby and raised on Mars. Since the gravity there is low, Rose Rita would explain, Bill grew to be a beanpole. The Martians brought him back when they discovered he was a human. They

had wanted a monkey and had made a natural mistake.

Rose Rita had lots of wild stories like that one, but even though Lewis encouraged her to tell him one, she refused. Unlike Rose Rita, Lewis could never decide what he wanted to be when he grew up. Sometimes he thought it would be fun to be a photographer for *National Geographic* and go all over the globe taking pictures of dusty herds of elephants, lofty snowcapped mountains, and exotic dancers in Thailand or Tahiti. At other times he wanted to be an airline pilot, a research chemist, or an astronomer. Usually he could tease Rose Rita into making up a story about what life would be like if he were photographing crocodiles on the banks of the Nile or bending over a telescope on Mount Palomar, searching the night sky for comets. Lately, however, she didn't even seem to listen to him.

The week of the talent show was so hectic that Lewis almost forgot to worry about Rose Rita. For many years the junior high students had performed the show in the school cafeteria. This year they would put it on in the municipal auditorium, the refurbished New Zebedee Opera House. Lewis had bad memories of that stage, and just standing on it made him nervous, but all the kids would have to perform there. The teachers had planned the talent show for the evening of October 9, a Friday. On Thursday afternoon they all had a dress rehearsal in the auditorium.

The New Zebedee Opera House was an old theater in the top two stories of the Farmers' Feed & Seed building. It had a horseshoe-shaped balcony, rows of red-

velvet-covered seats, and an ornate stage. The walls had been painted pink, with intricate designs in gold framing the stage. On one side was the grieving theatrical mask of tragedy, and on the other the laughing mask of comedy. Uncle Jonathan helped Lewis carry all his magical paraphernalia upstairs and put it out of the way backstage. The two of them had found two big cardboard boxes, which Lewis and Rose Rita had painted with tempera. One was red and yellow, and the other blue and purple. Rose Rita would climb into the red-and-yellow one, and after some hocus-pocus on Lewis's part she would reappear in the blue-and-purple one. They also hauled up a sort of low sofa that Uncle Jonathan had knocked together from some scrap lumber, some cotton stuffing, and some upholstery material. It had casters so that it could roll on and off the stage, and Rose Rita would lie on it before the levitation stunt. Finally, they brought up the chair and the mirror for the last trick, the one in which Rose Rita's head would seem to float in midair.

As rehearsal began, Lewis got into his costume and paced around backstage while Dave Shellenberger and Tom Lutz practiced their comedy act. They were imitating the comedians Bud Abbott and Lou Costello doing a baseball skit called "Who's on first?" The other kids stood in the wings listening and laughing their heads off, but Lewis was too tense to watch. He saw James Gensterblum tuning up his guitar. James was wearing a gray-and-black striped shirt and gray pants, and his blue eyes were narrowed in concentration. "Hey, James," Lewis whispered, "have you seen Timmy around?"

James shook his head. "Not since we left school. He should be here, though. He's gonna juggle."

For a few minutes Lewis watched James lower his head over his guitar and listen carefully as he tuned.

"Hey, Lewis," James said suddenly. "Timmy just came in."

Lewis looked in the direction James pointed. Timmy, an easygoing, tubby boy with curly black hair and a freckled nose, came backstage. He lugged a canvas bag, which he set down in a corner. Lewis hurried over to him, asking, "Did you bring it?"

Timmy sighed. "Aw, gee, I forgot, Lewis. I'm sorry."

"I need that chicken," said Lewis, annoyed at Timmy's absentmindedness.

"I'll get one for you. I just forgot." Timmy took some bowling-pin-shaped Indian clubs from his bag. He rolled up the sleeves of his blue shirt. "I gotta practice now."

Lewis frowned as Timmy began to toss and catch the three clubs. Timmy was pretty good at juggling, but he had a lousy memory.

Rose Rita came out of the girls' dressing room. She had changed into her costume. James and Timmy looked at her and grinned, but she didn't seem to notice them. "You ready?" Lewis asked her.

Rose Rita just nodded.

Their magic act came after Tom and Dave's "Who's on first?" routine. Mrs. Fogarty, their English teacher, sat in the auditorium, along with Uncle Jonathan and a few parents. One of the parents, Mr. Lutz, was helping backstage. He put on a record that Lewis gave him, "Saber

Dance." As soon as the music started, Lewis stepped out from behind the curtains.

Footlights and spotlights shone in his face, dazzling him. He could hardly see anything out in the audience—just the gleam of light reflected in Mrs. Fogarty's spectacles. "Ladies and gentlemen," he said in a squeaky, frightened voice, "I am the Mystifying Mysto, Master of Illusion! Let me introduce you to my beautiful assistant, the Fantastic Fatima!"

Rose Rita came out from the wings holding the newspaper. She went through the act just as they had practiced for weeks, and Lewis produced the sock, calling it "a live chick, produced by magic!" He began to feel better when someone, probably his uncle Jonathan, applauded. They did the other tricks without a hitch and then took their bows. The curtain fell, and Lewis and Rose Rita got their stuff offstage with James's help. "That was great," James whispered as Timmy's juggling music began.

"Thanks," Lewis said. He felt drained. Now that his turn was over, his knees began to shake, and he was dizzy. To Rose Rita he said, "I think we've finally got it down."

Rose Rita just shrugged, as if she didn't really care.

Friday was horrible. All day long the talent show tormented Lewis. He hated the thought of going out onstage in front of everyone. Though he tried to tell himself that everything would go well, doubts and fears kept nagging him. He decided that Rose Rita was right. She often called him a worrywart and accused him of

always looking on the dark side. Lewis hated when he did that, but he couldn't help himself. Now he kept imagining all kinds of disasters that could happen. Whenever he thought about forgetting his lines or making some stupid mistake, his hands felt cold and his stomach churned. He could not keep his mind on school, and his math teacher snapped at him, "Lewis, pay attention!"

Lewis wanted to practice after school, but Rose Rita shook her head and drifted away, walking toward home. Lewis slouched along behind her with his hands in his pockets. Because of the talent show none of the teachers had given homework, and he had no books to carry, but he was in a foul mood. Deliberately walking slowly, he watched Rose Rita up ahead. He was beginning to think she wasn't much of a friend. She didn't seem to care about their act enough to practice one last time.

As they headed up Mansion Street, with Lewis fifty feet behind Rose Rita, he felt cold all over. Rose Rita was walking beside the privet hedge in front of Martha Westley's house. The yard was Mrs. Westley's pride and joy, and the hedge was neatly trimmed. Lewis squinted. Something dark was creeping along at the base of the hedge, right beside Rose Rita. It looked like a steel-gray kitten or puppy, except that it moved strangely, in jerky darts. It looked more like an impossibly big insect than anything else.

Rose Rita passed the hedge, and the dark blob moved out of its shadow. Lewis's throat was dry. When the shape moved from the shade into the sunshine, it simply vanished, becoming as transparent as a soap bubble. Rose

Rita walked on alone. Still, Lewis had a hard time getting his breath. In the single instant before it had disappeared, the shape had looked as if it had long, busy legs and a round, shiny body. It looked like a spider the size of a kitten.

Rose Rita turned at her house and went up the steps and inside. Walking slowly past, Lewis peered this way and that, staring hard at the piles of autumn leaves along the curb, at the roots of hedges and bushes. He could smell the fall scent of burning leaves, and he could hear the dry rustling of more leaves overhead. The rustling made him jerk his gaze upward. What if the sound wasn't just the wind? What if that horrible creature was lurking up there, ready to drop its cold, clutching body onto the back of his neck? Lewis broke into a frantic run. He did not stop until he had slammed the door of his house safely behind him.

Late that afternoon Uncle Jonathan and Lewis piled into Jonathan's big, old-fashioned car, a black 1935 Muggins Simoom. They pulled out into the street in a cloud of exhaust fumes and drove to Mansion Street to pick up a glum and withdrawn Rose Rita. Then they drove downtown, where Jonathan found a parking slot near the Feed & Seed store. With his stomach already feeling queasy from stage fright, Lewis climbed out of the car. Mrs. Zimmermann had driven in earlier to help prepare the refreshments, and Lewis saw her car parked nearby.

They hurried upstairs. As he headed for the stage, Lewis thought that the mask of tragedy painted on the

wall looked just about as upset as he felt. He went to the boys' dressing room and got into his costume. Then he checked all his magic props. Everything was ready. Now if only Timmy would remember to bring the chick, Lewis was all set to go.

Timmy was late, as always. Lewis impatiently paced back and forth backstage, pausing every now and then to part the curtains and peep out at the growing crowd. All the elementary-school kids and their parents were coming in, together with the parents of the performers. Lewis had a big hard lump in his throat that he couldn't seem to swallow. Just the thought of doing his act in front of nearly five hundred people terrified him. His legs felt rubbery and weak, his head spun, and the breath caught in his lungs.

At last Timmy came hurrying down the aisle, carrying two bags. One was his canvas bag of juggling clubs and balls, and the other was a burlap sack. Lewis rushed to meet him. "Hi," said Timmy with a grin as soon as he was backstage. "I brought your chicken." He handed Lewis the burlap bag, which felt surprisingly heavy.

Lewis opened the bag and looked inside. A white hen stared back at him, her head tilted sideways, her little chicken eyes bright. "Timmy!" exploded Lewis. "This is a full-grown chicken!"

Timmy looked confused. "Huh? Didn't you want a chicken? You kept asking me to bring one."

"I wanted a *baby* chick," wailed Lewis. "Not a grown-up hen!"

With a shrug, Timmy said, "Henrietta will be okay.

She's a good chicken. She's just like a pet. You can pick her up and everything. Anyway, you'll have to use her, because I don't have time to go back and get another one. I gotta practice my juggling."

Timmy unpacked his clubs and started tossing them through the air. Lewis found a dark corner. He peered down into the burlap bag uncertainly. Henrietta stared back at him. Lewis was not at all sure that this would work. He wished he had brought a bouquet of flowers along, just in case something like this happened. But since he hadn't, Lewis decided that he'd better practice the trick with Henrietta. Getting one of the sheets of newspaper from the prop table, Lewis hooked the string-and-handkerchief swing around his thumb and then reached into the bag. Henrietta was feathery, soft, and hot. He pulled her out of the bag. She was a very calm chicken. Lewis looped the handkerchief swing around her, so she was sort of lying in it, and tucked her under his robe. It was hard for him to hold her with his elbow, because she was so large and heavy.

Lewis held the newspaper, then spread it. The swing swooped out from his elbow, he crushed the paper into a loose ball that barely covered Henrietta, and then he tore it away. Henrietta cocked her head this way and that and clucked once. Lewis had been holding his breath. He whooshed it out in relief. Maybe, he thought, the trick was going to work after all.

The talent show began when Miss White, the music teacher, played an overture on the piano and announced to everyone that the junior high students were pleased to

carry on the tradition here in this wonderful new auditorium. Then the curtain went up and the first talent act started. Lewis stood in the wings, watching, with Henrietta tucked beneath his robes and under his arm. Her body heat made him uncomfortably warm, and he started to sweat. Henrietta must have felt hot too, because soon she began to squirm and complain. Rose Rita came over and stood beside Lewis as Tom and Dave did their comedy routine. They wore goofy-looking old-fashioned baseball uniforms, and they had pasted fake mustaches under their noses. They got lots of laughter and applause. Then Miss White said, "Next we have a real treat—a magic act that will leave you baffled and bewildered!" Mr. Lutz started "Saber Dance" on the phonograph, and Lewis stumbled out onstage, under the hot glare of the lights.

"Ladies and gentlemen," rasped Lewis. He swallowed and squeaked, "Ladies and gentlemen," again. Taking a deep breath, Lewis blurted, "I am, uh, the Mystifying Mysto, Master of Illusion!"

From beneath his right arm Henrietta commented, "Bu-u-u-u-ck!"

Lewis squeezed the hen a little more securely. He said, "Let me introduce you to my beautiful assistant, the Fantastic Fatima!"

Rose Rita, looking as if she were in a trance, came out from the wings holding the newspaper. Lewis said, "I will ask the Fantastic Fatima to show you, uh, this perfectly, uh, ordinary—" He was really squirming, because Henrietta was trying to escape. He could feel her writhing

and kicking, and he held on to her desperately. "This, uh, ordinary newspaper, and then I'll ask her to give it to me right now!" he finished in a rush.

Rose Rita took her time, just as they had rehearsed. Meanwhile, Henrietta was making determined efforts to find a way out from under those hot robes. Lewis felt his face get hot and red as he wriggled and squirmed, trying to control the hen. At last Rose Rita gave him the newspaper. He reached for it with a feeling of relief.

And everyone started to laugh. In a flurry of feathers, Henrietta dropped out from beneath Lewis's robe. She flapped and squawked. Lewis hadn't even started the trick. He stared at Rose Rita, wondering what to do. She just stared back at him. Out in the audience some kid yelled, "Fake!" Other people started to jeer.

Lewis felt panicky. The chicken stood in the spotlight, jerking her head left and right. People were laughing and calling out things like "Why did the chicken cross the road?" and "Which came first, the chicken or the egg?"

Rose Rita gave Lewis a sharp nudge. "Uh, a live chicken, produced by magic," Lewis said lamely. "Now my assistant will lie down on this magic sofa, and we will perform for you the ancient art of levitation." He took Rose Rita's hand and escorted her to the sofa. Everyone was still laughing. Henrietta was pacing back and forth near the front of the stage, emitting long, contented clucks.

Rose Rita lay down, and Lewis picked up the sheet that would cover her. He spread it out, and as he did, Rose

Rita moved her own feet down to either side of the low sofa and picked up the fake feet. Trying hard to ignore the chicken, which was sitting in the middle of the stage, Lewis covered Rose Rita and turned to the audience. "Now with the mystic words—"

Henrietta was right beside Lewis. She suddenly stood up, cackling, "Bu-buck! Bu-buck! Bu-buck!" A gleaming white egg rested on the stage. Then people really began to hoot and cheer. More kids were shouting, "Lewis is a fake! Boo-ooo!"

A humiliated Lewis thought he was going to die. He held up his hands, forgot the magic words he was supposed to say, and yelled, "Rise up! Rise up!"

With her back bent and the fake legs held out beneath the sheet, Rose Rita raised herself off the sofa. Usually the illusion looked really good—just as if Rose Rita had mysteriously begun to float a few feet in the air under the sheet. But this time Lewis was distracted, and he did not notice he was standing on a corner of the sheet. When Rose Rita lifted herself up, the sheet fell away, revealing her holding those stupid-looking fake legs.

"It's a trick!" yelled someone in the audience. "Get off the stage! Boo!" Other kids joined in the catcalls. "You're no magician!" "Go back to the farm!" "Take your chicken home and cook it!"

Rose Rita dropped the legs and stood up, her face still burning red. She scowled out at the audience. Now all the elementary-school kids were shrieking, "Boo! Boo!"

Henrietta flapped her wings and cackled again. A sin-

gle white feather floated in the air, twirling and twisting.

Lewis wanted to shrivel up and creep into a hole somewhere.

And then, to his shock, he heard Rose Rita shout above all the noise, "Shut up! I hate you all! I'm going to make you pay!"

Mercifully, the curtain dropped. Rose Rita turned and glared at Lewis, then stalked away. Lewis thought his heart had stopped.

In that terrifying moment Rose Rita hadn't looked like herself at all. Her eyes had been completely black and glittery, as if they were made up of thousands of facets, like the eyes of a spider. A spider in human form.

CHAPTER SIX

Rose Rita huddled in the smelly dark, seething with anger. She hated Lewis for making her look ridiculous. She hated the school for having the stupid talent contest in the first place. Most of all, she hated the kids and even the grown-ups in the audience who had made fun of her. "I'll make them pay," she growled to herself. She sat in a hunched-up position, hugging her knees. Her hiding place was cramped and hot, but she didn't care. She didn't even care that it smelled bad—mildew and disinfectant and sweeping compound all mixed together. Rose Rita was trying hard to think up ways of getting back at everyone who had made her a laughingstock.

Someone knocked at the door, making her jump. She bumped her head but bit her lip to keep from yelling and

giving herself away. Then she heard Mrs. Zimmermann's kindly voice: "Are you in there, Rose Rita?"

"No!" snapped Rose Rita, though she knew how dumb that would sound. "Go away."

"I don't think I should. May I come in?"

Rose Rita didn't say anything. She shrugged in the dark. She should have realized there was no way to hide from Mrs. Zimmermann. Mrs. Zimmermann had all sorts of spells she could use to find anything lost or in hiding. The doorknob rattled, and Mrs. Zimmermann swung open the door of the janitor's closet. She looked down at Rose Rita, who was crouched in the corner under a thick plywood shelf stacked with cans of Old Dutch cleanser, boxes of lightbulbs and steel wool, and wadded cleaning rags. Mrs. Zimmermann wrinkled her nose as she peered into the darkness. "I might have expected to find you just about anywhere but here. Good heavens, but you picked a smelly place to hide!"

"I don't care," replied Rose Rita grumpily. She was still wearing her costume, though the talent show had ended half an hour earlier. She pulled her legs a little closer, scrunching as far back into her corner as she could.

"Well, if you don't care, then I don't either," said Mrs. Zimmermann brightly. She crouched down slowly until she was sitting in the doorway, her legs bent to the side. "What happened up on the stage isn't the end of the world, you know."

"It might as well be for me," grumbled Rose Rita. She punched her glasses back into place on her nose and

sniffled a little. After a little while she quietly asked, "Is everyone gone now?"

"Just about," said Mrs. Zimmermann. The janitor's closet was at the end of a short hall, where only one dim bulb gave any illumination. The faint light made Mrs. Zimmermann's white hair glow, and it reflected in the lenses of her spectacles, making them little white circles. She squirmed, trying to make herself more comfortable. "I told your mother and father that I'd bring you home," she said. "I thought you might like some time to cool off."

Rose Rita took a deep breath, and it caught in her throat. She fought back a sob. "Why does everyone have to be so mean?" she asked in a forlorn voice.

Mrs. Zimmermann looked down. She pinched the material of her purple dress and started to pleat it absent-mindedly. "I don't believe they think of themselves as mean," she said slowly. "It's more a case of thank-heavens-it-isn't-me. Everyone has embarrassing moments, Rose Rita. When something especially horrible and embarrassing happens, sometimes people forget how others feel. They see the whole event not as a catastrophe, but as a show meant to entertain them. They also feel relieved that they are not the one who is the center of attention, so they laugh. I don't think anyone really meant you to take it personally."

"Well, I did." Rose Rita could feel her lower lip trembling. Tears blurred her eyes. "Th-they made f-fun of me!"

Mrs. Zimmermann held her arms open, and Rose Rita crept forward and hugged her. Mrs. Zimmermann's dress smelled faintly of peppermint. "There, there," said Mrs.

Zimmermann gently, patting her shoulder. "They made fun of you, but they didn't really hurt you."

Rose Rita straightened up. Her glasses had fogged up from her hot tears. "Y-yes they did!"

Mrs. Zimmermann smiled in a sad kind of way. "Oh, I know they hurt your *feelings*. I know that when they were yelling and booing, they made you feel about six inches tall. And I know that you don't think you can face anyone at school on Monday. Still, people forget, Rose Rita. This reminds me of the time I went to a dance when I was sixteen years old. A handsome fellow named Ben Quackenbush asked me to dance. Well, he was rugged but clumsy, and he stepped on the hem of my long skirt with his big black brogans. My skirt fell right down to my ankles. There I was, waltzing with my petticoat showing, for all the world to see. That was really scandalous back then!"

With a weak smile Rose Rita said, "It'd be pretty bad even today."

"Well, I don't know," replied Mrs. Zimmermann thoughtfully, a glint in her eye. "It might not attract as much attention nowadays. My legs aren't as shapely as they used to be!"

Despite herself Rose Rita giggled. "What happened next?"

Mrs. Zimmermann shrugged. "Everyone laughed at me. At school the girls started calling me 'Little Egypt.' Do you know who Little Egypt was?" When Rose Rita shook her head, Mrs. Zimmermann smiled. "She was what people used to call a hootchie-kootchie dancer. Her specialty was dancing onstage while wearing very little

clothing. You can imagine how that made me feel. Still, I got over it, and now I even think that what happened with Ben Quackenbush had its funny side. I think in time you'll get over what happened tonight too."

Rose Rita looked down at the dirty floor. In her secret heart she doubted that she would ever get over being laughed at and booed. She didn't want to say that to Mrs. Zimmermann, who was only trying to be kind. "Where's Lewis?" she asked in a small voice.

Mrs. Zimmermann smiled. "Jonathan drove him home not long after the two of you came offstage. Lewis is going to have a hard time living this down too, you know."

Rose Rita nodded, though privately she felt as if Lewis were to blame for the whole mess.

"Come on," said Mrs. Zimmermann, getting slowly to her feet. "You need to change, and we have to get out of here so they can lock this place up for the night." She held out her hand, and Rose Rita let Mrs. Zimmermann help her up. Rose Rita had been hiding in the closet so long that her legs were cramped and stiff. Glumly, she went to the girls' dressing room and changed back into her jeans and sweatshirt. Then she and Mrs. Zimmermann went down to Mrs. Zimmermann's purple 1950 Plymouth Cranbrook. Rose Rita carried her costume balled up, and she tossed it into the backseat.

Mrs. Zimmermann was quiet on the short drive to Mansion Street. She stopped in front of Rose Rita's house. The porch light was on, its yellow glare making harsh shadows on the lawn. "Don't take your anger out on Lewis," said Mrs. Zimmermann softly. "Remember,

they were laughing at him too. He feels just as bad as you do. The two of you are friends, and friends have to stick together when bad times come along."

Rose Rita just grunted. She opened the passenger door and got out of the car. For a second she thought about getting her costume, but then she decided she never wanted to see it again. Without even thanking Mrs. Zimmermann, Rose Rita slammed the car door and ran across the lawn. The front door was unlocked, and she burst through. From the parlor her mother called, "Rose Rita? Is that you?"

"I'm home," Rose Rita called back, and then she ran upstairs to her room. She locked the door and stood with her back against it. Closing her eyes, Rose Rita imagined seeing the darkened theater, the white chicken, the white gleaming egg. She thought she could almost hear the sniggers and the cruel laughter. She felt the dull heat of anger rising inside her again. "I'll make them pay," she whispered. She began to plan what she could do to humiliate everyone who had laughed at her.

Rose Rita's mother came to her door and asked if she was all right. "I'm fine," Rose Rita called back. "I'm going to bed."

She changed into pajamas and turned out the light. Lying in the dark, she thought of the weeks she had spent at Camp Kitchi-Itti-Kippi last summer. Rose Rita despised camp, and she had gone only because Lewis was away at Boy Scout camp. She had felt homesick much of the time. In Rose Rita's opinion the other girls at the camp were silly and irritating, but some activities had

been fun. At night as they had sat around the campfire, they had sung all sorts of funny camp songs. Then it didn't matter if her voice was on key or so far off that she couldn't have found the right note with a flashlight. Sometimes Rose Rita thought of the songs when she was feeling blue, and they usually helped cheer her up. One came to her as she lay in the darkness. It was sung to the tune of "The Battle Hymn of the Republic":

Oh, I wear my pink pajamas in the summer when
    it's hot,
And I wear my flannel nightie in the winter when
    it's not,
But when it's warm in springtime, and when
    it's cool in fall,
I jump right in between the sheets with nothing
    on at all!
Glory, glory, hallelujah,
Glory, glory, what's it to ya?
Glory, glory, hallelujah,
I jump right in between the sheets with nothing
    on at all!

The silly song usually made her smile. But after what she had been through, it seemed to have lost its power. Rose Rita lay awake and angry for hours.

The streetlight outside the house seemed unusually bright that night. Rose Rita stared at the window, and as time went by, the window began to gleam in the silvery light of the foggy streetlamp. Inside her room Rose Rita couldn't really see anything—just black shapes where she knew her chair, desk, and bureau were. Her eyes began

to feel heavy, until opening them seemed to be too much effort. Her breathing became slower and slower.

As Rose Rita nodded off, she tried in a dreamy, drifting kind of way to figure out what another dark shape was. She sensed it close by, and she forced her weary eyes open just a fraction to look for it. Yes, the shape was very close. It was tall and next to her bed. It might have been a coat rack with a coat or two hanging on it, except that she did not have one in her bedroom. Whatever it was, the form looked unfamiliar, as if it did not belong, and yet Rose Rita felt no surprise at glimpsing it there. A spicy scent wafted from it, dry and tingling in her nose, a little like sage and a little like cloves. She could have reached out and touched the form—it was that close to her bed—but she felt far too tired.

Instead, Rose Rita closed her eyes again and felt something touch her. The soft, dry hand on her forehead was Mrs. Zimmermann's, she thought in drowsy confusion, touching her brow in soft, soothing strokes. "I hate them all," murmured Rose Rita.

"I know you do." The voice was just a breathy whisper, so soft it might have come from inside Rose Rita's head. "Hatred is good. It can make you strong."

"Mm." Rose Rita felt keenly aware of her breathing, deep and regular. Her body felt as though it were floating on a cloud, billowy and soft.

"Your hatred can grow," said the whispery voice. "It can do your will and be your eyes and ears. You can set it free. I can show you how to send it forth to do your bidding." The dry hand stroked her forehead, soothing and

light, barely touching her. "I come from the grave to tell you this."

Cold fingers gripped Rose Rita's heart. Her breath stopped. She struggled to breathe again, but she was paralyzed.

"It is airless in the grave, dusty and quiet. And you cannot move, cannot scream. You can only think. Think of the power you possessed once and will possess again. I know!"

Rose Rita felt as if her lungs were about to burst. She was suffocating; she fought for air. But the hand pressed against her forehead, hard, pushing her down, down.

The relentless voice went on: "I bring a gift. You have been chosen. Feed your hate! Make it strong! Call me back!"

The hand pressed down even harder, and Rose Rita lost consciousness. She tumbled into a terrible nightmare, full of scuttling spiders, sticky webs, and dark, misshapen creatures, partly human and partly animal. Hands that were partly claws tore at her. Faces with black bug eyes, with the grimacing mouths of lions, snarled at her. She heard laughter, mocking and hateful. Then everything grew quiet.

Rose Rita dreamed that she stood before a strange sculpture. It was a many-sided pillar taller than her. Atop the pillar rested a stone ball, pitted and worn—a ball so large that Rose Rita could not have encircled it with her arms. Letters had been carved in the base of the pillar, but because of its shape Rose Rita could not read them. She circled the sculpture, trying to follow one line

of letters and make sense of them, but they were a jumble.

"Find me," said the breathy, whispery voice she had heard in her bedroom. "Come and free me."

Rose Rita looked around, but she could see no one. The dark ground stretched bare all the way to the horizon. The world might have been flat, with the sculpture at the very center. "Where are you?" Rose Rita called, her voice lost and tiny in the vast world.

"Find me," repeated the voice.

Rose Rita turned back to the sculpture. She gazed at the stone ball. Was it turning, slowly rotating? She couldn't be sure. For a long time she watched it. It was like staring at the minute hand of a clock, trying to see whether it was moving or not. Standing on tiptoe, Rose Rita reached up to touch the strange dark-gray sphere. The stone felt rough and cold beneath her palm.

And then something happened.

Two eyes opened. Eyes in the solid stone.

They stared at Rose Rita with a deep, piercing glare of hatred, looking so evil that Rose Rita gasped.

And then a stone hand emerged from the sphere near the eyes. It seized Rose Rita's hand and froze around it. The grip was solid, cold, rough, and unforgiving. Rose Rita tried to pull away. She could not budge an inch.

Rose Rita stared in horror. Her arm was turning gray and brittle. In a terrible wave, moving past her elbow to her shoulder, her body was changing.

Her flesh was turning to stone.

CHAPTER SEVEN

The next week passed as if Rose Rita had never awakened from that terrible nightmare. She almost felt that she really had been turned to stone. At least, her feelings were as cold as stone. She went to school every day. The other girls talked about her and giggled. Rose Rita ignored them. Lewis, who was suffering from merciless teasing himself, tried to apologize to her. She looked at him as though he were a mile away and didn't say anything. When the teachers gave assignments, Rose Rita did them automatically, like a machine. She didn't speak to anyone—not her mother or father, not Mrs. Zimmermann—about the hot little flame of hatred deep down inside her. It seemed to Rose Rita that the angry feeling was the only thing human about her, and she greedily kept it going.

Lewis invited her to his house for dinner a couple of

times, but Rose Rita just shook her head. She was waiting for something—she did not know what it might be—but somehow she knew that if she talked and laughed with her friends, her precious hot flame of hatred might die. So she kept to herself more than ever, biding her time.

On the Monday afternoon ten days after the talent show, Rose Rita came home from school and found a basket of newly laundered clothes in her room. She began to put them away. She hung blouses and skirts in her closet. She put folded jeans on a shelf. And then she began to match her socks into pairs. Rose Rita opened her bureau drawer and saw something sticking out from under the socks. Something that looked like faded purple velvet. Frowning, Rose Rita burrowed down and came up with the scroll.

"I put this back," muttered Rose Rita, turning the worn velvet cover this way and that. "I know I put this back in the museum."

She trembled, feeling the skin on her arms break out in gooseflesh. From deep inside her mind came again a sinister, whispery voice: *I bring a gift. You have been chosen.* Rose Rita watched her hands pull the brittle old scroll from its cover. She felt she had no control over them. Her fingers unrolled the scroll as if someone else were making them move. She scanned the crumply tan-colored scroll that bore letters and figures drawn in ink that had once been black but over the years had faded to a rusty iron shade. Before, Rose Rita had read only the first part of the scroll, which said that it was the final tes-

tament of Belle Frisson. Now she was looking at the rest. It made no sense.

The marks were not letters or numbers or even pictures, but just random-seeming strokes. Some of them led right off the top edge of the scroll, and others off the bottom. More nonsense chicken scratches covered the middle. Rose Rita had learned a little about foreign languages in school. She could read some Latin and French. In her schoolbooks she had seen reproductions of Egyptian hieroglyphs, Chinese pictographs, and other kinds of writing. The marks on the scroll did not look like any of them. They looked closer to Hebrew or Arabic than anything else, but Rose Rita did not think they were in either of those languages. She continued to unroll the scroll until she came to the very end, and then she gasped.

She saw something she recognized. She had seen it before in her nightmare: a many-sided pillar crowned with a huge ball. Rose Rita's hands began to shake as she remembered the awful feeling of turning into stone. She hastily rolled the scroll back up and thrust it into its cover. Something moved in her room, just at the corner of her vision. Rose Rita whirled. Did a dark shadow, the size of a small dog, dart into her closet? She could not be sure. Rose Rita dropped the scroll onto her bed and reached for her desk chair.

Holding it the same way a lion tamer holds a chair to ward off the dangerous big cats, Rose Rita threw her closet door wide open. Her clothing hung there. Nothing moved. She saw no shadowy shape. However, on the

floor of the closet lay the old green book she had borrowed from Mr. Hardwick at the museum. With everything that had happened, Rose Rita had not even looked at it. She set the chair down and picked up the old volume. Its leather cover felt pebbly and strangely slick. Rose Rita sat on the edge of her bed and opened the book and read the title page:

Forty Years Among the Magicians
or, My Friends the Fakirs, the Fakers, and the Fabulous Frauds

⚬∞⚬

by Joseph W. Winston
Stage Manager, Director, and Theatrical Producer

⚬∞⚬

The Leavitt Press, Inc.
Chicago, Illinois
1885

Rose Rita turned a few pages and then began to read what Mr. Winston had to say about magicians:

Stage conjurors are among the cleverest people on earth. They delight in controlled confusion, misdirection, and wonderful sleights that deceive us and delight us. Time after time I have witnessed some seeming miracle and have been utterly baffled, only to learn later of the absurdly simple means the artist has used to create the illusion of the miracle. I must admit to curiously mixed feelings in such cases, for part of me is delighted at the cleverness of the per-

former, whilst another part is annoyed at my own credulity and lack of observation.

And yet, on a few memorable occasions in my four decades of traveling from theater to theater, often in the company of such wonder workers, I have encountered what just possibly might be the real thing. Does magic truly exist? Gentle reader, I will leave the question to you. I intend only to bear witness to the half dozen or so performers whose tricks I could never fathom, whose sleights I could never penetrate. Were they tricksters only, or were they perhaps masters of powers most of us cannot even imagine? You be the judge.

Rose Rita turned more pages. She found a whole long chapter headed "Belle Frisson: Or, Speaking to the Spirits." Before reading it, Rose Rita stopped at an old-fashioned steel engraving, all dark cross-hatched lines. It showed a woman with a thin, oval face, large, piercing, dark eyes, and jet-black hair. She wore an Egyptian headband with a round medallion in front, and on the medallion was an engraving of a spider. Her somber eyes seemed to stare right into Rose Rita's. Rose Rita turned the page very quickly.

And then she stared at another picture, a grainy photograph this time. It showed a flat cemetery with headstones crowded thick. At the center of the picture was a monument far taller than the stones around it. Rose Rita had seen it before. It was the many-sided pillar with the stone ball on top. The caption of the photograph read, "Belle Frisson, née Elizabeth Proctor, lies buried beneath

this strange monument. People report that the ball slowly revolves, with no visible power. Does her spirit still strive to reach us? Who can say?"

Feeling very odd indeed, as if *she* might be the only one who could answer that question for sure, Rose Rita began to read the chapter about Belle Frisson.

As for Lewis, he despaired more and more as the days went past. Surprisingly, the source of his trouble was not teasing. He found that the other kids didn't make fun of him nearly as much as he expected. The talent show was soon forgotten as other topics came up, such as the high-school football games and the approach of Halloween. Oh, every once in a while someone would cluck like a chicken as Lewis walked past, but more people seemed to remember the "Who's on first?" routine that Dave and Tom had done. The boys had come in third, and lots of people thought they should have won the contest.

Lewis's growing concern came from the way his best friend was behaving. Rose Rita's coolness bothered Lewis a lot. He did not have very many friends, and Rose Rita was the one who understood and liked him best. One afternoon as he and his uncle were raking leaves, Lewis talked to Jonathan about her, and his uncle sympathized. "Growing up is a very rough process," Jonathan told him, leaning on his rake. "Your feelings get bruised, and you don't think you can ever make it, but somehow most people do. Give Rose Rita time to live down her embarrassment, and things will be fine."

"I messed everything up," said Lewis sorrowfully, sweeping wet maple leaves into a musty-smelling scarlet-and-yellow pile.

Jonathan patted him on the shoulder. "Accidents happen. Do you know the notion I had when everything started to go wrong? I thought, 'Lewis and Rose Rita could still save the day if they just turn the whole act into a comedy routine.' But I had no way of telling you that."

Lewis piled his batch of leaves onto the large heap that the two of them had made in a corner of the yard. He considered what his uncle had said, and he wondered why he had not had the same idea at the time. It was true—people had laughed more loudly at him and Rose Rita than they had at Tom and Dave, who had been trying to be funny. If only Lewis had come up with some way to make his bumbling seem part of the act, everything might have turned out differently. Only he hadn't, and the talent show had been the worst night of his life.

That Friday Mrs. Zimmermann invited everyone down to her cottage on Lyon Lake. It was too late in the year for swimming, but the cottage was a peaceful place, with a nice view and a cozy atmosphere, and Mrs. Zimmermann said she hoped Rose Rita would come along. Rose Rita turned her down, though, so the party consisted of just Mrs. Zimmermann, Uncle Jonathan, and a subdued Lewis. Mrs. Zimmermann outdid herself at making a tasty dinner, with grilled pork chops, fluffy stuffed baked potatoes, tangy sauerkraut, freshly baked bread, sweet creamy butter, and an enormous apple pie

with ice cream for dessert. They ate everything off her purple plates, wiped their lips with purple napkins, and sighed in contentment.

"That was wonderful, Florence," said Jonathan with a broad smile that shone through his red beard. "I don't think you've ever done better."

"Why, thank you, Weird Beard," returned Mrs. Zimmermann. Then she sighed too, and her expression became serious. "I'm only sorry that Rose Rita wouldn't come. I'm worried about her."

Stuffed and happy for the moment, Lewis felt his heart sink. "I am too," he admitted. "She barely talks to me anymore."

"Well," said Mrs. Zimmermann, sipping a cup of coffee, "Rose Rita is at an age when she hates to be embarrassed. It may take her quite a while to get over it."

Jonathan put his hand on Lewis's shoulder. "Lewis is having a rough time too," he said. "He's going to have to put up with all sorts of corny jokes about his act laying an egg for a long, long time."

Lewis couldn't help grinning. It really helped that neither his uncle nor Mrs. Zimmermann played down what had happened, or tried to tiptoe around it. They talked about it right out in the open, just as if Lewis were an adult. He liked that about his uncle. Jonathan Barnavelt had a knack for making Lewis feel comfortable even about horrible things like his failure in the talent show.

"Well, Lewis," said Mrs. Zimmermann playfully, "do you plan to give up the stage forever?"

Lewis shrugged and used his fork to toy with a few

crumbs of pie crust still on his plate. "I don't know. I think everything would've been all right if I hadn't tried to use that chicken. Learning the tricks was a lot of fun."

"Hmm," said Jonathan. "You know, every year there's a big magicians' meeting over in Colon, where a magic-supply house, Abbot's, is located. Maybe next year we can drive over and you can pick up some tricks—that is, if you want to."

Lewis laid his fork down. "I'll have to think about it. Right now I sort of want to be an astronomer. That way I could work in an observatory at night, when everyone else is asleep, and I could look at planets and stars through a telescope instead of being looked at."

"There's a lot to be said for that too," said Jonathan, chuckling. "And now I think it's only fair if we do the dishes to show our appreciation for this magnificent meal." He took a quarter from his pocket. "We'll flip to see who washes and who wipes."

"Uncle Jonathan," said Lewis, "is that your trick two-headed quarter?"

For a second Jonathan looked utterly flummoxed. Then he threw his head back and laughed. "Curses! Foiled again! Your choice, Lewis—wash or wipe?"

They had driven down to Lyon Lake in Bessie, Mrs. Zimmermann's purple Plymouth, because Mrs. Zimmermann said she didn't trust Jonathan Barnavelt's driving or his antique car. They drove back late at night. The oaks and maples grew close to the shoulder of Homer Road, making dark tunnels through which the car whizzed.

Lewis knew the moon was just about full, but the thick, dark clouds covered it completely. Now and then a gusty wind swept whirling dry leaves through the glare of the headlights. Lewis, sitting in the backseat, looked between Mrs. Zimmermann and Jonathan to peer out at the road ahead.

They bumped across the railroad tracks and back into New Zebedee. All the stores were dark and locked. Mrs. Zimmermann turned onto Mansion Street, and a moment later Lewis glanced at Rose Rita's house. He felt frozen for an instant, and then he yelped.

Mrs. Zimmermann stepped hard on the brake, and Bessie screeched to a halt. "What in the name of Heaven?"

"Look!" said Lewis. "Look at Rose Rita's house!"

Jonathan rolled down the passenger window. In a shaky voice he asked, "Is that a dog?"

"No," replied Lewis. The dark shape moving in jerks and starts on Rose Rita's porch was big enough to be a collie or a Labrador, but it was no dog. It had stalky legs, far too many of them.

"It's a shadow," said Mrs. Zimmermann uncertainly. "Just the shadow of a tree."

The dark shape ran straight up the wall in unnerving silence.

"No," Jonathan said tensely. "It's no shadow. It's a spider—a spider as big as a steamer trunk!"

Lewis gasped, his heart racing. The creature scrambled up to the roof and then rose into the sky, as if it were

climbing an invisible strand of spiderweb. "What is it doing here?" he asked nervously.

"I have no idea," said Jonathan, craning his head out and looking into the sky. "Whatever it is, it's gone now. Florence, I think we have to have a council of war about this. That was no real spider. It's a creature of magic—and of evil. And I have the feeling that Rose Rita is in terrible danger."

CHAPTER EIGHT

The next day was a cool, breezy Saturday. Lewis had taken to dropping in at the National Museum of Magic for half an hour every weekend to talk to Mr. Hardwick and his poker friends. On this Saturday he did not go but hung around the house, fighting the feeling that something horrible was coming, like a storm building up on the horizon.

Uncle Jonathan and Mrs. Zimmermann were deep in conversation in the study. Lewis had told them all about what he had seen, and they were worried. They were so busy that Lewis felt like an intruder. Finally Jonathan kindly told Lewis it might be better if he paid his usual visit to the museum. "Florence and I aren't much company for you right now," explained Jonathan, "and I really think Mr. Hardwick appreciates your interest in his

museum. It might take your mind off your troubles, anyway."

Lewis wanted to forget his troubles more than anything else. He found his windbreaker and stepped out into the crisp morning. He walked toward downtown thoughtfully, and when he passed Rose Rita's house, he crossed to the other side of the street and kept looking anxiously at the trees, half expecting to see a horrible gray shape there, ready to drop down and seize him.

Nothing happened, though. He saw nothing in the trees more strange or frightening than dead leaves, a few fat black squirrels, and one or two old, ratty-looking birds' nests. When Lewis got to the museum, he found that Mr. Perkins was late, and the other three men were sitting around trying to fool each other with card tricks while they waited for him to arrive. "You never did tell us how your magic show came out," said Mr. Hardwick as he shuffled the deck of cards and then made the jacks pop up from the top one by one. Lewis sighed and told the whole ghastly story.

All three of the magicians listened sympathetically. Mr. Mussenberger assured Lewis that such accidents were common. "Try dressing up in a floppy clown outfit and doing tricks on live TV," he said comfortingly in his rumbling voice. "I've had rabbits misbehave and children give away the secrets of my tricks on the air, and once I produced a big, delicious bottle of Twin Oaks milk, took a huge swig, and spat all over the camera lens because it had turned sour!"

"Even Houdini made mistakes," little Johnny Stone

said, reaching for the cards. "Once or twice he had to be rescued when his escapes went wrong. He used to tell a story about how he was doing an underwater escape in the winter, and when he got out of the crate he was locked in, he found himself trapped under the ice in the river! He said he had to swim half a mile on his back, breathing the little bit of air sandwiched between the ice and the water. He got back to shore only seconds before he would have frozen."

Lewis could picture only too clearly the dark water and the terrible barrier of ice, and he could almost feel the deadly embrace of the frigid river. "Did that really happen?" asked Lewis in awe.

Mr. Stone winked. "It made a good story, anyway," he said. "Did you see Houdini's milk can downstairs?"

Lewis shook his head. Mr. Hardwick got to his feet. "Well, there's no time like the present!" he said. They trooped downstairs, and Mr. Hardwick showed Lewis the big galvanized milk can, as tall as Lewis. Eight Mammoth padlocks held the lid tightly closed. "Imagine climbing into that thing and letting someone lock you in," said Mr. Hardwick. "Imagine how dark and tight it would be in there. No light and no air."

Lewis shuddered at the thought. And then something else struck him. Mrs. Zimmermann had spoken about finding Rose Rita in the janitor's closet after the talent show. Lewis remembered that Rose Rita was claustrophobic—being in closed-in places gave her the screaming meemies. Hiding in a closet was a very unlikely thing

for Rose Rita to do. "Excuse me?" Lewis asked. Mr. Hardwick had stopped talking and was looking at him.

"I can see you were imagining being inside this thing," said the museum owner. "I asked, Can you also imagine how in the world Houdini managed to escape when it was locked this way?"

Lewis shook his head. "It looks impossible."

"It can be done," said Mr. Stone smugly.

Mr. Hardwick agreed, "Oh, of course it can be done. Still, Houdini did it with *style*. He may have been more an escape artist than a magician, but you have to admit, he did everything with style."

Someone tapped on the door, and Mr. Hardwick grinned. "That must be the *late* Mr. Thomas Perkins," he said, going to the front of the store.

It wasn't Mr. Perkins. Lewis was amazed when Mr. Hardwick opened the door and Rose Rita stepped inside. She looked as if she hadn't slept very well for days. Dark circles made her eyes look tired and sunken, and her hair was even stringier than usual. She held a green book close to her chest. "Hi," she said quietly as she handed the book to Mr. Hardwick. "Thanks for lending this to me."

"You're certainly welcome," replied Mr. Hardwick.

Rose Rita had not noticed Lewis. She licked her lips. "I'd like to keep it a little longer, if you don't mind. Uh, do you ever go to that cemetery you were telling us about? The one where Belle Frisson is buried?"

"Now and then," said Mr. Hardwick. "Some of my old friends are buried nearby, and my wife and I visit their

graves. A surprising number of magicians have chosen to be buried there and over in Colon, you know." He handed the book back to Rose Rita. "Keep this as long as you want."

"Are you going soon?" Rose Rita asked anxiously.

Mr. Hardwick thought for a moment. "Hmm. Now that you mention it, I haven't made the trip in a while. Maybe Ellen and I will drive down tomorrow."

"May I go too, please?" asked Rose Rita.

Mr. Hardwick said, "Why, sure, if your parents don't mind." He turned and asked, "Lewis, would you like to tag along?"

Lewis could not answer for a moment. Rose Rita's eyes had darted toward him when Mr. Hardwick had spoken, and an expression of furious anger had flickered across her face. Then, like a flash of lightning, it was gone, and her face had the worrisome, slack expression Lewis had seen too often lately. He stammered, "S-sure, I guess. I'll have to ask my uncle."

"By all means," said Mr. Hardwick. He looked out the door. "Well, Tom Perkins is parking his old rattletrap across the street, so our poker game can begin at last."

Lewis said good-bye to Mr. Hardwick and the others, and he and Rose Rita walked away. Lewis murmured a few words to her, but Rose Rita either grunted or shrugged in response. When they got to her house, she just walked away from Lewis without a word. Lewis had the eerie feeling that somehow the person he had walked from the museum with really wasn't Rose Rita. She's like a walking corpse, he thought. The idea made him feel

nauseated and weak. If Rose Rita was not living inside her body, then who was?

Or, even worse—*what* was?

When he got home, Lewis found Mrs. Zimmermann and Uncle Jonathan still sitting in the study. Jonathan was behind the big desk with the green-shaded lamp, an untidy stack of books at his elbow. Mrs. Zimmermann sat in one of the big armchairs, busily knitting something that looked like a long purple scarf. She rarely knitted, but sometimes when she had to do a lot of thinking, she dragged out her yarn and her needles and started to work on something that might turn out to be a baggy sweater, a comforter, or a shawl. She always said that whatever turned out surprised her just as much as anybody, since she simply began to knit with no object in mind.

Both Mrs. Zimmermann and Uncle Jonathan glanced up as Lewis came in and settled into the other armchair. "You look bewitched, bothered, and bewildered, Lewis," said Mrs. Zimmermann as her needles clicked away.

Lewis nodded. "I thought about something a while ago," he said, and told Mrs. Zimmermann how odd it was that Rose Rita had chosen to hide in a broom closet.

"I've already mentioned that," replied Mrs. Zimmermann. "In fact, Jonathan and I have been talking about how strangely Rose Rita has been acting lately—she isn't quite herself. We've been doing a little research on that—and on the spider thing we all saw at her house." Lewis shivered when Mrs. Zimmermann said that. She gave him a strained sort of smile, as if she were trying to look

happier than she really felt. "Cheer up! Fuzzy Face and I have been looking through his volumes of mystic lore, and we think that whatever that grim gray beastie was, it probably can't hurt Rose Rita."

"It isn't that, exactly," said Lewis with a sigh. He told them about meeting Rose Rita at the museum. "She wants to go with Mr. Hardwick to this grave tomorrow," he finished. "And I don't want to go along." He bit his lower lip. If he had dared, he would have confessed that the idea of traveling down to Cristobal scared the wits out of him. He did not like spooky cemeteries. Nor did he relish riding twenty miles into the country in the backseat of a car with Rose Rita—not when she was acting so odd.

Jonathan Barnavelt exchanged glances with Mrs. Zimmermann. "Haggy Face," he said, "this opportunity might be the very answer to our problem. Do you agree?"

Mrs. Zimmermann perked up. "I surely do. Enough sitting around and moping and wondering what disaster is going to happen next! I say it's time for action, and I say that Lewis can be a big help."

Jonathan tugged at his red beard. "I think Florence is right, Lewis," he said slowly. "You see, we believe that Rose Rita has somehow come under a magical attack. In order to fight it, we have to know what's behind it—or more to the point, *who's* behind it. So you'll have to be our eyes and ears. I think you should go along on this trip and see what you can get out of Rose Rita."

Lewis sighed helplessly. "She won't even talk to me," he said.

Mrs. Zimmermann clicked her tongue irritably as she dropped a stitch. She worked back over it and said, "That's why you'll have to be sort of a secret agent, Lewis. Oh, I know it's not nice to spy on your friends, and ordinarily I'd never suggest such a thing. In this case, though, Jonathan is right. I can practically feel my thumbs pricking, like the witches' thumbs in *Macbeth*. Something wicked is coming our way, and we'll be sunk if we don't learn what we're dealing with. You'll have to be observant, and you'll have to remember every little thing. But it could save Rose Rita."

Lewis pondered that as he watched Mrs. Zimmermann's needles busily add another row of stitches to the growing garment. Finally he took a deep breath. "Okay," he said at last. "I don't like it, but I'll do it."

And so it was settled. Jonathan and Mrs. Zimmermann conferred all afternoon, and dinner was a hurried affair of cold chicken sandwiches and potato chips. Throughout the evening Lewis was restless. He wandered around the house, searching for something he could not name and would not recognize if he saw it.

The old mansion was a great place to live, and Lewis loved it there. Each room had its own fireplace, and every fireplace was made of marble of a different color. The upstairs rooms were rarely used, and a great variety of junk was stored there, including trunks of Barnavelt stuff that dated from before the Civil War, a wheezy antique parlor organ, and a stereopticon with about five hundred three-D sepia-toned photographs of everything from the Pyramids of Egypt to a tightrope walker poised on a wire

high above Niagara Falls. Usually Lewis could while away a rainy day very happily, just exploring and trying out the wonderful things he found.

But that Saturday evening he felt at loose ends. He was too nervous to sit still, and he had nothing to keep him occupied. So he roamed instead. He spent a little while sitting on the back stairs, gazing at the stained-glass window. Jonathan had cast a spell on it, and it changed every time you looked. Sometimes there were strange scenes that might be from another planet—tall smoking volcanoes, weird twisted trees, and inexplicable buildings in the shapes of spheres, cones, and cylinders. Usually there were more earthly subjects—a knight slaying a dragon; shepherds playing lyres, tambouras, and syrinxes while tending their sheep; or four angels dancing the tango.

That evening the stained-glass window showed a road stretching through a landscape of rolling, wooded hills. The sky above the road was a dark purply blue, about the color of a Vicks VapoRub jar. The hills were a deep, gloomy green, and the road wound between them like a flat gray snake. The picture seemed to pull Lewis in, and he imagined traveling down that mysterious road under the strange and threatening sky. What would lie at the end? He sighed, got up, and went to see if there was something to watch on TV.

Later that night, in bed, Lewis brooded over his sense of coming doom. He was frightened without knowing what frightened him. He felt trapped. He sensed that some evil intelligence was watching him, knowing what he would do and planning to destroy him. The sinister

image of that winding road kept returning to his mind, and he kept wondering what terrifying end the road might have. Lewis tried to tell himself not to be such a coward, but that did no good. Lewis just wasn't the kind of person who could ignore doubt and danger. His chest ached, and he felt terribly alone. A prayer came into his mind, the one that began *Omnipotens sempiterne Deus*, and as he lay in the dark he whispered it aloud. He finished with the words *"Quaesumus, ut eiusdem fidei firmitate ab omnibus semper muniamur adversis."*

In English they meant "We beseech Thee that by our steadfastness in this same faith, we may evermore be defended from all adversities."

After his prayer Lewis felt a little better. He faced an adversity that he couldn't even begin to understand, and he hoped that his plea for help would be answered. At last, still tossing and turning, he fell into a light and troubled sleep.

CHAPTER NINE

Sunday was one of those fall days with a deep blue sky and the kind of high, wispy, streaky cirrus clouds called mares' tails. Mr. Hardwick and his wife, Ellen, a slight, brown-eyed woman who wore slacks and a straw sun hat, called for Lewis in their blue-and-white Chevrolet. Rose Rita was already in the backseat, and Lewis joined her. They didn't talk much on the trip to Cristobal; Rose Rita was still distant and quiet. Lewis stared out the car window instead as they passed farms with old red barns, their roofs bearing "Chew Mail Pouch" advertising signs. Mr. Hardwick was a good, careful driver, and they took their time.

Cristobal was hardly a town at all. New Zebedee was pretty small, but Cristobal was just a crossroads with a feed store, a general store, and a gas station. Maybe be-

cause New Zebedee had once been in the running to be named the capital city of Michigan, its houses tended to be old and rather elegant, Victorian affairs with towers, gingerbread decorations, and gabled roofs. The houses in Cristobal were more modest, little white frame buildings with small yards.

Mr. Hardwick drove through Cristobal. They passed a big brick church with a cemetery nearby, but they didn't stop. Then they were out in the country again, and Mr. Hardwick turned down a winding side road. After a mile or so the road simply ended at another cemetery, this one small and square. A freshly painted old white wooden fence encircled the graveyard. Mr. Hardwick stopped the car, and everyone got out. Lewis looked around. The cemetery had no trees at all. Many of the tombstones were old and granite. They were not fancy. Instead of being carved into angels, urns, and monuments, these stones were simple slabs with rounded tops, weathered and gray and splotched with green circles of lichen. One marker stood out.

Mr. Hardwick had taken a basket out of the Chevrolet's trunk. It contained two pairs of gardening gloves, grass clippers, and a few other tools. "Ellen and I will tidy up some of the graves," he said. "Both of you can wander around if you like. Rose Rita, that big monument in the middle is Belle Frisson's grave. It's pretty strange. You might want to have a look."

The grass was a little high in the cemetery. Lewis thought that people probably came out occasionally to keep things neat. Many of the graves had flowers on

them, some bright and fresh, others brown and withered. He and Rose Rita walked slowly toward the center of the cemetery, the gravel crunching under their feet. One of Lewis's superstitions was that something bad would happen to him if he stepped on a grave, so he trod carefully.

"Sure is big," said Lewis as he and Rose Rita stopped in front of the mysterious tombstone. The whole monument rested on a square base ten feet long on each side. Atop the base was a stone cube five feet on each facet, then a many-sided pillar that rose for about ten feet, and finally at the summit a gray ball at least three feet in diameter. For some reason it had several faint chalk marks on it. Everything, from the base to the ball, was a gloomy-looking dark gray granite. The cube that supported both the pillar and the ball had words engraved on it:

BELLE FRISSON
(Born Elizabeth Proctor)
1822–1878
She Waits to Live Again

Lewis could hear the *click-click* of grass clippers behind him. He looked up from the inscription. The pillar on top of the cube wasn't very thick, maybe two feet or so in diameter. It had marks carved deeply into it, curlicues and lines, but they were not letters. Lewis looked at the ball again. Something about it made him feel very apprehensive.

Rose Rita was slowly walking around the grave, study-

ing the pillar intently. Lewis had had enough. He turned and hurried back down the gravel path to the Hardwicks, who were trimming the grass around a headstone inscribed with the name "Frederick Jeremy McCandles: The Great Candelini."

"Weird monument, isn't it?" Mr. Hardwick asked Lewis. The museum owner patted his forehead with a handkerchief. "Belle Frisson's, I mean. She died here, you know."

Lewis shook his head.

"Tell him the story," Mrs. Hardwick urged. "Halloween's coming soon! It's a good time to hear it."

"Well," said Mr. Hardwick, clipping more grass, "back in 1878 Belle Frisson was touring the country, doing her communicating-with-the-dead act. She had made an appearance in Detroit and was heading west by train. Just outside Cristobal the train jumped the tracks. Quite a few people were hurt."

"It was a famous accident," Mrs. Hardwick added. "It happened in the middle of October on a clear, dry night, and no one ever discovered the cause."

Mr. Hardwick agreed. "It was very puzzling. Many injuries, as I said, but only Belle Frisson's were serious. There used to be a farm right here, owned by a doctor. He and his wife took Belle Frisson in to treat her injuries. She regained consciousness, but she knew she wasn't going to make it. So on her deathbed she did something very eccentric. She arranged to buy the doctor's farm from him."

"Was she rich?" asked Lewis.

"Rich enough," replied Mr. Hardwick. "She spent nearly a week sketching out her tombstone, ordering it to be made exactly the way she drew it. Then strange people came to the farm—people the doctor had certainly not telegraphed, people whom Belle Frisson couldn't possibly have contacted in any normal way. She saw them one at a time and gave them some kind of orders. She also told the doctor that she was going to be buried in the front yard of the farm. And she wrote out her will. She also created a very peculiar scroll that I have in the museum. She died on Halloween night, 1878. The next day the doctor and his wife moved away. Those outsiders came—stonemasons, carpenters, an undertaker, I don't know what—and they spent a month burying Belle and putting up that monument. Then they dismantled the house and went away."

"They left just the one grave," said Mrs. Hardwick. "Over the years, that changed. Belle Frisson's will said that anyone who couldn't afford a burial anywhere else could have a plot for free. Any magician could also be buried in this cemetery."

Mr. Hardwick continued. "About six or seven conjurors have taken her up on the offer." He patted the grave that he was working on. "Freddy, here, better known as the Great Candelini, is one of them. I knew him back before the war. He passed away in 1943, at the ripe old age of eighty-seven, and he asked to be buried here. He had a great act that used lighted candles. You would have liked him, Lewis."

Lewis nodded. "Why are there chalk marks on the ball on top of Belle Frisson's monument?" he asked.

Mr. Hardwick put the clippers back in the basket and got up. "That's another peculiar thing. The ball rotates. It moves very slowly. It makes one complete revolution about every six weeks. Nobody can tell how it works, though one science teacher told me it probably has to do with the way the granite expands when the weather is warm and contracts when it cools off again."

"People put chalk marks on the ball to prove that it moves," explained Mrs. Hardwick. "And sure enough, it does."

The two of them began to clean up another grave, and Lewis walked back toward Belle Frisson's monument. He could not shake a creepy sensation that something was very wrong, and he was worried about Rose Rita. He stopped dead in his tracks when he saw her, standing on the far side of the monument. She had her arms spread out, her palms turned toward the sky, and her head thrown back. The sunlight glinted on her glasses. She seemed to be staring at the ball atop the monument.

"Hi," he said, coming up to her. She did not answer. "Pretty strange tombstone."

Rose Rita glared at him. "You don't know anything about it," she snapped.

Lewis raised his eyebrows. "What? What's eating you? I just said—"

"Forget it."

Lewis went on, "Mr. Hardwick says the ball up there

rotates. It turns all by itself. That's why people have put chalk marks on it. Weird, huh?"

"Where movement is, there is life also," replied Rose Rita in a strange, hoarse voice. "Blood is the life, and as from one it may be taken, to another it shall be given."

"What are you talking about?" asked Lewis.

Rose Rita shook her head. "Nothing."

The day began to feel very cold to Lewis, though the sun still shone through the clouds. The *snip-snip* of the garden shears, the rustle of a breeze through the grass, were the only sounds. "What do you suppose those marks are?" asked Lewis, trying to fill in the silence. He pointed to the curves and swirls carved into the granite shaft.

"A mystery," replied Rose Rita in that same harsh, dreamy voice. "One that may be wrapped up or un-wrapped in time. One whose answer may be fetched from afar."

Something tickled Lewis's neck. He slapped at it, thinking it was a bug. He felt something stringy and looked at his fingers. A thin strand of cobweb connected them. Grimacing in revulsion, he stooped and scrubbed his hand on the grass. Then he felt another light touch on his face, and another. Crying out in alarm, Lewis began to flail the air. It was full of wispy, floating strands of cobweb—and at the end of each strand was a tiny, almost invisible, gray spider. Lewis hated spiders. He grabbed Rose Rita's arm. "Let's get out of here!" he said, dragging her down the path.

The floating baby spiders vanished as soon as they were a few steps away from the Frisson grave. Lewis told

the Hardwicks about them, and they thought the baby spiders were probably just migrating. "I've heard of them doing that," said Mr. Hardwick. "Thought they did it in the spring, though."

Rose Rita didn't say anything, and she said very little on the way back to New Zebedee. Lewis watched her, tried to remember her exact words, and brooded.

That evening he told Uncle Jonathan and Mrs. Zimmermann about everything that he remembered. They listened gravely, and when he finished, they exchanged long looks. "Does this tomb with its revolving ball sound familiar to you, Jonathan?" asked Mrs. Zimmermann.

"It sounds like something out of the Egyptian Book of the Dead," responded Jonathan. "What about the spiders? Wasn't there something about spiders in Egyptian mythology?"

Mrs. Zimmermann touched a finger to her chin. "Hmm. I don't remember anything especially about spiders. Of course, the Egyptians placed great store in the scarab, which is a type of beetle, but spiders aren't even insects, so that wouldn't apply. I'm coming up blank. I can remember the myth of Arachne, whom the gods turned into a spider, and I can recall the African folk tales about Anansi, the trickster spider, but that's all."

"It's a mystery," pronounced Jonathan.

"One whose answer may be fetched from afar," said Lewis solemnly. Both Uncle Jonathan and Mrs. Zimmermann stared at him as though he had suddenly sprouted an extra head. "What is it?" he asked, a little alarmed.

"That was a mighty odd thing to say," replied Jonathan. "One whose answer may be fetched from afar? What is that supposed to mean?"

"I don't know," confessed Lewis. "It's something Rose Rita said."

"She used those exact words?" asked Jonathan, his voice troubled.

"Yes, I'm pretty sure," Lewis said. "If not those words, almost the same ones."

Jonathan took a pipe cleaner—he still carried them around, though he never smoked anymore—from his vest and twisted it into the shape of a spring. He pressed the ends together until the pipe cleaner slipped out of his fingers and leaped away. Then he said tightly, "Florence, I may be a fussbudget and a gloomy Gus, but that has a bad sound to me. You know all about fetches, of course."

"Ye-s-s," she said. "Still, it could be a coincidence."

"What are fetches?" asked Lewis.

Jonathan looked somberly at Mrs. Zimmermann. "You explain them, Haggy. You're the professional here."

"Well, Lewis," Mrs. Zimmermann began, "a fetch is a kind of apparition or spirit. In England and Ireland fetches take the form of a person. In fact they are identical to the person they apply to. That kind of fetch is what the Germans call a *Doppelgänger*, which more or less means 'walking double.' Anyway, usually a friend or family member sees the fetch of a victim—"

"V-victim?" stammered Lewis. Now he knew he wasn't going to like learning about fetches.

Jonathan nodded. "Sometimes even the victim himself

or herself sees the fetch. Usually other people mistake it for the victim."

"That's a human kind of fetch," said Mrs. Zimmermann. "In other countries and other time periods, though, people believed in other kinds. They might be animals, or birds, or insects."

"Or s-spiders?" guessed Lewis.

"Yes, or spiders," answered Mrs. Zimmermann. "All fetches, whether animal or bird or creepy-crawler, have one job to do, and that is how they get their name. They are sent forth to fetch the soul of a doomed person."

"And the person dies?" asked Lewis in a small voice.

Softly, Uncle Jonathan replied, "That's right, Lewis. The person dies."

Lewis didn't say anything. He could only think of his friend, Rose Rita, and of the terrible spider they had seen outside her house. Was it truly a fetch? Was Rose Rita doomed to die?

CHAPTER TEN

That Sunday afternoon Rose Rita was getting ready to leave the house. Her mother called, "Where are you going, dear?"

Rose Rita was wearing jeans, a bulky jacket, and a purple knit cap that Mrs. Zimmermann had made for her. She yelled back, "Lewis and I are going to study for a big test. I probably won't be back until late."

"Don't be too late," Mrs. Pottinger called.

Rose Rita dashed outside. She had several things stuffed inside her jacket: the scroll, the book, a flashlight, and a couple of sandwiches wrapped in waxed paper. In a way she felt very guilty about what she was going to do. Rose Rita liked to tell outrageous stories, but she almost never lied to her parents. She climbed onto her bike and rode downtown, pumping away like a machine. She

headed west, past the fountain and the National House Hotel, and then out into the countryside.

She rode for maybe three or four miles before finally climbing off her bike. She looked around. Just north of the highway was a cornfield, with the brown, dry cornstalks still standing. It had a three-rail fence around it, but that was no problem. Rose Rita climbed the fence, then wrestled her bike through. It was easy to hide the bike in the corn. Rose Rita headed back down to the highway and began to hitchhike.

Six cars zoomed past without even slowing. Then a rusty red Ford pickup came sputtering along, slowed, and pulled over. A plump woman opened the passenger door. "Need a ride, dearie?" she asked in a cheerful voice. "Climb in!"

Rose Rita did. "Thank you," she said.

The woman banged the truck into gear. "That's all right, dearie. My name's Susanna Seidler. What's yours?"

"Rowena Potter," declared Rose Rita, who had already made up the fake name.

"Well, Rowena Potter, where are you bound?"

"I'm trying to get back to Cristobal," said Rose Rita.

Mrs. Seidler had the broad, red face of a farmer, and she wore a red-and-black checked flannel shirt and overalls with a big red bandanna tied around her neck. Her hair was short, straight, and copper red. She gave Rose Rita a surprised look from cornflower-blue eyes. "My stars, Rowena, that's quite a ways. How'd you get clear over to New Zebedee?"

Rose Rita stared ahead at the highway. "Well, that's a

long story," she said slowly, her mind working furiously. "My uncle had to come into New Zebedee yesterday to see the doctor. He asked me if I'd ride along with him, so I did. But the doctor decided he had to have his appendix out right then, so he stuck my uncle in the hospital. It was so sudden that nobody thought about me. Anyway, today my uncle asked me if I could get back home to feed his chickens and pigs and let my mom and dad know he's all right."

"You could've just phoned," said Mrs. Seidler.

"We don't have a phone," replied Rose Rita. "Both of my parents are deaf."

"My stars!" cried Mrs. Seidler. "You certainly have a rough time of it! Why didn't you ask the doctor for help?"

"He's not in New Zebedee anymore," said Rose Rita. "As soon as he operated on my uncle, he went off for a week-long fishing trip on the Upper Peninsula."

"I never heard of such a thing!" exclaimed Mrs. Seidler indignantly. "Well, Rowena, just you relax. I'll take you right to your front door, because I'm passing through Cristobal. My husband and I have a farm about ten miles past there, so it's no trouble."

Rose Rita bit her lip in consternation. Sometimes her stories were *too* good. She didn't say much else about her family but instead asked Mrs. Seidler about hers. Mrs. Seidler loved to talk about her children, and as the miles rolled past, Rose Rita heard all about Hiram and Ernst and Clara and Velma, the baby, whom everyone called "Snookums." They drove through Cristobal just before

sunset. Rose Rita began to feel anxious. Then she saw a farmhouse on the left. "That's my house," she said hurriedly, stopping Mrs. Seidler in the middle of a story about how Snookums had painted the kitchen walls with ketchup.

"I'll drive up and say howdy," said Mrs. Seidler, slowing the truck.

"No, that's all right," replied Rose Rita. "They're probably at church anyhow. Thanks for the ride." She insisted until Mrs. Seidler just pulled over and let her out of the truck. Rose Rita stood and waved until the rusty old Ford had driven away out of sight. Then she began to walk. The turnoff to the cemetery was not far past the farmhouse.

Once she got onto the turnoff road, it was a long way, and Rose Rita got hotter and hotter. The sun sank low, and her shadow stretched out long and dark. At last she stood before the strange monument. Squinting up at it, Rose Rita thought the chalk marks had moved a little. The mysterious ball atop the monument had revolved half an inch or so in the few hours since she had been here. The rugged, pitted gray globe was halfway in ruddy sunlight and halfway in deep shadow. Rose Rita reached inside her jacket and pulled out the scroll. She took it out of its embroidered wrapper and began to unroll it. "Now what do I do?" she muttered aloud.

The answer was startling. Rose Rita squeaked out in surprise as she felt a tug. The scroll seemed to have come to life. It yanked and jerked in her grasp, trying to tear itself free. Holding it was like holding a piece of iron near

a very strong magnet. The scroll wanted to leap out of her hands and fly toward the monument. Rose Rita let go.

Whoosh! The scroll unwound! It stretched out to more than twelve feet. It snaked through the air, rippling and fluttering. One end of it caught at the very base of the many-sided pillar, and the other began to fly around and around the shaft. The scroll stretched out, longer and longer, as it wrapped itself around the pillar in a spiral. About an inch of the stone showed between the bands of the scroll. With a final slap the free end of the scroll plastered itself just beneath the sphere. The sun set at that moment, leaving Rose Rita in the sudden chill of twilight.

There was still enough light to see. Rose Rita walked around the pillar, looking up. She gasped. The marks along the edges of the scroll had lined up with those carved into the stone. Together, they made up letters. Rose Rita began to speak them, her heart bursting with terror. Some spell was at work. She could not stop reading the words aloud:

~~IN THE NAME OF NEITH,~~
~~IN THE NAME OF ANUBIS,~~
~~IN THE NAME OF OSIRIS, HEAR!~~

Rose Rita's vision became blurry, though the letters of the chant burned bright and clear. Slowly she walked around the stone shaft in a counterclockwise direction,

reading strange, ancient-Egyptian-sounding words in a voice edged with grief and fear.

The air around her seemed to shimmer. The sandwiches and the flashlight fell from her jacket, but she did not notice. When she tried to stop walking, something drew her on. She had the weird feeling that hundreds of tiny ropes had been tied to her arms and legs, and they dragged her along like a living puppet. She screamed out the last words of the chant, "UR-NIPISHTIM! HORLA! THUT-IM-SHOLA!" Then she stood reeling and exhausted.

Silence dropped around her. Rose Rita had no sense that any time had passed, but overhead, stars shone in a dark sky, and a gibbous moon was rising in the east. In its light everything looked different. The tombstones were like snaggly teeth jutting from ancient gums. The tomb before her resembled a tall, standing figure glaring down at her. The sphere on the top began to spin faster and faster. Sparks began to fly. The sound grew sharper, until Rose Rita fell to her knees and clamped her hands over her ears.

Then, with a rumble that made the ground tremble, the whole monument—cube, shaft, and sphere—shifted, pivoting to the left. The moving cube uncovered a dark, square opening beneath it. Again feeling as if she were being pulled by strings, Rose Rita jerked to her feet and lurched forward onto stairs carved from stone. They led down into the earth.

"No!" she cried, but it was no use. She hated closed-in

spaces, and the opening was more frightening than anything she had known. She tried to scream, but something soft and clinging, something like yards and yards of cobweb, closed her mouth, reducing her to terrified squeaks.

And then she stepped down into the darkness. Overhead, the monument shuddered as it slid back into place. The last rays of light died.

Rose Rita was trapped inside the tomb.

CHAPTER ELEVEN

Lewis was in bed reading when he heard the phone ring. The Westclox alarm clock beside his bed said the time was nine forty-four. Curious, Lewis got out of bed and padded downstairs barefoot to find out who was calling so late.

His uncle stood in the front hall, speaking into the receiver: "No, she hasn't. . . . Yes, that's what I'd do. . . . I wouldn't worry just yet. I tell you what, Mrs. Pottinger, I'll call Mrs. Zimmermann. She may have an idea or two. . . . I understand. Certainly. . . . Yes, you do that. Good-bye." Jonathan hung up the phone and turned to Lewis, looking very upset. "That was Louise Pottinger. She said Rose Rita came over here around four o'clock to study for a test with you. She didn't, did she?"

Lewis felt cold. "No," he uttered. "I haven't seen her

since about two thirty, when the Hardwicks dropped her off at her house. What's happened?"

"She's disappeared," said Jonathan gravely. "Go get dressed, Lewis. I'm going to call Florence. This doesn't sound very good at all."

Lewis hurried back upstairs and got into a fresh pair of corduroy pants, a shirt, socks, and sneakers. By the time he got down to the study, Mrs. Zimmermann was already there. "I was afraid something like this might happen," she was saying. She looked up as he came in and gave him a sad kind of smile. "Hello, Lewis! I was just telling your uncle that Rose Rita may be in real trouble."

"I bet it has something to do with that Belle Frisson," said Lewis. "Rose Rita acted really weird at the cemetery. It was like the monument fascinated her."

"Jonathan and I have checked all our books on magic," Mrs. Zimmermann said. "Belle Frisson, whoever she was, doesn't show up in any of them. If she was a real sorceress, she was not one who associated with any other true magicians."

"To tell you the truth," revealed Jonathan, "both Florence and I think that Belle Frisson was just a stage magician—a conjuror, like your friends at the magic museum. I found a mention or two of her name in books on spiritualism and mediums, but that was all. I figured she was like the 'trance mediums' whom Houdini used to expose. He was sort of a detective, you know, specializing in unmasking fakes who claimed to have real powers."

"I didn't know that," replied Lewis.

"Well, be that as it may," said Mrs. Zimmermann firmly, "it doesn't help us with our problem. Louise Pottinger is asking the police to find Rose Rita, but if magic is tied up in this, they won't be able to help. It seems to be sorcery of a special kind too—Egyptian magic. If only Dr. Walsh were in town, we could consult him."

Dr. David Walsh was a great local celebrity. He was an archaeologist who specialized in the history and lore of ancient Egypt, and he had been on many expeditions. In fact, at that moment he was away, excavating a tomb somewhere on the banks of the Nile River in Egypt.

Lewis said, "His son, Chris, goes to the elementary school. I know him."

"That might help," said Jonathan. "Lewis, tomorrow I'd like you to ask Chris if we might take a look at some of his father's books. Dr. Walsh has a huge collection dealing with Egypt, and maybe something will be of help."

"Tomorrow? Can't we do anything tonight?" Lewis pleaded.

"Like what?" asked Mrs. Zimmermann. "Lewis, we all like Rose Rita a great deal, and we'd do anything to help her. When you're up against the unknown, though, it doesn't do to go charging in. You have to arm yourself so that you can fight if necessary. Besides, Rose Rita will be all right, at least for a while. Jonathan and I have learned something about fetches. If one has summoned Rose Rita away, that's all it can do for the time being. She will be safe until the next phase of the moon."

"When is that?" asked Lewis, dreading to hear.

"Friday night," said Jonathan. "That's when the moon goes into its last quarter."

"The night before Halloween," whispered Lewis.

"Yes," replied Jonathan in a solemn voice. "The night before Halloween."

If Jonathan and Mrs. Zimmermann had guessed right, that meant they had only five days to rescue Rose Rita. Lewis hoped it would be enough.

The next day school dragged on forever. Rose Rita was absent, and everyone knew she was missing. Many people thought she had run away, and others thought she might have been kidnapped. Some of the kids in Lewis's classes asked him about Rose Rita, but he didn't want to speak about her.

After school Lewis headed over to the Walshes' house. They lived on Michigan Street, several blocks west of High Street. As he walked along, Lewis had the uncanny sense that he was being watched. He turned and looked behind him, but he saw no one. Then he stuck his hands deeper into his jacket pockets, hunched his shoulders, and crunched over dry leaves. He turned a corner suddenly and jumped behind a tree. He waited there, holding his breath.

Half a minute later a hurrying figure came around the corner. Lewis let his breath out and relaxed. He stepped out from behind the tree. "Hey, Chad," he said. "Are you following me?"

Chad Britton, a blond, brown-eyed kid wearing a tan trench coat buttoned up tight, stopped and grinned. "Well, I was," he said ruefully. "I'm practicing."

Lewis sighed. Chad wanted to be a detective when he grew up, and he liked to practice by following people around. He was getting pretty good at it. Sometimes he gave older people the willies when they realized he had been silently observing them for an hour or more. "Well, stop it," said Lewis. "I'm not doing anything."

"But you're one of Rose Rita Pottinger's friends," replied Chad reasonably. "Everyone says she's been kidnapped and crooks are holding her for ransom. That's why I was following you."

"*I* wouldn't kidnap Rose Rita," said Lewis angrily.

"I know you wouldn't. But your uncle is rich, so I figured they might kidnap you too and ask him for a lot of ransom money. Then I could get the crooks' license number and report it to the police." Chad smiled as if that were the most logical thing in the world.

"I don't think it's going to be that easy," said Lewis. "Anyway, I'm busy right now. Tomorrow I'll tell you everything I know about the case, okay?"

"Great!" Chad consented. "Keep me posted!"

Shaking his head, Lewis walked on to the Walsh house. Chris Walsh, a ten-year-old boy with short, brown hair, was standing in front of the big stone house tossing a football up and catching it. He grinned when he saw Lewis and threw the ball to him. Lewis flinched, missed the ball, and picked it up. Laughing, Chris said, "Hi, Lewis."

"Hi yourself," Lewis replied, tossing him the football. Chris caught it expertly.

"Want to play?" Chris asked.

"I can't right now," Lewis said. "Is your mom home?"

Chris said, "Yes," and Lewis explained what he needed. "My uncle is interested in Egypt," he finished, "and he'd like to borrow a book or two. Especially books on Egyptian magic."

"Oh, sure," said Chris right away. "Dad has lots of those. Come on in."

The house was big, with high ceilings, wainscotted walls, and many Egyptian artifacts. There were urns and statuettes, and on the walls were pieces of ancient bronze armor, funeral masks, and framed sheets of papyrus covered with hieroglyphs. Chris's mother said that Lewis could borrow as many books as he wanted, so they went to the study. Chris walked over to a bookcase and said, "Here's some of the real stuff. This is *The Book of Going Forth by Day*, which most people call the Book of the Dead. And this one is about animal magic. Here's another one. . . ."

By the time they had finished, Lewis had a stack of six books, two of them large and heavy. He thanked Chris and his mother and headed back across town. Before he had gotten even halfway home, Chad Britton started to shadow him again. Lewis ignored him and hurried on to High Street.

Mrs. Zimmermann returned, and she and Jonathan pored over the books, taking time only for another hurried dinner of sandwiches. At last Mrs. Zimmermann

looked up from her book. "Here's something," she said. "Listen to this." She cleared her throat and began to read:

> In predynastic times the curious cult of Neith began in ancient Sais. The followers of the goddess Neith were caught up in the study of the mysteries of life and death. Neith was the Weaver of the World, the terrible Opener of the Way between life and death, and her representative creature, the spider, was a symbolic connection between the two states, with her web the bridge between the here and now and the hereafter. Some worshippers believed that the web of the Great Spider, like the skein of Ariadne, could thread the maze between this world and the dark world of death. They judged that, by following the strand backward, it might be possible for a departed soul to return to life.
>
> Such a passage would be costly, however. To begin, it would demand the spilling of blood and the creation of the spectral Death Spider. At the termination of the process a human sacrifice would have to be made, blood for blood and life for life. Only by sending a victim into death could the soul anxious to return be granted a passage back to life.

Jonathan Barnavelt whistled. "That sounds pretty ominous. Is there more?"

Mrs. Zimmermann read silently for several minutes. Then she looked up. "Yes. This Death Spider is a creature half spirit, half real—a kind of specter. Just as we guessed, it behaves like a fetch, and its power is tied to

the phases of the moon. Rose Rita will be safe until the turning of the moon—or at least she won't be sacrificed until then. That doesn't give us much time. But there's more, I'm afraid."

In a harsh voice, Jonathan said, "Let's have it."

"The spider has magical powers," Mrs. Zimmermann said slowly. "Physically, it is very weak, but it can create illusions, it can mislead and trick us, and if it bites us, it could very well kill us. We'll have to be on our guard."

"When do we go?" asked Lewis.

Jonathan shook his head. "Lewis, I can't ask you to help in this. It's too dangerous." In a kindly voice, he added, "It might be very frightening."

Lewis said quietly, "I know: I'm terrified already. Only, Rose Rita is my friend. Back when that evil spirit nearly lured me into a well, she showed up to help. She needs me now."

Mrs. Zimmermann agreed briskly. "I think Lewis is right, Jonathan. The powers of evil have dreadful tricks up their sleeves, but they don't always count on simple things that might foul them up. One of the simplest and most powerful is friendship. All for one and one for all, I say."

Jonathan Barnavelt tugged at his red beard. "All for one and one for all it is, then," he said. "Lewis, go get our flashlights. Florence, maybe you'd better go home and pick up some especially powerful amulets and talismans. If we're going up against this Death Spider, we'll need every bit of help we can get!"

CHAPTER TWELVE

When Rose Rita stepped into the dark hollow of the tomb, she had a moment of pure panic. She had the feeling that the walls were slowly coming together to crush her. The air turned dead and stale, and it was hard to breathe. Her lungs throbbed, and her heart felt squeezed, as if it were about to burst in her chest. The world began to spin around and around, and she staggered, dazed and dizzy.

Then some force pulled her along. The passageway slanted downward, like a ramp, and then became a kind of tunnel. To her astonishment, Rose Rita could see. No light from the surface could come through the earth and stone around her, but some strange, dim, greenish illumination let her glimpse walls made of crumbling gray tiles, with roots and earth bulging through here and

there. The floor underfoot was unpleasantly soft and spongy, and things squelched under her feet, popping in a horrible liquid way. A bad smell filled her nostrils, earthy, damp, and moldy, reminding her of mildew, of rot and decay. Ahead of her the passage turned, but the muted green light—it was almost like a faintly glowing haze in the air—let her see only dimly. Rose Rita took step after unwilling step, her path turning left, then right, then left again, and always leading down, down, down.

She walked for what seemed like hours. At last the light began to grow stronger. She had the sense of tons of earth above her, cutting her off from the surface and from life. As the light increased, Rose Rita could see dark, slimy streaks where water had oozed down the tiled walls of the passage. She could see, too, that she was walking on a leathery carpet of fungi—bloated, pale toadstools that were an ugly, fleshy color and that released a sickening stench when she stepped on them and made them pop.

The passageway widened to at least ten feet and led to an arch. A filmy curtain swayed softly and gently in the air. As she came closer, Rose Rita held her breath. The swagging silk was not a curtain. It was an enormous spiderweb. Small bones were stuck throughout, perhaps the bones of bats, rats, or snakes that had come down here. The arch was far above her head, but even so, Rose Rita cringed as she passed under it.

She stepped out into a strange, round room. The arched ceiling soared high overhead, its hollow center lost in darkness. In the middle of the room was a round

marble platform, with steps leading up to it from all sides. A tall white pillar was centered on the platform, and a broad, white marble bowl rested on top of it. In this marble cauldron something burned with a slow, green flame. Glowing green smoke rose, spread lazily, and drifted through the air. The flame and the vapor were the sources of the bizarre dim light.

"Come!"

Rose Rita gasped. She could not tell if the voice was in her head or if the word had been spoken aloud. The deadly force that gripped her made her move around the edge of the platform. Against the wall on the far side stood two thrones. They gleamed dully, like gold. Both thrones had high backs, and crowning each was an odd bust. It looked like a creature with a man's shoulders but the head of some fox-faced animal with enormous ears. Rose Rita had seen pictures of such a being in books. It was Anubis, an ancient Egyptian god, she thought as she moved slowly forward. She vaguely recalled that Anubis guarded the passageway from life to death. . . .

"Welcome," said the harsh, whispering voice, and Rose Rita jerked her attention back to the two thrones. The one on the right was empty. A spectral figure, as erect and proud as a queen, sat in the other.

"Stop."

Rose Rita halted. She stared at the seated figure. From this close she could tell the figure was a woman, slim and regal looking. She wore a flowing white robe. Her arms rested on the arms of the throne, each hand on top of a golden globe. The skin on her hands and fingers looked

unhealthy, gray and strangely pebbly in texture. Her face was in shadow, and she remained motionless.

"Welcome."

Rose Rita swayed and collapsed to her hands and knees. She felt as though a string had been supporting her and had suddenly been cut. She shuddered as her hands touched the squelchy toadstools, plunging down into their cold slime up to her wrists. Crying out, she scrambled backward, up onto the steps of the platform. "Who—who are you?" Rose Rita screamed.

Laughter came from the figure—hissing, cold laughter. "You know who I am."

Rose Rita's teeth chattered. Her hands felt cold. She frantically scrubbed them against her jeans legs, trying to remove the awful fluids of the fungi. The air in the cavernous room was freezing, and she could not stop shaking. "Belle Frisson," said Rose Rita in a low growl. "What are you doing to me?"

"Nothing that you have not cheerfully done to yourself," the voice said callously. "Did you not want revenge? Did you not hate those who mocked you? Did you not wish to loose the Death Spider?"

"N-no," stammered Rose Rita. "Maybe I daydreamed—"

"You will have all eternity to dream now," responded the whispery voice. "This, though, I promise you: When I go forth once more into the waking world, my first task will be to destroy those who mistreated you. You may reflect on that as you rest here forever."

Rose Rita reeled. Visions flashed before her eyes. Vi-

sions of the other girls in her class screaming in terror. Visions of the whole school flaring into flame, burning though it was made of stone. Visions of New Zebedee itself laid waste, everything broken, shattered, ruined, with spiders creeping over the rubble. Then it all cleared away. "You can't do that!" shouted Rose Rita, angry and terrified at the same time.

"I have waited too long," replied the still figure. "I will live again, oh, I will live! But first I will destroy!"

"W-why?" wailed Rose Rita.

The voice was cruel, remorseless. "When I lived the life of flesh, I spoke to spirits! Had I had time to refine my studies, I might have become most powerful, the ruler of the universe—but I had to perform for fools to earn my bread. Ancient spirits taught me, nurtured me, showed me a way of perhaps holding off death. I— arranged for certain procedures to be done in the event of my death. My apparent death. For the vessel was broken, yet the spirit continued."

"I don't understand," complained Rose Rita. Her arms and legs were beginning to feel numb from the terrible cold.

"Of course not!" The voice was a whiplash that made Rose Rita flinch. "Foolish girl, how could you understand the thread of the spider? How could you appreciate how it may hold and bind a spirit, saving it from the final journey to the realms of the dead? *I* understood! *I* prepared! And now here you are, to take my place, that I may again don flesh and walk forth among the living! Do you know how a spider lives? How she traps prey and

then drinks the blood from it? A small fly's life might last a few weeks, but trapped and wrapped by a spider, the fly lives many times that span! So shall you live, here, seated on the Throne of Anubis, and your long, long life shall be mine, for I am as the spider, drinking from your strength and life!"

Something chittered behind Rose Rita. She turned, dreading what she might see.

A huge spider, the size of a horse, had climbed up onto the platform behind her. Its enormous dark-gray body pulsed in a hideous way. Its five bulging black eyes glittered in the unearthly light. Its jaws quivered and clenched, revealing sharp, scarlet-tipped fangs that glistened with venom. The hairy beast moved toward Rose Rita.

Rose Rita backed away, her heart thundering. The spider crept forward. Rose Rita's lungs were paralyzed. She wanted to scream, but she could not. She took another step back, off the platform, and another—

And a bony hand seized her arm!

Gasping, Rose Rita turned to fight.

The creature on the throne held her arm in her deadly grip. Rose Rita stared at the woman and felt as if she were going insane.

A skeleton was inside the white linen robe—a skeleton with hollow eye sockets and a fierce grin. The skeleton had a horrible kind of flesh on its bones—for over every inch of its face, swarming and spinning, crawled millions and millions of tiny spiders, their eyes shimmering, their busy legs thrashing.

The skeleton's grinning mouth moved, and the whispery voice said, "They weave me new flesh to wear. It will do. It will do."

And then Rose Rita felt the firm clutch of two of the huge spider's legs, one on each of her shoulders. Everything went dark. She fainted dead away.

CHAPTER THIRTEEN

"Turn here," said Lewis. Mrs. Zimmermann turned the wheel, and Bessie rolled off the highway and onto the lane leading out to the cemetery.

Jonathan Barnavelt, sitting in the backseat, said, "This is certainly a deserted patch of ground."

Mrs. Zimmermann sniffed. "When villains and evildoers want to set up housekeeping, they don't march right into the center of town, Weird Beard. They like to keep their nefarious activity under the cover of darkness and loneliness."

Lewis stared straight ahead. The headlights made a wavering tunnel of light in the night. Finally the lane widened, and Lewis could see the jutting, rounded forms of headstones. "The big one in the middle is Belle Frisson's grave," whispered Lewis. Though he was willing to

do anything to help Rose Rita, he had to face the fact that he was sick with anxiety.

The car jounced to a stop, and Mrs. Zimmermann turned the key in the ignition. "Well," she said, "here we are. I suppose there's no sense putting things off. Have you got the flashlights, Jonathan?"

"Right here." He handed two long chrome-plated flashlights forward, and he kept another for himself. They were powerful six-cell lights, and they could throw a beam a long way. Before they had left New Zebedee, Jonathan had put new D-cell batteries into all three flashlights. When Lewis switched his on, the car flooded with bright white light.

"Let's go," said Mrs. Zimmermann, opening her door. They all got out.

The countryside was quiet. A light wind ruffled the dry leaves clinging to the trees. A solitary cricket chirped, its song slow, sad, and soft. Four or five silvery clouds drifted across the sky, faintly lit by starlight. The moon was low in the sky. Lewis stood for a few seconds, breathing in great lungfuls of the crisp, cool October air. His uncle put a hand on his shoulder, making Lewis jump a mile.

"Sorry, Lewis," said Jonathan.

"That's okay," croaked Lewis, his throat dry.

They went down the central path of the cemetery. Halfway to Belle Frisson's strange monument, Uncle Jonathan turned his light to the left. "What in the world is that?" he asked, and he walked between the headstones toward something long, brown, and snaky. Lewis heard a dry rustle as Jonathan picked up whatever it was. Then

there was a rattling sound, and in a moment Jonathan was back.

"What is it?" asked Mrs. Zimmermann, shining her light toward Jonathan.

"It's a scroll," answered Jonathan. "A long, dry, brown scroll, made of parchment, I think."

"That's the one we saw in the museum!" cried Lewis. "The testament of Belle Frisson I told you about! Oh, my gosh, Rose Rita must have stolen it back again!"

"Don't jump to conclusions," said Mrs. Zimmermann. "Here, hold my flashlight."

Lewis took it and shined it on the parchment as Mrs. Zimmermann unrolled it a little at a time. "Hmm," she murmured, and "Oh," and "Aha."

"Come on, Haggy," complained Uncle Jonathan. "This crumply dumpling means something to you. Tell us what the Cracker Jack prize is!"

"It's a spell of unsealing," she said slowly. "Its function is to unlock magically sealed secret places. But it's strangely incomplete. And the parchment seems oddly . . . *stretched*. It's as if it had been used in a tug-of-war by demons. I think all its magic may have been used up."

"Let's go," said Jonathan urgently, taking the rolled-up scroll from her. "Let's see what else we can find."

They circled the monument. When he turned his flashlight on the central pillar, Lewis thought it looked different somehow, chipped and rugged. Then he realized that the carvings were no longer there. The stone looked as if someone had taken a hammer and a chisel

and pulverized the pillar's surface, erasing all the markings. He moved the circle of his flashlight lower and saw that a litter of stone chips now covered the top of the cube on which the pillar rested.

Mrs. Zimmermann touched his shoulder. "Lewis," she said in a strange voice, "switch off your light. You too, Jonathan."

Lewis did, and the darkness fell like a velvet curtain. Off in the distance an owl cried out, a low, lonesome *Hu-hu-huuuu!* Very faintly came a faraway train whistle, mournful and low. "Look up," said Mrs. Zimmermann in little more than a whisper. "Look at that globe on top of the pillar."

Squinting into the darkness, Lewis felt the hair on his neck and arms bristle. The dark stone sphere at the top of the pillar was—*steaming*. Green, faintly glowing vapors boiled from it, tendrils of mist that thinned and vanished as they evaporated. Jonathan cleared his throat. "Something is going on here," he said. "Something evil. Are those fumes the ones you'd get from the Lamp of Osiris spell?"

"A–plus, Jonathan," replied Mrs. Zimmermann. "And you know what that means."

"I don't," said Lewis in a hushed tone.

Mrs. Zimmermann turned her flashlight back on as Jonathan walked around the grave. "It means sacrifice," she said. "Someone has been killed here. Oh, maybe not lately—not this year, or even this century. Still, an unholy rite was performed here. That's the kind of light people used to call a 'corpse candle,' or sometimes a

'will-o'-the-wisp.' It's a product of sudden death—a kind of unfocused haunting."

From the other side of the monument, Jonathan Barnavelt called, "Take a look at this."

They went around. Jonathan was shining his flashlight at the ground. There, resting on the grass, was a flashlight, two waxed-paper-wrapped sandwiches—and a green-bound book. Jonathan picked it up, and opened it. "*Forty Years Among the Magicians,*" he read aloud. He leafed through the book. "It has a chapter on Belle Frisson," he said.

"Rose Rita got that from Mr. Hardwick at the museum," Lewis recollected. "So she *has* been back here."

Mrs. Zimmermann turned the beam of her flashlight back toward the tomb. "I'll bet anything she brought the scroll and worked the spell. Or the spell worked itself, more likely. Lewis, is that pillar all bashed up?"

"Yes," said Lewis, "it is. It had marks on it—carvings that didn't really make any sense. They're all gone now."

"A self-activating spell," said Mrs. Zimmermann thoughtfully. "Wherever Rose Rita is, she's gone through some magical portal. We've got to find out how to follow."

"How do we do that?" asked Jonathan, sounding frustrated and angry. "You said all the magic is gone from the parchment scroll."

"We do it," said Mrs. Zimmermann, "by becoming detectives. Jonathan, Lewis, we can't do anything else here, at least not tonight. I have an idea or two about discover-

ing how to work that spell again—because a magician *can* activate the spell, you know. It doesn't have to work itself. However, I have to figure out exactly how it was worded, and that might take some time. Let's head home. We have until Friday night."

Four days, thought Lewis. Only four more days!

As soon as school was over on Tuesday, Lewis hurried home. Mrs. Zimmermann was there, sitting at the dining-room table. She had stacks of paper around her, and she had scribbled all over them. The scroll was there too, looking very fragile and brittle now. Jonathan Barnavelt sat quietly on the other side of the table, deeply engrossed in the book he had retrieved from the cemetery. He looked up and gave Lewis a weak smile. "Hi," he said.

"Have you done it?" asked Lewis.

"Partly," responded Mrs. Zimmermann. She looked exhausted. Her wrinkled face was strained and drawn. "From the picture of the tomb in that book, and from the parts of the letters on the scroll, I've got about eighty-five percent of the spell figured out." She showed Lewis how the edges of the scroll had been meant to line up with the carvings on the tomb. Together, the markings on the tomb and the scroll came together to make up letters, which literally spelled out the incantation. The trouble was that some of the markings on the scroll were just vertical lines. There was no telling if they were meant to be the downward strokes of T's or I's, or per-

haps lower-case l's. Other markings might be the tops of F's or E's, or of B's or R's. Guesswork could fill in a lot of the words, but some were very strange indeed.

Mrs. Zimmermann rubbed her eyes. "If only I knew what the tomb markings were," she said. "That would make life easy!"

"Can't we try what you've got?" asked Lewis. "It might work!"

Jonathan shook his head. "Sorry, Lewis. It has to be the complete spell or nothing. You see, a spell controls and binds the magic. If you tried a spell without all the words, it might not work at all, or the magic might react in uncontrollable ways. You might accidentally turn yourself into a frog, or let demons loose in the world, or produce a live chicken from under your robes."

Lewis groaned.

With a forced laugh Jonathan said, "I'm sorry about that chicken crack. I'm tired, I guess. I'll fix us some dinner, and then we'll go back to studying this sinister scroll."

Mrs. Zimmermann pushed a stack of papers away. "*I'll* fix the dinner," she said. "I'm tired of Fuzzy Face's gourmet ham sandwiches! Tell me what the book says about Belle Frisson while I cook, Jonathan."

Jonathan summarized for them. The information was meager and not very helpful. "The author of the book thought she was probably just another trickster," Jonathan finished, "although he admitted she did some very startling and baffling effects. No wonder. Clearly, Elizabeth Proctor—or Belle Frisson, as she called her-

self—was in touch with mysterious powers and forces. There's one odd thing. She seems to have amassed a fortune over the years, but it was all spent on her funeral. Years before her fatal accident she'd arranged for a strange troupe of people to come whenever and wherever she died to prepare her tomb and bury her. That sounds like she was plotting something."

"I agree," said Mrs. Zimmermann, rattling pots and pans. "I believe Belle Frisson was determined to come back from the dead."

"I think you've hit it, Florence," declared Jonathan. He turned and stared at the kitchen calendar. "She died on Halloween 1878. I think she's planning to come back this Halloween. So on Friday at midnight, when the date changes from the thirtieth to the thirty-first—"

He left the rest of the thought unspoken. He didn't need to say any more. The idea was too terrible to put into words.

CHAPTER FOURTEEN

Rose Rita rose from unconsciousness like a diver slowly swimming to the surface of deep, dark waters. Her first impression was that she had been dreaming. Everything that had happened since the day she had first found the scroll seemed faraway and hazy, like a dimly recalled nightmare. For just a few seconds, Rose Rita felt safe and cozy and warm.

Then she opened her eyes to the repellent green light, and she knew it had all been real. She found herself sitting on one of the two thrones, and she tried to get up. She could not stir. She could barely even move her head. She looked down at herself, and her eyes grew wide with terror.

Rose Rita's whole body had been wrapped in glistening spider silk. Except for her head she was encased in a co-

coon. She might have been a mummy, wrapped in yards and yards of bandages pulled tight around her. Her stomach lurched as she remembered the touch of that huge spider's prickly legs on her shoulders. It had spun its silk around her, the way an ordinary garden spider would spin silk around a trapped insect. Even her hair felt as if it had been plastered to the back of the throne with more silk. Rose Rita had just enough slack to breathe. Her arms had been tied to the arms of the throne, her hands bound to two balls that felt like polished metal. She could not even turn her head.

From the corner of her eye she could glimpse another figure, seated beside her. It was the horrible spider-crawling skeleton. From it came a breathy voice: "There is no need to struggle. You will have no lasting pain, and after that you will not even care. Your mind will continue to work as your body withers away, slowly, slowly, over a hundred years. Its life force will feed me. You will be a part of me in a way. You should be flattered."

"Let me go," said Rose Rita. No longer terrified, no longer paralyzed, now she was just plain angry. "You let me go, or you'll be sorry!"

The insinuating voice ignored her. "What will you think of, here in the dark, as I have been for all these years? I believe you will go mad very quickly. Alone in the tomb, with only a spider for company. Yes, I believe you will be quite insane before many weeks have passed."

Rose Rita did not answer. She struggled fiercely to break free, but the clinging spider silk was tough. She could barely wriggle. "Let me go!" she yelled again.

"Foolish child," sneered the voice. "When my body was broken, I reached through the curtain of death to work my will. At my bidding was my tomb fashioned, and at my bidding did my slaves sacrifice one who had been my best friend to Neith, the Weaver of the World. Do you think that I, who would not hesitate to command that, would allow you to escape? No, child, you are my lifeline, my tie to the world. Not for all the treasures of the East would I release you!" The voice chortled, a harrowing, raspy sound. "When the time comes, and it is very close now, my pet will seize you and bend you forward. It will bite you just once, on the back of the neck, and I am afraid that will be very painful. Then I shall leave you. Behold, already I grow strong."

Rose Rita gritted her teeth to keep from crying out. The skeleton beside her *moved*! With creaky, slow jerks, it raised itself to its feet. It took a wobbling step, and Rose Rita shut her eyes.

The tiny spiders had woven a skin of white spiderweb over the skeleton. They were beneath it, for the creature's flesh literally crawled. The empty eye sockets glowed with a red inner light. The mouth had become a straight slit, revealing dry, yellowed teeth. Beneath the linen robe the chest heaved, as if the monstrous thing were breathing.

"You do not think I am lovely?" mocked the voice. "Wait, child. When you have been . . . prepared, when I draw strength and sustenance from you, then this flesh will seem as real as yours. I shall be beautiful! I shall walk the Earth again! This time I shall master the weak mor-

tals around me. After your usefulness has been drained, there will be another, and another. I shall live forever!"

Rose Rita opened her eyes. The skeleton stood before her, swaying, as if it were hardly strong enough to stand. It stepped aside, collapsing back onto the throne with a muffled clatter of bones. "My pet is coming," the voice whispered.

With dread in her heart Rose Rita glared out at the room. Creeping over the round platform was the enormous spider. "No!" screamed Rose Rita.

"The time draws near," said the voice. "The time draws very near."

By Friday, the day before Halloween, Lewis was growing frantic. The police were searching everywhere for Rose Rita, without success. Mr. and Mrs. Pottinger had offered a reward, but of course that would do no good. Jonathan and Mrs. Zimmermann were at the end of their rope. They had tried everything from books on cryptography and code breaking to the most powerful spells that Mrs. Zimmermann could think of, but nothing helped.

Lewis stayed home from school that day, too anxious to attend. Late that afternoon the phone rang, and Jonathan answered it. He came back to the kitchen, where Mrs. Zimmermann and Lewis waited, with his face set in a grim expression. "That was George Pottinger," he said. "The police have found something after all. A woman named Seidler picked up a girl who said her name was Rowena Potter out west of town, and she dropped her off near the cemetery. The state police searched

around and found Rose Rita's bicycle in a cornfield. Now they believe that Rose Rita has run away."

Mrs. Zimmermann sighed. "Oh, if only we knew the rest of this blasted spell. I think I have everything except seven words, but they are words of power. Jonathan, if worse comes to worst, we simply have to work the spell. God help us, I don't know what it might do, but we'll have to try."

Lewis said, "Why don't we ask Mr. Hardwick if he has pictures?"

Both Jonathan and Mrs. Zimmermann looked at him. "Pictures?" asked Uncle Jonathan. "You mean pictures of the monument?"

Mrs. Zimmermann asked, "Why do you think he'd take pictures?"

With a shrug, Lewis answered, "I know it's a long shot. Still, Mr. and Mrs. Hardwick visit the cemetery a lot, and they have friends buried there. And Mr. Hardwick does make a point of collecting everything he can about magic—everything from wands and books to posters and Houdini's old milk can."

Jonathan got to his feet. "It's worth a try. Let me call him." He went to the study and made the call, and a minute later he was back. "Let's go!" he hastened them. "Lewis may have saved the day."

Mrs. Zimmermann did not even object when Jonathan opened the garage. They drove the few blocks to the National Museum of Magic in Jonathan's boxy old car, and they hurried inside. Mr. Hardwick was waiting there for them. He opened the door and ushered them in. "Wel-

come, welcome," he said, shaking hands with all of them. "Jonathan, it's good to see you again. My, I did admire that trick you did at the Chamber of Commerce meeting last summer—the floating handkerchief. I think I've about figured out how you did it, but it was a great stunt. I—"

With a tight smile Jonathan said, "Thank you very much, Bob, but we'd really like to see—what we talked about on the phone, if it isn't too much trouble."

"Oh, sure," replied Mr. Hardwick, leading them to a doorway. "They're in the basement. Has your friend turned up yet, Lewis?"

"No," Lewis said mournfully.

"I'm sorry." Mr. Hardwick opened the door and reached inside to flick on a light. "Come on, and watch your step. The stairs are pretty steep. Well, I'm sure Rose Rita will show up. She probably ran away from home. Lots of young people do that, and most of them return again safe and sound." As he talked, Mr. Hardwick led them down into a brick-walled cellar. It was lined with dozens of file cabinets, each drawer labeled. Mr. Hardwick waved at them. "This is my collection of letters and manuscripts," he explained. "There are also playbills and advertisements for magic shows. Photographs of famous magicians, many of them autographed. Scrapbooks and handwritten instructions about how to perform tricks. And this one, of course. This cabinet is full of rubbings."

He pulled open a file drawer and rummaged inside, finally producing a thick green file folder. "Is that it?" asked Jonathan urgently.

"Yes," replied Mr. Hardwick. "The folder is labeled right here: *Rubbing of the Belle Frisson tomb, done June 1, 1938*." He opened the file and took out a big sheet of thin paper. Lewis stared as his uncle took one end of it and unfolded it. The sheet was actually several sheets taped together, and it had been smeared with charcoal.

Lewis realized that it was a tombstone rubbing—Mr. Hardwick had placed the paper against the shaft of Belle Frisson's monument and had rubbed a piece of charcoal back and forth over it. The result was a replica in charcoal of all the markings. Mrs. Zimmermann was already tracing her finger over the lines of marks. "That's one!" she said.

There were many more folded sheets of paper in the file folder, one for each side of the shaft. Mrs. Zimmermann found another partial word, then another and another. In five minutes, she had found them all. "Thank you!" she said to a puzzled-looking Mr. Hardwick. "Now we have to go!"

Mr. Hardwick gave her a curious smile. "Can't you even tell me why this was so urgent?" he asked.

Jonathan Barnavelt clapped him on the shoulder. "Later, Bob. Right now, all I can say is God bless you for being such a fanatical collector—and for being so fantastically well organized! Lewis, come on!"

Lewis followed him up the stairs. He realized two things. First, it was terribly late—the sun was ready to set.

Second, Mrs. Zimmermann now had the complete

spell. They had to go back to the deserted cemetery. They had to use that spell to try to save Rose Rita.

And what would happen? What would they face in that terrifying graveyard? A Death Spider? A sorceress returned from beyond the tomb?

Or something even worse—something so horrible that Lewis could not even imagine it?

CHAPTER FIFTEEN

Jonathan Barnavelt drove like a madman. Lewis hung on as the old car lurched around curves, its tires screeching. Farmhouses and fields flashed past. The sun was setting as they turned into the long lane that led to the cemetery, and by the time Jonathan had slammed on the brakes and brought his auto to a halt, it had vanished.

"We don't have much time," said Mrs. Zimmermann, climbing out of the car. "Here, Jonathan. Put this around your neck. Here's yours, Lewis, and here's one for me." From her collection of amulets Mrs. Zimmermann had selected three. One was a scarab, an ancient Egyptian symbol of life. Another was a tiny gold cross that had been blessed by a very holy monk in the fifteenth century. The third amulet—the one she gave to Lewis—was

a purple gemstone that glowed with a spark of her own magic.

She strode toward the monument carrying a plain black umbrella. It was folded, and its handle was a bronze griffin's talon gripping a crystal sphere. Jonathan and Lewis joined her as she carefully placed the umbrella on the ground. "Hold my hands," she said in a low voice. "Whatever happens, we are in this together."

"All for one," said Lewis in a timid voice. He tried to sound brave, but the attempt was as complete a failure as his magic act had been.

"And one for all," boomed Jonathan Barnavelt. "Florence, do your best. And let any wandering bogies, beasties, and creepy-crawling spiders look out!" He squeezed Lewis's hand, then took Mrs. Zimmermann's right hand in his. Lewis held her left hand.

In a clear, high voice Mrs. Zimmermann began to pronounce the words of the spell. Some were in English, some in Latin, some in Greek, and some in Coptic, a language spoken in Egypt. Lewis felt the earth beneath his feet shift as the words rang out. He heard a strange groaning, the sound that stone might make if it came to life and tried to stir. And as Mrs. Zimmermann pronounced the final syllables of the chant, he saw the sphere atop Belle Frisson's monument shake. It split into fragments with a great *crack!* and an explosion of dust. Lewis shouted in alarm. The pillar teetered and fell, and the cube of granite slowly pivoted to one side.

It revealed a dark opening leading down into the earth.

Mrs. Zimmermann cleared her throat. "So far so good," she said. "Let's go—and watch out for surprises. I'm sure Elizabeth Proctor would have some nasty watchdogs guarding her privacy! Lewis, if we should run into that huge spider, remember it's hardly real at all. It is made up of a pinch of ashes and one drop of living blood. It's just a specter."

"Th-then it can't hurt us?" asked Lewis.

Mrs. Zimmermann's expression was grave. "It can hurt us, all right," she said. "As a specter, it grows on bad emotions—hatred, fear, and anger. But it must have your belief to exist at all. If you don't believe, you take away its evil power. Remember that. . . . Everyone okay? Let's go." She picked up her umbrella, looking ready for action.

Jonathan Barnavelt led the way, his flashlight sending its strong beam down the tunnel, over the split and decaying tile walls, where green slime had grown. Over the horrible floor of rubbery toadstools. Over the whitened bones of small animals.

Lewis followed him, and Mrs. Zimmermann brought up the rear. The stench was appalling, and Lewis felt nauseated. He kept gulping air through his mouth. They followed the twisting tunnel for a long time, and then Jonathan halted. "Here's her watchdog, all right," he whispered. "Florence, see what you think!"

Lewis looked around from behind his uncle. What he saw froze the blood in his veins. The end of the tunnel was completely closed off by a billowing white spiderweb, and resting in the exact center of it was a huge spider. It was not the one they had glimpsed at Rose Rita's

house, because that one had been hairy and gray. This one was shiny black, and it had a red hourglass marking on its belly. It was a black widow, the deadliest spider in America.

And it was the size of a dinner plate. Its long legs stirred, and it began to creep down the web.

Mrs. Zimmermann stepped forward and held her umbrella in front of her. Suddenly the umbrella became a dark, long staff, crowned with a blinding sphere of purple light. Mrs. Zimmermann changed too—she wore flowing purple robes, with flames in the folds, and she stood tall and terrible. The spider seemed to sense that something was happening. It leaped forward, its legs stretched wide—

Power crackled from Mrs. Zimmermann. A bolt of purple energy shot from her hand and struck the hideous creature in midair. It tumbled away from them, bursting into flame, and it hit the web. With a *whoosh!* the web caught fire and sizzled away. The spider's body fell to the floor, a sputtering cinder.

Mrs. Zimmermann lowered the staff, and it was just an umbrella again. "She knows we're coming now," she said. "Let's not disappoint her!"

They stepped into a large round room. They could not see the far side because of a marble platform in the center. Slowly they edged around it. Then Mrs. Zimmermann stopped with a despairing cry. Lewis stared.

Rose Rita sat on a golden throne. Her body had been wrapped up like a mummy. Her eyes, behind the black-rimmed spectacles, were wide with horror.

The gray spider, far larger than it had been earlier, crouched above her. Its forelegs rested on her shoulders. Its dripping fangs were only inches from her neck. It clung to the wall, its abdomen pulsing slowly.

A figure stepped around the platform. "Fools," it said in a scornful, breathy voice. Lewis could not believe his eyes. The figure was like the dried corpse of a woman. The flesh was dead white and clung to the bones of the face. The eyes looked hollow, and the mouth was simply a dark slit. It moved as the creature said, "You are too late."

"No," proclaimed Jonathan. "I don't believe we are. Rose Rita, we're here! We've come to take you home!"

"You ignorant fat man!" exclaimed the walking corpse. "You three will join my guest here—join her for all eternity!"

"Let Rose Rita go," Mrs. Zimmermann said, stepping forward. "You don't want her. Take me instead."

"Why should I do that?" asked the creature.

"Because I am what you always desired to be," replied Mrs. Zimmermann. "I am a witch."

Light seemed to flare in the empty eye sockets of the thing that had once been Belle Frisson. "I shall have you *and* the girl," she said. "There is no bargain!"

Lewis saw Rose Rita start to squirm. She twisted, just under the fangs of the spider. Fiercely, she cried out, "You let Mrs. Zimmermann alone! I take back all my bad wishes! I take back that drop of blood! I won't let you hurt my friends!"

The walking corpse whirled, hissing. Mrs. Zimmer-

mann said, "So Rose Rita reclaims her drop of blood! Now I can deal with you, my friend!" She raised her umbrella, and from it a spark of intense purple fire leaped out. It struck across the room like a crackling bolt of purple lightning, and it hit the spider above Rose Rita squarely in the back.

Lewis screamed. The creature sprang from the wall, its legs thrashing madly. It scrambled toward them.

Mrs. Zimmermann was shouting a spell. Jonathan rushed around the spider and charged to help Rose Rita. The spider reared high over Mrs. Zimmermann, who thrust her hand out. Her fingers pierced the spider's skin. Then she jerked her hand away. The tip of one finger was red. "In Rose Rita's name, I reclaim her blood!" she shouted. "You have no power here!"

The mummy of Belle Frisson shrieked from somewhere in the darkness. The spider swayed for an instant, and then its skin crackled into a thousand zigzag lines. The creature collapsed in a dark cloud. In an instant it had vanished.

Jonathan had picked up Rose Rita. The cobwebs that had bound her were vanishing too, crumbling into powder. Jonathan yelled, "Look out, Florence!"

Too late! The mummified Belle Frisson had surged forward. Bony hands closed around the umbrella. With superhuman strength the shambling creature wrested it away from Mrs. Zimmermann. She wailed and fell to her hands and knees.

Laughing insanely, the undead Belle Frisson raised the umbrella over her head. "A magician's staff breaks when

she dies!" the creature screeched. "And sometimes it works the other way! If I smash this globe, you are dead!"

"Wait!" Lewis cried, stepping forward. His knees were knocking. He felt as if he were about to faint. But he knew he had to keep Belle Frisson from shattering the umbrella. He held up his empty hands. "Wait!" he said again. "I have a gift for you!"

"What?" The red eye sockets seemed to bore into him. "What would you have?"

"A talisman!" Lewis shouted, his voice breaking. "See, it's here! It's in my hand!"

"There is nothing in your hand!"

"That's because it's invisible!" Lewis screamed. "I am the Mystifying Mysto! Now you don't see it"—he flicked his hand, doing a movement he had practiced over and over for the magic show—"and now you do! Take that!" The powerful amulet swung out from his jacket. He grabbed it, lunged forward, and thrust it against the shambling creature's face!

The purple star flared to brilliant life. The living corpse howled as the crystal burned into it, creating a sizzling hole right between her eye sockets. She dropped the umbrella, which Lewis barely managed to catch.

"Get back!" yelled Mrs. Zimmermann, pulling Lewis away.

The creature staggered. Purple beams of light shone from her eyes, from her gaping mouth. Her skin billowed, crisped, burned away. Then she collapsed to a pile of bone; and in a silent, purple explosion, she flew into whirling dust.

The ground began to shake. Mrs. Zimmermann took her umbrella from Lewis, and the globe gave off its strong purple glow. "Rose Rita, are you all right?"

"I am now!" said Rose Rita.

"Let's get out of here," bellowed Uncle Jonathan. "This place is caving in!"

They raced for the tunnel. Lewis did not look back. From behind him came awful sounds of collapse and ruin, and he did not wish to see what was producing them.

CHAPTER SIXTEEN

"Is she really gone?" asked Rose Rita. Two weeks had passed since the underground struggle with the animated corpse of Belle Frisson, and she was still having nightmares.

"Yes!" replied Mrs. Zimmermann decisively. "We snapped her thread, you might say. She had connected her spirit to the land of the living with a magic spell, like a spider's web. When Lewis did his magic trick, he burned right through that magical web. Her spirit was banished to the domains of the dead, and that's why everything fell apart."

"Don't tell anyone around here that, though," said Jonathan Barnavelt with a laugh. "They all think it was a mighty unusual earthquake that toppled her monument!"

"We got out just in time," said Lewis.

It was an unseasonably warm Saturday in Novem-

ber. The four friends were sitting in the backyard of 100 High Street, enjoying the balmy Indian-summer day. Mrs. Zimmermann had baked a big plate of delicious double-fudge walnut brownies, and they were all munching happily and drinking tall glasses of milk. Rose Rita's sudden return had astonished everyone in New Zebedee, but she had risen to the occasion. She concocted a story of tumbling off her bike and getting amnesia. For several days, she told everyone, she had wandered around not knowing who she was. She said she had slept in barns.

Jonathan told the police that he, Mrs. Zimmermann, and Lewis had found Rose Rita when they had driven over the route that Mrs. Seidler had talked about. Rose Rita, who had been without food and water for several days, had to spend that Friday night in the hospital, but she made a rapid recovery. Even the tiny moon-shaped mark where she had cut her finger faded and vanished. Now everything at her house was more or less back to normal, except that Mrs. Pottinger would not allow Rose Rita to ride her bike for the rest of the fall and winter. Rose Rita said that was a small price to pay.

"Did you replace the scroll?" Mrs. Zimmermann asked.

"When I took the book back to Mr. Hardwick, I slipped the scroll into its box," Rose Rita admitted. "Do you really think it's safe now?"

"Yes. All its magic power is gone," Mrs. Zimmermann said. "Without that, the scroll is just a curiosity. And now that the tomb has been destroyed in the cave-in, it can't cause any more mischief."

Jonathan looked at Lewis. "You're very quiet," he said. "What are you thinking?"

Lewis grinned. "I'm thinking that I did pretty good for an amateur magician," he said. "I fooled Belle Frisson into letting me get close, and then I used the chicken trick to hit her with that amulet."

"That was fast thinking," Rose Rita said. "How did you know it would work?"

Lewis shrugged. "I didn't know—not really," he confessed. "Only it seemed to me that Mrs. Zimmermann's magic is good, and that it would destroy evil. So I took a chance. I didn't know what else to do."

"Your instincts were right on the money," said Mrs. Zimmermann. "I'm glad you didn't let her smash my umbrella. Ugh! It might not have killed me, but such a blow wouldn't have left me the same."

Rose Rita kept glancing around the yard nervously. Jonathan tilted his head and asked, "What's wrong, Rose Rita?"

She scowled. "I don't know. I keep having the creepy feeling that I'm being watched, but I guess that's impossible. Old Belle Frisson is long gone, and I hope her spiders have gone with her!"

"I'm sure they have," said Mrs. Zimmermann. She looked thoughtful. "Hmm. Now that you mention it, I think I have a sense of being watched too. Weird Beard, do you want to have a stab at finding out why?"

Grinning, Jonathan Barnavelt made a couple of magic passes. In the air in front of him a golden arrow appeared, floating with no support. It looked like an old-fashioned

weathervane. It spun around and around, and it wound up pointing toward the corner of the house. Jonathan got up and winked as the arrow disappeared. He tiptoed over to the house. Then he pounced, and Lewis heard a squeak.

Jonathan reappeared, chuckling. "Come along," he said. Chad Britton came around the corner, wearing his trench coat and looking embarrassed. "Cheer up," said Jonathan to the others. "It's only our neighborhood detective!"

"Chad, were you spying on us?" asked Lewis.

"No, not really," Chad said. "I just—well, I—I thought—"

Mrs. Zimmermann reached for the tray of brownies. "You thought you detected the smell of fudge," she said kindly.

"Yeah!" said Chad, beaming.

"Have one," Mrs. Zimmermann told him. "And next time just come up and ask."

Chad bit into a brownie and rolled his eyes. "This is great," he said. "Thanks, Mrs. Zimmermann!"

"You're welcome," replied Mrs. Zimmermann.

Lewis reached for a brownie too. "Well," he said, "maybe Chad and I are both on the right track. He detected these brownies, so he'd be a good detective. And I'm a great magician. Watch me make this brownie disappear!"

Chad laughed, and Rose Rita and the others joined in. The pleasant sound topped off a wonderful day.